LAMB OF THE FREE

"Drawing especially on important insights from Jacob Milgrom, Andrew Rillera relentlessly critiques faulty assumptions about sacrifice, substitution, and atonement that (mis)inform certain prevalent interpretations of Jesus's death. Anyone interested in these matters will need to grapple with Rillera's stimulating and provocative work."

—David M. Moffitt, reader in New Testament Studies, University of St. Andrews

"PSA for all Christians: PSA is dead, and Andrew Rillera just killed it. Christians who have been troubled by the implications of penal substitutionary atonement will want to read *Lamb of the Free*, while those who subscribe to PSA might not want to read it, but absolutely must!"

—Matthew Thiessen, associate professor of religious studies, McMaster University

"Andrew Rillera provides an essential primer to sacrifices and ritual purity situated within a compelling argument about various misreadings of New Testament texts. It is a great resource for anyone interested in Jewish rituals and concepts of 'atonement.'"

—Madison N. Pierce, associate professor of New Testament, Western Theological Seminary

"Beware! Don't read this book if you aren't ready for a head-exploding, previous-theology-mashing, and page-turning exposition of the saving significance of Jesus! Put it down and walk away if you'd rather hang on to penal substitutionary atonement (PSA) or something else similarly unbiblical. This is a book that will satisfy the academic as well as call the Christian into profound discipleship. You will end up using the words 'union' and 'participation' with more joy and depth than ever before as you think about the saving significance of Jesus."

—Chris Tilling, head of research and senior lecturer in New Testament, St. Mellitus College

"With this book, Andrew Rillera has given readers the best gift a scholar can give: a thoughtful, thorough, clearly written argument that demands attention. Those already familiar with the complex world of Jewish sacrifice will find yet more to explore due to Rillera's judicious and animated exposition, and due to his precision, any who disagree will be required to articulate a well-defended response. If matters about atonement in the Old or New Testament at all interest (or vex) you, read this book."

—Paul T. Sloan, associate professor of early Christianity, Houston Christian University

"Andrew Rillera's *Lamb of the Free* shows cogently that penal substitutionary atonement is not a New Testament teaching. Quite the opposite: Christ didn't suffer and die so that we don't have to; rather Christ enacted radical solidarity with us in our suffering and death so that, vanquished by the resurrection, these might no longer prevent us from truly loving even now. This is a work of considerable exegetical and theological significance."

—Jordan Daniel Wood, author of *The Whole Mystery of Christ: Creation as Incarnation in Maximus Confessor*

Lamb of the Free

Recovering the Varied Sacrificial Understandings of Jesus's Death

ANDREW REMINGTON RILLERA

With a foreword by
DOUGLAS A. CAMPBELL

CASCADE *Books* • Eugene, Oregon

LAMB OF THE FREE
Recovering the Varied Sacrificial Understandings of Jesus's Death

Copyright © 2024 Andrew Remington Rillera. All rights reserved. Except for brief quotations in critical publications or reviews, no part of this book may be reproduced in any manner without prior written permission from the publisher. Write: Permissions, Wipf and Stock Publishers, 199 W. 8th Ave., Suite 3, Eugene, OR 97401.

Cascade Books
An Imprint of Wipf and Stock Publishers
199 W. 8th Ave., Suite 3
Eugene, OR 97401

www.wipfandstock.com

PAPERBACK ISBN: 978-1-6667-0304-7
HARDCOVER ISBN: 978-1-6667-0305-4
EBOOK ISBN: 978-1-6667-0306-1

Cataloguing-in-Publication data:

Names: Rillera, Andrew Remington [author]. | Campbell, Douglas A. [foreword].

Title: Lamb of the free : recovering the varied sacrificial understandings of Jesus's death / Andrew Remington Rillera.

Description: Eugene, OR: Cascade Books, 2024 | Includes bibliographical references and index.

Identifiers: ISBN 978-1-6667-0304-7 (paperback) | ISBN 978-1-6667-0305-4 (hardcover) | ISBN 978-1-6667-0306-1 (ebook)

Subjects: LCSH: Jesus Christ—Crucifixion—Biblical teaching. | Sacrifice—Biblical teaching. | Sacrifice—Christianity. | Atonement. | Crucifixion—Biblical teaching. | Jesus Christ—Crucifixion.

Classification: BT450 R55 2024 (print) | BT450 (ebook)

To my wife, Karianne, and my children, Eden and Zion.
And for all my students, past, present, and future.

Contents

Foreword ix

Acknowledgments xxiii

Abbreviations xxvii

Introduction 1

1 Understanding Old Testament Sacrifices, Part 1: What Sacrifice Is *Not* 9

2 Understanding Old Testament Sacrifices, Part 2: The Non-Atoning Sacrifices 27

3 Understanding Old Testament Sacrifice, Part 3: Ritual Cosmology 69

4 Understanding Old Testament Sacrifice, Part 4: Atonement and the Prophets 88

5 Lamb of the Free: Jesus, Purity, and Non-Atoning Sacrifices 150

6 Jesus, Purgation Sacrifices, and the Day of Decontamination 209

7 When Jesus's Death Is Not a Sacrifice 243

8 Conclusion 272

Bibliography 287

Index 295

Foreword

A LOT OF SCHOLARS read and apply the New Testament with a particular account of Paul's gospel in mind. I, similarly to Andrew Rillera, was taught it as a convert, and have spent much of my subsequent career investigating its cogency and impact, as has he.[1] Needless to say, the model of the gospel we operate with is important. It speaks to the very heart of the God that the church attests to, hence to the center of its proclamation, and to all the critical social, cultural, and political endorsements the church goes on to enact. Indeed, to say it is "important" is understating matters: it is *absolutely critical*. Here *everything* is at stake. And it is of course why Andrew has written his important book.

Both Andrew and I have become convinced that the particular model we were first taught is, despite its good intentions, deeply flawed. Its presuppositions are problematic at the most important level in that its view of God is wrong! But, unsurprisingly in view of this mistake, it goes on to generate a weak and distorted ecclesiology that ultimately, in turn, complements a rather nasty political and cultural agenda. The key flaw exposed by Andrew here, however, is that its exegetical basis is wrong as well, and this is something the model prides itself on. A crucial set of connections that the model needs in order both to work as a model *and* to claim to be a fair account of what is said in the Bible is inaccurate, at which moment the model really falls apart in terms of its own lack of scriptural corroboration. So Andrew's book is an important one. It is probably not overstating things to suggest that it drives a biblical stake through the corrupt heart of a false account of the gospel. But a little more detail is necessary if these dramatic claims are to be comprehensible. So I will supply a quick sketch of the problematic theological model he engages with here, before going on to explain, in very broad terms, where Andrew is pointing to a critical biblical deficiency within its most central claims.

1. So, esp., my *The Deliverance of God* (Grand Rapids: Eerdmans, 2009).

1. SALVATION IN TERMS OF ATONEMENT AND SACRIFICE

No one within the church seriously disputes the claim that God's great act through his Son, Jesus, has saved us in some sense. Our God saves! Moreover, presumably few would seriously challenge the claim that this salvation involved Jesus's death. Jesus's death achieves something or effects something, and it does so, furthermore, *for us*—what the theologians tend to speak of as its "vicarious" function. To speak of Jesus's vicarious death means then, in agreement with almost every Jesus-follower, that his death is significant, accomplishing something, and that it accomplishes something that benefits us. So far so good. But now a potential problem emerges into view, although at this moment it is only a potential confusion.

When we speak of these matters we often use the language of "atonement," although this language can also appear as the cognate verb, "to atone," along with the corresponding adjective, "atoning." And atoning language needs to be understood precisely.

As Andrew explains, this word group began to emerge in the fourteenth century when John Wycliffe was translating the Bible into English for the first time (he spoke of "at onement"), and was further developed by William Tyndale, when he was translating the Bible into English in the sixteenth century (who pushed this phrase together into "atonement"). This happened because, like all translators, Wycliffe and Tyndale faced the struggle of rendering notions from the original biblical languages into their contemporary equivalents when sometimes the words for what exactly they wanted to say were lacking. "Atonement" was a neologism they formulated from the phrase "being made 'at one'" to get at the idea of some problem between God and humanity that needed to be fixed; we needed to be made "at one" again, and Jesus had done this.

If we leave things at this level of specification, no further harm necessarily ensues. The need for God acting through Jesus "to atone" in this sense simply suggests that some problem or disturbance in our relationship needs to be fixed; God and humanity are not perfectly and completely "at one" with one another, in the way that Jesus alone was. So the precise nature of this problem, and its corresponding solution, is not yet being specified, which is important. But whatever the problem, Jesus has solved it. However, Tyndale went on to create some immediate potential problems.

He used the new word "atonement" to translate texts in the OT, in Leviticus, that spoke of sacrifices and sacrificial acts with the Hebrew word *kipper*. The translators of the Greek version of the OT, the Septuagint, used the Greek *hilaskomai* at this point. But Tyndale *also* used the English word "atonement" to translate the Greek *katallassō* in the NT, which most NT translators render in terms of "reconciliation." And these are two rather different things. Nevertheless an equation was set up immediately in the minds of English readers between God's reconciling work on our behalf through Jesus in the NT, which is clearly closely related to his saving work on our behalf, and the sacrificial activity being described in Leviticus. To reconcile *was* to sacrifice (or, to benefit from a sacrifice). Reconciling atonement was achieved by means of sacrificial atonement. So it was as if train tracks were laid by Tyndale within our very language that ran from the NT description of God's saving actions through Jesus, which reconciled our relationship, to the sacrificial categories operative in the OT in relation to the temple. And any further accounts in the NT of how we have been saved now often ended up following those train tracks to the same place automatically. To be saved *was* at bottom to have had one's sin atoned for, which meant in turn that one was benefiting from Jesus's "sacrifice."

I. An acceptable equation

Salvation = a relational problem has been solved, so
Salvation = "at-one-ment" or atonement

II. Question-begging equations

Salvation = "atonement" and . . .
Atonement = (OT) sacrifice (!) and . . .
Salvation = (through) sacrifice (!)

These equations are potentially very problematic. They are both question-begging and inaccurate. Salvation in the NT is simply not reducible to sacrifice in the OT. They are not automatically the same thing. This, at its worst, is semantic sleight of hand. (Tyndale did not intend this of course, but the results of our words are sometimes very much not what we intended.) But the situation, as Andrew points out, is more serious than this.

This railroad has allowed the NT account of Jesus's saving death on our behalf to be *captured* by one particular model that has been loaded with problematic, and ultimately quite destructive, theological assumptions. A particular account of sacrifice has been pulled through from the OT, and has then spread out through its domination of atonement discussions, to colonize the NT witness to Jesus's saving activity. From sacrifice, the trajectory passes through atonement, to salvation, although in doing so it also focuses the NT discussions down narrowly on Jesus's death. But in order to appreciate how Andrew responds to this sinister situation we will need to grasp the model of salvation that this process puts in play in a little more detail.

2. SACRIFICE AND PENAL SUBSTITUTION

At the heart of the model Andrew targets here—a model that is very widespread—is a set of assumptions that are oriented by a particular account of sacrifice. Four, in particular, need to be understood:

I. Substitution. The animal in the sacrifice is accepted *in the place of* the offerer. So something happens to the animal that otherwise would happen to the offerer. In this way, the animal *substitutes* for the offerer, explicitly so that what should happen to the offerer happens to the animal instead. A notion of *transfer* is clearly critical here. And God must accept the legitimacy of this transfer. There is also a clear *separation* between the offerer and the offering. The notion of "substitution" summarizes all these interrelated elements.

II. Retribution. Wrongdoing or sin must ultimately be responded to with a *retributive* rationale. This is a critical notion, with several interrelated elements, so we will need to describe it in a little more detail.

At bottom, sin is being viewed here utilizing a set of quantitative metaphors and hence usually also in terms of money, which is obviously quantifiable.[2] Moreover, there is an obvious concrete and entirely reasonable practice in play here. If some piece of property is taken from someone then an appropriate response, assuming the thief has been caught, is to *repay* what has been taken. This goes a long way toward fixing the wrong that has been done. Alternatively, if the property has gone, an equivalent payment of money can be paid. So "I stole your car and got caught. I have, unfortunately for you, sold your car, but I can repay you the money you need to buy a new one—although it ought to be equivalent." Now, I don't pay vastly more than I took, although here we step into an important additional practice that we need to hold off from explaining for a moment. (See assumption III below.) The repayment must be equivalent or "fair."

2. See esp. George Lakoff, *Moral Politics* (3rd ed.; Chicago: University of Chicago Press, 2016). Lakoff's brilliant analysis underlies much that follows. The biblical and Jewish utilization of this analogy is charted helpfully by Gary A. Anderson in *Sin: A History* (New Haven, CT: Yale University Press, 2009).

This proportional repayment generates the vast legal field of compensation and generates a certain account of what is right or of "justice." Moreover, we can see straightaway why responses to sin and wrongdoing so often utilize monetary imagery. We *repay* someone, or *pay* for our crime, hence the very word "retribution" is derived from the Latin *retribuere*, which means "to pay." In this retributive practice we really do!

It is critical to grasp, however, that this is an account of *positive* retribution only. Positive retribution, where "payment" can be quite real, seems entirely reasonable, at least in general terms. But note carefully how it involves responding to what is really an absence with a positive action that fills a "gap" or "absence" that we have inflicted on someone unnecessarily and inappropriately. It is as if we steal from someone and thereby dig a hole in their well-being, and so we respond by filling the hole in again. Money flows into that space where value has been taken and fills it up.

With this account of how to respond to a certain type of wrongdoing in mind—in terms of repayment or retribution—we need now to introduce a further critical practice.

III. Punishment. Another form of retribution exists that is *symmetrical* to the positive account of retribution that we have just supplied and that is appropriately called *negative* retribution. Positive retribution pays something tangible back to someone who has been deprived of something. Negative retribution does something that seems very similar but is in fact *entirely different*. Recall that the thief has inflicted harm on the victim by stealing something from them. It is as if the victim's bank account of happiness has been depleted, although if the theft in question was money or had monetary value, then their actual bank account has been depleted as well! Positive retribution asks the thief to pay back the money stolen. But in negative retribution, the retributive response of payment is *not* to repay the victim back as much as to make the thief "pay" in other way—by experiencing the same amount of pain and harm that they have caused their victim. The way to respond to wrongdoing here then is *to actively inflict harm on the wrongdoer*. Now this further harm must again be strictly equivalent. The harm visited upon the thief must not exceed the harm inflicted by the thief on their victim. But it must not be less either. So usually a third party inflicts this harm, hopefully in a more impartial fashion, and we generally refer now to this entity as "the state." The pain must be *measured*, like money, and this and only this is fair and just.

It is vital to grasp how similar this negative retributive response to wrongdoing feels to positive retribution, how easily it can also utilize monetary imagery, although here that usage is metaphorical, and yet how different the underlying action really is. In a sense, this response to wrongdoing *reproduces* the initial act of wrongdoing, on the assumption that this is the correct response. As Leviticus famously puts this on one occasion (although the text quickly moves in fact to compensation) "an eye for an eye and a tooth for a tooth."

To return to our thief: one way of responding to the theft might be then, instead of forcing the thief to repay what has been stolen in the mode of positive retribution, to simply inflict a certain amount of harm and damage on the thief in an act of negative retribution. They are *punished*.

The mechanism operating at the heart of this type of response to wrongdoing is again very clear in the etymology. "Punishment" comes from the Latin *punio*, which means "I inflict punishment upon . . . ," and from *poena*, which means "penalty" or "punishment." But *poena* could also sometimes simply mean "pain." We can respond to wrongdoing punitively then, which means by inflicting a proportionate amount of pain on the person who committed the crime in the first place.

One of the advantages of responding to wrongdoing with negative retribution is that it allows non-monetary wrongs to receive some sort of reaction that then feels right because of its visceral and analogical similarities to positive compensation. The state cannot always make a perpetrator who has assaulted and wounded someone else pay their victim an amount of money to compensate for the harm done. The harm is not really monetary, although a bit of money might help; it is difficult to calculate just what the right repayment might be; and, most importantly, the perpetrator might have no money. So it is easier in a certain sense for the state simply to strike the perpetrator as well, in a proportional act of harm-infliction, and this act can then lay claim to a certain account of justice. This is "right" and "fair" and so "just." At least something has been done. The criminal has "paid" for their crime, and, as such, this should be the end of the matter. But that this response is usually violent in some sense should be carefully noted as we move forward in our introductory analysis.

The critical similarities and differences between positive and negative retribution are evident in the following mathematical summaries of how they work—and note carefully how positive retribution gets us all parties concerned to a reasonably good place. Conversely, although it employs valid math, negative retribution does not end up with an equally helpful sum.

> The math of positive retribution
>
> Victim: $10 - $5 (after theft) = $5; $5 + $5 (after compensation) = $10
>
> Thief: $5 + $5 (after theft) = $10; $10 - $5 (after compensation) = $5
>
> After these events we are back where we started and everyone is happy, or least happy enough. This is the "math" that underlies positive retribution.

> The math of negative retribution
>
> Victim: $10 - $5 (after theft) = $5; $5 + $0 (after punishment of thief) = $5
>
> Thief: $5 + $5 (after theft) = $10; $10 - $5 (after punishment) = $5
>
> The math here feels right in that it is proportional, but in fact the absence of addition and prevalence of subtraction means that the victim ends up in an unhelpful place (and thief will too if the state errs on the side of heavy harm-infliction, perhaps to "compensate" for the additional harm done to the victim).

If this is all clear, then we need to introduce one final cluster of assumptions, and this can be done relatively quickly.

IV. Justice. We have already noted that negative retribution can claim to be "just." Its response is proportional, hence it seems "fair," and many would claim that it is also the "right" response to wrongdoing. If it is right and fair then it seems to be just. Indeed, this approach seems to supply a convincing account of "justice." So in fact many people

> would argue fervently that it is *the* account of justice, and this is a very important step. Unfortunately, there is insufficient space here to press into the fascinating but complex question concerning just why so many people feel so strongly that this is the correct account of justice and hence the appropriate response, at bottom, to all wrongdoing.[3] We must simply acknowledge that this is the case. Negative retribution has, for many, a monopoly on responses to wrongdoing. It is *the* account and there is no other—or, at least, none of equal status and value. And in this context, many Bible readers would claim that these convictions are present in the Bible's account of sacrifice as well. OT sacrifice presupposes the correctness of negative retribution as *God's* response to wrongdoing: it is *the* response of the *just* God to sin.

With this realization all the pieces are in place for us to complete our brief account of the model of the atonement that Andrew is engaging in this book—the model that is so widespread and yet that he, I, and many others, find so problematic.

This solution works in detail—in terms of its mechanism—in ways that are now familiar to us if they were not already.

A sacrificial victim is offered in place of the offerer's own sin and wrongdoing. God accepts this *substitute* and redirects the appropriate response away from the offerer onto the offering. This response is governed, moreover, by the logic of negative retribution. It is *retributive* in that sin is viewed in quantitative terms, and analogized with money. Sin is therefore analogous to a "debt" that must be "paid." The logic of *negative* retribution dictates, however, that this debt will be paid if an amount of harm and pain equivalent to the debt of sin is visited by an impartial third party on the sinner—although here it is redirected on to the substitute. So the sacrifice pays the price for the sin in the sense that it suffers the harm-infliction and pain proportionate to the harm of the sin. The offering is punished in the offerer's stead. This suffering is, furthermore, proportional. The equivalent harm is inflicted, and no more and no less.

Once this process is complete, the wrongdoing has been dealt with and the relational impediment caused by that wrongdoing has been removed.

3. Although it is difficult, being embedded within Tomkins's particular, utterly brilliant, but complex, account of human nature, I have found this study to be unsurpassed in its insights at this point: Donald L. Mosher and Silvan S. Tomkins, "Scripting the Macho Man: Hypermasculine Socialization and Enculturation," *Journal of Sex Research* 25.1 (1988) 60–84. This work is summarized more accessibly by the Tomkins Institute, "The Ideology of Machismo," http://www.tomkins.org/what-tomkins-said/bio-quotes-excerpts/the-ideology- of-machismo/.

So, in this case, God and humanity are reconciled and "at one" with one another—and given that God is involved, inflicting the necessary harm on the offenders and/or their substitute(s), we can rest assured that the harm inflicted is proportionate and hence fair and just.

In sum then, sacrifice is God's solution to wrongdoing—or what the Bible calls "sin"—couched in terms of the logic of negative retribution, with the added assumption that it is substitutionary. This sacrificial response to sin is first seen in the OT. And the gospel proclaimed in the NT is then, in the main, the proclamation that Jesus—meaning by this specifically his death—is now *the* singular and uniquely complete sacrifice that responds appropriately to all wrongdoing in the entirety of human history. He pays the complete price for all sin, suffering the harm-infliction due us in our stead, and the demands of negative retribution are thereby satisfied. And after his one, definitive sacrifice, OT sacrifice and the temple are no longer necessary (and were clearly limited in any case). So they pass from view and God's saved community can move on.

This model is often summarized with the rubric "penal substitutionary atonement," and the accuracy of this rubric is plainly apparent. A response to wrongdoing in terms of negative retribution is being signaled by the word "penal." Quantitative analogies are also mobilized here immediately—talk of debt, payment, and so on—and it will be similarly assumed by those who hear the word "penal" that this account is the correct, right, and just account, here in a close relationship to fairness and proportionality. "Substitutionary" signals the critical twist the model's advocates find in the Bible that a sacrificial offering can be accepted by God in place of the sinner. The necessary punishment can be redirected. And "atonement" signals the monopoly that advocates of this model claim for the NT account of God's actions through Christ on our behalf. This is how God has made us "at one." Salvation and penal substitutionary atonement are coterminous (at least at their most fundamental level). Indeed, such is the phrase's appropriateness, we can refer to the model I have just described and that Andrew is engaging in his book as the PSA model. As we turn to consider his engagement, however, we should quickly recall the key conceptual equations in play since the linkages here will be the central concern of Andrew's argument.

Salvation = atonement
Atonement = sacrifice
Sacrifice = substitution + retribution + punishment + proportionality (+ monopoly)

With these clarifications, we are ready to pivot to a brief account of Andrew's concerns, and to a summary of his measured and significant response in this book.

3. IMPLICATIONS

There is no question that the PSA model of salvation has strengths. It is clear. It is simple. It utilizes several obvious concrete cultural analogies—money and proportional justice (et cetera). It addresses sin directly and seriously. And it emphasizes the importance of Jesus's death. But closer analysis suggests that these strengths have been purchased for a terrible price.

It follows from its endorsement that the main problem from which Jesus saves us is God's pending violent retributive action against our sins. This problem is *the* problem that lies behind the "at-one-ment" we all seek. Hence, it follows further that God's retributive nature, along with its endorsement of proportional violent action to correct any wrongdoing, is absolutely basic. This is deep down who God really is. God is then, essentially, like a monarch or ruler and a judge (bearing in mind that prior to the modern industrial state, rulers combined political and judicial rule in their single person). God is really a head of state. All other attributes are secondary and must ultimately conform to this disposition, at which moment we must ask, what has happened to the God of love? But our problems are only just beginning.

It follows further that the heart of the gospel is a political and retributive God and arrangement—*and hence that all politics should be fundamentally retributive as well.* God, we might say, is a God who is wholly committed to law and order, to the appropriate coercive order, and ultimately to the correctness of the death penalty, *and this says the most important thing about who he is.* Righteous violence *defines* him, as that is deployed in support of laws. This model of the gospel then, underwrites *political authoritarianism* and God is essentially a dictator. He is a fair dictator, but a dictator nonetheless, who wields the sword appropriately. Jesus, of course, was not a dictator, although he was crucified by one. But there are important knock-on effects for discipleship as well.

This view of the atonement is "external." It changes God's *attitude* toward us—although only *conditionally* and hence possibly also only *temporarily*—but it does not change *us*. It is not an intimate, internal account of the atonement.[4] God's great act on our behalf through Jesus is not a

4. Peerlessly lucid and insightful in this regard are the essays of James B. Torrance, "Covenant or Contract: A Study of the Theological Background of Worship in

transformational event. So the church amounts now to a confessional society, that acknowledges this change within God's attitude, from violence to benevolence, and presumably appreciates it, but when it comes to ethics, it is oriented primarily by laws and, in terms of capacity, left very much up to its own devices. Further, given these dynamics, discipleship often amounts now to the endorsement of the model's politics, and to any earthly representatives of the same, while violent defense of those representatives is legitimate and even necessary.

In fact, the place where this model's assumptions play out most commonly will be in the construction of the family and in parenting.[5] This authoritarian model authorizes the arrangement of families in hierarchical terms, and permits parents to enforce its principles. Indeed, more than this, they *ought* to. Punitive parenting will be the result, sometimes in defense of a hierarchical family order. And those who do *not* parent punitively and order their families hierarchically are doing their children a disservice as they violate the basic order of the cosmos.

Andrew and I—and not a few others—find all this rather horrific and deeply destructive. Something has clearly gone wrong. This is not the gospel, the gospel's politics, or the correct account of God at all. But what are we to do?

The short answer is, to follow the argumentative trail through this book, which identifies and knocks out one of this dangerous model's key supporting structures.

4. THE SCHOLARLY REEVALUATION OF SACRIFICE

Andrew begins his response by summarizing an important recent scholarly trajectory that has yet to have its full impact on the PSA model that has just been outlined—although his book essentially delivers that impact. Although there were antecedents, this trajectory is associated most strongly with the work of Jacob Milgrom (1923–2010), a deeply insightful scholar who inspired a generation of students, followers, and interlocutors. Milgrom's climactic publications appear in the Anchor Bible Commentary

---

Seventeenth-Century Scotland," *Scottish Journal of Theology* 23 (1970) 51–76; "The Contribution of McLeod Campbell to Scottish Theology," *Scottish Journal of Theology* 26 (1973) 295–311; and "The Vicarious Humanity of Christ," in *The Incarnation: Ecumenical Studies in the Nicene-Constantinopolitan Creed A.D. 381* (ed. T. F. Torrance; Edinburgh: Handsel Press, 1981), 127–47.

5. For details, again consult Lakoff's *Moral Politics*. Also rather fascinating in this relation is Kristin Kobes du Mez, *Jesus and John Wayne: How White Evangelicals Corrupted a Faith and Fractured a Nation* (New York: Liveright, 2020).

series, namely, a series of commentaries on Leviticus. (The three volumes appeared in 1998; 2000; and 2000, respectively.) And although his findings are not perfect—there are gaps and wrinkles in his explanations—they easily provide enough material to underwrite a particular interpretative paradigm concerning the nature and logic of OT sacrifice. Many other scholars—whose work Andrew utilizes—have then been able to build on this.

Andrew will summarize the key discoveries of this trajectory concerning the logic of OT sacrifice in what follows—and they are fascinating—so I do not need to do so here. The key point for us to grasp in this preliminary discussion is that this careful, historical work by Milgrom, along with those who argue like him, exposes the fact that the set of equations at the heart of the PSA model is, quite simply, untrue. The practice and logic of OT sacrifice *has nothing to do with substitution, retribution, or punishment* (i.e., *negative* retribution). Neither is it supplying a universal account of justice. The mechanism, logic, and concerns of OT sacrifice *are completely different*.

As Andrew goes on to show, a number of significant reinterpretative tasks are set in motion by this realization, although I will mention just the key moves here since it will be better just to read what he says:

1. Where sacrifice is used in the NT, we now need to reorient our interpretations. What is going on in these texts is *not* PSA. A different logic is in play. Needless to say, the meaning of a lot of key texts utilizing sacrificial imagery shifts subtly but significantly—for example, the meaning of Romans 3:25. Andrew traces the most important such shifts in what follows.

2. Sacrifice disappears from many texts and arguments where previously we thought it was present. Simply because a passage discusses "atonement," or even "salvation," we no longer need to assume that the underlying logic and metaphorical register is actually "sacrifice." Many NT texts are consequently set free to make their own, more individuated contributions to our understanding of God's saving activity through Christ. They can find different metaphorical fields and intertexts to be illuminated by. The discussion of soteriology, as Andrew shows, is diversified, complexified, and thereby enriched.

3. Financial metaphors and analogies are also caught up in this reevaluation. Simply because a text analogizes God's work in Christ in terms of money no longer entails that God is enacting an event constrained by the parameters of negative retribution. God is not always exacting the payment of a debt from sinners meted out with pain. Something very different might be going on. Money and the financial system are, after

> all, very complicated metaphorical fields. They can speak much more clearly now of God's gracious benefaction.[6]

The final critical result of all this reevaluation is, of course, that the account of the atonement in terms of PSA is damaged beyond all hope of redemption. Its account of sacrifice is incorrect; its reach, presupposing sacrifice, is false; and its account of financial metaphors is false as well. At bottom, it has lost its biblical base almost entirely. (Andrew does not address appeals by PSA to non-sacrificial registers, but these will be limited and desperate.) It remains only then to press this good news through for all the rest of our thinking. We must press, that is, more deeply into a God of love, not retribution; into a God who eschews violence, rather than practicing it proportionately; and into a gospel rooted in divine benevolence and covenant, not in retribution and contract. And we must advocate, and preach, and teach, the same. But these practices must follow on from a lucid and thorough appropriation of Andrew's important expositions and arguments. So I exhort you, as a matter of some urgency, to press into that task immediately. At the end of that road a joyful gospel awaits.

Douglas Campbell
Duke Divinity School

6. See (i.a.) Nathan Eubank, *Wages of Cross-Bearing and the Debt of Sin* (Berlin: de Gruyter, 2013); and T. J. Lang, "Disbursing the Account of God: Fiscal Terminology and the Economy of God in Colossians 1,24–25," *ZNW* 107 (2016) 116–36.

Acknowledgments

DEPENDING ON WHICH DETAILS I highlight, the story of how this book happened might be seen as the immediate result of a COVID-restrictions-induced hyperfocus episode in the middle of the spring 2020 semester teaching New Testament Survey. I accidentally wrote fourteen thousand words over twelve hours to provide my students with extra explanation on "Sacrifices and Atonement in the Bible." I thought I was just going to write a one- to two-thousand word explainer . . . whoops! Or, this book could be seen as the inevitable culmination of pondering and studying the scholarship on the saving significance of Jesus's death and sacrifice and purity in the Bible for over a decade.

Nevertheless, I was able to write this book thanks to several people in my life, both near and far. I shared and worked through many of my initial observations on this topic with Colby Truesdell, my good friend and seminary colleague. We would have great discussions both in between classes and on our hour-long carpool trips since 2011. Many of them were about how and why notions of salvation often were collapsed into "atonement" when atonement itself barely features in the NT. We were both taught to emphasize what is itself emphasized in the Bible. So why was there all this talk by biblical scholars and theologians about "atonement" when it was rarely ever mentioned in the NT and it's not even mentioned in any evangelical speech in Acts? This is when I started to realize the importance of distinguishing between the broader meaning of atonement and the more specific *sacrificial* notion (see the introduction). Colby also came up with the title *Lamb of the Free* (though it was initially for another book idea, but we thought it fit better for this one). I am grateful to him not only for his cleverness with the title, but even more for his and his wife Crystal's friendship and support, both spiritual and material, for my family over the years.

During my second semester of doctoral coursework in NT at Duke, Susan Eastman graciously agreed to do a directed study with me on the relation of Jesus's death and ethical formation in Paul's letters. I ended up writing an essay on the so-called "atonement" passages in Paul where I argued that Paul does not comprehend the death of Jesus within a register of sacrificial atonement. I am thankful for Susan's guidance and support while I was a student and for her many incisive remarks both on that essay and throughout my time at Duke.

That essay eventually became the basis for a paper I gave in the Pauline section at the SBL Annual Meeting in 2021 titled "Paul Does Not Have a *Kipper* Theology: Understanding Paul's Sacrificial Imagery Applied to Jesus." I am grateful for those who provided feedback in the Q&A and/or afterward who read my manuscript, especially Paul Sloan, Logan Williams, Stephen Finlan, and Kathy Ehrensperger.

In between that directed study and the SBL presentation was the spring 2020 New Testament Survey course I was teaching online for my alma mater, Eternity Bible College. I need to also thank EBC's academic dean, Joshua Walker, for hiring me to teach several courses as an adjunct and encouraging me to keep following the Scriptures wherever they lead, even if it upsets the theological status quo. Spring 2020 was my third time teaching the course and a student had asked for more information on something I had said about sacrifices in one of my lectures. The COVID restrictions did not impact our class because it was already online so with the extra time I had on my hands I set out to write a brief explainer on sacrifices and atonement in the Bible. I ended up writing for over seven hours straight late into the night, woke up, and then finished with an obviously way-too-large fourteen-thousand-word document. I knew right then that this could easily become a book, but I hadn't yet finished my dissertation (on Romans).

Since COVID was wreaking havoc, I figured I needed some "productive procrastination" from my dissertation. After using almost every bit of spare time I had over the next few weeks diving more deeply into the scholarship of sacrifice and purity, I contacted Wipf & Stock editor Robin Parry. Robin had thankfully taken an interest in me and my work after I met him at an event at Fuller Seminary in 2015, so before I "wasted" more time on this research, I wanted to ask if he thought this idea had legs. To my delight he loved it and encouraged me to submit an official proposal and I was offered a contract in the summer of 2020. Words cannot express how thankful I am to Robin and the entire Wipf & Stock team for providing me the opportunity to write this book, especially since I was still ABD at the time. Their decision to offer me a contract was no doubt helped due to the support of my doctoral advisor, Douglas Campbell, who also graciously agreed to write the foreword. Douglas has been way more than a great PhD advisor to me and I am filled with gratitude for his unwavering guidance and friendship.

I want to acknowledge that having this project in the pipeline most definitely contributed to me landing a tenure-track job at The King's University (Edmonton, AB). There are obviously many other factors that go into obtaining a tenure-track job (luck most of all), but I will always cherish Robin, Douglas, and everyone at Wipf & Stock for their part in bringing this idea to life, especially because it has already had a life-changing impact on my teaching career.

I am grateful for Will Van Arragon (my dean) and Kris Ooms (vice president academic and research) for a course release my first semester and relaxed service requirements during my first year. These are standard for new faculty at King's and I am grateful to work for an institution that provides humane benefits like these to give new faculty adequate space to do our jobs well. This gave me the time necessary to stay on top of my research and writing. I was also permitted to teach a "Special Topics in Theology" elective in the winter semester of 2022 on sacrifice and sacrificial imagery in the Bible, which further helped me process all these ideas with a great group of motivated students: Braeden, Thaler, Holly, Elisha, Ben, Shaina, and Melanie. Thank you all for your contributions that made for a wonderful class. (No, I did not subject them to reading my chapter drafts! But we did read quite a lot of the scholarship I engage in this book.)

A special thanks are also due to Robin (again) and Matthew Wimer for their undying patience as I had to keep pushing back my manuscript deadline. While I definitely take personal responsibility for many of those delays, a major delay was due to me finding out about a similar book brilliantly written by Scott Shauf in April 2022: *Jesus the Sacrifice: A Historical and Theological Study*. I reached out to Scott that May, telling him about my project and sharing my SBL paper with him. He kindly shared his manuscript with me and I quickly devoured it and started incorporating his work into my current chapter drafts. Scott and I often agree, and I learned quite a lot from him. My book is better for having engaged with his scholarship.

I want to thank and acknowledge those who read or offered critical feedback on earlier versions or portions of my work, saving me from several mishaps: David Moffitt, Madison Pierce, Paul Sloan, Chris Tilling, Colby Truesdell, Douglas Campbell, Josh Dykstra (my unofficial student at King's), and Jonathan Nicolai-deKoning. Jonathan, my colleague, friend, and Ultimate teammate, deserves special recognition for reading and commenting on the entire (bloated) full draft. Although boilerplate, it is nevertheless true that all enduring errors remain my own.

Finally, I am supremely thankful for my family. My mom, Linda, first taught me to read the Bible and question old paradigms and has always been my biggest supporter and encourager. I regret that my stepdad, Pat, passed away this past April and did not get to see this book published. But I am so thankful he would constantly express his praise of me as his son and for my work as a scholar. I know he is proud of me and I am grateful he was a father to me. My dad, Richie, has been an unwavering supporter of mine even though, as he is a Jehovah's Witness, we have deep theological disagreements. My wife, Karianne, has been my best friend and partner for almost seventeen years now and has listened to me externally process all these ideas (sometimes patiently and sometimes politely impatiently!). I am thankful she taught me that it is okay to be "slow," to take my time writing this book. I may have burned out before really beginning if it wasn't for her drawing me into her steady, tranquil presence. She helped me take actual breaks, (somewhat) free from anxiety to have fun together and as a family. My children, Eden and Zion, keep me grounded and humble. They are simultaneously impressed that I wrote a big book and unimpressed since I'm not writing anything near as thrilling or cool as Cressida Cowell, Rick Riordan, or Erin Hunter.

I have dedicated this book to my wife and children because I hope we can embody, however incompletely, a family that lives into the freedom of the Lamb. I hope to be a family that cultivates a shared life that is "free" from the fear-based and pseudo-justice of so many theologies of "atonement" that pass as "Christian," but that actually nurture antichrist authoritarian household environments. Rather, we strive, with the Lamb's help, to be participants in the broken body and shed blood of the Lamb for the life of the world.

And I have dedicated this book as well to all my students, past, present, and future, because I hope I can be an adequate witness for them of the truth in Christ Jesus in all aspects of my teaching and scholarship.

Abbreviations

Abbreviations of ancient texts follow *The SBL Handbook of Style* (2nd ed., Atlanta: SBL, 2014).

Introduction

"Jesus died as a substitutionary (atoning) sacrifice for our sins." This assertion seems to be taken for granted as an accurate summary of a key Christian claim. However, while it may accurately describe the beliefs of certain sectors of the Christian tradition, it is an inaccurate summary of *the New Testament's* claims about the meaning of Jesus's death. There is something mistaken about each one of the key terms here.

Now, to be clear up front, the NT univocally claims that Jesus's death has *saving significance*, but the mistake is collapsing this into notions of "substitution," "sacrifice," and "atonement." And an even bigger mistake is thinking biblical sacrifice has anything to do with "substitution" at all, let alone that all sacrifices are about "atonement." This book is an attempt to untangle the various knotted and interrelated misunderstandings about sacrifice in the OT and Second Temple Judaism so that we can more clearly see how various NT authors reflect on the meaning of Jesus's death when they make use of sacrificial imagery. Often, the NT authors do not even bring up sacrificial imagery at all, but this fact goes unnoticed even by many NT scholars because it has become commonplace to conflate anything "saving" about Jesus's death with the concept of "sacrifice." To untangle this interpretive mess, we need to patiently examine the biblical texts and to observe what is and what is not happening in the descriptions of various sacrifices found in the Bible and other pertinent contemporaneous texts.

The research presented here, especially the first half, serves dual purposes. First, it functions as a (relatively) concise reference resource for the Levitical sacrificial and purity system for its own sake, breaking down its key nuances and distinctions. Second, it grounds and substantiates the theses about Jesus in the second half of the book, demonstrating how careful attention to the nuances within the Levitical system, coupled with the prophetic appropriation of its themes, sheds light on how early followers of

Jesus actually employed sacrificial imagery to articulate the significance and purpose of Jesus's death (and resurrection).

While this book is written from a Christian perspective,[1] and I hope it will be read by Christians, I hope non-Christians interested in ancient and contemporary religions will engage this project too since it is a descriptive study of ancient texts, along with, ultimately, how their interpretation impacts current realities. Thus, this book is primarily written for students of the Bible, whether hopeful, former, or enrolled students, as well as teachers who have the privilege of being lifelong students. For all such readers, I wish to demonstrate how a lot of Christian theology in many Western (mainly Protestant) traditions, as it mobilizes the notions of "sacrifice" and "atonement," has little to no anchorage in the biblical texts themselves.

However, before diving into the various intricacies and nuances of sacrifice in the Bible, I want to frame this project in broader terms. The title *Lamb of the Free* is an intentional, if unclever, pun on the self-conception and identity the United States projects into the world in its national anthem as the "land of the free" ("and the home of the brave"). Although this study will remain focused on understanding sacrifice as it is presented in the Old Testament, in order to rediscover afresh how various New Testament authors make use of these conceptual frameworks for understanding the saving significance of Jesus's death, I want to be up front about a deeper reason underneath this inquiry. My aim is ultimately to showcase the liberating message of the gospel as an act of resistance to other notions of "freedom" on offer in the world as represented in the US national anthem. I will return to this concern in my conclusion and discuss how this study matters beyond just clearing up common misunderstandings of ancient texts for their own sake. However, the bulk of this project will be demonstrating how many assumptions about biblical sacrifice are just that—(false) *assumptions*—since they lack justification in the actual texts available to us. And this matters.

It turns out many theologies about God's salvation in Jesus Christ and justice are based on these mistaken understandings about sacrifice and justice. For instance, John G. Stackhouse Jr. claims that "God cannot 'just forgive' our sins without anyone suffering" on the supposed basis that "the elaborate sacrificial system of the Torah was ordained by God to symbolize this fundamental reality" and he calls this "[t]he logic of justice."[2] Each of these three claims, not to mention the ostensible relationships assumed between them, is mistaken. And I hope clearing up misunderstandings like these will play a small part in rediscovering a view of justice that is informed

1. I am a Christian in the Anglican tradition.

2. Stackhouse, "Terminal Punishment," 77.

by a more accurate understanding of the way sacrifice functions in Christian scripture. Hence, although my immediate purpose is to help us better understand NT author's sacrificial claims about Jesus, this all plays into a larger vision about how Christians ought to go about enacting distinctively Christian notions of justice and renewal.

Put another way, I don't think either the OT's or the NT's views of sacrifice have much to do with "justice" *per se*, but too many Christians, like Stackhouse, derive their view of what justice is from a mistaken understanding of sacrifice in the Christian canon. For some, justice is retributive and has to do with punishment. And a sacrifice, so it is thought, is bringing justice by punishing some other blood-filled mammal as a substitutionary death, construed as the just punishment for the sinner.

For instance, Hannah Bowman has recently demonstrated how "American penal culture" and "American mass incarceration has been driven by many ideological factors, including the pernicious influence of theological conceptions of 'penal substitutionary atonement,'" in opposition to which she offers an alternative model of atonement via solidarity.[3] I hope to ultimately dismantle these misunderstandings of justice and "the mutually-reinforcing ways in which atonement theology has acted in the service of racialized narratives of punishment and control"[4] by being clear about what is and what is not actually happening in OT sacrifice and then how NT authors (along with other Second Temple texts) make use of these sacrificial concepts.

I believe taking the time to sow these seeds to help those of us who are Christians hear more accurately what is in our Bible will reap a bountiful spiritual and theological harvest that can sustain ongoing Christian formation and our common mission of renewal and reconciliation in the name of Jesus Christ. As Isaiah says, God's word does not return empty (Isa 55:11).

WHAT DOES "ATONEMENT" EVEN MEAN?

In English, the word "atonement" means too many things at once. And this is a result, in part, of how this word came into the English vocabulary. I have no inherent problems with this word, but because it can be used in *both* a sacrificial register (e.g., to translate the Hebrew word *kipper*) and in a non-sacrificial register (to convey anything that falls within the broad realm of "the saving significance of Jesus's death"), these conceptually separate domains are often conflated. And this conflation results in some major

3. Bowman, "From Substitution to Solidarity," 1–19, here 1.

4. Bowman, "From Substitution," 1.

misinterpretations of NT texts, which in turn have resulted in problematic theologies about the nature of salvation.

Following John Wycliffe's Middle English translation of the Bible in the fourteenth century, which used phrases like "to one" and "one-ment," William Tyndale in the sixteenth century first standardized "atone" and "atonement" (at-one-ment). It was first used as a translation of the Greek word *katallassō*, which means "reconciliation," in texts like 2 Cor 5:18–20 and Rom 5:10. *Katallassō*, "at-one-ment," "reconciliation." This all makes good sense. So far, so good.

But Tyndale then used the noun "atonement," and the verb form "to atone," to translate the Hebrew root word *k-p-r* in the Torah (Genesis–Deuteronomy). But this already makes theological assumptions about the function of Israel's sacrificial system that Hebrew Bible scholars almost unanimously have demonstrated to be misunderstandings, as will be developed in the next chapter. For a quick teaser: In the *piel* form, *kipper* means "remove" most broadly, but when used in the sacrificial system it more specifically conveys the idea of "decontaminate" or "purify" or "purge" (i.e., removing a contamination clinging to something). Hence, *kipper* does not mean "reconcile," nor "save," nor "forgive." Equally importantly, only holy objects within the sacred dwelling place,[5] or later the temple, receive the ritual action of *kipper*. In other words, when *kipper* happens, what is decontaminated or purified is a holy object in the sanctuary, *not people*.

More on all of this in due course. For now I only want to signal that because many modern English translations follow Tyndale and use "atonement" and "atone" to translate *kipper* in books like Leviticus, "atonement" has come to mean, for NT scholars and Christian theologians alike, both "the totality of Jesus's saving work" *and* "*kipper*." This has led to an unfortunate set of misunderstandings, which in turn have resulted in problematic theologies.

All too often, as evidenced by Stackhouse above, when people are discussing the saving significance of Jesus's death, false equivalencies are made in rapid succession: "saving" is assumed to mean "atoning," and "atoning" is taken to mean "sacrifice," and "sacrifice," so it is thought, always has a *kipper* function and is then assumed to be equivalent to "forgiveness." So everything about the salvific meaning of Jesus's death gets reduced to and

5. Following Liane Feldman's suggestion, I am using "dwelling place" rather than the usual "tabernacle" to translate *miškān* to productively defamiliarize readers, since "tabernacle" fails to convey the function (and therefore meaning) of *miškān*. The verbal forms of the root *š-k-n* convey the act of "dwelling" or "settling" (*šākan*) and the *mem* (*m*) prefix signifies the *place* where the verbal action happens. Thus, the *miškān* functions as the physical and geographical place of YHWH's dwelling among Israel.

conflated with "an atoning, *kipper*, sacrifice." These inaccurate conflations are what I aim to correct.[6]

This matters because many of the go-to NT texts assumed to be supporting something like "penal substitutionary atonement" (e.g., Rom 3:25; 8:3, Gal 3:13, 2 Cor 5:21) are demonstrably not about sacrificial atonement (nor are they about substitution).[7] They are about the saving significance of Jesus's death, but they utilize a completely different conceptual framework than sacrifice in general or *kipper* in particular to explain that saving significance.

To be sure, and as I will develop more shortly, atonement—in the sense found in Leviticus (*kipper*)—is indeed present in the NT. But it is underappreciated how *rarely* it is actually mentioned. It is only explicitly mentioned in two texts written toward the end of the first century: Hebrews and 1 John. There is *other* sacrificial imagery used throughout the NT, but I will demonstrate why it is important to notice the difference between sacrificial atonement (*kipper*) and other types of sacrificial imagery—because not all Levitical sacrifices have an atoning function. Too many interpreters betray their lack of awareness of this and thereby replicate and pass on distorted notions of sacrifice in their exegesis of NT texts.

CHARTING A PATH FORWARD

When I use "atonement," "atone," "atoning," and so on, I am restricting this word group's meaning to the Levitical concept of *kipper*. And this study aims to show how differentiating between atoning and non-atoning sacrifices is crucial to understanding the sacrificial imagery applied to Jesus by various NT authors. Moreover, this project is not about interpreting the meaning of Jesus's *death per se*, in all its metaphorical varieties present in all the NT texts that touch its meaning. Many NT texts use some metaphorical register other than the sacrificial to convey the significance of Jesus's death. But the point of this study is to focus particularly on the *sacrificial* understandings

6. Similarly, from Scott Shauf: "One of the main barriers to understanding sacrifice in general and Jesus's death as a sacrifice in particular is a too-easy equation between sacrifice and atonement. Christians are accustomed to thinking of Jesus's death as a sacrifice solely in the sense of an atoning sacrifice, as achieving forgiveness for sins, without even being aware that sacrifice was more commonly performed for purposes other than atonement, especially for the purposes of communion and gift" (*Jesus the Sacrifice*, 195).

7. I discuss each of these and more in chapter 7. But see also, e.g., McLean, "The Absence of an Atoning Sacrifice in Paul's Soteriology," 531–53; Streett, "Cursed by God? Galatians 3:13," 189–209; McMurray, *Sacrifice*, 57–94.

of Jesus's death in the NT. To do this well, however, I will also have to debunk the interpretations of some texts that scholars often mistakenly read as being about sacrifice but that, upon investigation, turn out to be set in another metaphorical register altogether.

Therefore, when we encounter a NT text, our main guiding questions in the background will be:

1. Is this text using *sacrificial* imagery, or is it employing language from another conceptual domain?
2. If it is employing sacrificial imagery, is it drawing upon the *atoning* or *non-atoning* sacrifices?

The result of all of this will be greater clarity concerning the diverse ways NT authors speak about the saving significance of Jesus's death in terms of both types of sacrificial imagery—both atoning and non-atoning—as well as imagery from other conceptual frameworks. It will also highlight the prominence the non-atoning sacrifices had for early Jesus-followers since these were the sacrifices associated with Jesus's death in the earliest strands of the NT literature. These sacrifices are the determinative framework for comprehending the Lord's Supper (and Paul's instructions and warnings in 1 Cor 11 in particular).

A secondary, but no less important, result is that this study will end up dismantling the ostensible exegetical basis for "penal substitutionary atonement." This will mainly be indirect because the exegetical arguments to be presented are going to focus on expositing the biblical texts and the way the words run on the page.[8] But the results of these endeavors will prove how penal substitutionary atonement is left with no scriptural anchor. This study will demonstrate how, from a biblical-studies perspective, penal substitutionary atonement has problems with each one of its key terms—penal, substitutionary, and atonement. I shall argue that it is predicated on a complete misunderstanding of the sacrificial system in the scriptures. And I do mean *complete*. It misinterprets how atonement is accomplished and what it is for (and it also falls victim to the imprecision of the word "atonement" by conflating all sorts of meanings with it).

At this point it will be helpful to chart my path for arriving at these conclusions in a little more detail. In chapters 1–4, I clear up common misunderstandings about OT sacrifice and the two forms of (im)purity (ritual vs. moral) in the process of providing an account of the meaning, logic, and limits of the various functions of Levitical sacrifices.[9] In chapter 4 I also

8. Cf. Hauerwas, "Why 'The Way Words Run' Matters."

9. I am neither assuming the OT represents, nor am I attempting through a critical

discuss the so-called prophetic critique of sacrifice and the expectation of "restoration" when utilizing cultic imagery, as well as the fact that forgiveness can and did occur apart from the atoning apparatus of cultic sacrifice.

Chapter 5 explores Jesus's relation to the sacrificial and purity systems in the Gospels. I demonstrate how the understanding of the Lord's Supper in both the Gospels and 1 Corinthians derives exclusively from the *non-atoning* sacrifices. I also deconstruct arguments that try to find allusions to sacrificial atonement in the Lord's Supper and the crucifixion accounts in the Gospels.

Then I address, in chapter 6, how atonement is used in 1 John and Hebrews. I also show how Hebrews employs this framework to depict followers of Jesus as being made into both co-high priests and co-purgation sacrifices with Jesus. Hebrews has a thick atonement theology, but it is *not* a *substitutionary* atonement theology. It is a participatory atonement, or solidarity atonement theology.

In chapter 7 I examine several key NT texts that are commonly misunderstood to be about sacrifice and/or atonement. I show why they are best comprehended within another conceptual framework: 1 Pet 2:24; Mark 10:45//Matt 20:28; 2 Cor 5:21; Gal 3:13; Rom 8:3; and 3:25. There are more passages than these, but space does not permit me to tackle every single text misunderstood in this way. Nevertheless, I hope these case studies provide sufficient examples of how to analyze NT passages in relation to the preceding study of OT sacrifices.

By way of conclusion, I directly address the notion of "substitution." By this point, it will have become more than clear that the NT authors, whether they make use of sacrificial imagery, or whether they make use of the atoning sacrifices, all agree on one fundamental point: Jesus's death is a *participatory* phenomenon; it is something all are called to *share in experientially.* The logic is not: Jesus died so we don't have to. Rather it is: Jesus died so that we, together, can follow in his steps and die with him and like him, having full fellowship with his sufferings so that we might share in the likeness of his resurrection (e.g., Phil 3:10–11; Gal 2:20; 6:14; Rom 6:3–8; 1 Pet 2:21; Mark 8:34–35 with 10:38–29; 1 John 2:6; 3:16–18; etc.).

In short, while Jesus did die *for* us, this does not mean that Jesus died *instead of* us. It means that he died *ahead of* and *with* us.

---

use of the biblical texts to reconstruct, what ancient Israelites "really did" or "really taught/thought." Rather, since this book is primarily about understanding how the NT authors appropriate the OT's sacrificial and purity language and themes to comprehend the saving significance of Jesus, my aim in these chapters is detailed exegesis of the biblical texts themselves in conversation with their interpretive legacies/reception history, especially in the Second Temple period.

This why I find "substitution" to be inadequate, incoherent, and inherently misleading as a summarizing conceptualization of the saving significance of Jesus's death in the NT. As a former college ministry pastor and now an undergraduate professor, I have seen first- and secondhand how much destruction is caused by Christians because their essentialized substitutionary framework prevents them from even *wanting* to be conformed and transformed into the cruciform image of Christ. Substitutionary frameworks—whether intentionally or not—corrode the logic of Christian discipleship among everyday Christians. Substitution makes conformity to the cruciform image of Christ incoherent. If Jesus is my substitute, why do I need to take up a cross? Why do I need to have fellowship with his sufferings? Why do I need to be co-crucified?

The seeds for my arguments in the conclusion are planted in the chapters that precede, but the conclusion will provide the needed space to cultivate those seeds into a more developed discussion and to show how this study has important ramifications for Christian discipleship—especially in contexts where much of the church itself is hamstrung in the pursuit of God's kingdom justice (Matt 6:33) by being beholden to warped notions of justice based on penal substitutionary atonement.

1

Understanding Old Testament Sacrifices, Part 1

What Sacrifice Is *Not*

ALTHOUGH HAVING EARLIER ANTECEDENTS,[1] a lot of misunderstandings carried forth today about ancient Israelite sacrifices as presented in the OT, and in Leviticus and Numbers in particular, are reinforced in René Girard's influential theory of sacrifice. Girard thinks all sacrificial systems reduce to the infliction of violence on a scapegoat substitutionary figure (which can be a human or animal victim).[2] According to Girard, what is fundamentally taking place in sacrifice is a ritual mitigation of a society's violent tendencies by directing it upon a "surrogate victim."[3] Girard admits, however, that his theory partly derives from his reading of the passion narratives in the Gospels,[4] and also concedes that his use of "scapegoat" is different from what is found in Lev 16.[5] Nevertheless, Girard's theory of sacrifice, developed in

1. There is no need to delve into the history of penal substitutionary atonement for this study, but it is worth flagging here that contrary to popular belief Anselm is *not* the progenitor of it. He vehemently rejects any semblance of what will later be known as penal substitutionary atonement in *Cur Deus Homo?* 1.8.

2. Girard, *Violence and the Sacred*, cf., e.g., 5–11, 101–3; Girard, "Generative Scapegoating," 73–105.

3. Girard, *Violence and the Sacred*, 92. "Surrogate victim" is used throughout, e.g., 2, 5, 68–88.

4. Girard, in conversation after his paper "Generative Scapegoating" transcribed in Hamerton-Kelly, *Violent Origins*, 141–42.

5. Girard, "Generative Scapegoating," 73–78.

large part by reading a certain interpretation of Jesus's crucifixion back into the accounts of sacrifice in the Torah, has influenced biblical scholarship directly and indirectly.[6] Somewhat ironically, Girard's view of Jesus's death is that it exposed Israel's sacrificial system for the deplorable violent system of scapegoating that it is (and thus Jesus saves humanity from it by ending sacrifice). As Jonathan Klawans summarizes, "according to Girard, Jesus' death finally put the lie to deceptive rituals of sacrifice" and thereby unmasks, cancels, and opposes Israel's ostensible deep logic of sacrificial violence.[7] Moreover, Bowman has shown how it is specifically this "Girardian reading of the crucifixion" that both influences one's understanding of sacrifice in the Torah, and "the American criminal punishment system."[8] So the stakes are high for getting things right—or, at the very least, back on the right track. But whatever the merits or demerits of Girard's inquiries into other cultures' sacrificial rituals, he gets sacrifice in the OT completely wrong, and this fact undermines all understandings of Jesus's death that are based on Girardian theories.[9]

Over the course of the next four chapters I will present an overview of what is happening in the OT sacrifices (the positive argument) and what is not happening (the negative argument) thereby dispelling several common misunderstandings of sacrifices. In this chapter I focus on certain negative arguments in order to prove that there is no such thing as a "substitutionary death" sacrifice in the Torah. The theses I argue are:

(1) There is no such thing as a "substitutionary death" sacrifice in the Torah.

(2) The hand-laying ritual is not saying "this is me; this is my substitute," but rather, "this is mine; I own this and I'm giving it to God [for various distinct purposes]."

(3) Sacrificial slaughter is itself not focused on the biological death of the animal. Sacrificial slaughter is separated from any notion of simply being a "death" and it is explicitly reconceptualized via specific ritual actions as something *other than a killing* of a blood-bearing creature.

6. For lists of scholars who endorse a Girardian theory of sacrifice, see, e.g., Klawans, *Purity, Sacrifice*, 22, 238n52; Bowman, "From Substitution," 7n29.

7. Klawans, *Purity, Sacrifice*, 44.

8. Bowman, "From Substitution," 7–9, 16, here 7.

9. For direct critiques of Girard, see, e.g., Klawans, *Purity, Sacrifice*, 22–26, 44, 47; Boersma, *Violence, Hospitality, and the Cross*, 133–51; Smith, "The Domestication of Sacrifice," 191–205.

(4) Sacrificial slaughter is not at all about making the animal "suffer" (let alone suffer as a substitute).

SACRIFICE IS NOT ABOUT SUBSTITUTIONARY DEATH

There is no such thing as a substitutionary death sacrifice in the Torah.[10] We will accumulate more supporting reasons below and in the following chapters for why substitutionary death cannot be the logic of Levitical sacrifices, but the following three are important to realize straightaway.

(1) Whenever something calls for capital punishment, or for the sinner to be "cut off,"[11] there is no sacrifice that can be made to rectify the situation (see esp. Num 15:30–31; 35:32–33). This already rules out the idea that the death of the sacrificial animal is substituting for the death of the offerer. If "substitutionary death" was the logic of animal sacrifice, then the one thing we could expect to be remedied by sacrifice would be capital offenses when the death of the offender is on the line. The fact that this is explicitly not the case means we need to rethink the OT sacrificial system and to analyze the NT's sacrificial metaphors with this in mind.

(2) It is not as if God desires human blood on the altar, but settles for animal blood instead. In fact, *human* blood on the altar or in the temple does just the *opposite* of what sacrificial animal blood does; rather than purging the sancta from pollution, human blood "defiles" it, even if it is the blood of sinners who "deserve" death (e.g., Ezek 9:7). The idea that human blood on the altar is a sacrilege precedes the priest-prophet Ezekiel by centuries; this is why clinging to the altar was a common ancient way to claim asylum (Exod 21:14).[12] Nobody would dare to defile the altar by shedding human blood upon it, even if it was the blood of a person guilty of murder. The guilty person needs to be "taken away from my altar" before being "put to death" (21:14). This is why Adonijah (Solomon's older half-brother and eldest living heir of David at the time) grabs hold of the horns of the altar for safety (1 Kgs 1:50–53). The idea is that Solomon would not dare kill

10. Contra Morales, *Who Shall Ascend*, 127–29. For a detailed defense that substitution is not part of the sacrificial logic as it comes up at various interpretive avenues in the Torah (especially against the Israel's Mesopotamian context), see Milgrom, *Leviticus 1–16*, 440–42, 1021, 1072–79; see also Shauf, *Jesus the Sacrifice*, 32–35.

11. These are technically two different forms of punishment, but getting to the details of their distinctions need not concern us here. In brief, capital punishment is carried out by the community, but being "cut off" is seen as a divine prerogative only (i.e., God will take care of the situation, however it happens).

12. Sarna, *Exodus*, 122.

Adonijah next to the altar because his blood would then be all over the altar, desecrating it.[13]

And (3), according to the OT, the God of Israel abhors human sacrifice; it is the pinnacle of false worship (e.g., Lev 18:21; 20:2–5; Deut 12:31; 2 Kgs 21:6; Jer 7:31). Logically then, the atoning blood of atoning sacrifices cannot be construed as substituting for the death/blood of the offerer.

There is no warrant *anywhere* in the OT that through animal sacrifice God is accepting animal blood on the altar instead of the ostensibly more ideal human blood.[14] The notion that Levitical sacrifice is a ritual of substitu-

13. Though see a similar story with Joab in 1 Kgs 2:28–34. Benaiah initially refuses to kill Joab because Joab will not leave the altar. He tells Solomon this is the reason he couldn't kill Joab there. But then Solomon instructs Benaiah to kill Joab anyway. The text is unclear if Benaiah killed Joab while he was still upon the altar or if Benaiah wrestled Joab away from it first and then executed him (per Exod 21:14). Nevertheless, this whole scenario illustrates that it was taken for granted that human blood does *not* belong on the altar (even for guilty people).

14. The story of Abraham nearly sacrificing Isaac (Gen 22:1–19) cannot be used (a) to warrant the idea that God is accepting animal blood on the altar instead of the ostensibly more ideal human blood nor (b) does it serve as an interpretive key for Levitical sacrifices. Taking these in reverse order, Gen 22 cannot be linked directly with Levitical sacrifices because the ritual slaughter in Gen 22 is different from the way ritual slaughter happens in Leviticus. Animals are not slaughtered *on* the altar, like Isaac was about to be (22:9–10); rather they are slaughtered *away from* the altar and only the necessary components are brought to the altar to be burned upon it (cf. Milgrom, *Leviticus 1–16*, 249; and see a little further below [p. 21, where I discuss animal slaughter vis-à-vis the altar). Levitical sacrificial practices are therefore not patterned after Gen 22, which presupposes a different means of ritual slaughter and a different function for an altar. Further, although Gen 22:2 says this takes places in "the land of Moriah" and 2 Chr 3:1 says Solomon built the temple on "Mount Moriah," "it is striking that the passage in Chronicles defines the place where the angel appeared to David and not the place of our story, which would, of course, have given the place a much more ancient consecration" (von Rad, *Genesis*, 240). It is highly doubtful, then, that the Chronicler is intending an allusion to Abraham and Isaac, let alone the differences between Moriah as "a land" in Genesis, but "a specific hill" in 2 Chronicles (Levenson, *Death and Resurrection of the Beloved Son*, 119). No matter whether "[t]he name Moriah was inserted into [Gen 22:2] from II Chron. 3.1 only subsequently in order to claim it as an ancient tradition of Jerusalem" (von Rad, *Genesis*, 240), "the land of Moriah" in Gen 22:2 does not support a link with the Levitical system since it assumes a traveling cultic space at the dwelling place. And even the expectation in Deut 12 of a final location for the dwelling place for sacrifice does not give any hint that this place will be where Abraham was willing to sacrifice Isaac. In fact, it can be within the territory of any tribe (12:5, 11, 14). Finally, while "Moriah" may be intended to identify the *place* of Abraham's near-sacrifice of Isaac as occurring at the same place where Solomon built the temple in Jerusalem (if "Moriah" is a post-2 Chr 3:1 addition), the point remains that this cannot be conflated with the notion that it also "serves an etiology of animal rather than human sacrifice" (Levenson, *Death and Resurrection of the Beloved Son*, 111–24, here 113) since this is "another category of etiology" (114). This segues to the next point.

Regarding issue (a): Isaac's question, "Where is the lamb for the burnt offering?"

tionary death is an altogether foreign concept; this idea simply needs to be "substituted" with something more congruent with the biblical texts.

What about Hand Laying?

One reason some assume sacrifice is a substitutionary death is because certain sacrifices call for the offerer to lay a single hand on the animal. The mistaken idea is that this gesture means the animal is substituting for the offerer who should really be the one to die.[15] But the fact that there is no such thing as a substitutionary death sacrifice automatically excludes this as a possibility.

(Gen 22:7), actually serves to underscore my point that the sacrificial animal was never logically the substitute for the human worshiper. Whatever else is going on here in Gen 22, the *odd* thing within the story world of the pericope itself is that *a human being* (Isaac) is supposedly about to be a *substitute* for the expected and normative use of an animal for sacrifice. To read this pericope as if it is reversing this substitutionary framework—as if it is supposed to teach the readers that animal sacrifices are substituting for the expected and normative use of human beings—is, quite frankly, unintelligible nonsense from within the internal plot of the pericope itself. This story, as Levenson notes, is not "intended as an etiology of animal instead of human sacrifice" (*Death and Resurrection of the Beloved Son*, 126; cf. 111–14). The drama of the story necessitates that sacrificing a human being is, at the very least, *not normal or expected* for either the characters in the story or its audience. The fact that Abraham is asked to substitute the expected *animal* sacrifice with Isaac is what charges this story with the ethical moral gravitas it has. As we know, the story resolves with the resumption of the normative sacrificial practice—Abraham sacrifices a ram. But this act of ultimately sacrificing an animal is not presented as, "So now you, the audience, can see why we now offer animals instead of human beings" (cf. von Rad, *Genesis*, 238–39, 243). According to the narrative, God never actually wanted Abraham to sacrifice Isaac (or any other human being for that matter). This was just a "test" (22:1). But this potential abnormal substitution of a human being instead of an animal is ultimately rescinded and it becomes clear again (since it is already clear with the language of "test" at the start of the episode) that animal sacrifice is the norm and not a second-rate substitution for the more ideal human sacrifice. The surprise of the story as it stands in Genesis is not that an animal is ultimately sacrificed as a burnt offering, but rather (1) that God would even ask Abraham for a human substitute and (2) that Abraham would acquiesce. The story only works because animal sacrifice is presumed as the standard such that offering up Isaac is understood within the narrative as a break from what is normal.

For a provocative and compelling reading of Gen 22 that engages and responds to Levenson's landmark study of the binding of Isaac in the *Death and Resurrection of the Beloved Son*, see Middleton, *Abraham's Silence*, 131–225. I also respond to Levenson's views regarding the practice of firstborn child sacrifice in chapter 2, where I deal with the redemption of firstborn males in the subsection "The Passover Is Not a Substitutionary Death" (see especially footnote 78).

15. E.g., Morales, *Who Shall Ascend*, 128–29.

Notice that the "well-being" sacrifices (*šəlāmîm*) (Lev 3), which have no atoning function (because they have nothing to do with sins),[16] are one of the sacrifices that require a single-hand-laying gesture (3:2, 8, 13). This means the single-hand gesture cannot be understood as substitutionary death or transferring sin or whatever else because "sin" is excluded from view for these non-atoning well-being sacrifices.[17] Moreover, as Scott Shauf notes, these well-being offerings are "made on joyous occasions and ha[ve] nothing to do with atonement. For these sacrifices, the idea that the animal's life substitutes for the life of the offerer does not even make sense."[18] Additionally, the guilt offering, which is one of the atoning sacrifices, does *not* require a hand gesture (5:14–6:7 Eng. [5:14–26 MT]). These two offerings prove that whatever the single-hand gesture means, it cannot mean "substitutionary death" or "transfer of sins": the non-atoning well-being offering requires the hand gesture, whereas the atoning guilt offering does not.

What does the hand gesture mean then? Quite simply, it is a gesture of ownership.[19] The single-hand gesture is distinguished from the double-hand gesture, which occurs on the Day of Atonement, although only upon the goat that is *not* sacrificed and remains alive (16:21).[20] As Klawans summarizes, "Drawing on the biblical and ancient Near Eastern sources, David P. Wright argues that the two-handed rite conveys a notion of designation . . . as when Moses appoints Joshua as his successor (Num. 27:18, 23, Deut. 34:9; cf. Lev. 24:14)."[21] In this way then,

> while the laying of two hands connotes designation, the laying of a single hand conveys the notion of ownership. The rite is not intended to express some abstract identification between the

16. More on these non-atoning sacrifices in chapter 2.

17. Similarly, Shauf, *Jesus the Sacrifice*, 33–34.

18. Shauf, *Jesus the Sacrifice*, 33.

19. Wright, "The Gesture of Hand Placement," 433–46; Milgrom, *Leviticus 1–16*, 150–53; Milgrom, *Leviticus*, 24; Milgrom, "The Modus Operandi of the *Ḥaṭṭāʾt*," 112; Feldman, *The Story of Sacrifice*, 53, 55; Klawans, *Purity, Sacrifice*, 85; Balberg, *Blood for Thought*, 50. Contra Morales, who does not engage any of this evidence when discussing hand-laying (*Who Shall Ascend*, 127–29).

20. See Wright, "Gesture," 436: "Though this [double-hand-laying] ritual results in the placement of the sins on the goat's head, it should not be considered a transfer of sins in a strict sense. That is, the sins are not passed from Aaron through his hands to the goat. Aaron never carries or embodies these evils. Consequently, one cannot say that sins are *transferred*. Rather, the placement of the sins is effected by both the hand placement gesture which designates where the sins are to rest *and* the spoken confession which concretizes the sins which then fall on the head of the goat" (his emphasis; see also 434–39). See also Feldman, *Story*, 164.

21. Klawans, *Purity, Sacrifice*, 85.

> offerer and the offering—it is not intended to say "This offering represents me." Rather, the statement is more concrete and practical. The offerer puts his single hand on the offering to state: "This offering is mine."[22]

Wright provides helpful observations to support this thesis:

> This interpretation allows us to make sense of the lack of hand placement with birds and cereal [grain] offerings (cf. Lev. 1:14–17; 2; 5:7–10, 11–13). These offerings are small and can be carried by the offerer alone in his or her hand. The offerer brings these items and gives them directly to the priest. The presentation of the small offerings in the hand of the offerer is enough to designate the offering as pertaining to that person. No hand placement rite is therefore necessary. In contrast, one can imagine that with the larger quadrupeds, several persons may have been required to move a stubborn animal into proper position, or in the case of a woman bringing an offering (cf. Lev. 12) other men may have led the animal into the sanctuary court. Confusion as to who was actually bringing the animal may have ensued. Therefore, hand placement needed to be performed with the larger animals to initiate the sacrifice and allay any possible confusion of attribution.[23]

We will return to this notion of proper and legal ownership when dealing with the so-called prophetic critique of sacrifice in chapter 4 since, as Klawans argues, this is what much of the prophetic critique of sacrifice is premised on.[24] Nevertheless, at this point it suffices to conclude that the single-hand-laying gesture cannot be used as evidence that sacrifice serves as a substitutionary death for the offerer. The fact that non-atoning sacrifices require it, but certain atoning sacrifices do not, as well as the textually and contextually validated distinctive functions of single- versus double-hand-laying, all militate against a substitutionary understanding.

SACRIFICE IS NOT ABOUT "DEATH"

Another reason sacrifice cannot be construed as a substitutionary death is because the (obvious) biological death of the animal sacrifice is reconceptualized in Lev 17 into something explicitly other than a "killing" and a

22. Klawans, *Purity, Sacrifice*, 85.

23. Wright, "Gesture," 439.

24. E.g., Klawans, *Purity, Sacrifice*, 86–89, 91.

"death." As hand-laying cannot be used in support of *substitutionary* death, this section argues that sacrifice cannot be about substitutionary *death*. The ritual is all about accessing "life" and bringing that "life" into the presence of the Living God (17:11, 14).

Death *qua* "death" cannot be brought into sacred space without defiling it (see esp. Num 19; Exod 21:14; Ezek 9:7). As will be discussed more in the chapter 3, the sources of ritual impurity are all related to (non-sinful) conditions that convey "the forces of death," as Jacob Milgrom phrased it.[25] Not only can *death* itself not be brought into sacred space, but also nothing and no one associated with death via *ritual impurity* can be brought into sacred space (Lev 7:20–21; 21:1–6, 10–12; 22:3–9; Num 19:13, 20). Therefore, thinking that a sacrifice is conceptualized as a *death* (substitutionary or not)—the greatest and most potent source of ritual impurity—which is then brought into the direct presence of God fundamentally misunderstands the conceptual framework of Leviticus's ritual ontology.

So how does the Torah deal with this seeming contradiction that "death" cannot be brought into sacred space, but that animal sacrifice rather obviously necessitates the biological death of the animal? It does this by capitalizing on the basic notions of what rituals do, namely, as Jonathan Z. Smith argues, providing the "means of overcoming this contradiction between 'word and deed.'"[26] In brief, according to Leviticus, although in "deed" an animal literally dies, in "word" via the whole ritual process (how the animal dies, where it dies, what happens to its body and blood afterwards, etc.) the death of the animal is reconceptualized and reconfigured so that what just took place was a not-killing, but a "sacrifice." And the "sacrifice" itself will take on different meaning and significance depending on the function

25. Milgrom, *Leviticus 1–16*, 686, 733, 767–68, 865, 889, cf. 1000–1004; Milgrom, *Leviticus*, 135; Milgrom, "The Rationale for Biblical Impurity," 107–11; cf. Thiessen, *Jesus and the Forces of Death*, 14–18; Klawans, *Purity, Sacrifice*, 53–58. But I do not think ritual impurity is reducible to "death" or "mortality" *per se*. I discuss the purity framework further in chapter 3, but here I just note that those aspects of ritual impurity more obviously relating to death (corpse impurity in Num 19 and scale disease in Lev 13–14, which makes one's skin look like a rotting corpse, Num 12:12) can be subsumed under a broader understanding of human *finitude* (human beings both *begin* and *end*) in contrast to God's infiniteness (God not only does not procreate, but did not have a beginning and will not have an ending). (My thanks to my former student Braeden Holmstrom for this initial observation.) This better explains why sex and childbirth also convey ritual impurity (Lev 12, 15), not so much because they are associated with "death" or "mortality," but rather more because they are associated with human finite *beginnings*. This view is found in Jub. 3:8–14, which highlights Adam and Eve's presumed initial impurity since they need to remain outside of the holy garden of Eden (vv. 9–14), for the same proscribed days of impurity in Lev 12 (cf. Luke 2:22).

26. Smith, "The Bare Facts of Ritual," 124.

of the particular sacrifice being offered. So a "sacrifice" is further construed either as a "sacred gift" or, when used for *kipper*, into a "ritual detergent" for decontaminating sancta (sacred objects/places).[27] But the validity of either of these purposes depends upon the sacrifice being transfigured into something completely separate from anything having to do with the concept of "death." In short, Lev 17 makes it clear that "sacrifice" functions within a ritual ontology wholly distinct from the realm of "death."

To build to this conclusion, recall that according to the priestly account of creation in Gen 1, humans were originally supposed to be vegetarians (Gen 1:29; 2:16; 3:18–19). Even though God permits humans to consume meat after the flood so long as they do not consume any blood, which is its "life" (9:3–6), it is apparent that Lev 17 is still very uncomfortable with the fact that eating meat requires an animal to actually *die* and it therefore seeks a ritual solution to this conundrum. In other words, eating meat, which obviously requires the death of the animal, needed a theological rationale. Leviticus gives its readers an ingenious way to reconceptualize the death of the sacrificial animals so that it is no longer conceived of as a "death." It is difficult to capture the ritual reconfiguration happening, but in short, they conceptualized the death of the sacrificial animal as "*not*-a-killing."

Granted, this at first seems paradoxical and counterintuitive. This is why it is helpful to understand the transformative power of rituals—because it allows us to see the ethical motivation behind the instructions in Lev 17. As Smith argues, "one major function of ritual" is specifically to deal with seeming "hypocrisy" or "contradiction."[28] Smith goes on to explain:

> [*R*]*itual represents the creation of a controlled environment* where the variables (i.e., the accidents) of ordinary life have been displaced *precisely* because they are felt to be so overwhelmingly present and powerful. *Ritual is a means of performing the way things ought to be in conscious tension to the way things are in such a way that this ritualized perfection is recollected in the ordinary, uncontrolled, course of things.*[29]

In this article, Smith uses examples from hunting societies for how they ritually perceive and rationalize what they in fact *do* with what they *want to have happened*. Hunting rituals allow them to "face the gap," the "incongruity between their ideological statement of how they *ought* to hunt

27. See chapter 4.

28. Smith, "The Bare Facts of Ritual," 124.

29. Smith, "The Bare Facts of Ritual," 124–25; his emphasis.

and their actual behavior while hunting."[30] According to the rituals and liturgies of these societies, the ideal hunt can be summarized thus:

> The hunter is a host inviting the animal to feast on the gift of its own meat. The animal is host to the hunters as they feed on its flesh. The animal is a gift from the "Master of the Animals," it is a visitor from the spirit world. The animal gives itself to the hunters. The hunter, by killing the animal, enables it to return to its "Supernatural Owner" and to its home, from which it has come to earth as a visitor. . . . [T]he Kill . . . is likewise governed by strict rules of etiquette. Most of the regulations seem designed to insure that the animal is killed in hand-to-hand, face-to-face combat. . . . The controlling idea is that the animal is not killed by the hunter's initiative, rather the animal freely offers itself to the hunter's weapon.[31]

But in reality most hunters "do not, in fact, hunt bears face-to-face [and the bear subsequently willingly and without a fight gives up its life to the hunter] but [rather the hunters] make extensive use of traps, pitfalls, self-triggering bows, and snares" and even brag about their cunning and/or their strength to overpower these predators.[32] This is what generates "a gap, an incongruity between their ideological statements of how they *ought* to hunt and their actual behavior while hunting."[33]

But it is noticing how they deal with this gap that illumines the reconceptualizing role rituals play for communities: "It is far more important and interesting that they say this is the way they hunt than that they actually do so. For now we are obligated to find out how *they* resolve this discrepancy."[34] This is instructive for our purposes because we can see how Leviticus deals with its own "incongruity" as it concerns the slaughter of animals used in sacrifices.

Leviticus has an analogous yet different way of handling the tension between "the way things are" with "the way things ought to be" within its distinctive conceptual framework of reality. In Leviticus's "controlled environment" of sacrifice the "tension to way things are" (an animal is being killed) with "the way things ought to be" (humans living in harmony with and not killing animals for food, per Gen 1:29; 2:16; 3:18–19) is dissolved because the cultic ritual makes it possible to reorient the whole process

30. Smith, "The Bare Facts of Ritual," 123; his emphasis.

31. Smith, "The Bare Facts of Ritual," 120.

32. Smith, "The Bare Facts of Ritual," 122–24, here 122.

33. Smith, "The Bare Facts of Ritual," 123; his emphasis.

34. Smith, "The Bare Facts of Ritual," 123.

around accessing "life." That is, the rituals make it so that the event of sacrifice is *not at all about death* but rather is *a presentation of life* (Lev 17:11, 14).[35]

Leviticus accomplishes this very thing by raising the stakes and letting the reader know just where the notions of "death," "killing," and "murder" come into view. According to 17:3–4 the act of killing a domesticated animal that could be used as a sacrifice (bull, s/he-goat, ram, lamb) simply to eat it—even if you pour out its blood—without ritually presenting it as an offering at the dwelling place means that this act is not only considered a killing, but "bloodshed" or "murder" (17:4). Let this sink in:

> If anyone of the house of Israel slaughters an ox or a lamb or a goat in the camp, or slaughters it outside the camp, and does not bring it to the entrance of the tent of meeting, to present it as an offering to the LORD before the tabernacle of the LORD, he shall be held guilty of bloodshed; he has shed blood, and he shall be cut off from the people. (Lev 17:3–4 NRSV)

According to Leviticus, *killing a domesticated animal is morally equivalent to murdering a human being*.[36] That is the basic ethical claim here. Failure to comprehend the significance of Leviticus's ritual reconfiguration of these seemingly "mundane" events, which to the untrained eye makes ritual sacrifice look like a plain and simple "death," has led to interpretations and Christian theologies that are not only exegetically inaccurate, but, as pointed out in the introduction, can be downright dangerous.

There is only one circumstance in which killing a domesticated animal is not considered murder and that is when it is offered as a sacrifice *at the right place* and its blood is deposited *in the right manner* somewhere on the outer altar (17:5–6, 8–9, 11).[37] Killing a domesticated animal for a meal or trying to offer one at another altar in any other place than at the entrance to the dwelling place is not a "sacrifice" but a "murder" (17:3–5, 8–9; cf.

35. Similarly, Willi-Plein, "Some Remarks on Hebrews," 33.

36. Levine, *Leviticus*, 113; Milgrom, "Sacrifices and Offerings, OT," 770; Douglas, *Leviticus as Literature*, 232; Schwartz, "Leviticus," 236. Non-Israelites would simply be subject to Gen 9:3–6 such that so long as they do not consume any blood, then they will not incur bloodguilt and have their own blood required of them.

37. Both *where* the blood goes and *how* it gets placed depends on which type of sacrifice it is, since the blood carries different functions depending on the ritual. The subtle distinctions here will matter (more on this in due course), but they do not matter presently. The point for now is that the sacrificial slaughter and the placement of the blood needs to happen for a certain purpose (an offering) at a certain place (the altar at the dwelling place); otherwise, the mundane "reality" of what just happened—an animal was killed—would still be considered "murder."

Deut 12:11–14, 17–18). It is not that Lev 17:3–5 conceptualizes "sacrifice" as "the right/acceptable way to commit a murder." Or, as Ina Willi-Plein expresses, sacrifice "is no act of violence, no expiatory killing," but "[r]ather, it is a presentation of life."[38] Leviticus 17 makes an ontological distinction between "sacrifice" and "killing/death" by means of the reconceptualization made possible by the power of ritual.

Supporting this view is the fact that the death of the animal—the slaughter itself—is given no ritual or theological meaning by any biblical text.[39] Scott Shauf's incisive observation about the role of the priest as opposed to the offerer in Lev 4:27–31 makes this clear:

> Note that the slaughter of the animal is mentioned only in v. 29. The great part of the ritual focuses on what is to be done with the different parts of the animal *after* it is killed. . . . Note also that it is the offerer, the one who has sinned, who slaughters the animal, while the priest performs all the rituals with the blood and the fat[. S]ince it is the priest who is said to make atonement for the offerer in v. 31, the implication clearly is that it is the post-slaughter rituals that are central to the act of atonement, not the slaughter itself. This does not square well with the idea that the sacrifice atones via substitution, because in the idea of substitution, the death of the animal in place of the offerer is the focus. If the substitution of the animal for the offerer were the key to understanding the whole act, why would the rituals performed *after* the slaughter be identified specifically as what atones? Moreover, why would not the priest do the slaughtering?[40]

Therefore, as Christian A. Eberhart puts it, "The priestly texts lack any indication that this ritual element [i.e., 'the act of *killing* the animal'] had special significance. . . . This means that *ritualized killing is not the purpose of cultic sacrifices* in the Hebrew Bible, and killing alone does not qualify a given set of activities as a sacrifice."[41] The fact that sacrificial killing involves accessing *blood* means that something other than death *qua* death is being activated. As Moffitt puts it, "the blood is the vehicle or agent of the victim's life" and "[t]he converse of this point is that the death or slaughter of the victim, while necessary to procure the blood, has no particular atoning significance

38. Willi-Plein, "Some Remarks on Hebrews," 33.

39. E.g., Moffitt, "It Is Not Finished," 163–64; Moffitt, "Blood, Life, and Atonement," 219; Eberhart, "Characteristics of Sacrificial Metaphors in Hebrews," 39, 43–44, 49–50, 52–53, 58; Willi-Plein, "Some Remarks on Hebrews," 33.

40. Shauf, *Jesus the Sacrifice*, 32; his emphasis.

41. Eberhart, *The Sacrifice of Jesus*, 96; his emphasis.

in and of itself."[42] A bloodless breaking of the animal's neck or some such would suffice as a "sacrifice" if all that mattered was the *death* of the animal. However, breaking an animal's neck is a non-sacrificial slaughter used only in special circumstances that are also ritually construed (and thus the ritualized action again renders it no longer a killing/murder), but it is explicitly not a *sacrificial* ritual (Exod 13:13; 34:20; Deut 21:4).[43]

Eberhart observes additionally how sacrificial "animal slaughter is never to be carried out on the central altar, but somewhere in the forecourt or on the side of the altar (Lev 1:11; Ezek 40:39–41), which are areas of lesser sanctity."[44] Further, the outer altar (that is, not the smaller altar inside the holy place, which is for burning incense only) is simply called "the altar of burnt offering" (Lev 1:9, 13; 8:21; cf. "altar of the burnt offering," 3:5; 4:7, 10, 18, 25, 30, 34). This "indicates that the burning of the sacrificial material is the main ritual element to be carried out there," which is why vegetable and grain offerings are "sacrifices" even though there is obviously no slaughter happening with these, and thus, there are no blood rites with these either, even though they can serve a bloodless-atoning function in 5:11–13.[45] The key conclusion to be drawn from these observations "is that the slaughter of animals is rather insignificant."[46] The blood rites from animal sacrifices, though they differ depending on the specific sacrifice and its specific function, come into play precisely as a way of ritually reconceptualizing the slaughter away from the realm of "death," transforming the event into a "non-killing" and the procurement of the life-giving and purifying blood.

This conceptual framework proves that whatever is going on in the ritualized *sacrificial* death of an animal, it is *not* conceptualized as a "killing," let alone a substitutionary killing. "Killing," as a concept, is what happens when an animal is slaughtered for any other reason or in any other place or when its blood is not properly handled. If any one of the requirements from Lev 17 is violated, then the entire event is perceived as belonging to the realm of "death" and thus the person is guilty of shedding blood (akin to homicide). And it carries the same bloodguilt as if a human has been killed (Lev 17:4).

42. Moffitt, "Blood, Life, and Atonement," 219.

43. Sarna, *Exodus*, 67; Tigay, *Deuteronomy*, 192.

44. Eberhart, "Characteristics," 43.

45. Eberhart, "Characteristics," 43–44, 49, here 43; see also Eberhart, *The Sacrifice*, 97–98.

46. Eberhart, "Characteristics," 44.

There is much more to say regarding Lev 17, but to summarize thus far: the only way to transform the death of a domesticated animal into something other than killing/murder is if (a) it dies as a result of being offered as a sacrifice (b) in the right ritual manner and (c) if its blood is handled in the right ritual manner (d) at the right ritual place. *This necessarily means that the death of a sacrificial animal is conceptualized in Leviticus as something other than killing or being put to death.* In turn, *this means that whatever is happening for atoning sacrifices, they most definitely cannot be conceptualized as a "substitutionary death" because the whole "reality" of the event has been transfigured via ritual so that it has nothing to do whatsoever with "death."*

The *rituals* of sacrifice are what allows this seeming "contradiction" to be resolved. The theological reasoning is that since the animal's blood is on the outer altar in some fashion this transforms the death of the animal from being a "killing" and a "murder" to being "*not*-a-killing" (and thus not a sin and bloodguilt-free). Ignoring these observations in favor of a theological interpretation of sacrifice that trades in the concepts of "death" and "substitution" fails to attend to the historical and cultural embeddedness of these sacrificial rituals. All of this gets to the point that when an animal is used in Levitical sacrifice, then, ontologically speaking, from within that conceptual framework, it is being *offered/sacrificed*; it is not being *killed*.

The Importance of Non-Sacrificial Blood Rituals

There is another corroborating observation from Lev 17 that reinforces the point about how ritual reconfigures and transforms what under any other circumstances would be considered part of the realm of "death" and "murder."[47]

After discussing the ritual (re)configuration of domesticated animal death, Lev 17 ends with instructions for hunting (clean) game (vv. 12–16). Importantly, the instruction is not just about not consuming blood (cf. Gen 9:3–5), but also specifies that certain actions with the blood need to take place otherwise the hunters are liable to being "cut off" (Lev 17:14). The blood needs to be (a) "poured out" and (b) "covered with dirt" (v. 13). As William K. Gilders asks and responds, "But why is the blood disposed of in this specific way? Clearly, we have to do with ritualized activity here—that is, the text prescribes a definite mode of dealing with the blood, which differs from the normal and casual disposal of other waste products from a

47. Ritual reconfiguration is also what is happening with the ritual breaking of an animal's neck in Exod 13:13, 34:20, and Deut 21:4 as discussed briefly above (footnote 43).

slaughtered animal, such as excrement in the digestive tract, or the bones."[48] Also, Mary Douglas has noted the "telling verbal cross-references" between "homicide" and "eating" in Gen 4:11, Lev 7:22–27, 17:3–4, 13–14, and 19:16, 26.[49] This, as others have surmised, suggests that the reason the instructions for hunting game go beyond simply refraining from literally consuming blood and include extra ritualized actions of handling the blood ("pouring out" and "covering") is because failure to perform these rituals amounts to *consuming* the blood, which itself amounts to *murder*.[50]

In fact, Deuteronomy borrows from the logic of handling the blood from hunted game in Lev 17:13–14 in order to deal with the new reality that Israelites who now live in the promised land and live so far away from the centralized sanctuary and altar would never be permitted to eat from their flocks and herds since the meat from these can only be eaten when they are offered as well-being sacrifices at the sanctuary, per Lev 17:3–6 (Deut 12:15–16, 21–25; cf. 15:21–23).[51] Living too far away from the dwelling place makes journeying there unfeasible any time the Israelites wanted to eat meat and so Deuteronomy stipulates that eating meat from the flock and herds can be treated in the same way Lev 17:13–14 deals with hunted game. Deuteronomy only specifies "pouring out" of the blood on the ground and lacks the additional activity of "covering" it from Lev 17:13. Nevertheless, as Gilders observes, "the deliberate act of not doing anything with the blood except disposing of it by pouring it out on the ground is ritualized activity, since it is strategically distinguished from another assumed type of activity and a privileged opposition is established."[52] In this way, the necessary biological death of a herd or flock animal for a meal in Deuteronomy is no longer a "killing"/"homicide," but neither is it a "sacrifice." It just becomes a "non-killing-meal," like hunted game.

Therefore, it this direct *ritualized handling of the blood* in both Lev 17 and Deut 12 that redirects attention away from the obvious "death" of the animal and transforms it into an inoffensive not-murder. As Smith outlines,

48. Gilders, *Blood Ritual*, 23–24; see also 15 when Gilders comments on the similar instructions found in Deut 12:16, 24; 15:23.

49. Douglas, *Leviticus*, 231–33.

50. Gilders, *Blood Ritual*, 24, 144. Leviticus 17:3–6 already unequivocally says killing animals is no different than killing a human being, but Ezek 24:7–8, Job 16:18, and Isa 26:21 together corroborate this reading because it shows how the act of "covering" the blood per Lev 17:13 would be an intelligible ritual act that prevents this event—hunting an animal for food—from being reckoned *as* a killing/homicide. The book of Jubilees similarly corroborates this understanding of the meaning of "covering" animal blood (Jub. 7:30–31; 21:1–25).

51. Milgrom, *Leviticus*, 192; Gilders, *Blood Ritual*, 14–17.

52. Gilders, *Blood Ritual*, 15.

"The ordinary (which remain, to the [outside] observer's eye, wholly ordinary)," i.e., the death of the animal, "becomes significant, becomes sacred . . . by having our attention directed to it in a special way" through ritual actions.[53] Apart from this ritual action with the blood (which slightly changes if this is a sacrifice or hunted game), the person is liable to bloodguilt and thus will be "cut off" even if he literally abstained from consuming any blood. It is "by having our attention directed" to the blood that the blood ritual transforms the entire event so that it is no longer a murder.[54]

This transformation of what (to an outsider) might seem like the brute facts of the matter—an animal is being intentionally killed—into something entirely incompatible and incongruent with those brute facts is a major function of ritual activity itself. Smith puts it this way: "Ritual gains its force where incongruency is perceived."[55] This is how it becomes possible for the death of an animal to be ritually transformed into a sacred gift to God—a non-killing, a non-murder. The meaning and function of the sacrifice depends upon several distinct ritual actions with respect to the blood and the carcass discussed in the following chapters, but there is no meaning attached to the animal's actual death other than that its death is reconceptualized through these various ritual actions to convey something other than "death." According to Leviticus, "death" is what happens *apart from* the sacrificial system.

Therefore, it is not even proper to call sacrifice a "ritual *death*" because the ritual depends on it not actually being comprehended as a *death*, which would bring impurity into the dwelling place. Sacrifice is rather a way to access *"life"* and avoid all associations with "death." Sacrifice is a process by which to transform the mundane into a sacred gift. "Death" has no intelligibility in this ritual framework of perceiving the truth of the matter. Meaning, the presence or absence of these ritual actions determines the "truth" of what happened; it might be a homicide, or it might be a sacrifice. What the "truth" is all depends on the ritual factors discussed above.

SACRIFICE IS NOT ABOUT "SUFFERING"

Not only is sacrifice separated from having anything to do with the concept of "death," it is also separated from the notion of "suffering."[56] As David

53. Smith, "The Bare Facts of Ritual," 115.

54. Smith, "The Bare Facts of Ritual," 115. For more on the importance of ritual directing "attention," see Smith, *To Take Place*, 104.

55. Smith, "Bare Facts," 125.

56. Contra Stackhouse, "Terminal Punishment," 77.

Moffitt explains, "To maltreat a sacrificial animal would be to render it ineligible to be offered to God, since a sacrificial victim that suffered physical damage from abuse would no longer be ἄμωμος ('without blemish')."[57] Hence, the "attempt to read suffering and the centrality of death back into Jewish sacrifice leads to all manner of misunderstanding about sacrifice as Leviticus portrays it."[58]

Sacrificial slaughter was meant to be painless, quick, and humane by means of a swift cut to the throat. In fact, rabbinic instructions for animal slaughter (*shehitah*), building on the basic notions for humane animal slaughter in the Torah, demonstrates how foreign the notion of "suffering" is to animal slaughter (let alone animal sacrifice) because every effort is made to preclude suffering taking place. Just as animals that cannot be sacrificed nevertheless have a *ritual* means of transforming their necessary deaths for a meal into a "non-killing/non-murder" (Lev 17:13–14), *shehitah* transforms what could be considered "suffering" from an outsider's perspective (because the death of the animal may be comprehended as inherently involving suffering) into a non-suffering and painless event from an insider's perspective by stipulating how all the various aspects before, during, and after, the slaughter are to be done so that the animal does not suffer pain. Once again, we encounter the transformative power of ritual activity. So, as Moffitt highlights, in the Torah "there is no hint that the animal is made to suffer, nor that the victim is an object of abuse or wrath. Inflicting suffering on the sacrificial victim is not a part of the biblical sacrificial system."[59]

This is significant because we can now see that when it comes to sacrificial understandings of Jesus's death in the NT, these never occur in the context of Jesus's sufferings and passion. Put another way: when Jesus's *sufferings* and/or death *qua death* are the topic, then sacrificial metaphors are *avoided*.[60]

57. Moffitt, "It Is Not Finished," 164.

58. Moffitt, "It Is Not Finished," 165n23.

59. Moffitt, "It Is Not Finished," 164.

60. "In sacrificial images, therefore, Christ's death is not the actual salvific event. . . . The author of Hebrews provides indirect proof of this subtle distinction. His/her general Christological program that salvation is accomplished through Christ's death (Heb 2:14) is stated again in Heb 9:15. . . . But in order to prove this statement, the author of Hebrews needs to change the imagery that has been so thoroughly developed throughout the entire chapter. Hence s/he leaves cultic metaphors and chooses a secular legal background when arguing that succession takes effect upon the death of the testator [in 9:16–17]. . . . This legal metaphor provides a sufficient background to argue that somebody's death has a positive effect. Based solely on cultic metaphors, this argument would have been impossible" (Eberhart, "Characteristics," 59). See also Moffitt, "It Is Not Finished," 164n19.

CONCLUSION

Israel makes a big deal about bloodguilt, and, as we will see soon enough, not even the Day of Atonement can atone for it. Leviticus 17:3–5 says that killing and eating a domesticated animal is considered killing/murder and thus incurs bloodguilt upon the person. The only way for this not to be killing/murder is if the animal is sacrificed at the dwelling place and its blood is placed in some fashion in relation to the altar. This transforms the death of the animal into a *sacrifice* and thus the offerer is not guilty of bloodshed.

At the end of the day, it is crucial to realize that the Torah explicitly reconceptualizes the death of the sacrificial animal into a "non-killing." This explains why the Torah does not give the death of the animal itself any ritual or theological significance. *And this all thereby proves that there simply is no warrant for the view that the sacrifice is standing in for the death of someone who is ostensibly worthy of death.* This is because (a) the death of a sacrificial animal is explicitly *not* to be recognized as shedding blood and thus logically cannot be understood as substituting for shedding the blood of the offerer. And (b), there is no sacrifice (not even the Day of Atonement) that can be made to substitute for when someone is to be put to death or "cut off."

Any way we come at this, the Levitical sacrificial system was not about substituting for someone who was supposed to be put to death (let alone substituting for someone else's deserved suffering).

We can turn now to a more positive account about what the functions of Levitical sacrifices are, even as we expose and dismantle more common mistakes.

2

Understanding Old Testament Sacrifices, Part 2

The Non-Atoning Sacrifices

Now that we know what Levitical sacrifice is *not*—it cannot be about substitutionary death—here I provide a description of what *is* going on in the Torah's sacrificial system in terms of the non-atoning sacrifices (the atoning sacrifices will be addressed in chapter 4). As in the last chapter, I will not be able to say everything that should be said, not even for the limited goals of this book. When discussing various NT passages in the following chapters, I will offer more supplementary observations regarding certain sacrifices. This chapter serves to establish a necessary foundation for moving forward. Here I argue for the following theses:

(1) Not all sacrifices have an atoning function. There are non-atoning sacrifices that have separate rationales and functions. These are most of the burnt offerings and all of the well-being offerings.

(2) The purpose of the regular burnt offerings is "divine attraction" or "invitation."

(3) The purpose of the well-being offerings is sacred feasting between God and people.

(4) The Passover is neither about atonement nor substitutionary death. Rather, it is a non-atoning well-being sacrifice commemorating God's

past act of deliverance. More specifically, it is most like the "thanksgiving" well-being sacrifice.

(5) The covenant-inauguration and renewal ceremonies only use non-atoning sacrifices.

(6) The blood sprinkling on the people (Exod 24:8) is neither about atonement nor about substitutionary death. Rather, it is a way to signify and ratify the bond between two covenantal parties (God and Israel here).

(7) Whenever blood is placed on people, it is never blood from the atoning sacrifice used to atone (purge) sancta (the *ḥaṭṭāʾt*). The use of non-atoning sacrificial blood on people is to ritually mark specific metaphysical transitions.

THERE ARE NON-ATONING SACRIFICES

It is all too common to think that there is only one purpose for Levitical sacrifice; namely, to atone. However, *not all sacrifices have an atoning function.* Without getting into the history of religions, origins of sacrifice in general, or ancient Israelite sacrifice in particular, it suffices for our purposes to note that there are two main categories for sacrifices broadly speaking:[1] these are "the categories of gift-offering-display and/or pollution removal."[2] In the terms I have been using thus far, in the Torah these are the "non-atoning well-being sacrifices" and the "atoning sacrifices," respectively. There is merit and value for further nuancing these categories into various subdivisions for other analytic endeavors—and I will do some of this myself shortly—but it is still apparent from the proposed lists of other scholars that they in fact reduce to the above two umbrella categories.[3] Keeping the categories broadly simplified in this way will help focus our attention when we get to the NT since we will be able to distinguish between the atoning and non-atoning sacrifices with ease.

Moreover, the assumption that sacrifice always has an "atoning function" is not only inaccurate, but this misconception has also prevented NT scholars from noticing one of the most obvious and significant observations when it comes to comprehending the sacrificial understandings of Jesus: the

1. Space requires the focus of this study to be aimed at what will be most relevant for analyzing NT texts. For further study into all the other details of the history of ancient Israelite sacrifice, the reader is encouraged to consult the various secondary sources I have catalogued in these footnotes.

2. Smith, "Domestication," 197.

3. E.g., Shauf, *Jesus the Sacrifice*, 18, 26; Sanders, *Judaism*, 104.

earliest NT texts associate Jesus with the *non-atoning* sacrifices. These non-atoning sacrifices are also the most prevalent ones linked to Jesus's death across the NT. These non-atoning sacrifices are a covenant-inaugurating sacrifice and the Passover.[4] I will discuss these further below, but for now we are just noting that both are categorized as types of the non-atoning "well-being" sacrifices (*šəlāmîm*, Lev 3; 7:11–18).[5]

Conveniently, it is straightforward to recognize if a sacrifice is atoning or non-atoning: if the laity *eat* from it, then it *cannot* be an atoning sacrifice. This is how we know, for example, that the Passover is a type of communal well-being sacrifice since it is *eaten* by the laity. This is why these sacrifices are sometimes translated as "fellowship" or "communion" offerings, since these are a way for the worshiper to commune or have fellowship with God at the sanctuary.

I will discuss the purpose and function of atonement in chapter 4, but what is crucial for now is that if a sacrifice has an atoning function, then the laity never eat from it.[6] And, if the atoning sacrifice is atoning for the priest himself (or priests as a group), then the priest(s) is not permitted to eat from it either.[7] As Jacob Milgrom comments, "[priests] are not to benefit from their own offenses," which is why "priests are not to eat their own expiatory [atoning] sacrifices."[8] After the appropriate parts are burned on the altar and the appropriate blood ritual manipulations are made, then the carcass must be burned "outside the camp" (*not* on the altar) (4:12, 21; 6:30). Basically, the sinner (priest or lay) cannot receive a tangible benefit (i.e., the meat) from a sacrifice whose purpose is to purge the sanctuary from their own sin-contamination.

4. The Sinai covenant inauguration in Exod 24 is celebrated with a communal well-being offering (24:5). The elders ate a meal in the presence of God on the mountain from these well-being sacrifices (24:9–11; cf. Gen 26:30; 31:54; Exod 34:15). The covenant was also commemorated with well-being offerings under Joshua for the reciting of the blessings and curses (Deut 27:7).

5. Cf. Milgrom, *Leviticus 1–16*, 219.

6. Milgrom, *Leviticus 1–16*, 221.

7. Priests are supposed to eat from the atoning sacrifices for *other individuals* (Lev 6:25–29 [6:18–22 MT]). This is part of the priestly compensation for their duties (priests have no land/income apart from sharing in some of the offerings brought by the people), but they are strictly forbidden to eat from any atoning sacrifices that are offered for *their own* sins/impurities and from any atoning sacrifice whose purgation blood is brought inside either the holy place or holy of holies, regardless if the sacrifice is specifically for their own sins or the sins of others (e.g., 6:30 [6:23 MT] with 4:3, 5–7, 12, 13, 16–18, 21; cf. 10:18). Simply put, if the type of atoning sacrifice requires blood to be taken inside the sanctuary itself, then no priest can eat from it, period. The remaining meat and carcass all need to be burned outside the camp.

8. Milgrom, *Leviticus 1–16*, 264.

Another way to look at this is if there is a sacrificial feast, then we can be sure "atonement" is not taking place with those sacrifices. Whenever "atonement" is happening for someone, they are not feasting on the atoning sacrifice. Insofar as nobody is permitted to eat from an atoning sacrifice that is offered for them (priest or lay), it is not feasting but rather a sort of *fasting*—in the sense of not consuming the sacrifice—that is connected with atoning sacrifices. This fasting aspect of not being allowed to partake from atoning sacrifices that purge one's own sins from the sanctuary is taken to its logical conclusion on the Day of Atonement in which fasting from all meals throughout the day is required (16:29, 31; 23:32; Num 29:7; cf. Isa 58:3).[9] Since it is a day dedicated to *atonement* writ large, then it makes perfect sense that it would be a day dedicated to *fasting*. Fasting and atonement were so closely tethered together that the Day of Atonement became known simply as "the Fast" (e.g., Acts 27:9; cf. Josephus, *Ant.* 3.240). Conversely, joyous *feasting*—the opposite of fasting—is connected with the non-atoning well-being sacrifices (Num 10:10). As we will see, these sacrificial feasts usually celebrate and commemorate a past act of divine deliverance. They are joyous feasts that have nothing to do with atonement.

THE PURPOSE FOR THE REGULAR BURNT OFFERINGS

This almost brings us to the purpose and occasions of the non-atoning well-being offerings, but before getting into that we need to understand the function of the regular prescribed daily burnt offerings, the *tāmîd* (Exod 29:38–46; Num 28:1–8), because these illumine the logic behind the well-being offerings.

A burnt offering is one where the entire animal—except for its hide, which goes to the officiating priest (Lev 1:6 with 7:8)—is burned up on the altar in the courtyard of the dwelling place (1:1–17). The required *tāmîd* in particular is in the non-atoning category.[10] This is because (a) atonement (*kipper*) is never mentioned in relation to these, nor the other regularly prescribed burnt offerings that seem to be based on the *tāmîd* for each week (on the Sabbath), each new moon (month), and during the annual convocations (Num 28–29; cf. Lev 12:8, 12–18, 36–37).[11] (b) When atonement (*kipper*) is

9. Cf. Milgrom, *Leviticus 1–16*, 1054–58, 1065–67.

10. Similarly, Shauf, *Jesus the Sacrifice*, 137.

11. Atonement (*kipper*) is mentioned with respect to a burnt offering only on the Day of Atonement (Lev 16:24) and for the *voluntary* sacrifice from an *individual* Israelite (Lev 1:2–4). But this latter is case is peculiar for the very reason that burnt offerings in

mentioned in the catalogue of sacrifices for these festivals, it is always only linked with the specific purgation offerings (*ḥaṭṭāʾt*, Num 28:22, 30; 29:5, 11). And (c), the only purpose that is mentioned repeatedly for all of these regular required burnt offerings is to provide "a pleasing aroma" to God (Exod 29:41; Num 28:2, 6, 8, 13, 24, 27; 29:2, 6, 8, 13, 36; Lev 23:13, 18).[12]

This last point clues us into the function of these regularly prescribed burnt offerings. Jonathan Klawans shows how the pervasive misunderstanding that all sacrifices have an atoning function have prevented some from realizing the distinctive purpose of the regular burnt offerings.[13] As we will discuss, atonement deals with the pollution certain sins create on the sanctuary as well as the impurity certain forms of ritual impurity produce on the sanctuary, but these burnt offerings evidently have another function having nothing to do with atonement, as the above observations showcase. As Klawans puts it: "It is not that the daily sacrifice [the *tāmîd*—and I would add those other regular burnt offerings like it] undoes the damage done by grave transgression. Quite the contrary: grave transgression undoes what the daily sacrifice produces," namely, that the *tāmîd* "attracts . . . the divine presence."[14] Given the tight correspondence between the twice-daily burnt offerings (the *tāmîd*) and the other regular prescribed burnt offerings noted above, I agree with Baruch Levine that "[t]he essential role of the ʿ*ôlāh* [burnt offering] seems to have been that of *attraction*."[15]

This is corroborated by one of the first laws given after ten commandments about building altars. There are only two types of sacrifices mentioned here—the burnt offering and the well-being offering—and only one purpose given: "I *will come* to you and bless you" (Exod 20:24 NRSV).[16] We will discuss the well-being sacrifice in the next section, but it is unambiguous from this that the purpose of these sacrifices is to elicit God's presence (and thereby God's blessing)—hence, "attraction" is more than warranted.

This purpose for divine attraction aligns with the Hebrew word for the burnt offering, ʿ*ôlâ*, which "means 'that which ascends.'"[17] Thus, the "pleasing aroma" *ascends* to heaven and thereby *attracts*—in a manner of speaking—God to the altar so that he can "meet with the Israelites there" (Exod

general seem to have a non-atoning function (cf. Milgrom, *Levitius 1–16*, 153, 175–77). Basically, although these two particular burnt offerings can have an atoning function, the *tāmîd* burnt offerings are never said to have an atoning function.

12. Similarly, Shauf, *Jesus the Sacrifice*, 52–53.

13. Klawans, *Purity, Sacrifice*, 71–72.

14. Klawans, *Purity, Sacrifice*, 71.

15. Levine, *In the Presence*, 22–26, here 22; his emphasis.

16. My emphasis.

17. Milgrom, *Leviticus 1–16*, 172; see also 146, 161, 173.

29:42–45, here v. 43).[18] That's it. That's its function. Once the dwelling place is inaugurated (Exod 40:35; Lev 9:22–24; cf. Solomon's temple inauguration in 1 Kgs 8:10–11 and 2 Chr 7:1–2), then the purpose is probably best understood as *continuance* of this divine presence. As Klawans concludes, "The purpose of the daily burnt offering—and perhaps some other sacrifices as well—is to provide regular and constant pleasing odors to the Lord, so that the divine presence will continually remain in the sanctuary."[19]

The stability of God's presence cannot be sustained by regular burnt offerings alone, however. This is why there is a need for the category of atoning sacrifices. This need for a category of sacrifice with the specific function to remove various pollutions from God's dwelling place (so that God is not driven to abandon it) already implies that these regular burnt offerings have no atoning function. Their only function is divine "attraction" so to speak through their "pleasing aroma." And so, as Klawans summarizes, "transgression undoes what the daily sacrifice produces."[20] The regular burnt offerings are *not* the sacrificial solution to sins, but rather sins pose a *problem* for what the daily burnt offerings accomplish (attracting God's presence) and for which another solution is necessary (hence the atoning category for sacrifices).

But why does burning an animal (or grain) produce a "pleasing aroma" that "attracts" God's presence? This is fairly straightforward once we realize that the ubiquitous rationale for ancient Mesopotamian and Greek sacrifice is that this provided foods for the god(s).[21] Although the Torah (and the OT as a whole) rejects the notion that God literally "eats" the sacrifices (e.g., Ps 50:12–13),[22] nevertheless the ancient notion of sacrifice as "food" is the

18. See also David's burnt offerings on an altar he built on Ornan's threshing floor in 1 Chr 21:26 (cf. 2 Sam 24:24–25) and Elijah's burnt offerings on the altar on Mount Carmel in 1 Kgs 18:38.

19. Klawans, *Purity, Sacrifice*, 72.

20. Klawans, *Purity, Sacrifice*, 71.

21. Milgrom, *Leviticus*, 17, 21; Shauf, *Jesus the Sacrifice*, 11–13.

22. The Torah rejects the notion that God literally eats the sacrifices more obliquely. See Milgrom, *Leviticus*, 21: "A. L. Oppenheim succinctly characterized Mesopotamian religion as 'the care and feeding of the god.' We owe Israel's priesthood for eviscerating every trace of this notion from the sacrificial system. Pagans regularly set food and drink on their god's table, but the Priestly legists banned all food rites inside the shrine [i.e., the dwelling place proper: the holy place and most holy place]. All sacrifices were to be offered on the outer altar in the open courtyard . . . , visible to all worshipers and removed from the tent, YHWH's purported domicile. The text specifically prohibited the burnt offering (flesh), the cereal offering (bread), and all libations (drink) on the inner altar (Exod 30:9). Further, the frankincense, a precious spice, offered with the bread of the Presence, is not placed on the bread, as is the case with other cereal offerings (Lev 2:1, 15; 6:8) but is uniquely set apart from it, so that the bread can be eaten in its

controlling metaphor in the Torah (Lev 3:11, 16; 21:6, 8, 17, 21–22; 22:25; Num 28:2, 24).[23] Many of these are in close proximity to the idea that these sacrifices produce a "pleasing aroma" for God (e.g., Lev 3:16; Num 28:2, 24). (Put baldly, the idea is that God senses the pleasing smell of the BBQ cookout and, like those classic cartoon portrayals, follows the smoke/scent to its source.)

In fact, the term often translated as "offering by fire" (e.g., NASB, NRSV), *ʾiššeh*, for the (non-atoning version of) burnt offerings, the grain offerings, and the well-being offerings is best translated as "food gift." The word *ʾiššeh* more than likely does not derive from the word for "fire" (*ʾēš*) "but from a root meaning 'gift'"[24] from Ugaritic or Arabic.[25] It is also connected with the priestly food portions allotted to them for their service (Deut 18:1). Further, "fire offering" is inadequate since the term *ʾiššeh* is not used for other sacrifices that are burned on the altar (e.g., purgation and reparation offerings) and some offerings that are *not* burned are nevertheless designated as *ʾiššeh* (e.g., the wine drink-offering, Num 15:10; the priest's portion from the well-being offering, Lev 7:30, 35–36; and the bread of the Presence, 24:7, 9).[26] The term *ʾiššeh* (3:3, 9, 14; 7:30) is probably an abbreviation of "food gift" (*leḥem ʾiššeh*) (3:11, 16);[27] and it is also connected to being a "pleasing aroma" (e.g., Lev 1:9, 13, 17; 2:2, 9; 3:5, 16; 23:13, 18; Num 15:3, 7, 10, 13, 14; 28:2, 24). All of this strengthens the idea that "food" is the foundational underlying rationale of Levitical sacrifice.

At its most basic level, then, Israelite sacrifice is about preparing sacred "food" for God to consume (metaphorically) and sometimes for worshipers—priests and lay—to consume (literally) with God. The burnt offerings are solely for God to consume, but the well-being sacrifices (discussed in the next section) are consumed by God, the officiating priest, and the offerer. Risking oversimplification, the dwelling place is a divine residence outfitted with a sacred kitchen and dining space as well as a takeout restaurant (for

entirety by the priests (Lev 24:9), while the frankincense alone is burned on the inner altar (Exod 30:7–8). Thus all food gifts brought as sacrifices are conspicuously removed from the tent, YWHH's purported domicile, thereby erasing any suspicion that Israel's God consumed the sacrifices (see Psalm 50)."

23. Note also how the outer altar (rather than the literal table *inside* the holy place upon which the bread of the Presence is placed) is called God's "table" in Ezek 41:22; 44:16; Mal 1:7, 12. The "food" metaphor remains the underlying logic of sacrifice even in the postexilic period.

24. Schwartz, "Leviticus," 197.

25. Milgrom, *Leviticus 1–16*, 162.

26. Observations from Milgrom, *Leviticus 1–16*, 161.

27. Milgrom, *Leviticus 1–16*, 162.

laity). Sometimes God is the only one being served a meal (burnt offerings) and sometimes lay Israelites, priests, and God are all dining together (well-being offerings).

As we will soon see, and worth noting briefly in this context, the notion of im/purity comes in as a criterion for who is fit to enter/access the holy restaurant and dine with God. And atonement comes in when this sacred kitchen and restaurant gets contaminated and needs to be purged/disinfected. Crucially, the concept of "food" nearly disappears with the atoning sacrifices. The word *ʾiššeh* "is not used for the purification and reparation offerings, [since these] are not gifts but rituals of expiation."[28] Or, as Milgrom explains, "[an atoning] sacrifice that purges the sanctuary of the pollution caused by the accumulation of sin . . . can hardly be called a gift. Conversely, because the burnt offering functions primarily as a gift . . . , there is no better designation for it than *ʾiššeh*."[29]

This further supports the above criterion for distinguishing between atoning and non-atoning sacrifices: what is eaten by the laity cannot be an atoning sacrifice. Hence the notion of "food" is dropped when discussing the atoning sacrifices in Leviticus. Only when a sacrifice does not have an atoning function is it labeled a "food gift" ([*leḥem*] *ʾiššeh*).

Furthermore, this means that the atoning function of these other sacrifices gains its larger significance from the more basic "sacred food" rationale of sacrifice. That is, the atoning sacrifices come in to solve the problem of potentially being barred for various reasons (either due to sins contaminating the dwelling place and/or ritual impurities contaminating both the dwelling place and the person) from both providing God his "food"/"pleasing aroma" and having a sacred meal with God.

Keeping with the residence-restaurant image, atonement is what is needed for this holy residence-restaurant to maintain its grade A health score. The place itself (the dwelling place), its butchers, cooks, and servers (the priests), and its customers (the people) all need to be in a state of purity for the sacred meals to happen. Atonement rituals decontaminate the dwelling place and ritual purity regulations ensure that human beings (both priest and lay) are fit to access the sacred space and foods.

We are getting ahead of ourselves, however. In any case, now that we understand how the inauguration of the dwelling place and then all the regular burnt offerings are what "attract" God's presence and how this is

28. Schwartz, "Leviticus," 197. But see Num 15:25, which may be the lone exception (that proves the rule).

29. Milgrom, *Leviticus 1–16*, 162.

all tethered to the notion of sacred meals, we can discuss the purpose and occasion of both the voluntary and required well-being sacrifices.

THE PURPOSE AND OCCASIONS FOR THE WELL-BEING OFFERINGS

It is now easy to understand the function of the well-being offerings (*šəlāmîm*) since the regular burnt offerings function to "attract" or "invite" God's ongoing presence at the dwelling place. Since God is the only one "consuming" the burnt offerings, it makes sense that there would be a type of offering from which the offerers share in as well. This is what the well-being sacrifices are. As Gary A. Anderson explains:

> The role of human consumption constitutes the primary level of meaning for this sacrifice and helps to explain why the *ʿôlâ* and the *šĕlāmîm* are routinely paired in biblical (and Ugaritic) ritual. The *ʿôlâ* was the sacrifice that constituted the basic nourishment for the deity, while the *šĕlāmîm* in turn nourished the people.[30]

Moreover, the function and sequential priority of the burnt offering supports this understanding. From what we can observe from the Hebrew Bible, in practice the well-being sacrifices always come *after* a burnt offering.[31] As Levine illuminates, "this pattern reveals . . . [the] meaning of the *šelāmîm*" by how the burnt offering "invited the deity to a common, shared sacrificial meal [which will be the well-being sacrifice] after he had been invoked by means of an *ʿôlâh*."[32] This brings us back to Exod 20:24 where only these two sacrifices are mentioned and the sole purpose is inviting God's presence to the altar for divine blessing.

Moreover, the term *šəlāmîm* is an umbrella category for three distinct sacrifices (thanksgiving, freewill, vowed offerings, Lev 7:11–21). Before getting to the distinctions, as a main category, the well-being offerings can be either private (for a family or clan unit) or public (communal) (cf. Josephus, *Ant.* 3.224). A public well-being sacrifice marks or commemorates

30. Anderson, "Sacrifice and Sacrificial Offerings," 879.

31. This is the case whether individual worshipers come with both an individual burnt offering and a well-being offering or if they simply bring a well-being sacrifice, since the morning *tāmîd* is always the first sacrifice of any given day. And, at public communal festivals the burnt offerings are always offered first and then the well-being ones comes after (see, for example, the two very important public events, the covenant inauguration at Sinai in Exod 24 and the inauguration of the dwelling place in Lev 9). No matter what, a burnt offering *always precedes* any well-being offerings.

32. Levine, *In the Presence*, 26.

"significant beginnings" and thus it often "appears as a rite largely reserved for royal and/or confederative-national celebrations of a dedicatory or commemorative character" (with Moses in Exod 24:5; Joshua in Deut 27:1–8 and Josh 8:30–35; Samuel and Saul in 1 Sam 10:8; 11:14–15; David in 2 Sam 6:17–18; 24:25; 1 Chr 16:1–2; 21:26; Solomon in 1 Kgs 8:63–64; 9:25; 2 Chr 7:7; Ahaz in 15:11–13; Hezekiah in 2 Chr 29:35; 30:22; 31:2; Manasseh in 2 Chr 33:16).[33] Hence, as we will explore shortly, the well-being offering is used for both the Passover and the covenant-inauguration (and covenant-renewal) ceremonies.

It is important to emphasize that these are the *only* sacrifices from which the laity eat (and these are split three ways between God, the priests, and the offerer/s). For example, when explaining Jewish sacrificial practices to outsiders, Josephus clumps all the well-being sacrifices under the name "thanksgiving" (*charistērios*)[34] and makes a concerted effort to say that only these offerings can be eaten by the laity. He specifies that they are "performed with the intention of providing a feast for those who have offered it" (*Ant.* 3.225, cf. 228). While feasting is named as the function of the well-being sacrifices, he then clarifies how all other sacrifices "for sins" (*hyper hamartadōn*) are their own category and cannot be eaten by the laity (3.230–32).

Also, the term *zebaḥ* is used in the Hebrew Bible synonymously with *šəlāmîm*.[35] The *zebaḥ* "is limited to the meaning 'slain offering whose meat is eaten by the worshiper'" (cf. Jer 7:21).[36] These two terms may have originated in separate sources or ancient Israelite "schools,"[37] but they are unambiguously synonymous in the compiled Hebrew Bible. Neither term is ever confused with or attributed to an atoning sacrifice.

33. Levine, *In the Presence*, 52 and 46, respectively.

34. Confusingly, this is not the sub-type of well-being sacrifice called the "thanksgiving" (*tôdâ*) offering in Lev 7:11–15, which the Greek Septuagint (LXX) translates as a "offering of praise" (*tēs thysias tēs aineseōs*). (The Septuagint is the Greek translation of the Hebrew Bible completed around the mid-second century BCE; it also includes some works that are originally composed in Greek like 1–4 Maccabees.) I will outline this further below, but the *tôdâ*/*ainesis* has a one-day expiration—everything has to be eaten or otherwise burned before morning—whereas the other two well-being offerings (vowed and freewill) have a two-day expiration (Lev 7:11–18). Josephus says the *charistērios* has a two-day expiration (*Ant.* 3.228), but knows of other eaten sacrifices, which he does not name, but says they have a one-day expiration (3.236).

35. Levine, *In the Presence*, 3, 11; Milgrom, *Leviticus 1–16*, 217–18.

36. Milgrom, *Leviticus 1–16*, 218.

37. For more on the possible source histories of these terms and how they were combined, see Levine, *In the Presence*, 3–22, Milgrom, *Leviticus 1–16*, 217–25.

The relationship between the word for a sacrifice that is eaten by the people (*zebaḥ*) and the altar (*mizbēaḥ*) further supports the point that sacred eating is the most basic rationale for Israelite sacrifice. The altar is named in relation to the eaten-sacrifice since the *mem* (*m*) prefix signifies the *place* where the root action (*z-b-ḥ*) occurs; this is the place where the *zebaḥ* is offered for God to "consume." The altar is called the "place for the *zebaḥ*," not the "place for *kipper*." While not a lot of weight should be placed on etymology alone, given all the other evidence thus far this datum serves a corroborating function, strengthening the case that the core logic of OT sacrifice is sacred eating—either God alone or God and humans feasting together.[38]

Also, Num 15:1–13 stipulates that all of these "food gift" (*ʾiššeh*) offerings (burnt offerings and well-being offerings) need to be accompanied by a grain offering (described in Lev 2) and a drink offering. The grain and wine complement the animal (protein) with carbohydrates (grain) and drink (wine). This is a full meal. This all reinforces the fact that sacrifice is fundamentally about sacred meals. Again, God's "eating" and "drinking" is always considered metaphorical and symbolic in all the biblical texts. Still, the power of the symbolic framework is that the worshipers who themselves are eating and drinking are sharing in a sacred meal with God even if God's "consumption" of the meal is qualitatively different from literal "eating" (and "drinking").

Importantly, well-being sacrifices are the only meals that lay people need to be in a state of ritual purity in order to eat (7:20–21).[39] I will discuss ritual im/purity further in the following chapter, but for now it is useful to note these four things regarding the regulations for eating from these:

1) Any sacrifices that are to be eaten (by priests or lay persons) require the person to be ritually pure.
2) Laypersons are only able to eat from the non-atoning well-being sacrifices.
3) No Israelite is required to be ritually pure to eat regular meals.

38. The logic of atonement (which I will define more carefully in chapter 4) gains its full sense in relation to this more basic meaning. Atonement makes it so that this sacred feasting can still happen even though humans are either regularly contracting forms of impurity or committing certain sins that pollute the sacred dwelling place from afar, thereby threatening God's continued dwelling there. Atonement removes these ritual pollutants so that the sacred feasting can continue.

39. To be thorough, priests need to be ritually pure to eat any of their allotted sacrificial meals as well (22:3–7).

4) The consequence for eating a well-being sacrifice in a state of ritual impurity is severe: the person will be "cut off" (7:20–21).[40]

Also, before discussing the subcategories of well-being offerings, it is likewise important to emphasize that atonement (*kipper*) is never attributed to any of these sacrifices as it is with the others. They have nothing to do with sin and nothing to do with atonement (cf. Josephus, *Ant.* 3.224–32).[41] For instance, Josephus is careful to note how different blood rituals for the atoning sacrifices for sins differ from the non-atoning well-being sacrifices (3.226, 228, 231). Whereas for the non-atoning sacrifices the blood is "tossed" or "dashed" (*zāraq*) on the *sides* of the altar (e.g., Lev 3:2, 8), Josephus specifies that for the atoning *ḥaṭṭā ʾt* sacrifice: "with the blood the priest sprinkles the altar, not, however, as before [with the well-being sacrifices], but only the projecting corners [on the *top* of the altar]" (*Ant.* 3.231, LCL; cf. Lev 4:25, 30, 34). Though he leaves out some details that will be important later, the pertinent observation here is that Josephus considered it worthwhile to expressly flag how the different functions of the atoning and non-atoning sacrifices are indexed and enacted by different blood rituals pertaining to each.[42]

It is also worth recalling the discussion on Lev 17 in chapter 1 where we learned that eating meat from the flock or herd apart from the context of sacrificial worship is conceptualized as murder (17:3–6). This helps us see how "[t]he main [practical] function of the well-being offering is to provide meat for the table"[43] in the context of sacrifice at the dwelling place. Although the blood for the well-being sacrifices has no atoning function, their blood rituals are vital since they serve to transfigure the death of the animal into "not-a-killing" per the logic of Lev 17 discussed in chapter 1.[44]

Besides the practicality of allowing for meat consumption from clean domesticated (i.e., eligible for sacrifice) animals, Milgrom also notes that the "well-being offering is, at its core, an offering of thankfulness" and is "the joyous sacrifice par excellence."[45] And this brings us back to the (non-

40. This datum will be important when analyzing Paul's comments in 1 Cor 11.

41. Milgrom, *Leviticus 1–16*, 221–22; Gilders, *Blood Ritual*, 88–89, 94; Anderson, "Sacrifice," 878; Feldman, *Story of Sacrifice*, 64; Shauf, *Jesus the Sacrifice*, 47. And Baruch Levine treats the well-being sacrifices separately in his part 1 from all the "sacrifices of expiation" in part 2 of *In the Presence*.

42. For more on the key differences between the non-atoning blood rituals of the well-being offerings and the atoning *ḥaṭṭā ʾt* offerings, see Gilders, *Blood Ritual*, 88–89, 94.

43. Milgrom, *Leviticus 1–16*, 221.

44. I will discuss another function of the blood for well-being sacrifices below.

45. Milgrom, *Leviticus*, 28 and 29 respectively; see also Milgrom, *Leviticus 1–16*, 224; Anderson, "Sacrifice," 879.

atoning) function of the burnt offerings and how it logically relates to the (non-atoning) function of the well-being offerings: "i.e., that the *ʿôlāh* was . . . utilized for the purpose of invoking the deity preparatory to joining with [God] in a fellowship of sacrifice [the well-being offering], which was the context for petition and thanksgiving, and for the expression of other religious attitudes of this character."[46] Importantly, while the burnt offering can be offered by itself and the "divine attraction" function can relate to the worshiper's desire to petition God (now that God is "there" and thus "attentive," cf. Exod 20:24), the well-being sacrifice is almost always a *retrospective* offering to rejoice and thank God for some antecedent act of deliverance and/or general well-being. In fact, the LXX calls the well-being offerings "sacrifices of deliverance/salvation" (*thysia sōtēriou*). These are not sacrifices that petition God *to* deliver or rescue; rather, they commemorate and memorialize a *past* act of divine deliverance, whether individual or communal (e.g., Pss 56:12–13; 107:2–9 with v. 22; Josephus, *Ant.* 3.236).

In other words, the sacrifice itself is neither the saving event nor the catalyst for a future act of salvation, rather, a prior saving event is joyfully celebrated with a well-being sacrifice. This is why, for all the subcategories of the well-being offering (thanksgiving, freewill, and vowed offerings), "[t]he common denominator of all three categories is joy. 'You shall sacrifice the well-being offering and eat them, *rejoicing* before the Lord your God' (Deut 27:7)."[47] The offerer(s) is looking back on a past event and, by means of a burnt offering (individual or more generally via the *tāmîd*), inviting God to a sacred celebratory feast so that the offerer(s) can rejoice specifically in the "well-being" God brought about for them by means of a well-being sacrifice. This is confirmed by observing the celebratory contexts in which these sacrifices occur (e.g., Exod 24:5; Judg 20:26; 21:4; 1 Sam 10:8; 11:5; 2 Sam 6:17–18; 24:25; 1 Kgs 3:15; 8:63–64; 9:25; 2 Kgs 16:13; Ezek 45:15, 17; 2 Chr 29:31–35; 30:22–27; 33:16).[48]

The three subcategories of well-being offerings can be distinguished in terms of occasion, expiration date of the meat, and presence/absence of unleavened bread. Both the vowed and freewill offerings do not have an unleavened bread component, and both have a two-day expiration, which means that any leftover meat that has not been eaten has to be burned on the third day (Lev 7:16–18; 19:5–8). The difference between these two is the

46. Levine, *In the Presence*, 26.

47. Milgrom, *Leviticus*, 28; his emphasis. See also Levine, *Presence*, 27–35.

48. Some of these are covenant-renewal ceremonies, which only gain their intelligibility by looking back on and celebrating the initial covenant inauguration (Exod 24:1–11) and rejoicing that there is a covenant to renew/rededicate themselves to in the first place.

occasion. The freewill is self-explanatory: it has no occasion other than the spontaneous desire of the worshiper to offer this joyous sacrifice. The vowed offering is brought if the conditions of a vow are met. The offerer makes a vow to God like "If such-and-such happens, then I will offer a (vowed) well-being offering in gratitude for you having brought those conditions to pass." A good example of this type is when Absalom tells David, "'Please let me go to Hebron and pay the vow that I have made to the LORD. For your servant made a vow while I lived at Geshur in Aram: If the LORD will indeed bring me back to Jerusalem, then I will worship the LORD in Hebron'" (2 Sam 15:7–8 NRSV).[49] Neither the freewill nor the vowed offering are required. They are completely voluntary. Though, of course, once someone *voluntarily* makes a vow to offer a sacrifice if certain conditions come to pass, then if those conditions are met at that point they are under *obligation* to fulfill their vow (e.g., Num 6:21; Pss 50:14b; 116:18; Jonah 2:10b [v. 9b Eng.]).

The thanksgiving offering is unique because it requires an unleavened bread component (7:12) and it only has a one-day expiration (all leftover meat must be burned before the next morning, 7:15; 22:29–30). It is offered when one is thankful for a particular previous act of divine deliverance (e.g., Pss 50:14–15, 23; 56:12–13; 107:21–22; 116:17–18; Jonah 2:10 [v. 9 Eng.]; Josephus, *Ant.* 3.236).[50]

Since this well-being sacrifice will be relevant for understanding the NT's claims about Jesus's death, it is worth noting the rabbinic teaching that because thanksgiving offerings are not offered for sin, this means in the world to come the thanksgiving offerings will be the only kind of remaining

49. I am using this example from Milgrom, *Leviticus 1–16*, 219.

50. Levine, *In the Presence*, 43. Also, the well-being sacrifices were most likely accompanied by songs of thanksgiving (e.g., Pss 42:5 [v. 4 Eng.]; 95:2; 100:1; 107; Jonah 2:10a [v. 9a Eng.]). In fact, Ps 107 is a thanksgiving song outlining several occasions for giving thanks, which the rabbis use as specific occasions to offer the thanksgiving sacrifice per v. 22 (b. Ber. 54b). There are five broad occasions mentioned (*pace* Milgrom, who does not include vv. 2–3 [*Leviticus*, 28 and *Leviticus 1–16*, 219]): redemption from enemies by being gathered from the four compass points (vv. 2–3), deliverance and sustenance through the wilderness (vv. 4–9), deliverance from a prison of darkness and death (vv. 10–16), salvation from severe affliction/illness (vv. 17–22), and being brought safely home from a hazardous sea voyage (vv. 23–32). All of these can be applicable on the individual level, but the first three echo communal acts of deliverance that either refer to the exodus and/or the return from exile or use these as paradigms for any sort of communal deliverance. Psalm 107:2–3 is a straightforward description of gathering from exile, vv. 4–9 alludes to the exodus and wilderness wandering, and vv. 10–16 can be read similarly if exile is construed as a type of imprisonment. These descriptions of deliverance are patterned after the exodus (as even "return from exile" is conceptualized in relation to the exodus) and can be applicable to both individuals and the community whenever God acts to deliver them from whatever peril they find themselves in.

offering (Lev. Rab. 9:1, 7), always praising God for saving us from the old age.[51]

Now we can turn to two specific types of communal well-being offerings that will be most relevant for analyzing NT texts in relation to Jesus's death: the Passover and the covenant-inauguration/renewal ceremonies.

THE PASSOVER

The Passover is a required annual sacrificial feast for all Israel to celebrate their deliverance from Egypt (Exod 12). Here I will discuss what the Passover is and is not (removing prevalent misconceptions). As I will show, the Passover is best categorized as a unique type of thanksgiving well-being sacrifice.

Strictly speaking, however, the ritual prescribed in Exod 12:1–23 for the first Passover is *not* a sacrifice. Not only is the first one not called a "sacrifice" (*zebaḥ*), it cannot be one by definition because there is no priest and no altar (thus none of it can be burned and translated into smoke to produce a "pleasing aroma" for God).[52] Moreover, the fact that the first Passover was categorically not a sacrifice solves a longstanding interpretive conundrum caused by a discrepancy between the instructions in Exod 12:8–9 to roast the meat directly over fire and *not* "boil" (*bāšēl*) it and the contradictory instruction in Deut 16:7 to "boil" (*bāšal*) the meat. All *sacrificial* meat that is eaten by humans needs to be boiled (*bāšal*, e.g., Exod 29:31; Lev 6:28; 8:31; Num 6:19; 1 Kgs 19:21; Ezek 46:20, 24; Zech 14:21; 2 Chr 35:13). Roasting *sacrificial* meat for human consumption is sacrilege (1 Sam 2:12–17). This is because only God's portion is to be in direct contact with the fire, whereas the portions allotted for human consumption requires mediating objects between it and the fire (a boiling pot and water).[53] Ronald S. Hendel concludes that "an essential difference that separates the humans from their God" is enacted through these distinct modes of ritual "cooking."[54] While "both the Israelites and Yahweh share in the consumption of the sacrificial animal" and "in this sense the deity and the people are joined," there nevertheless remains a distinction between God and humans because "they consume different portions that are prepared differently"—"the human portion

51. Similarly, the author of Hebrews thinks some form of the thanksgiving sacrifice persists even after Jesus's once-for-all-time sacrifice of atonement (13:15).

52. Eberhart, *The Sacrifice*, 120.

53. Hendel, "Sacrifice as a Cultural System," 382–84.

54. Hendel, "Sacrifice as a Cultural System," 384.

is boiled while Yahweh's portion is burned."[55] Since cooking sacrificial meat in the same manner God's portion is "cooked" is sacrilege (1 Sam 2:12–17), then the requirement to cook the Passover over a direct flame indexes it in a non-sacrificial category. By repeating the instruction to roast the meat and explicitly prohibiting boiling in Exod 12:8–9, it almost seems as if the author is waving their hands wildly shouting: *"The first Passover was not a sacrifice!"* There is no priesthood yet, there is no altar, and they cooked it in a non-sacrificial manner. Everything about the first Passover is categorically not a sacrifice.

However, the author notes that each *subsequent* Passover will be celebrated as a "sacrifice" (*zebaḥ*, Exod 12:27) when it is incorporated into the sacrificial and calendrical framework. The verbal form *zābaḥ* is used throughout Deut 16:1–8 ("*sacrifice* the Passover") because now there is an ordained priesthood, a sanctuary, and an altar upon which the fat is to be burned and whose sides the blood is to be dashed on.[56] And this is then why Deut 16:7 specifies that the Passover needs to be "boiled" since it is now categorized as a "sacrifice" and thus the portions for human consumption have to be boiled and cannot be in direct contact with fire. So there is no real contradiction between Exod 12:8–9 and Deut 16:7 since the difference in cooking instructions function to index the Passover differently in its different contexts (from the last meal before the exodus to a memorial of the exodus incorporated within Israel's liturgical calendar). That is, the function of "roasting" in Exod 12 necessarily indexes it outside of the sacrificial system (and having non-priests sacrifice, let alone sacrifice without an altar for the fat and a portion of the meat to be burned up for God, would be a major cultic problem); whereas since Deut 16 is incorporating Passover within the sacrificial calendar, the instructions need to index it accordingly by changing the manner in which the meat is cooked. "Boiling" the meat for human consumption is the necessary way to indicate that it is now a "sacrifice" because it matches how sacrificial meat is prepared for human consumption.

Also, although Num 9 does not use the words *zebaḥ* or *šəlāmîm*, it does call it "the LORD's offering [*qorbān*]" (v. 7), which is the largest umbrella term for every type of sacrifice in the Torah (Lev 1:2).[57] Additionally,

55. Hendel, "Sacrifice as a Cultural System," 384.

56. Though there is some evidence that some Diaspora Jews ignored Deut 16 and Num 9 and relied on Exod 12 so that they could celebrate and eat a Passover meal outside of Jerusalem. E.g., Philo, *Spec.* 2.145–49; Josephus, *Ant.* 14.260; and Jub. 49:16, 18, 20, and 21 seems to be denouncing this practice repeatedly precisely because enough families were actually doing it (references found in Sanders, *Judaism*, 133–34).

57. *Pace*, Eberhart, who incorrectly asserts that "the Passover is never called an

the Passover instructions in Num 9 (and the instructions for an emergency alternative Passover a month later) precede the summative statement in 10:10 about the "appointed times of feasting" that require "your sacrifices of well-being [*zibḥê šalmêkem*]." Since the Passover is one such "appointed times of feasting," then it is best understood as belonging to these sacrifices of well-being. Additionally, the fact that the Passover participants need to be "clean/pure" (*ṭāhôr*) (9:13) to eat the Passover necessarily indexes it as belonging to the category of well-being sacrifices as noted earlier (Lev 7:20–21; 22:3–7).[58] Therefore, although the first Passover was evidently *not* a sacrifice, it subsequently belongs to the well-being sacrifices.

Not only is the Passover indexed as a general well-being sacrifice, but it is also specifically indexed as a unique kind of thanksgiving well-being sacrifice because it likewise has a one-day expiration (Exod 12:8, 10; 34:25; Num 9:12; Deut 16:4; cf. Lev 7:15; 22:29–30) and needs to be accompanied with unleavened bread (Exod 12:8; Num 9:11; Deut 16:3; cf. Lev 7:12–13).[59] It makes sense that of the three types of well-being offerings the Passover would be related to the thanksgiving offering. This is because the other two are unprompted—the freewill offering is "purely spontaneous" and the vowed offering is also spontaneously promised by the offerer if certain conditions come about—whereas the thanksgiving offering is for celebrating a particular prior act of divine deliverance.[60] Thus, the Passover and the thanksgiving offering also "share the same motivation: thanksgiving for deliverance, both national *(pesaḥ)* and individual."[61]

Again, Passover has nothing to do with atonement.[62] This word is never used in either the initial ritual or in the subsequent explanations of it. This is unsurprising now given what has been laid out so far, yet Christian scholars in particular seem especially predisposed to conflate sacrificial categories here.[63] Since the laity eat from it and since it is more specifically aligned

'offering [*qorbān*] for God' and is not counted among the cultic sacrifices in the priestly cult system" (*The Sacrifice*, 120; his brackets).

58. Note also how being "unclean/impure" (Num 9:6, 10) likewise disqualifies the person from being about to eat the Passover. Similarly, Balberg, *Blood for Thought*, 147.

59. Similarly, Milgrom, *Leviticus 1–16*, 219–20.

60. Milgrom, *Leviticus 1–16*, 220.

61. Milgrom, *Leviticus 1–16*, 220.

62. Similarly, Milgrom, *Leviticus 1–16*, 1081; Shauf, *Jesus the Sacrifice*, 137; Marianne Meye Thompson, *John*, 47, 47n15.

63. E.g., Morales claims without argument or warrant that "atonement" is one of "three distinct elements of the Passover ritual found in Exodus 12:6–11" and takes this even further by asserting "[t]he sacrifice involved the concept of substitutionary atonement, the animal's death being regarded as 'in the stead of' the firstborn male within each Israelite household, atoning for sin" (*Who Shall Ascend*, 80). Below I rebut the

with the non-atoning thanksgiving well-being sacrifice, then it cannot have an atoning function. If it had an atoning function, then the people would be prohibited from eating from it. The Passover is a distinctive thanksgiving well-being sacrifice thanking God for Israel's liberation from Egypt.[64]

Notably, and to anticipate chapter 5, just like the first Passover was a *proleptic* celebration for what was immediately about to happen, so too is the first Lord's Supper. Jesus not only tethers the meaning of his death with the Passover feast in general with the timing of his death and with the unleavened bread and wine, but that final meal itself was similarly explained as a proleptic celebration for what was immediately about to take place. All subsequent celebration feasts take on a "memorial" function (Exod 12:14; cf. Luke 22:19; 1 Cor 11:24–25)—and the well-being offerings are the only kind of sacrifices said to have a memorial function in the Torah (Num 10:10).[65] This memorial function per Num 10:10 is why "all joyous celebrations that would have been marked by the well-being offering, the joyous sacrifice par excellence" since they commemorate acts of deliverance both national and individual.[66]

The Passover Is Not a Substitutionary Death

Some of the common (mostly Christian) misunderstandings of Passover have already been indirectly corrected in the foregoing observations, but it is worth connecting the dots more explicitly here to address the most pressing misunderstanding for our purposes: the interpretation that the "lamb dies in the place of the firstborn of Israel and its substitutionary death is indicated by the blood on the doorposts and lintel."[67] This reading is, as Gilders notes, "heavily dependent on the Western Christian doctrine of

---

claim that the Passover has anything to do with a substitutionary death.

64. I say "*distinctive* thanksgiving well-being sacrifice" here (and "unique kind of thanksgiving well-being offering above") to flag that there are a couple differences between Passover and the regular thanksgiving offering. E.g., (a) Passover requires "bitter herbs" (Exod 12:8) that are not part of the thanksgiving offering and (b) a thanksgiving offering has both unleavened and leavened bread components (Lev 7:13), but all leaven is strictly forbidden for the Passover (Exod 12:15, 19; 13:6–7). Nevertheless, the Passover most resembles the thanksgiving well-being offering. But even if someone is disinclined to link them as closely as I and others, like Milgrom, do, the fact remains that the Passover is a non-atoning sacrifice from which the laity eat.

65. Milgrom, *Leviticus 1–16*, 224; Barber and Kincaid, "Cultic Theosis in Paul," 252, 252n57.

66. Milgrom, *Leviticus 1–16*, 252.

67. Gilders, *Blood Ritual*, 46. Gilders disagrees with this interpretation.

'substitutionary atonement.'"[68] But this reading is already hamstrung by the fact that the Passover (along with all other well-being sacrifices) was not about "atonement" (*kipper*).[69] But what else might be going on besides celebrating divine deliverance, especially as Exod 12 describes the first Passover?

Whatever is happening, "substitutionary death" is less than plausible. This is because, as Gilders further observes, "there is little evidence for 'the magic of sympathetic substitution.' The text never indicates that the blood substitutes for the blood of those in the house."[70] The only explicit statements about the function of the blood are unambiguous and have nothing to do with "substitutionary death." These comments are in Exod 12:13 and 23. Both comment that the blood functions as a signal for God to "see" it and either not directly smite the Israelite home (v. 13) or for God to "see" it and so restrain the "destroyer" from smiting the house (v. 23).[71] Verse 13 calls it as "sign" and so, the most the text decidedly claims is that "the blood signals the presence of the Israelites in the houses."[72] The blood is only said to "serve as a tangible sign of . . . remembrance" because at first "Yahweh will *see* the blood and will *remember* the Israelites"[73] and then all subsequent Passovers are themselves a celebratory sacrificial "remembrance" (12:14). Loading more meaning into the blood here simply goes beyond what is written; it "requires conceptual gap filling."[74]

Now, not all "gap filling" is inherently problematic. It all depends on the method and rationale of using any information outside the immediate context. But the logic of thinking, "Well, if they didn't have blood smeared on the door frames, the firstborn would die and this therefore means the blood is a substitutionary death" is fallacious.[75] For one, the text claims that failure to observe the Passover will mean not only the death of the firstborn male in the family, but the death of the firstborns of all their livestock too (11:5; 12:12, 29; 13:15). So is the lamb, which itself does not have to be

68. Gilders, *Blood Ritual*, 46.

69. See also Thompson, *John*, 47.

70. Gilders, *Blood Ritual*, 45; cf. 46.

71. "The text offers no explanation except that Yahweh sees the blood and restrains the 'destroyer'" (Gilders, *Blood Ritual*, 46).

72. Gilders, *Blood Ritual*, 49.

73. Hendel, "Sacrifice as a Cultural System," 387; my emphasis.

74. Gilders, *Blood Ritual*, 46.

75. E.g., "Apart from the slaying of the lamb, it is evident that the firstborn sons of Israel would have died. . . . The sacrifice therefore involved the concept of substitutionary atonement, the animal's death being regarded as 'in the stead of' the firstborn male within each Israelite household, atoning for sin" (Morales, *Who Shall Ascend*, 80).

"firstborn" (!), a substitutionary firstborn cow, bull, goat, ram, and donkey as well? For another, this same substitutionary logic would also mean that all the Passover instructions are necessarily substituting for the death of the firstborn and all family members since failure to do any of the other instructions likewise results in being "cut off" (12:15, 19; Num 9:13). Consuming bitter herbs is not "substituting" for their deaths. Refraining from all leaven is not "substituting" for their deaths. Eating or otherwise burning any leftovers before morning is not "substituting" for their deaths. Yet failure to observe any of these would result in the firstborn dying and the household being "cut off" according to the text.

Put another way, just because something averts being cut off does not mean it is "substitutionary." If an Israelite family only did the blood smearing bit with the lamb, but neglected eating bitter tasting herbs and/or ate plumb-risen bread and/or didn't eat or burn all the leftovers before morning, then the firstborn along with the whole family would perish. This means the lamb was not really "substituting" for the firstborn, otherwise that would be sufficient to automatically have spared him even though everything else was neglected. The consequences for not partaking of the Passover properly cannot be reduced to a logic of an isolated discrete instance of the lamb substituting for the firstborn. The feast needs to be understood as a whole.

Further, it is not the case that a stated consequence for a failure to do this-or-that instruction means that positively obeying those instructions "substitutes" for the consequence. This is a non sequitur. Cause and effect relationships work in many ways; so to reduce the Passover to "substitution" is question begging. This might be easier to understand if we change the consequence from the firstborn dying and/or the unobservant Israelite from being cut off to being struck with something else, say, paralysis. I find it hard to believe that someone would assert that the blood ritual is a "substitutionary paralysis" and this is because in any other context we know that cause and effects do not inherently reduce to the logic of substitution. The only basis for connecting the death of the firstborn and what happens to the lamb is a misunderstanding regarding OT sacrifice that was debunked in chapter 1; namely, the mistaken idea that sacrifice is about "death" at all, let alone a *substitutionary* death. Yes, a lamb has to literally die to be eaten, but its *death* is given no ritual significance in Exod 12 just like the death of any sacrificial animal is not given any ritual or theological significance in the Torah, as discussed in chapter 1. However, the proper use of its blood, roasting its meat, burning any leftovers before morning, etc., are all given explicit ritual meaning (e.g., "roasting" its meat overtly marks the first Passover ritually as a "non-sacrificial" event—it might need to be said that there are such things as non-sacrificial rituals).

Before discussing the plausible meaning and rationale of the blood further, it is worth observing another way in which the logic that the lamb is substituting for the firstborn breaks down upon closer inspection.[76] If the Passover lamb "substituted" for or "redeemed" all the firstborns for an Israelite family (human and animal), then why does Israel still need to "redeem" their firstborns, human and animal, later and in a *completely alternative manner* (Exod 13:2, 11–16; 34:19–20; cf. 22:29–30; Num 18:15–17)? This makes it obvious that the Passover lamb was not substituting for any of the firstborns, otherwise the annual Passover ceremony would itself *be* how the firstborns (human and animal) are "redeemed" by dedicating the Passover lamb to God instead each year.

In fact, these passages in Exodus do not specify how to "redeem" the firstborn humans (13:2, 11–16; 34:19–20) or "give" them to God (22:29–30), but, ironically enough given the context of our present discussion, it is explicitly clear in 13:13 that "lambs" will not do. This is because lambs can only substitute for the redemption of non-sacrificial firstborn *animals*, such as donkeys.[77]

Even though the Passover is actually rather uncomplicated—it is a ritual celebratory commemoration of a past act of divine deliverance that makes use of the standard cultic meals of thanksgiving, the thanksgiving well-being sacrifices—it takes a while to untangle the notion that the Passover lamb is substituting for the redemption of the human firstborn males since it is layered with several misunderstandings by failing to observe what is actually written in the Torah on such matters.

In any case, although left unexplained in Exodus, the Torah goes on to specify how to "redeem" Israel's human male firstborns (13:2, 11–16; 22:28–29 [Eng. 29–30]; 34:19–20). First, we are told it happens by substituting the firstborns with the Levites (Num 3:12–13, 45; 8:14–18).[78] We learn

76. Contra Morales, *Who Shall Ascend*, 80.

77. Morales misses this and writes: "For the firstborn sons of Israel . . . God commanded the Israelites to redeem them by the substitute sacrifice of a lamb commemorating the redemption of Passover" (*Who Shall Ascend*, 80n12). But this is *not* what the text of Exod 13:11–16 says. Only *animals ineligible* for sacrifice, such as donkeys, can be redeemed with a lamb. As Nahum m. Sarna notes, "[t]he mode of redemption [for human male firstborns] is not given" in Exod 13:13 (*Exodus*, 67), but it is specified elsewhere (e.g., in Numbers).

78. Exodus 22:28–29 (Eng. 29–30) is not about child sacrifice; contra those like Jon Levenson and John J. Collins, who read this as a primitive artifact that Israel used to practice child sacrifice (Levenson, *Death and Resurrection of the Beloved Son*, 3–17, 43–52; *Inheriting Abraham*, 70; Collins, *What Are Biblical Values?*, 44). The problem is that they overdetermine what "go to God" means (thanks to Joel Baden for this observation). It is an obvious mistake to think that everything that "goes to God" means it is incinerated on the altar. What happens to each thing dedicated to God (wine, animals,

from this that the firstborns were supposed to be given to God as permanent sanctuary workers, but now the tribe of Levi substitutes for all the firstborns. Second, since the firstborns outnumber the Levites in that first generation, these remaining firstborns are financially redeemed rather than joining the Levites (3:45–51). The redemption cost is not ransoming their lives from *death* as if it were a monetary "substitutionary death." Rather, it is buying back their workload. It is compensation to the sanctuary since it is losing out on the services of more (literal) manpower. This is why we are then told that each firstborn human male subsequently requires a redemption price, which just means that instead of them going to serve at the dwelling place their parents make a payment that goes to the necessary costs of running it instead (18:15–16).

It is not as if the firstborn of every household was threatened every year with death unless a substitute lamb was offered in his place on Passover by the family. The only thing the first Passover established is God's "right" to all the firstborns (human and animal) (Exod 13:2, 15; 34:18–20; Num 3:13; 8:17). Given all these laws about God's right to the firstborns it is clear that whatever the Passover lamb is doing, it is definitely *not* "substituting" for these firstborns because *they are all still owed to God* (and "lambs" can only substitute for unclean animals like donkeys). This necessarily refutes the idea that the Passover lamb is substituting for firstborn *deaths*, which is also strengthened by the fact that we know the firstborns are meant to *live* in dedicated service to God's dwelling place. As we saw, in Exod 13:13 and 34:20 the human male firstborn aspect takes the form of redemption. And how to "redeem" the firstborn is not spelled out in Exodus, but we are told

humans) *depends on what it is*. Thus, animals eligible for sacrifice get sacrificed, but animals that cannot be sacrificed are (obviously) not sacrificed and burned on the altar (hence, either substituting a lamb for a donkey or breaking the donkey's neck, which is the ritual way of indexing the death of the animal as a non-sacrificial death; cf. Sarna, *Exodus*, 67; Tigay, *Deuteronomy*, 192). Wine cannot touch the top of the altar and be burned because nothing fermented is permitted on the altar (Lev 2:11) and the fire on the altar cannot be put out (6:6) (Milgrom, *Leviticus*, 26; Milgrom, *Leviticus 1–16*, 188–89). So the wine is poured out on the ground at the base of the altar (Josephus, *Ant.* 3.234). Therefore, what happens to each thing dedicated to God is different according to what it is. Same with humans. Humans are not the sort of thing that can get sacrificed and Israel is not told to substitute their firstborn males for an animal that can be sacrificed (as in the case of a donkey). When firstborn males "go to God" they are dedicated as *permanent sanctuary workers* in every instance in the Bible about this happening. When Samuel is "given to God" and arrives at the dwelling place he is not slaughtered and offered up on the altar. Rather he is dedicated to serve in the dwelling place perpetually (1 Sam 1–2). Similarly, with the Levites in Num 8: the Levites serve in the sanctuary in place of the firstborns from every Israelite family (Num 3:12–13, 45; 8:14–18). Firstborn redemption, therefore, has nothing to do with either human (child) sacrifice in general, or substitutionary death in particular.

right away lambs cannot be used (13:13a). This all eventually gets taken up in Numbers with the dedication of the Levites for service at the dwelling place, which redeems the obligation of the firstborn from each family having to do this work (Num 3:12–13, 45; 8:14–18). The excess firstborns and subsequent firstborns then require a redemption payment to the sanctuary to compensate for their service obligation (3:45–51; 18:15–16).

Therefore, no matter which way we come at this, the Passover lamb cannot be substituting for Israelite firstborns, let alone substituting for their *deaths*, because the dedication and/or redemption of all firstborns occurs completely apart from the Passover ritual and human firstborns are clearly meant to *live* and be dedicated sanctuary workers. This is explicit once we learn that the Levites substitute for God's claim on all the Israelite firstborn males. And the Levitical substitution is not that they are "killed" or "sacrificed" instead of the firstborns. Rather, the Levites fulfill the obligation for Israel to give over all firstborn males to God for permanent service of the sanctuary.

So then, the firstborn aspect of the first Passover is never part of any subsequent Passover celebrations since the firstborn aspect is fulfilled by the Levites' service for human male firstborns (and animal firstborns must be dealt with in their own specific ways). Therefore, to continue to insist on a substitutionary death framework for the Passover lamb despite all the evidence to the contrary is tendentious and unwarranted theological special pleading. There is no scriptural warrant for this. The only warrant for this view comes from an external (and, I will argue, a diametrically opposed) theological framework that has decided beforehand what the form of "salvation" *must* be like (i.e., substitutionary [and perhaps penal as well]) and trying to anchor that in debunked interpretations of biblical practices like sacrifice in general or the Passover in particular.

The Role of the Passover Lamb's Blood

I claimed above that not all "gap filling" is inherently problematic, but I demonstrated why gap filling vis-à-vis the *death* of the lamb is misguided because the death of sacrificial animals never holds any ritual or theological significance in the Torah. The preceding discussion, however, also exhibited how gap filling can be done responsibly regarding God's claim on the firstborns (human and animal). By attending to how the redemption of firstborns is explained and developed outside of Exod 12 and across the Torah and 1 Samuel, we were able to both understand that concept better and simultaneously debunk more misunderstandings. Similarly, I think attending to certain other details in the account of Passover in Exod 12 might help us "gap fill" and ascertain another layer of meaning to the blood ritual in addition to it serving as a tangible "sign" to signal to God that this is an Israelite household, which is the only explicit comment made in the narrative (12:13, 23).

First, although I have been using "Passover" since that is now the accepted English name for this celebration, the root *p-s-ḥ* more than likely does not mean "pass over," but rather "protect/ion."[79] This is supported by the verbal use of *p-s-ḥ* in Isa 31:5: "Like birds hovering overhead, so the LORD of hosts will protect Jerusalem; he will protect and deliver it, he will spare [*pāsōaḥ*] and rescue it." The "pass over" connotation is a retrospective gloss specific to the narrative of Exod 12 where God's "protection" of Israel can be thought of as "skipping over" or "passing over" the Israelite houses. But the *p-s-ḥ* root "was originally independent of the Exodus events"[80] so "pass over" is not its basic denotation even if this is the particular way God's protection is imagined to have looked like during the tenth plague.

The point here, though, is that the Passover meal is memorializing an event when Israel was "protected." When we examine the peculiar use of blood for the first Passover, its usefulness as a "protective" agent, *only when combined with another key ingredient*, becomes clear. Put another way, although the function of blood is not for the purpose of "atonement" (*kipper*) this does not mean it has no ritual function. We have already seen how it functions at least as a visible and tangible "sign" for God to recognize the house as an Israelite one (12:13, cf. v. 23), and now we can see how it also has the particular function of "protection" (*pesaḥ*, 12:11, 21).

Second, this protective function is supported, not only by the word *pesaḥ*, but also by observing that "hyssop" (*ʾēzôv*) is used in combination with the blood (12:22). Hyssop is not used for many biblical rituals, but in every other ritual besides the first Passover where hyssop is dipped in blood and used as the sprinkling instrument, it serves a "purifying" or even an apotropaic, "protective" or "warding off," function (cf. the mention of hyssop in Ps 51:9 [v. 7 Eng.]). The hyssop-blood combination is only used in purification rites for people that have already recovered from scale disease (*ṣāraʿat*)[81] (Lev 14:3–6), for houses that have recovered from fungus (also

79. Sarna, *Exodus*, 56; Tigay, "Exodus," 117–18; Milgrom, *Leviticus 1–16*, 1081.

80. Sarna, *Exodus*, 56.

81. This can refer to a variety of skin conditions that "produce scales" (Milgrom, *Leviticus*, 127) of "[w]hite, flaky skin" (Thiessen, *Jesus and the Forces of Death*, 46). *Ṣāraʿat* is commonly translated as "leprosy," but this is incorrect because it makes it seem as if Leviticus is talking about what is today called Hansen's disease, which is severe contagious bacterial infection that likely postdates Leviticus (Thiessen, *Jesus and the Forces of Death*, 44–46). Even so, what Leviticus is describing is not "leprosy" but a medically

labeled as *ṣāraʿat*, 14:34, 44, 54–55) (14:48–52), and finally for people who have contracted corpse impurity and need to be purified to worship at the dwelling place again (Num 19:6, 18).[82]

Without getting bogged down in the nuances of these rituals, we only need to observe four points. (1) "Sin(s)" is never brought up in these texts (e.g., scale disease is not punishment for sin).[83]

(2) None of this blood is *sacrificial* blood because none of it comes from an animal that is offered up on the altar (and thus none of its blood goes on any part of the altar either).[84] As I will emphasize in chapter 4 on

---

minor skin condition that only has ritual significance. Those whose skin qualifies as *ṣāraʿat* cannot offer sacrifices at the dwelling place until the condition dissipates and they subsequently go through the necessary purity rituals set forth in Lev 13–14. For more, see Milgrom, *Leviticus* , 127–29; Thiessen, *Jesus and the Forces of Death*, 43–54.

82. For more on the historical cultural-religious context to these rituals and further details see, Milgrom, *Leviticus 1–16*, 835, 837–38, 863–65; Milgrom, *Numbers*, 157–63, 438–44.

83. Baden and Moss, "The Origin and Interpretation of *Ṣāraʿat* in Leviticus," 643–62.

84. Milgrom concludes that because the noun *ḥaṭṭāʾt* is used in Num 19:9 and 17 that the red cow is to be considered a purgation sacrifice proper since this is also what Leviticus calls the atoning purgation sacrifices (Lev 4–5, 16) (Milgrom, *Numbers*, 160, 162, 438). But the ritual procedures for the red cow themselves render the whole thing a *quasi*-sacrifice at best. Milgrom even admits that the red cow ritual "does not appear to be a sacrifice at all" since "[t]he blood of the red cow is not offered up on the altar in the same manner as is the blood of every *hattaʾt* and, indeed, of every other animal sacrifice. Rather, the whole cow, together with its blood, is incinerated outside the camp" (*Numbers*, 438). In another place he further destabilizes the notion that it is a sacrifice by noting that this means "nothing is given to God via the altar" and so asks, "How could the ritual of the red cow be a purification [*ḥaṭṭāʾt*] offering if nothing is offered to God?" (*Leviticus*, 34). I think the rationale for calling the red cow a *ḥaṭṭāʾt* even though the ritual procedures make it clear that it is not a *ḥaṭṭāʾt sacrifice* (like the *ḥaṭṭāʾt* sacrifices outlined in Lev 4–5, 16) makes sense given the meaning of the root as a verb. The *piel* verbal construction of the root *ḥ-ṭ-ʾ* means "purify, purge" (e.g., Exod 29:36; Lev 8:15; 14:52; Num 8:21; 19:12, 13, 19, 20; 31:19; Ezek 43:20, 22, 23, 26; 45:18; 2 Chr 29:24; Ps 51:9 [v. 7 Eng.]) (see also Milgrom, *Leviticus 1–16*, 253; Gilders, *Blood Ritual*, 31). Therefore, the most likely (and rather unspectacular) reason for calling the burning of the red cow, along with all the other necessary ingredients, a *ḥaṭṭāʾt* is not because it is a "purgation *sacrifice*," but rather because it is simply a "purgation *procedure*" or a "purification *rite*." It is something that "purges/purifies," but because (a) it is not purging sancta and (b) its blood does not go on the altar nor (c) is its fat burned on the altar, then it is not indexed as a *sacrifice*, let alone a purgation sacrifice. It is just a special purgation ritual for people who have come in contact with a corpse and so cannot come to the dwelling place to worship (Num 19:13, 20).

It is worth noting, in fact, that in a psalm that questions the efficacy of sacrifices (Ps 51:18–19 [vv. 16–17 Eng.]), hyssop is said to "purify" the person (*ḥiṭṭēʾ*, Ps 51:9 [v. 7 Eng.]). The effect of purification, then, does not require that a *sacrifice* was its cause. Since hyssop seems to inherently purify (*ḥiṭṭēʾ*), a ritual that uses hyssop twice in order to purify people (first it is burned along with everything else to create ashes in Num

atoning sacrifices, the blood used to decontaminate the dwelling place from sins and severe impurities comes from a *ḥaṭṭāʾt* ("purgation") sacrifice, but this *ḥaṭṭāʾt* blood is never placed on any people.[85]

(3) Given that these are the only places where hyssop is used with blood, it is apparent that using these together is the taken-for-granted standard ingredients to use in non-sacrificial purification rituals (a practice that likely predates these writings). Hyssop-blood is the common denominator between all of these and the first (non-sacrificial) Passover.[86] By observing the functions and contexts of these rituals besides Passover, we can see that the hyssop-blood combination offers some sort of generalized protection. This does not mean it is warding off the *same* thing in each ritual. This combination is incorporated into specific rituals aimed at warding off specific threats. Since the *ṣāraʿat* person and/or house has to be physically healed of the infection *prior* to the hyssop-blood rituals (Lev 14:3–4, 48), then the hyssop-blood cannot be conceived of as actually healing the person/house. It may have been a folk ritual used proactively to inoculate against scale disease or reactively to heal it (and perhaps this was an exorcism, since similar rites are attested in other Mesopotamian exorcism rituals), but once it gets incorporated into the Levitical priestly system these possible functions have disappeared.[87] In Leviticus it is either purifying any remaining invisible (symbolic?) miasma from these people/houses or warding off reinfection (or perhaps both) of the person/house. Whatever else can be said about what is going on here, the hyssop-blood is at the very least offering some sort of post-infection and post-healing protection from any possible lingering effects of the impurity of *ṣāraʿat*. For corpse impurity, however, the hyssop-ash (Num 19:6) and the hyssop dipped in the hyssop-ash-water that is then sprinkled on the person (19:17–18) can be said to actually purify the

---

19:6 and then, in v. 18, it is used as the sprinkling instrument that is dipped in the hyssop-ash-water) is understandably called a *ḥaṭṭāʾt* (19:9, 17) to indicate that it is a purification procedure (19:12, 13, 19, 20). True, the red cow ritual has quasi-sacrificial-like aspects, but so do the bird rituals for scale disease. And Milgrom argues convincingly that these bird rituals are definitely not sacrifices, let alone *ḥaṭṭāʾt* offerings, for similar reasons I am refusing to do so for the red cow ritual (Milgrom, *Leviticus 1–16*, 833–35, 888).

Therefore, Milgrom's conclusion that the red cow is a purgation *sacrifice* simply on the basis of the use of the word *ḥaṭṭāʾt* is mistaken. There need not be any more rationale to call the red cow ritual a *ḥaṭṭāʾt* (Num 19:9, 17) other than that it is a procedure that *purifies* (19:12, 13, 19, 20).

85. The only blood that gets placed on people is either non-sacrificial blood (like in the case of the non-sacrificial bird blood for the person just healed from scale disease [see above note]), or non-*ḥaṭṭāʾt* blood.

86. Balberg, *Blood for Thought*, 147.

87. Milgrom, *Leviticus 1–16*, 835, 837–38, 863–65.

person from the impurity (*ṭāmēʾ*) adhering to their bodies by contact with a corpse (19:13, 20).

For the first Passover, then, using hyssop to sprinkle the blood on the doorposts and lintel of a house (Exod 12:22) is most like the ritual for the *ṣāraʿat* house in Lev 14:48–52. The Passover ritual with hyssop, therefore, which is also unique to the first Passover since *hyssop is not used in any subsequent Passovers*, can be reasonably conceived of as purifying the house to protect it from "the destroyer" coming in, which is exactly what Exod 12:22–23 conveys. It is a preventative apotropaic ritual warding off this specific one-off threat.[88] Hence, calling this meal celebrating this event "the Protection" (*hapāsaḥ*, Exod 12:21) makes good sense because God will "see" the hyssop-tossed blood and "protect" the house from "the destroyer" who will then not be able to "enter" (12:22–23; cf. v. 13).

Finally, (4) the concept of substitutionary death is never present in any of these hyssop rituals. The (non-sacrificial) blood is not functioning as a "substitutionary death" for those whom the hyssop-blood is protecting/purifying. Using hyssop to dip in blood (or ash-water with blood and hyssop-as-ash components) and sprinkle on things is simply taken for granted as a non-sacrificial purification procedure. What it purges and/or wards off is different depending on the ritual context. In any case, the hyssop-blood only happens at that first (non-sacrificial) Passover. Once Passover becomes incorporated as a sacrifice in Israel's liturgical calendar, there is no hyssop-blood and no door frames are supposed to be smeared with it (neither is the altar dashed with hyssop-blood). In fact, after setting forth all this information, then along with the previous observations about why the first Passover is not a sacrifice (no priesthood, no altar, not boiling the meat), the *presence* of hyssop only at the first Passover is yet another way the text indexes that first Passover as "not a sacrifice." The absence of hyssop at all subsequent Passovers, therefore, makes sense if hyssop is only used in non-sacrificial rituals (i.e., rituals whose blood/animal components are not offered up to God on the altar).

Therefore, the Passover does not have an atoning function, but the first Passover is depicted as having a protective (*pesaḥ*) apotropaic function,

88. Since the first Passover ritual was actually apotropaic (a proactive procedure to ward off a future threat), it might be how the hyssop-blood rituals for *ṣāraʿat* were used originally before they were incorporated into the priestly system. In other words, the hyssop-blood combination for purification of people and houses might have originally been used in the same proactive manner depicted in Exod 12 (and they might even have been used to try to cure the disease itself once present). But once these rituals were included as part of the formal priestly purity and sacrificial system, then their proactive and healing uses were discarded in favor of a post-hoc ritual purification after the disease was already healed on its own.

anchored as it is in the standard non-sacrificial ritual ingredients and procedures for warding off a threat, applying blood on a house with hyssop branches. All subsequent Passovers function as sacrificial commemorations of this event, celebrated by feasting on a unique type of (non-atoning) thanksgiving well-being offering.

COVENANT-INAUGURATION AND COVENANT-RENEWAL CEREMONIES

The covenant at Sinai was inaugurated with burnt offerings and well-being offerings (Exod 24:5). Now that we understand the relationship between these, it makes sense that the relationship between God and Israel would be initiated with these sacrifices because their main function is the meeting of God and people through sacred feasting (cf. 24:11). In general, these are sacrifices of *invitation* and *celebration* and cannot have an atoning function.[89] In particular, these are celebrating the ratification of the so-called "Mosaic" or "Sinaitic" covenant. It is this particularity that accounts for a peculiar blood ritual that is unique to Exod 24: in addition to the altar, blood is also sprinkled upon the people (v. 8).

Before discussing that unique blood ritual, it is worth seeing how future covenant-renewal ceremonies feature *only* these same non-atoning sacrifices, but without the blood-sprinkling ritual. For example, Moses instructs Joshua to facilitate one such covenant-renewal ceremony upon crossing the Jordan river (Deut 27:4–8), which Joshua does (Josh 8:30–35). We see similar covenant-renewal ceremonies with King Asa (2 Chr 15:10–15), King Hezekiah (29:30–36, esp. vv. 31, 35), and again at the re-institution of the Passover with another covenant renewal (30:1–27, esp. v. 22), and King Manasseh after his repentance (2 Chr 33:16). The common denominator for all these is the well-being (*šəlāmîm*)/eaten-sacrifice (*zebaḥ*). This is the standard covenant-ratifying sacrifice according to Ps 50:5 (NRSV): "Gather to me my faithful ones, who made a covenant with me by sacrifice [*zebaḥ*]!"[90]

Further, once the Maccabees successfully defeated Antiochus IV, they rededicate the altar for eight days and only burnt offerings and well-being offerings are mentioned (1 Macc 4:56). Even if this is not quite the same

89. Similarly, Shauf, *Jesus the Sacrifice*, 123.

90. The burnt offerings seem to function as the invitation for God to come meet with the people (i.e., the function of divine "attraction") per Exod 20:24, but the ratification of the covenant-renewal ceremony happens when the people feast together with God from the well-being sacrifices, since this is the only one consumed by both parties (God and the people).

as a covenant-renewal ceremony, it is a re-dedication to "the law" (4:53) and commemorating their deliverance from Antiochus (4:59). Thus, only sacrificing burnt and well-being offerings is expected, since these are the appropriate sacrifices for such purposes and occasions.

The main idea is that when a leader wants to mark the renewal of the covenant, they use well-being sacrifices because one of the key functions of those sacrifices is to serve as communal feasts of commemoration and celebration. Now that we understand their broad use in contexts that have great national significance, we can examine the role of the distinct blood ritual associated with the well-being sacrifices for this function.

The Visible Memorial Function

Even though the blood ritual for the covenant-inauguration is not about atonement, it still has a significant function as a sign of the bond being ratified or renewed. This becomes clear when we attend to two aspects of the blood ritual described in Exod 24:6 and 8. The first is "dashing" (*zāraq*) on the sides of the altar (v. 6) and the second is "dashing" it upon the people (v. 8). Dashing the blood on the sides of the altar is standard protocol for burnt and well-being sacrifices (e.g., Lev 1:5, 11; 3:2, 8), but dashing it on people only happens here; it is not in any of the covenant-renewal ceremonies.

Regarding the first aspect, "dashing" blood on the sides of the altar does not happen with the atoning purgation sacrifices (*ḥaṭṭāʾt*). As Josephus was careful to highlight, when the blood from the purgation sacrifices goes on an altar (there are two altars, the outer altar for animal sacrifices and the altar inside the holy place for burning incense only), then it only goes on their protruding "horns," not its sides (e.g., Lev 4:7, 18, 25, 30, 34; cf. Josephus, *Ant.* 3.231).[91] The blood manipulations between these sacrifices are further distinguished by the use of different verbs. Whereas the burnt and well-being sacrifices have their blood "dashed" or "tossed" (*zāraq*) on the altar's sides, the purgation sacrifice has its blood "daubed," "smeared," or more generally "put" (*nātan*) on the altar's horns.[92] The different actions

91. As discussed later, the purgation sacrifice blood goes on a different altar depending on who it is for. But whenever it goes on either altar it is only daubed on its four horns.

92. For more on the distinctions between the various blood manipulation terminology in Leviticus, see Gilders, *Blood Ritual*, 25–32.

with the blood and the different locations it contacts both index the distinct functions of these sacrifices.[93]

The visibility of these different blood rituals is important.[94] From the perspective of the laity, who cannot "come near" the outer altar (this is only accessible to *priests*, not even Levites, Num 18:2, 7, 22; 1:51), they cannot see the horns of the altar from above, which means they cannot see the blood daubed on top of them. This is especially the case since the altar is elevated, built on a platform, and so required a long ramp up to it (Exod 20:26). And for the atoning blood rituals that take place inside the dwelling place proper (the holy place and holy of holies), the laity cannot see any of it. It is completely hidden from view behind the curtain blocking access to the dwelling place. But the laity can see the *sides* of the outer altar from afar. This means the only sacrificial blood visible to the laity is the blood dashed on its sides for the burnt and well-being sacrifices, making it look red. Hence, when describing the unique blood ritual of the well-being sacrifices, Josephus says the priests "redden [*phoinissō*] the altar with the blood" (*Ant.* 3.228, my translation).

Ronald S. Hendel argues that it is specifically the *visibility* of the "blood splashed on the side of the altar" that allows it to function as "a tangible, visible reminder of the performance of the sacrifice."[95] He connects this visibility back to the only stated function of the burnt and well-being offerings in Exod 20:24; namely, that God will "come" to Israel there to bless them. In this way, "The blood that remains on the side of the altar long after the ceremony is concluded serves as a tangible sign of the remembrance and corresponding blessing. It [the blood dashing] is not only a part of the ceremony, but a remnant and symbol of it."[96]

Importantly, 20:24 is the only comment we get regarding the purpose of sacrifices (and only the burnt and well-being sacrifices are named) in the so-called "Covenant Code" (all the laws from Exod 20:22—23:19, or more precisely 21:1—22:16), which is what immediately precedes the covenant-inauguration ceremony in 24:3–8 that features these two sacrifices. Exodus 24:3 says that Moses recounts to Israel all the things God told him, which is all the laws in 20:22—23:19, before ratifying the covenant with these sacrifices. This means that the blood-dashing on the sides of the altar for the covenant inauguration in 24:6 functions, first, as Hendel puts, "not only [as]

93. See also Gilders, *Blood Ritual*, 88–96, 109.

94. For an excellent study for how the (in)visibility of sacrificial blood matters in various Second Temple Jewish texts, including Leviticus, see Feldman, "Sanitized Sacrifice in Aramaic Levi's Law of the Priesthood," 343–68.

95. Hendel, "Sacrifice as a Cultural System," 387.

96. Hendel, "Sacrifice as a Cultural System," 387.

part of the ceremony, but a remnant and symbol of it."[97] Recall that well-being sacrifices have a memorial and remembrance function (e.g., Num 10:10; cf. Exod 12:14) and thus, the blood-dashed sides of the altar plays a visible role to that end. The significance of the blood-dashing ritual is that is serves a "communicative function" of "remembrance" precisely because of its visibility to the people to see.[98]

The Bonding Function

But what about the second, and utterly unique, aspect of the covenant-inauguration blood ritual? What purpose does dashing the blood on the people serve (24:8)? In short, I agree with Umberto Cassuto's basic conclusion: "The throwing of half of the blood of the offerings against the altar, which represented the Lord, and half on the people, or that which represented them, signifies a joining together of the two contracting parties (*communio*), and symbolized the execution of the deed of covenant between them."[99] That is, "the application of blood to *both* the altar and the people indexes a bond between the covenant parties."[100] This is a common view among OT scholars.[101]

This interpretation is supported by two further observations. The first is noting how the two blood manipulations bookend the covenant-inauguration ceremony (Exod 24:3–8). Moses first dashes the altar with the blood (24:6), then reads "the book of the covenant" (i.e., the Covenant Code in Exod 20:22—23:19), which the people affirm to obey (24:7), and after this affirmation he dashes the people with the same blood (24:8). These two blood manipulations frame the covenant-making ceremony and thus "mark the bounds of a time in which Yahweh's words are offered to the people in a concrete written form and the people express their acceptance of Yahweh as suzerain."[102] The blood-dashing ritually marks either that the covenant bond is being created in and through the blood manipulations, or that it has already been made (forged by verbal assent to God's words) and the blood is the tangible ratification and memorial of that bond. For our purposes, it

97. Hendel, "Sacrifice as a Cultural System," 387.

98. Hendel, "Sacrifice as a Cultural System," 387.

99. Cassuto, *Exodus*, 312. For the links between the altar and God (or at least as representing God's presence), see Exod 20:25, Ps 42:3 with 43:4; 1 Kgs 8:22, 31, 54; 2 Kgs 18:22–39; Isa 19:19–20.

100. Gilders, *Blood Ritual*, 90, his emphasis; cf. 39–41, 89, 102–3.

101. Sarna, *Exodus*, 152; Tigay, "Exodus," 154.

102. Gilders, *Blood Ritual*, 40.

does not matter which one is preferred. Either way, whether the blood dashing on both the altar and the people forges, ratifies, or signals a "bond," the blood ritual at the very least "index[es] a relationship between the people and that altar."[103]

The second observation is technically a set of observations and requires expanded discussion.

Sacrificial Blood Application to People Elsewhere: The Metaphysical-Transition Function

By looking at what happens in two other instances when blood is applied to both the altar and people, we can not only strengthen the above point, but we can also plausibly say more than just that this shared blood ritual between the altar and the people "indexes" a relationship. One happens at the ordination of Aaron and his sons as priests (Exod 29; Lev 8) and the other is part of the post-healing ritual purification process for the person recovered from scale disease (Lev 14).[104] For all the differences between these three rituals, what they have in common is that the people who have blood applied to them undergo a metaphysical transition. They transfer from one realm into another, always in the direction of holiness (though at different levels).

The first of these is instructed right after the covenant-inauguration ceremony when Moses goes back up the mountain to receive the instructions for constructing the dwelling place and consecrating the priesthood (Exod 25–29), which is then carried out after the dwelling place has been built (Lev 8). As part of a multistep priesthood-consecration process, Moses is instructed to take the blood from a ram used as an "ordination" sacrifice (Exod 29:22, 26; Lev 8:22, 29),[105] and "put" or "daub" (*nātan*) it on the right

103. Gilders, *Blood Ritual*, 103.

104. I am not including the corpse purification rite in Num 19 because (a) it is not a sacrifice, as discussed in footnote 84. And (b) what is sprinkled on the people undergoing corpse purification is only ever called "water," not "blood" (19:9, 13, 18, 20–21). Burnt blood is technically an ingredient in the "ash" that is made (19:5, 9), but it is no more emphasized than the animal hide, bones, flesh, hyssop, cedar wood, or scarlet yarn (19:5–6). That being said, even if we wanted to loosen the parameters of comparison, the corpse purification would still mark a metaphysical transition from being impure at the furthest extreme of the im/purity spectrum to being pure.

105. Technically it is called the "ram of filling" (*ʾel milluʾîm*, Exod 29:22, 26; Lev 8:22, 29). We know from its use elsewhere that the "filling" is shorthand for "filling the hands" of the priests (Exod 28:41; 29:9, 29, 35; 32:29; Lev 8:33; 16:32; Num 3:3). It is an idiom for priestly ordination because they are given a portion of the sacrifices in their "hands" (e.g., Exod 29:24–25, 28; Lev 8:22–29). Having sacrificial portions filling their

side earlobes, thumbs, and big toes of Aaron and his sons and then "dash" (*zāraq*) the rest against the sides of the altar (Exod 29:20; Lev 8:23–24). This "ram of ordination" is a one-off special instance of a well-being sacrifice (Exod 29:28) and the distinctive ritual action of "dashing" the blood against the sides of the altar confirms this.

Although the ritual action of "daubing" the blood on soon-to-be priests differs from the "dashing" or "tossing" on the people in Exod 24:8, these "can [be] fruitfully compare[d]" on the basis that these are two of the three times "blood is applied to people and to an altar."[106] It is apparent that these blood rituals are "indexing a relationship between the people [that have blood applied to them] and the altar."[107] Or, as Nahum Sarna expresses, "in both these ceremonies—covenant and ordination—the blood functions mysteriously to cement the bond between the involved parties."[108]

Moreover, although both the covenant-inauguration ceremony and the priestly ordination index a relationship between the people and the altar (God), these relational indexes are different for each group. The different action on Aaron and his sons need not indicate more than the fact that their relationship to God, represented by the altar, is that of *priests*, who mediate even the laity's access to the altar. In other words, the difference in ritual indicates a difference in office and access to the altar. The people have blood "dashed" on them and they will only be able to eat a portion of the non-atoning sacrifices of well-being whose blood is similarly "dashed" on the altar. Perhaps similarly, then, the priests, who also had blood "dashed" on them at the covenant ceremony, have blood "daubed" on them because they will also get to have a portion of certain purgation sacrifices whose blood is "daubed" on the horns of the altar. In any case, the similar "indexing power of the [blood] action is still evident" between these two events.[109]

Pausing over what is taking effect with Aaron and his sons, however, sharpens what we can say is happening when blood is applied to them. From the priestly perspective of the world, everything can be mapped onto two binaries: (a) "common/ordinary" (*ḥōl*) or "holy" (*qōdeš*) and (b) "pure/clean" (*ṭāhôr*) or "impure/unclean" (*ṭāmē*ʾ) (Lev 10:10; 11:47; 20:25; Ezek

---

hands is a symbol of their God-ordained right to offer sacrifices on behalf of the people and to make their living by being fed by portions from them (6:9 [v. 16 Eng.], 11, [v. 18 Eng.], 19 [v. 26 Eng.], 22 [v. 29 Eng.]; 7:6–10, 34–36). For more on this, see Milgrom, *Leviticus 1–16*, 526–27, 538–39.

106. Gilders, *Blood Ritual*, 102–3.

107. Gilders, *Blood Ritual*, 103.

108. Sarna, *Exodus*, 152.

109. Gilders, *Blood Ritual*, 102.

22:26; 44:23).[110] Aaron and his sons are transitioning from one metaphysical realm to another. They are going from the realm of the "common" (*ḥōl*) to the realm of the "holy" (*qōdeš*).[111] The blood applied to Aaron and his sons is one integral part of this transition;[112] it is part of what "sanctifies" or "consecrates" (*qādaš*) them (Exod 29:21; Lev 8:30). By this process of metaphysical transition, they are essentially becoming walking sacred-dwelling-place furniture.[113]

The idea is that the blood ritual applied to Aaron and his sons is part of a "rite of passage"[114] that facilitates, effects, or otherwise marks their transfer from the metaphysical realm of the "common" and into the realm of the "holy."[115] My point does not depend on which of these verbs (or perhaps another) is most accurate. I want to leave room for a (delimited) range of meaning. But the main idea at the very least is that the "indexing" function is not simply a "relationship" between the priests and the altar, but that it

110. The holiness binary is sometimes expressed as "profane" and "holy." But "profane" carries unnecessary negative connotations in English. Something that is *ḥōl* is not bad. It just means it is not related to the sanctuary in some way. Also, a thing or person cannot be both antitheses at once (e.g., nothing and no one can be simultaneously "common/ordinary" *and* "holy," or "pure/clean" *and* "impure/unclean"). But a thing or a person is always either (a) holy and impure/unclean, (b) or holy and pure/clean, (c) or common and impure/unclean, (d) or common and pure/clean. According to the priestly theology, everything in the world always exists in one of these four states. I will discuss these terms along with the purity system in more detail in the next chapter. See also Thiessen, *Forces of Death*, 10–11.

111. What it means for something to be "holy" (*qōdeš*) in the Torah is that it is dedicated for special use in relation to God and/or the dwelling place. The dwelling place is sometimes called a *miqdāš*, "holy space" (i.e., "sanctuary") (e.g., Exod 25:8; Lev 12:4; 16:33; 19:30). Note the same root, *q-d-š*, with the *m*- prefix, like the pattern we saw for "sacrifice" (*zebaḥ*) and "altar" (*mizbēaḥ*), and "to dwell" (*šākan*) and "dwelling place" (*miškān*). What is *ḥōl* belongs to the "common" or "ordinary" sphere and what is holy belongs to sacred sphere (the Sabbath day is an instance of a *time* being dedicated to God; Exod 31:14).

112. Special "holy" anointing oil is also used for their consecration (Exod 29:7, 21; 30:30; Lev 8:12, 30).

113. The high priest's unique vestments are made from the very same materials as the fabrics used in the most sacred parts of the dwelling place (cf. Exod 25:1–7; 26:1–6, 31–37; 28:1—29:30). Similarly, the regular priestly garments, which also get sprinkled with blood (and oil), are also getting turned into "sacred furniture" (Exod 29:21; Lev 8:30). These garments are to be handed down to each generation of priests (Exod 29:9, 29; 40:14–15) such that putting on the garments constitute the ordination of each new generation (29:29).

114. Milgrom, *Leviticus*, 137.

115. See Gilders, *Blood Ritual*, 182: "Exodus 29:21 and Lev 8:30 indicate that the act of sprinkling blood mixed with oil onto Aaron, his sons, and their liturgical vestments effects their transition to a state of holiness."

also indexes a "metaphysical transition" in the priestly conception of the world.[116] As Sarna conveys, "the life of the recipient is thought to take on a new dimension and to be elevated to a higher level of intimate relationship with the Deity."[117] This "new dimension" and "higher level" is what I am calling a "metaphysical transition" because this new dimension for Aaron and his sons is mapped onto the priestly metaphysics of the common and the holy (e.g., Lev 10:10).

This brings us to the only other time blood is ritually applied to people in the Torah: when it is used as part of the ritual purification process for a person who has recently recovered from scale disease (14:12–14, 25, 28). And for all the distinctives this ritual has with respect to the covenant-inauguration ceremony and the priestly consecration rite, it similarly evinces that when blood is applied to people in a ritual context it indicates that a metaphysical transition is happening. We already discussed the non-sacrificial blood ritual involving birds and hyssop above but revisiting it here will support the present point.

This non-sacrificial bird-blood ritual is the first ritual in a three-step purification process that parallels ritual purification from corpse impurity (and the ritual at the first Passover).[118] Its similarity with the process for

116. This consecration rite is never repeated for new priests. The metaphysical transition is so potent that sons born to priests simply don the already-consecrated priestly garments when they take on priestly work (Exod 29:9; 40:15; Num 20:26–28). Each new high priest, however, is anointed with the sacred anointing oil. And "high priest" is not the title in Hebrew. After the initial consecration anointing of Aaron and his sons, what we in English call the "high priest" is called "the anointed priest" (Lev 4:3, 5, 16; 6:15 [v. 22 Eng.]; 16:32; 21:10; Num 35:25). There is even a distinction in oil anointing at the initial consecration of Aaron and his sons. Whereas Aaron's *head* is anointed with oil (Lev 8:12), his sons only have the oil sprinkled on them and their garments (8:30). The anointing of the new high priest happens after the previous one dies and they succeed him. But no other regular priests are anointed with the holy oil again after the initial consecration ceremony in Lev 8:30. For more, see Milgrom, *Leviticus 1–16*, 554–55.

117. Sarna, *Exodus*, 152.

118. The person is declared "pure/clean" (*ṭāhēr*) at the end of each of the three purification stages (Lev 14:8, 9, 20). Again, this is not physically healing them of the disease. The disease has to already "be healed" (*nirpāʾ*) prior to the first stage (14:3); it is the precondition for the ritual purification processes. The first purification step is the ritual with birds and hyssop that culminates in water-washing (14:4–8). While the person had scale disease they had to live outside the camp because they transmit impurity to everything, common or holy, that is under the same roof (Lev 13:46; cf. Num 5:2–3). This first purification step is only one day and it removes one layer of impurity so the person can re-enter the camp, since they can only transmit ritual impurity (to common things) by direct contact (Lev 14:8). But they must remain outside their "tent" (house) for a week (14:8) because they still transmit impurity by overhang to holy things, such as the holy food from a well-being offering or objects dedicated but yet to be delivered to the

dealing with corpse impurity is instructive for our current purposes. As Milgrom observes, "the fact that the same life-enhancing ingredients are used in purificatory rites [for the first stage of three] for those contaminated by a corpse or by scale disease . . . supports the theory that the scale diseased person is regarded as a corpse . . . and that impurity, in general, is associated with death."[119] Further:

> The main clue for understanding the place of scale disease in the impurity system is that it is an aspect of death: its bearer is treated like a corpse. This equation is expressly stated by Aaron in his prayer on behalf of Miriam when she is stricken with scale disease: "Let her not be like a corpse" (Num 12:12[; cf. Job 18:13, 18–23]). In addition, both scale disease and the corpse contaminate not only by direct contact but, unlike all other impurity bearers, also contaminate by overhang, that is, by being under the same roof.[120]

This connection with death is significant because it means that the overall effect of this "symbolic ritual" is "a *rite of passage*, marking the transition from death to life."[121] This is a "symbolic ritual" and *not a cure* for scale disease because the disease already has to be gone and healed before the first step in the purification process (Lev 14:3).[122] This means the ritual purification overall is indexing and facilitating another metaphysical transition, but this time from the realm of the impure, which is associated with "the forces of death,"[123] to the realm of the pure. While all other ways of traversing these two realms are ritually less complex (usually only involving the passage of

---

sanctuary (Milgrom, *Leviticus 1–16*, 842–43). The second purification stage takes place on the eighth day (Lev 14:9). The person must shave their entire bodies and bathe again (14:9). This removes yet another layer of impurity with the result that they can be back in their tents since they no longer can transmit impurity to holy things (such as sacred sacrificial food) by overhang, only by direct contact (Milgrom, *Leviticus 1–16*, 844). The third and final stage involves a series of sacrifices and oil anointing (not the same holy anointing oil used for priests) at the end of which the final declaration of being "pure/clean" is given and they are now fully reincorporated into community and rhythms of worship at the dwelling place (Lev 14:10–20). This third stage involves a blood ritual from one of the sacrifices that mimics the blood ritual for priestly consecration that is explained below.

119. Milgrom, *Leviticus 1–16*, 835.

120. Milgrom, *Leviticus*, 128–29; cf. Milgrom, *Leviticus 1–16*, 819–20.

121. Milgrom, *Leviticus*, 134; his emphasis.

122. As Milgrom observes, "the priest does nothing to promote the cure; his rituals commence only after the disease has passed" (*Leviticus 1–16*, 887).

123. Milgrom, *Leviticus*, 135; Milgrom, *Leviticus 1–16*, 686, 733, 767–68, 865, 889, cf. 1000–1004.

time and a water-washing), the fact that the scale diseased person is treated as a walking corpse accounts for the distinctive blood-application rituals applied to the person after the disease goes away.[124] From this overall context and what results from the whole purification process, we see that the common denominator in the rituals that apply blood directly to people is that it is used to index when a major metaphysical transition is taking place.

In fact, while the non-sacrificial blood ritual at the first stage (Lev 14:3–8) is similar to the ones for corpse impurity (Num 19), the first Passover (Exod 12:22–23), and (more obviously) the one for a fungal house (Lev 14:48–53),[125] the *sacrificial* blood ritual during the third and final stage of the purification process mimics the one for priestly ordination.[126] As we observed, the priestly consecration ritual involves the "ram of ordination," a type of well-being sacrifice, but the sacrificial blood applied to the formerly scale diseased individual comes from the "reparation offering" (*ʾāšām*) (14:12–14, 25). However, both rituals "place" (*nātan*) the blood as well as oil on the right-side earlobe, thumb, and big toe of the person.[127] These similarities with priestly consecration signal that an analogous major metaphysical transition is taking place. For Aaron and his sons, they move over from the common to the holy, but for the formerly scale diseased person they not only go from impure to pure generally, but from the realm of *death* to the realm of *life*. As Milgrom expresses, "the entire purification process is nothing but a ritual, a rite of passage, marking the transition from death to life."[128] They go from the walking dead, outcasted from the whole community, to becoming reintegrated as "full-fledged participant in his community and its worship."[129]

Moreover, the use of the reparation sacrifice (*ʾāšām*) (Lev 14:12–14, 25) is distinctive here for two other reasons, both of which serve to strengthen

124. The passage of time and water are used for both corpse impurity and scale disease. But note that while purification from corpse impurity only involves the passage of time and (a rather unique) "water" (Num 19:9, 13, 18, 20–21), actual blood is used at two different stages in the ritual purification process for the former scale diseased person (Lev 14:4–7, 12–14, 25, 28). This use of blood applied directly to the person makes it comparable to the priestly consecration and the covenant-inauguration ceremony. It is also important to note that neither ritual comes from the blood of a purgation sacrifice.

125. Both scale disease on a person and fungus on a house are called *ṣāraʿat* (Lev 14:3, 34, 44, cf. vv. 54–57).

126. Milgrom, *Leviticus 1–16*, 853; Gilders, *Blood Ritual*, 105–6.

127. The oil for laity is not the same holy anointing oil used on the first priests and to anoint sancta.

128. Milgrom, *Leviticus 1–16*, 889, cf. 853.

129. Milgrom, *Leviticus 1–16*, 859.

the idea these metaphysical transitions are mediated by means of the altar. It is already distinctive since its blood is applied to the person. And we have observed how when both the altar and the people receive sacrificial blood, this indexes both a "bond" between them as well as a metaphysical transition. A bond between the person and the altar is created and it seems that it is this connection to the altar that facilitates the person's metaphysical transition in the direction of holiness (i.e., toward the altar, which represents God's presence and holiness).

The first additional distinctive aspect regarding the reparation offering in relation to purification from scale disease is that it cannot be commuted into a monetary donation to the sanctuary as it can be with all other regular reparation offerings (see 5:15, 18, 25 [6:6 Eng.]; 1 Sam 6:3–17; 2 Kgs 12:17).[130] The reparation sacrifice has to be from a male lamb (the regular reparation offerings are either a ram or money) even if the person is poor (Lev 14:12, 21, 25).[131] My only point here is that blood from the reparation sacrifice is a *necessary* ingredient for this third and final stage of the purification process. Money cannot substitute in this ritual because *blood* is what indexes the bond between the person and the altar when the blood is applied to both from the same sacrifice.[132]

The second distinctive aspect of the reparation offering in Lev 14 is the order in which it is sacrificed relative to the other three sacrifices required. "All Sin[purgation]-offerings enjoined in the Law precede the Guilt[reparation]-offerings, excepting only the Guilt[reparation]-offering of the [scale diseased person]" (m. Zebaḥ. 10:5).[133] Only here in the third stage of the purification process in all of Torah is the reparation sacrifice offered first. The rabbis provide the best reason for this anomaly suggesting it is "since this is offered to render him fit" (m. Zebaḥ. 10:5), which in context has to do with being fit to "eat" sacred food (i.e., partake of sacrifices of well-being) (cf. m. Zebaḥ. 10:6).[134]

130. Milgrom, *Leviticus 1–16*, 327–28. The reparation offering for the Nazirite who contracts corpse impurity also cannot be commuted (arguably for similar reasons) (Num 6:9–12).

131. For the poor, the burnt and purgation offerings required can be substituted with turtledoves or pigeons (Lev 14:22, 30–31). On the rationale for why the reparation offering cannot be substituted with a bird, see Milgrom, *Leviticus 1–16*, 861.

132. Leviticus 14 does not reference the blood-dashing on the altar from the reparation offering, but it is assumed given the instruction for reparation offering in Lev 7:1–2 (similarly, Gilders, *Blood Ritual*, 105).

133. Translation from Herbert Danby, *The Mishnah*, 483; my brackets.

134. This is why Danby adds the explanatory gloss in brackets "fit [to enter the Temple and to eat of the Hallowed Things]" (*The Mishnah*, 483). Similarly, Milgrom concludes, "his daubing with the ʾāšām blood renders him henceforth fit to enter the sanctuary and partake of sacred food" (*Leviticus 1–16*, 851).

As part of the third and final stage in the purification process, something is needed to re-establish the link between the person to be reintegrated into the worship of the community and their access to the dwelling place since scale disease brought them so close to the realm of death that they were completely disconnected from the altar. This unique reparation offering, then, by means of being the first sacrifice offered by the person recently healed from scale disease and having the sacrificial blood applied to both the altar and to the offerer, serves to re-establish the bond between the person and the altar. Scale disease is as close to death as one can ritually get besides being literally dead, and because of this they have been severed from the altar and the camp (Num 5:2–3; Lev 13:46) so that they cannot "defile" or "make impure/unclean" (*yəṭammə ʾû*) this space where God dwells (Num 5:3). In this way, their reintegration into the community and its liturgical life mimics the covenant-inauguration ceremony. The application of the blood to both the offerer and the altar reinstates the bond between the person and the altar once again.

It is important to notice that blood from the purgation sacrifice (*ḥaṭṭā ʾt*) is never used on people.[135] Purgation sacrifice blood is only ever used on sancta, to purge the ritual vandalism that impurity and sin produces on these holy objects. This is important because this means none of these non-atoning blood rituals have anything to do with sin and thus with purging *people* from any "stain" of sin. I will develop this and bring in relevant nuances for the purgation sacrifices in the next two chapters, but here we only need to realize how the fact that no blood from this particular sacrifice is ever used on people necessarily means these blood rituals cannot have anything to do with "overcoming the problem of sin" let alone "substituting for their deserved death" or any other such similar yet mistaken (and problematic) notions.

What has become clear from the foregoing, and what will be useful for analyzing certain NT texts later, is that when blood is applied to people it always marks a transition from one metaphysical realm into another—in the direction of greater holiness. Thus, for the soon-to-be priests, this is a transition from being a regular lay Israelite to a consecrated priest. For the person who has recovered from scale disease, this is a transition from the realm of "death," from being the "walking dead"[136] and thus excluded from community and liturgical life, back to "life" as a full community member. Sacrificial blood used in this way indexes metaphysical transitions up the

135. See Milgrom, *Leviticus 1–16*, 255: "Its use is confined to the sanctuary, but *it is never applied to a person*" (his emphasis; for the full argument, see 254–58; cf. 290).

136. Thiessen, *Forces of Death*, 43, 51.

scale of holiness. None of this has nothing to do with a ritual or symbolic substitutionary death.

Conclusion to Covenant Inauguration

We have established the "indexing" function of the blood for all three of the sacrificial rituals that feature the distinctive action of applying the blood to both the people and the altar; namely, that it indexes a bond between them. We also further established how this ritual indexes a metaphysical transition, but only for the instance of Aaron and his sons moving from the common (as laity) to the holy (as priests) and for the person who has recovered from scale disease transitioning from death to life.

All this provides a strong warrant to comprehend the covenant inauguration as likewise being about a metaphysical transition for Israel as a whole. That is, the blood ritual is not only about forging a covenantal bond between Israel and God (via the altar), but is also indexing their metaphysical transition from being a regular people to a "treasured possession" (Exod 19:5; cf. Deut 7:6; 14:2; 26:18) and a "kingdom of priests and a holy nation" (Exod 19:6).[137] In Exod 19:5–6 God says that if they agree to the terms of the covenant, then they will become a new sort of people, they will transition into the realm of the "holy" (19:6), a status the priestly literature in Leviticus confirms in its own way (cf. Lev 20:26; 11:44; 19:2: 20:7).[138] The connection between Exod 19:5–6 and 24:3–8 might be missed due to there being a lot of intervening material, but this is simply all the instructions Israel needs to hear first before they can agree to the covenant, which is why Moses reads out the book of the covenant before dashing them with blood (24:3–4, 7). Once this narrative context is accounted for, then, it becomes clear that the

137. This interpretation holds even at the level of source analysis, since both of these texts (Exod 19:4–6 and 24:3–8) come from the same Pentateuchal source: E. For the best modern defense (and nuancing) of the Pentateuch documentary hypothesis and source analysis, see Baden, *The Composition of the Pentateuch*, esp. 117–18 for both Exod 19:4–6 and 24:3–8 being from E.

138. It is inappropriate to overinterpret the language of being "kingdom of priests" in Exod 19:6 as if that is a (not so) subtle jab at Israel's Aaronic priesthood. It is a metaphor for the distinctive relationship Israel has with God vis-à-vis the other peoples. Since they are closer in relationship, they are further up the holiness spectrum. Also, just like there are gradations of holiness for sacrifices and spaces in the dwelling place (e.g., the outer courtyard is less holy than the holy place, which is less holy that the holy of holies), there are gradations of holiness within Israel. Israel is holy relative to the nations, but within Israel Levites are more holy than the rest of the tribes, and Aaron's sons are more holy since they are priests. And only one priest in each generation is the most holy as the anointed high priest.

covenant ceremony is establishing not only Israel's covenantal bond with God, but also their metaphysical transition into a holy people.

From this vantage point, therefore, we can safely conclude that for all the differences between these blood rituals that feature sacrificial blood being applied to both people and the altar, they all share common functions. Pulling the various threads together we see that the blood:

(a) serves as a visible sign and memorial of the event and,

(b) at the very least, ritually indexes or ratifies a relationship between the people and the altar (representing God) (though perhaps it might do more than "index" and may even actualize or generate it), and

(c) indexes that a metaphysical transition has taken place (or actualizes this transition).

In none of these blood rituals would "substitutionary death" make any sense. It is a foreign concept that is completely out of context for all these rituals. As we saw, ritual blood manipulations are distinct. The blood from different sacrifices, and even blood from non-sacrifices (as in the case for the first purification stage for scale disease), brings about different outcomes. Also, the action the priest performs with it affects different outcomes. All the specific verbs signify different functions. Blood that is "dashed" does something different than when it is "put" or "sprinkled," or, as we will see in due course, "poured out." And it also matters *where* these ritual actions are taking place. Is it happening to the outer altar or the inner altar (on its horns or the sides)? The veil? The ground? We have yet to explain some of these actions, but the point here is that not all ritual blood is endowed with the same meaning and function. Therefore, attempting to reduce sacrificial blood to one thing, let alone "substitutionary death," is fundamentally mistaken. It conflates where the priestly system distinguishes. It misunderstands that nuance and distinction is at the very heart of priestly discernment (e.g., Lev 10:10; 11:47; 20:25; Ezek 22:26; 44:23), which is why there are various types of sacrifices, non-sacrificial rituals, different blood manipulations, etc.

CONCLUSION

As demonstrated, sacrifices have distinct rationales and functions apart from atonement. The daily burnt offerings, for instance, serve the purpose of drawing divine attention. Well-being offerings facilitate sacred feasting between God and humanity, enacting and fostering the union of God and the community. Both the Passover and the covenant inauguration and renewal ceremonies only employ non-atoning sacrifices. And, not only is the Passover a unique "thanksgiving" well-being sacrifice, commemorating God's deliverance of Israel in the exodus, the initial Paschal meal was not even a sacrifice, let alone some sort of atoning substitutionary death sacrifice. Furthermore, I argued rituals of blood-sprinkling on the people have nothing to do with atonement or substitutionary death. Whenever blood is applied to people, it ritually marks and facilitates specific metaphysical transitions, unique to each cultic context.

Now, keeping the larger aim of understanding how the NT authors make use of OT sacrificial imagery and to comprehend various meaning of Jesus's death, it needs to be appreciated that the only sacrificial interpretation of Jesus's death that claims to go back to Jesus, is his words at his last Passover. Jesus tethers it both to the non-atoning communal celebrations of Passover and the covenant inauguration by quoting or alluding to Exod 24:8 ("the blood of the covenant") (Matt 26:26–29; Mark 14:22–25; Luke 22:15–20; 1 Cor 11:23–26). And King Hezekiah already set the precedent for bringing these two celebrations—Passover and covenant renewal—together (2 Chr 29:30—30:27).

I address views that try to shoehorn atonement into the Lord's Supper accounts in chapter 5, but for now the fact that both the Passover and the covenant-inauguration sacrifice having nothing to do with atonement and so are communal sacrificial *meals* needs to be appreciated. The very act of *eating* these is a major hurdle for anyone who thinks "atonement" is part of the Lord's Supper. As we saw, feasting and fasting are diametrically opposed cultic activities. The former is associated with celebration and thanksgiving, whereas the latter is associated with sins and atonement. The fact that both Passover and covenant-inauguration sacrifices are non-atoning celebrations is the point of departure for further analyzing the sacrificial meaning various NT authors inscribe either into the Lord's Supper more specifically, or Jesus's death more broadly. Alas, there is still a while to go before delving into the NT.

To be sure, although I will defend the view that the Lord's Supper has no atoning significance, Jesus *is* linked with sacrificial atonement in a few other places in the NT. So we turn next to the ritual purity system and the means by which to purge the dwelling place from ritual impurities and sin-contamination via atonement protocols.

3

Understanding Old Testament Sacrifice, Part 3

Ritual Cosmology

We need to situate the atonement system within Israel's ritual cosmology before getting into the atoning sacrifices directly. Here I will argue the following:

(1) There are two binaries in Israel's priestly mapping of the word: (a) holy and common, and (b) pure and impure (e.g., Lev 10:10). This is Israel's "ritual cosmology" so to speak. While these are distinct binaries (e.g., "holy" does not mean "pure"), a major concern within the Torah's sacrificial and purity system is keeping what is holy free from contact with what is impure.

(2) "Ritual" and "moral" impurity are heuristic categories that attempt to categorize overlapping yet distinct concerns within the Torah. Ritual impurity has nothing to do with sins, but moral impurity does; however, only certain types of sins cause moral impurity.

(3) Ritual impurity is contagious and needs to be "removed" or "decontaminated" (*kipper*) from holy objects in the dwelling place, whereas moral impurity is not contagious and can never be decontaminated through sacrificial atonement (*kipper*) because it pollutes things beyond the capacity of atoning sacrifices to purge.

(4) This is because in addition to the sanctuary, moral impurity pollutes both the *person* and the *land*. However, the only things that can be

decontaminated through *kipper* are sancta (holy objects in the dwelling place), not people and not the land.

ISRAEL'S RITUAL COSMOLOGY: HOLINESS AND PURITY

Although belonging to distinct binaries (holy and common, pure and impure), "impurity and holiness are antonyms."[1] As we will see, similar to how impurity is closely identified with death, holiness aligns with life.[2] God, as the source of all life, is the supreme Holy One and source of holiness (Lev 11:44; 19:2; 20:26; 22:32; cf. Isa 41:14; 43:14; 48:17; 49:7, 26; 54:5, 8). "The category of the holy," for Israel then, as Matthew Thiessen helpfully summarizes, "pertains to that which is for special use—in this sense, related to Israel's cult and therefore to Israel's God (Lev. 11:44; 20:7, 26; 22:32)."[3] To be "holy" is to be dedicated in some sense for special use in proximity to God.

There is more to this than just being either "holy" or "not holy" (i.e., "common"), however. Holiness is a spectrum of varying degrees. This can be seen in the different designations of spaces in the dwelling place. Even though the dwelling place as a whole can be referred to as a "sanctuary" or "holy space" (*miqdāš*) (e.g., Exod 25:8; Lev 12:4; 16:33), there are increasing levels of holiness the closer one gets to God's presence. The innermost room, where the ark of the covenant and God's presence are (Exod 25:21–22; 30:6, 36; Lev 16:2; Num 7:89), is called the "holy of holies" or "most holy place" (*qōdeš haqŏdāšîm*) (Exod 26:33, 34; 1 Kgs 6:16; 7:50), which distinguishes the higher holiness it has with respect to the adjacent room where the incense altar, lampstand, and showbread table are called "the holy place" (*haqōdeš*) (Exod 26:33). Similarly, the outer altar for sacrifices is "most holy" (*qōdeš qādāšîm*) and it therefore consecrates whatever touches it, but those things only "become holy" (*yiqdāš*), not necessarily "most holy" (29:37; cf. 30:29).[4]

1. Milgrom, *Leviticus 1–16*, 46.

2. Milgrom, *Leviticus 1–16*, 46.

3. Thiessen, *Forces of Death*, 9.

4. This designation of merely "holy" only seems to apply to the meat of the well-being offerings that the laity can eat, but only if they are in a state of ritual purity (Lev 7:20–21; 19:8). The laity are not holy, since only priests are holy in the strict cultic sense (though all Israel is "holy" in a non-cultic sense as being God's special possession, Exod 19:6, Lev 11:44; 19:2; 20:7, 26; 22:32). People can only eat sacrifices that are equal to or at most one level of holiness ahead of them. For the laity this means sacrificial meat that is merely "holy," which only applies to the well-being sacrifices (Exod 29:37; Lev 21:22). The meat (or grain) from the rest of the sacrifices (besides the burnt offerings, since everything is turned into smoke on the altar) becomes "most holy" and is reserved

Moreover, God's presence to Israel in the dwelling place signals blessing (e.g., Exod 20:24; 25:8; 29:42–46). Therefore, a major concern within the Torah's sacrificial and purity system is keeping what is holy—especially God's holy dwelling place, but also any sacred thing—free from contact with what is ritually impure (Num 5:2–3; Lev 15:31; 7:20–21).[5] As Feldman explains, "Bringing impurity into contact with objects or entities that are holy threatens the careful delineation of boundaries within the tent of meeting, boundaries that exist to keep impurity and holiness as far apart as possible. The introduction of impurity into a sacred area can undermine the structural foundation of a cult that is built to keep them apart."[6] The logic at work (confirmed by the prophets) is that if enough impurity builds up on the dwelling place, then "God's presence will depart,"[7] which signals the opposite of blessing: disaster and curse (Jer 12:7; 18:17; 22:5; 23:33, 39; Ezek 7–10; cf. Exod 33:15–16).

This is why I have delayed discussing the concept of impurity (ritual and moral) more fully until here, where it can be appropriately linked with explaining sacrificial atonement. We need to understand that the concept of atonement is not so much tethered to (certain) sins, but rather to removing contaminations adhering to God's dwelling place. As Milgrom notes, "The sacrificial system is intimately connected with the impurity system."[8] This is because even if all of Israel was sinless, perfectly obedient to the covenant, atoning sacrifices would still be necessary, according to Leviticus, in order to decontaminate the dwelling place from the inevitable accumulation of (ritual) impurities. And, as Klawans notes, "it is not sinful to contract these [ritual] impurities."[9]

---

only for the (holy) priests who have to eat this "most holy" food in a "holy place" (2:3, 10; 6:17, 25, 29; 7:1, 6; 14:13; 21:22; 24:9).

5. I explain the difference between being ritually and morally impure shortly, but for now, "ritually" is a necessary qualifier above since, while ritually impure persons cannot enter the sanctuary (e.g., Lev 12:4; Num 5:2–3), the morally impure can. E.g., murder and adultery are moral impurities, but those suspected of adultery and murderers can enter the sanctuary (Num 5:11–31; Exod 21:14; 1 Kgs 1:50–53; 2:28–30).

6. Feldman, *Story of Sacrifice*, 61.

7. Milgrom, *Leviticus 1–16*, 258–61, here 260; see also Klawans, "Concepts of Purity in the Bible," 1999.

8. Milgrom, *Leviticus 1–16*, 49.

9. Klawans, *Purity, Sacrifice*, 54.

RITUAL AND MORAL IMPURITIES: UNDERSTANDING THEIR DISTINCT CAUSES, EFFECTS, AND REMEDIES

Scholars have resorted to the heuristic terms "ritual" and "moral" impurity—even though "neither one is a category as such in biblical or postbiblical Jewish literature"—to make it clear that, as Klawans puts it, "there are two kinds of impurity in ancient Israel, one of which is more associated with sin than the other."[10] In teaching contexts we need to be able to easily distinguish between these types of impurity since "[t]he biblical texts use the same terminology of defilement to describe two distinct phenomena."[11] Both types are designated with word *ṭāmēʾ*. This means that "unless we supply our own descriptive terminology, confusion about the nature of the relationship between impurity and sin will continue."[12]

But another confusion threatens to undermine this goal since some might be tempted to think that the "moral" category matters more than merely "ritual." So long as we are clear that "making a distinction between ritual and moral impurity should not be interpreted as taking a first step down the road of antiritualism," I agree with Klawans that these heuristic categories are useful "to articulate the meanings of messages of ancient texts in modern scholarly terms."[13]

From chapter 1, it ought to be clear that "ritual" is by no means outside the realm of the "moral" or "ethical." Recall it is precisely through proper *ritual*—rituals of slaughter, proper blood manipulations, and burning at the ritually appropriate place—that killing an animal is morally transformed from a murder into a "not-a-killing" that serves as a sacred gift or means of decontaminating the sanctuary (Lev 17). This moral framework is only possible and facilitated in and through ritual. Ritual is not amoral.

Nevertheless, for the purposes of comprehending two distinct types of impurity, the use of "ritual" versus "moral" is particularly helpful.[14] With

10. Klawans, *Impurity and Sin*, 22.

11. Klawans, *Impurity and Sin*, 22.

12. Klawans, *Impurity and Sin*, 22.

13. Klawans, *Impurity and Sin*, 22.

14. There is also a third type of impurity in the Torah, pertaining to pure and impure animals (Lev 11; Deut 14), but this is largely tangential to the project at hand. Other than the fact that impure animals cannot be sacrificed, animal purity and associated dietary laws are their own category. But neither can all pure animals be sacrificed (e.g., deer are pure, but ineligible for sacrifice). Again, the same language of purity is used in the biblical texts for clearly distinct phenomenon. Whereas ritual impurity can be removed, nothing can remove impurity from an impure animal to make it pure (i.e., donkeys and pigs cannot be made pure). While eating impure animals is prohibited, oddly but significantly, nowhere in these texts does it say eating them makes one ritually

respect to moral impurity, "moral" reminds us that this is the one that is associated with a particular set of sins—though, importantly, not all sins. And "ritual" impurity is useful since it pertains to the ritual practices that are or are not available to ritually impure persons. E.g., ritually impure persons cannot participate in the regular rituals of sacrifice, but they can become reintegrated as full participants in the worship life through specific rituals. Moral impurity, however, has no ritual remedy (sacrificial or otherwise). Only ritual impurity can be remedied through various rituals, some of them also requiring the ritual of sacrifice.

Ritual Impurity

We are not able to get into all the intricacies within the ritual purity system, but there are a few observations that need to be made that will pay dividends as we move along into the prophets and NT.[15]

Some of these impurities are minor and resolve with the coming of sundown and a bath, but some are so strong that the impurity leeches out from the person and adheres to the sancta in the dwelling place. Atonement (*kipper*) is a ritual procedure that removes the contamination of these impurities from the sanctuary so that God does not abandon it, thereby leaving Israel vulnerable to inevitable catastrophe. This is why atonement would be necessary even if everybody in the community never sinned. And this is also why thinking of atonement only in terms of doing something about sins is deficient. This is the first basic observation.

I will expand on atonement later, but second, it is helpful to think of the ritual categories of "pure" and "impure" as "clearance" versus "no clearance" with respect to the sanctuary (cf. Lev 12:4; Num 5:2–3). Bringing back

---

impure. Moreover, "violations of the dietary restrictions are never explicitly viewed as defiling the sanctuary, and violators are not commanded to bring a *chattat* [purgation] sacrifice or suffer the punishment of *karet* [being cut off]" (Klawans, *Impurity and Sin*, 32). The only overlap between animal impurity and ritual impurity is that touching the dead carcass of the impure animals renders one temporarily impure—and this impurity is easily removed by bathing and then the impurity dissipates by sundown (Lev 11:24–28; cf. 39–40). Unlike ritual impurity, which is transmitted by contact, impure animals do not communicate impurity to those who touch them (while they are alive). Israelites owned or rode impure animals, such as "donkeys, horses, and camels (e.g., Deut 5:14; 17:16; 1 Sam 27:9; Zech 9:19)" (Thiessen, *Forces of Death*, 188) and Jesus did as well (Mark 11:1–14). For more on this topic, see Klawans, *Impurity and Sin*, 31–32; Thiessen, *Forces of Death*, 187–95.

15. Great resources to consult on this topic are: Klawans, *Impurity and Sin*; Klawans, *Purity, Sacrifice*; Milgrom, "Biblical Impurity"; Douglas, *Purity and Danger*; Feder, *Purity and Pollution in the Hebrew Bible*.

the sacred restaurant analogy, the notion of purity functions as a criterion for who is fit to access the holy restaurant and dine with God. But again, "[i]t is not a sin to contract . . . ritual impurities" themselves.[16] Contracting ritual impurity is inevitable and occurred often. The main thing becoming ritually impure indicates is that the person could not come to the sanctuary and offer sacrifices until they removed their impurity through the proper purification ritual(s). But not all ritual impurities were equal, as hinted above.

Thus, third, there are two main types of ritual impurity, which some scholars have called "minor" and "major" in order to distinguish between an impurity that only affects the person and dissipates with time and water-washing ("minor") and an impurity that affects both the person and the sanctuary and so also requires an atoning purgation sacrifice to purify the sanctuary from the impurity ("major").[17] And, a minor impurity can develop into major impurity if not dealt with properly at first; and letting that happen, intentional or not, is considered a sin (e.g., Lev 5:2–3 with 11:24–28, 39–40, and 17:15–16). But since all it takes is time and a bath to purify minor impurities (e.g., 15:5–8, 10–11, 16 18, 21–22; 17:15), then so long as a person bathed each day, even just as a precaution, then they would never be responsible for causing a minor impurity to develop into a major one. That said, while it is a sin to *prolong* a minor impurity such that it becomes a major impurity that requires a purgation sacrifice, it is not a sin to contract a major impurity itself. Getting scale disease or giving birth are not sins and both are classified as major impurities, and as such require a purgation sacrifice in their purification process (12:6–8; 14:19, 22). Therefore, major impurity itself is not a sin; only failing to bathe by the evening after contracting a minor impurity is considered a sin (cf. 5:2–3; 17:15–16).[18]

Fourth, ritual impurity is the only type of impurity that is contagious. It spreads mainly through direct contact, but scale disease and corpse impurity spread by "overhang, that is, by being under the same roof,"[19] as a

16. Klawans, *Purity, Sacrifice*, 54. Priests, however, do have more restrictions when it comes to corpse impurity in particular (Lev 21:1–4) and the high priest has even more (21:10–12). But other impurities are understood as inevitable (e.g., 16:26, 28; Num 19:7–8), and they just have to make sure not to touch or eat any of the holy foods while they are in a state of ritual impurity (Lev 22:3–7).

17. E.g., "minor impurities [are those] where no sacrifices are involved" whereas "major ones [are those] polluting the sanctuary from afar" thus requiring "the purification offering" (Milgrom, *Leviticus 1–16*, 975, 978, respectively). Milgrom uses these categories throughout his commentary, but see especially pages 976–1000.

18. And, more obviously, it is a sin to simply disregard ritual purification and access the sanctuary and/or eat from a well-being sacrifice someone else is sharing (e.g., Lev 7:20–21; 22:3–7; Num 19:13, 20).

19. Milgrom, *Leviticus*, 128–29; cf. Milgrom, *Leviticus 1–16*, 819–20.

corpse or someone who has scale disease (*ṣāraʿat*) or in a house infected with fungus (*ṣāraʿat*) (Lev 13:46; 14:8, 46–47; Num 19:14–15; 5:2–3). This secondary contamination from any impure source is considered a minor impurity (e.g., Lev 14:46–47; 15:5–11, 20–24, 27; Num 19:22). Moral impurity is not contagious, however. Touching a morally impure person or being with them in the same room does not render one impure as well, ritually or morally. Someone who is morally impure can come to the sanctuary and offer any sacrifice so long as they are ritually pure.

Importantly, the contagious aspect of ritual impurity means most people would be ritually impure most of the time, especially because becoming impure was not itself sinful. There is no real gain to be fastidious about avoiding secondary impurity unless the person was planning on going to the sanctuary that very day.[20] Thus, as Klawans makes clear, "it is not accurate to say that Israelites are encouraged to limit their contacts with ritually impure substances or people."[21]

This is because, fifth, at base, impurity is closely related to "the forces of death."[22] A few sources of ritual impurity are more obviously related to death (corpse impurity in Num 19 and scale disease in Lev 13–14, which makes one skin look like a rotting corpse, Num 12:12). But these can be subsumed under a broader understanding of human *finitude* (human beings both "begin" and "end") in contrast to God's infinitude (God does not procreate and has no beginning or ending). This would better explain why, in addition to abnormal genital discharges (like gonorrhea), normal genital discharges relating to procreation—any seminal emission, menstruation, and lochia after childbirth—also convey ritual impurity (Lev 12, 15). It is not so much because they are associated with "death" or "mortality,"[23] but rather more because they are associated with human finite *beginnings*. As Hannah K. Harrington observes, "coming into the world brings impurity (even for Adam and Eve)" (cf. Jub. 3:8–14; 1QH^{a} IX, 21–22).[24] Jubilees 3:8–14 highlights Adam and Eve's need to remain separated from each other (v. 8) and

20. Note, the sanctuary "closes" at sundown at the evening *tāmîd*, which is also when minor impurities go away. Becoming pure at sundown makes one eligible to be at the sanctuary the next morning.

21. Klawans, *Impurity and Sin*, 24–25.

22. Milgrom, *Leviticus 1–16*, 686, 733, 767–68, 865, 889, cf. 1000–1004; see also Milgrom, "The Rationale for Biblical Impurity," 107–11; and the book title by Thiessen, *Forces of Death*.

23. Although these too can nevertheless be construed to be related to mortality from a certain perspective. See, e.g., Luke 20:35–36, which seems to relate the need for procreation with human mortality such that being immortal in the resurrection is thought to necessarily preclude marriage and procreation.

24. Harrington, *The Purity Texts*, 100.

remain outside of the most holy place, Eden (vv. 9–14; cf. Lev 12:4), for the same proscribed days of the two-stage purification for a parturient of each gender in Lev 12, presumably due to their initial impurity by virtue of coming into being. Thus, menstrual blood, whether taken as a sign of "death" in terms of failing to conceive or as a sign of "fertility," it is nevertheless associated with *procreation* in Lev 12:1, 5 and hence human finite beginnings.[25] In other words, ritual impurity is a way of naming certain symptoms or signs of human finitude. I will return to this point shortly, but since sexual intercourse, childbirth, scale diseases, and just being in the same room as a human corpse are all normal parts of human finite life, people will be ritually impure frequently. This is why it "is not the avoidance of ritual impurity, but awareness of ritual impurity" that matters.[26]

Per the second point, the only time being ritually impure was a requirement was when coming to the dwelling place, either to have a well-being sacrificial meal or to offer one of the atoning sacrifices (or both). This is why, as Klawans remarks, "Israelites are obligated to remain aware of their ritual status at all times, lest they accidentally come into contact with the sacred while in a state of impurity (Lev. 15:31). As long as they remain aware of their status, there is little chance of danger or transgression."[27] Israelites did not need to be ritually pure to eat regular meals; only when they were going to eat a well-being sacrifice (Lev 7:20–21; 22:3–7).

And this would not happen as often as some might expect initially. In fact, once in the land, and not tightly encamped in the wilderness close to the dwelling place, it was already expected that the people would rarely actually journey to sacrifice at the sanctuary and so instructions were provided accordingly, as discussed in chapter 1 (Deut 12:15–28). Even so, it was unsustainable to be constantly eating a quadruped anyway.[28] As E. P. Sanders comments, "Although sacrifice was a normal and standard part of worship, it was not a routine activity [for individuals]. Most Jews resident in Palestine probably sacrificed on only a few occasions each year,"[29] which was most likely one (or more) of the three pilgrimage festivals: Passover, the Festival of Weeks (Pentecost), and the Festival of Booths. This is why "only those who planned actually to visit the Temple need [to] worry about

25. This contrasts and expands the rationales offered by Thiessen, *Forces of Death*, 16–18, 30n32.

26. Klawans, *Impurity and Sin*, 24.

27. Klawans, *Impurity and Sin*, 25.

28. See Sanders, *Judaism*, 114: "Slaughter was not an everyday experience. Many people ate fowl once a week, but red meat only a few times a year."

29. Sanders, *Judaism*, 115.

purifying themselves."[30] Ideally, however, this "worry" would only apply to the major impurities, such as corpse impurity, which requires a full week of purification with baths taking place on the third and seventh days (Num 19:11–19), since all minor impurities should have been purified by a bath the day they contracted it before evening.

This sets up the sixth, and perhaps most surprising, point: the reason why a person needs to be in a state of ritual purity to access the sanctuary is because it symbolizes becoming like God, who is infinite, has no beginning, does not procreate or have sex, and does not die. Ritual purity is a ritually tangible way to enact "becoming holy, as God is holy" (cf. Lev 11:44; 19:2; 20:7–8, 25–26) specifically by having one's body ritually free from those aspects associated with sex and death. As Klawans argues:

> Because God is eternal, God does not die. . . . Because God has no consort, God cannot have sex. Therefore, . . . "in order to approach God, one has to leave the sexual realm."
>
> By separating from sex and death—by following the ritual purity regulations—ancient Israelites . . . separated themselves from what made them least God-like. In other words, the point of following these [ritual purity] regulations is nothing other than the theological underpinning of the entire Holiness Code: *imitatio Dei* (Lev. 11:44–45, 19:2, 20:7, 26).[31]

This is why it is mistaken to think the Torah's purity system is about health and hygiene. Urine, excrement, blood from a wound, other diseases, etc., are not sources of impurity. Whatever "health benefits" there might be from the Torah's purity laws, they are tangential. For instance, Israel knows excrement is unsanitary, but it is not a source of impurity (Deut 23:12–14). The camp should honor God's holiness by having designated places to defecate, but neither defecating nor contacting excrement makes one unable to access the dwelling place—i.e., become ritually impure. So ritual impurity is not about sanitation *per se*. The sources of ritual impurity are focused on a limited set of things such that being pure allows human beings to *ritually transcend their finitude* as they approach the everlasting God of life.

Seventh, returning to the first and third observations above, the process for full purification from major impurities (scale disease, childbirth, abnormal genital discharges from a male or female, priests or Nazirites who contract corpse impurity) all involve an atoning purgation sacrifice

30. Schwartz, "Leviticus," 221.

31. Klawans, *Purity, Sacrifice*, 58.

(the *ḥaṭṭāʾt*) as the final step.[32] We will get into atonement rituals in more depth in the following chapter, but here we need to make a few foundational points that will affect our understanding of how sacrificial atonement relates to both the sanctuary and the person (who was either previously ritually impure and/or responsible for some sin[s]).

(1) I will discuss *how* below, but it needs to be appreciated *that* the function of atoning sacrifices for these major impurities is to remove that ritual impurity from the sanctuary itself (Lev 15:31; cf. 16:16, 20). This also confirms the non-atoning function of the regular burnt offerings as discussed in chapter 2. Ritual impurity threatens to undo what these sacrifices produce; namely, attracting and maintaining God's presence at the dwelling place. *If these burnt offerings had an atoning function, then there would be no need for an atoning sacrifice for these major impurities since the burnt offerings would be twice daily removing any impurities getting on the sancta.* Thus, the stability of God's presence cannot be sustained by regular burnt offerings alone. This very need for a specific category of atoning sacrifices that removes impurities from God's dwelling place (so that God is not driven to abandon it) indicates that these regular burnt offerings have no atoning function. Their only function is divine "attraction" so to speak. In other words, the regular burnt offerings are *not* the sacrificial solution to ritual impurities (or sins), but rather ritual impurities (and sins) pose a *problem* for what the daily burnt offerings accomplish (attracting God's presence) and for which another solution is necessary (hence the atoning category for sacrifices).

Though it perhaps might go without saying, the fact that an atoning sacrifice is necessary at the very end of the purification process for these people indicates that impurity can adhere not only to people's bodies, but to sancta as well. Milgrom explains it this way: "Let electromagnetism serve as an illustrative analogy. The minus charge of impurity is attracted to the plus charge of the sanctuary, and if the former builds up enough force to

32. Milgrom, *Leviticus 1–16*, 986, 991–92. Recall from chapter 2, that purification of corpse impurity is anomalous. I argued that the red cow in Num 19 is not itself a purgation *sacrifice*, but merely a purification *procedure*. Also, "the corpse-contaminated person brings no sacrifice at the end of his purification. Unlike the parturient, the '[scale diseased person],' and the chronic genital discharger, who bring a purification offering no sooner than the eighth day of the purificatory period (Lev 12:6–8; 14:10, 21–23; 15:14, 29), the corpse-contaminated person completes purification in seven days and brings no purification offering" (Milgrom, *Leviticus*, 38). However, both priests (Ezek 44:26–27) and Nazirites (Num 6:9–12) who contract corpse impurity are required to bring a purgation sacrifice. This seems to be because they are "holy" so the corpse impurity appears to gain access to the sanctuary through their sanctified bodies (cf. Milgrom, *Leviticus 1–16*, 992, 996).

spark the gap, then, lightning-like, it will strike the sanctuary."[33] Hence the accumulating danger if impurities go unaddressed. The atoning sacrifice removes the "minus charge of impurity." Importantly, then, it is not enough for one's *body* to be ritually pure after contracting a major ritual impurity, the *sanctuary* needs to purified as well.

(2) Just like there are varying degrees of holiness, a person can be in varying degrees of ritual purity. It is more complex than being either "pure" or "impure." To better grasp this, we need to remember that what makes an impurity "major" is that it is so potent that it becomes "airborne"[34] as it were, and travels from the person's body onto the sanctuary. Even if the person no longer has scale disease, for instance, they are deemed ritually "pure" in one sense (Lev 14:2), even though they still have the responsibility to remove the impurity on the sanctuary generated by their body when they had scale disease. Hence the multistep purification process outlined in Lev 14 that was discussed in chapter 2. There are three stages in their purification and at each stage they are declared "pure" (Lev 14:7–8, 9, 20) in addition to being called "pure" once they no longer physically suffer from scale disease (14:2). This indicates there are increased degrees of ritual purity that the person goes through at each step.

What this means practically is that one can be ritually pure enough to not transmit secondary contamination to common things (14:8) or to holy things (14:9–11), but still not be considered fully ritually pure until the impurity one's body caused to adhere to the sanctuary is eliminated (14:20). Once a person recovers from the physical symptoms of their major impurity, they are ritually pure only to the extent that they are no longer contagious to varying degrees. For instance, once a person is free from an abnormal genital discharge for seven days, they gain one level of ritual purity such that they can no longer transmit secondary impurity after washing their clothes and taking a bath (15:13, 28). But they still need to offer the purgation sacrifice no sooner than eight days post healing to be fully ritually pure (15:14–15, 29–30). In the intervening time, between their bath and when they finally get around to offering the purgation sacrifice, they are in a penultimate stage of purity. At this penultimate stage, their *bodies* are "pure" because they are no longer a source of transmitting secondary impurity to anything (common or holy).

The rabbinic discussions of those who had a major ritual impurity but are currently between their bath and offering the purgation sacrifice confirm

33. Milgrom, *Leviticus 1–16*, 270.

34. Milgrom uses this throughout his commentary, but see, e.g., 317, 804, 913, 930, 967, 976–1000.

this point. They mark the ultimate stage of purity—reached immediately after offering the required purgation sacrifice—as being able to eat sacrificial foods (m. Ker. 1:7; 2:1; m. Meʿil. 2:1–9; m. Kelim 1:5; m. Zebaḥ. 12:1; m. Neg. 14:3).[35] The penultimate stage is when they have undergone everything except offering the purgation sacrifice and the rabbis consider this stage ritually equivalent to the time in between a ritual bath and coming of sundown for a person who had a minor ritual impurity, referred to a "*tevul yom*" (m. Ṭ. Yom).[36] During this penultimate stage of purity—whether it be a *tevul yom* or a person who has recovered from a major ritual impurity when their "expiation is incomplete" (m. Ker. 2:1) or they are "lacking atonement" (m. Zebaḥ. 2:1; 12:1; m. Meʿil. 2:1–9)—these persons cannot defile anything (common or sacred) because there is no longer any impurity *inhering in their bodies.* If there was, then they would remain a contagious source of impurity causing whatever they contact to contract secondary impurity. But they are not fully pure until sunset (for the *tevul yom*) or until they offer the required purgation sacrifice (for those with a major ritual impurity). What this *ultimate* stage of purity means is being able to participate in the sacrificial liturgical life of Israel and eat sacrificial food.

In order to mark the ultimate stage of purity as being able to eat from sacrifices yet reckoning with the fact that the people have reached a sufficient level of purity such that they are no longer capable of transmitting secondary impurity to anything, those at the penultimate stage of ritual purity render holy sacrificial foods they might contact *invalid*, but not *impure*. That is, these foods are *disqualified* from "counting" as *sacrificial* food, but they can still be eaten (they just count as regular common food for them) because these sacrificial foods are not considered *impure* such that they must be burned, per Lev 7:19 (cf. m. Ṭ. Yom 2:1–2; m. ʿEd. 2:1; 5:4; m. Kelim 1:5; m. Neg. 14:3; m. Zebaḥ 2:1). In other words, a person who has reached the penultimate degree of purity cannot make sacred food impure because they themselves are no longer impure. But their penultimate status still means they are ineligible to consume sacred food *as sacred* food. If they eat sacred food, it automatically becomes downgraded to normal common food.[37]

35. See also the comments on each of these in Cohen, Goldenberg, and Lapin, eds., *The Oxford Annotated Mishnah*.

36. "*Tevul yom*, lit. 'immersed of day,' refers to an impure person who has completed the ritual acts necessary for purification before nightfall. However, the period of impurity only lapses with sunset. Consequently, the *tevul yom* is treated as an in-between category neither fully impure nor fully pure" (David Levine, "Tractate Tevul Yom," 919). The halakhic letter from Qumran known as 4QMMT rejected this in-between category, considering the *tevul yom* as completely impure until sundown (cf. B 13–16, 71–72). But it testifies that the rabbinic view was being widely practiced.

37. A similar line of reasoning is behind Hezekiah's prayer in 2 Chr 30:17–20 for

For the person who has recovered from scale disease, they have more levels of ritual purity to pass through than the person with an abnormal genital discharge. A person who has just physically recovered from scale disease is called "pure" (Lev 14:2), but they are less pure at this stage than the person who recovered from an abnormal genital discharge. They still transmit secondary impurity by overhang to common things for however long it takes them to be sprinkled with the non-sacrificial bird-blood and take a bath; but even then they can only enter the camp, but not their tent/home for seven more days because they are still able to transmit secondary impurity by overhang to sacred things such as the meat from a well-being sacrifice that someone brought home or things dedicated to the sanctuary (14:2–8). Note, this level of semi-purity lasts a minimum of a week, but that is only if the person had access to a priest to carry out the bird ritual the same day their skin became pure. And, it is not until the eighth day after the bird ritual, i.e., after the evening of the seventh day that they shave and bathe, that they are eligible to enter both their home (14:9) and the dwelling place (14:10–11) because only then are they ritually pure enough to no longer transmit impurity to anything, common or holy (cf. m. Neg. 14:3 for these three stages of purity).

Therefore, both of these observations about the use of "pure" in Leviticus and the rabbinic interpretations indicate there are varying levels of ritual purity a person can be in. The penultimate stage of purity is when a person has done everything necessary for purification and is just either awaiting sundown or an opportunity to offer their purgation sacrifice. Crucially, reaching the penultimate stage of purity means the person no longer has impurity in or on his or her body.[38]

Further, this also means that for major ritual impurities (those that require the purgation sacrifice as the final step of purification) even when a person's *body* is ritually pure enough to no longer transmit secondary impurity, they are not considered fully ritually pure because *their impurity still exists* in the world. What is left is the impurity their bodies generated that is still on the sancta. Thus, they are still *responsible* to remove their impurity from the divine dwelling place. In other words, even though their impurity no longer exists *on them*, their impurity still exists, but it exists *extrinsically*, on the sanctuary. This is why it is only when their impurity is fully removed from *both* their own body *and* from the sancta that they are

those from the northern tribes who are in Jerusalem for the Passover but who were not pure. Their eating of the Passover meal in that state should technically not count, which is why he prays for God to accept their partaking of it anyway.

38. This is a crucial point that will be important soon for debunking a view promulgated against the framework (based on Milgrom and Klawans) argued for here.

considered ultimately ritually "pure" (e.g., Lev 14:20; 12:8). And again, letting a minor impurity fester turns it into a major impurity, which just means that because of the delay in bathing, the impurity has accumulated to such an extent that it became "airborne" and is now adhering to the sanctuary. Thus, an atoning sacrifice is needed to purge the sancta from the impurity. This person would have been transmitting secondary impurity to whatever they came into contact with up until the point they finally remembered to bathe (cf. m. ʿEd. 5:1, 4).[39] Once they bathe, they are no longer transmitting secondary impurity—they have gained a level of ritual purity—but because they let their once minor impurity grow into an "airborne" major impurity, they now have committed a sin and need to provide an atoning sacrifice that will remove their impurity from the sanctuary (5:2–3). Then they can be forgiven for inadvertently producing an unnecessary impurity on the sanctuary (5:10, 13).

Finally, (3) I state here what is already implied, but needs to be made as clear as possible: ritual impurity is removed from people's *bodies* through the passing of sufficient time and water-washing, but it is removed from the *sanctuary* through an atoning purgation sacrifice. That is, the *purgation sacrifices do not purify the person's body.* Their body already must be made pure *before* they can even access the sanctuary to offer the sacrifice.[40] The atoning purgation sacrifices only purge the *sanctuary.* But it is removing *that person's specific* impurity from the sanctuary. And until this final step in the process for major ritual impurities is completed, the person is necessarily isolated from the worshiping life of Israel because they cannot start enjoying, say, the well-being sacrifices until they have dealt with the impurity on the sanctuary for which they are responsible. This penultimate stage of purity is the stage when one's body is fully purified because they no longer transmit impurity to anything (common or holy). And the requirement to offer a purgation sacrifice for the ultimate stage of purification is not because it is inherently a sin to generate impurity on the sanctuary, but simply because impurity just needs to be eliminated from the holy dwelling place.[41]

The ultimate stage of purification means the person is now fully restored to the sanctuary. And this only happens once the impurity they are responsible for has been eliminated from the sanctuary. Once their bodies are purified, they are again able to access the sanctuary;[42] but they cannot,

39. Milgrom, *Leviticus 1–16*, 996–97.

40. Milgrom, *Leviticus 1–16*, 849.

41. Milgrom, *Leviticus 1–16*, 849.

42. This is necessarily the case if they are eligible to come to the dwelling place and offer a sacrifice (e.g., 14:10–11; 15:14–15, 29–30).

for instance, come to the sanctuary and offer a thanksgiving well-being sacrifice praising God for their recovery from scale disease or an abnormal genital discharge unless they first purge the last remaining vestiges of their major impurity from the sanctuary. Once this final step is complete the person is now considered fully purified (e.g., 14:20; 12:8) in the sense that they are "henceforth a full-fledged participant in [their] community and its worship."[43] Therefore, simply attaining the level of ritual purity where one's body is pure is insufficient to be restored to the sanctuary. Their ability to *access* the sanctuary after their bodies become ritually pure makes it so that they can provide the means necessary for completely eliminating their impurity from existence. It used to exist both on them and on the sanctuary. Once their bodies are ritually pure it still exists, but it only exists on the sanctuary.

Thus, for example, the ritual purification process for the scale diseased person functions as a ritual reset for the person. They were once fully part of the community's worship life, but the scale disease removed them from the camp entirely (13:46; Num 5:2–3). As we saw in chapter 2, the blood rituals applied to them after the physical disease is healed—neither of which are blood from a purgation sacrifice—facilitates their metaphysical transition from the realm of "death" to the realm of "life." The last step in the process is to remove the remainder of their impurity that clings to the sanctuary by providing a purgation sacrifice. This ritual reset finalizes their reintegration into the liturgical sacrificial rhythms of the community. It makes perfect sense that, although their bodies are fully ritually pure before the point of the purgation sacrifice, they cannot be fully reintegrated into the community's worship until the last vestiges of their impurity have been eliminated from the sanctuary.[44]

At the end of the day, it is necessary to realize that there are distinct ritual remedies for removing impurity from one's body and from the sanctuary. Removing impurity from the body, whether it be a minor or major impurity, is accomplished through the passing of sufficient time and a water-washing (hence, the repeated use of "water" for removing corpse impurity, Num 19:9, 13, 18, 20–21). But removing one's impurity from the sanctuary

43. Milgrom, *Leviticus 1–16*, 859.

44. Milgrom, *Leviticus 1–16*, 849. Nevertheless, as noted above, according to the rabbis and the logic of Leviticus, if this person ate sacred food it would not be a sin and they would not be defiling the food because they are no longer holding impurity within their bodies. The rabbis conclude that by contacting or eating sacred food, they are simply disqualifying it from counting as sacred food. But it has not become impure because it if had, then it would need to be burned (Lev 7:19) and anyone who is impure and eats sacred food is liable to being "cut off" (7:20–21). Hence, those at the penultimate stage of purity are no longer themselves impure.

is accomplished through a purgation sacrifice. This will be an important point when we come to discussing how atonement functions with respect to the sanctuary and the sinner as well as the prophetic appropriation of the purity and sacrificial system in the next chapter.

But before we get to discussing how the purgation sacrifices also purge sins from the sanctuary, we need to discuss the category of sins that *cannot* be remedied through sacrificial atonement: moral impurity.

Moral Impurity

Certain sins are treated analogously yet distinctly to ritual impurity. Like ritual impurity, these sins contaminate the sancta in the dwelling place and so need to be removed through the ritual decontamination process of "atonement" (*kipper*). But not all sins can be eliminated from the dwelling place in this way. As noted earlier, these sins are categorized as "moral impurity" by scholars to differentiate between those sins that can be removed from the sanctuary from those that cannot. Although the term "impure" (*ṭāmēʾ*) is used for both ritual and moral impurities, there are several significant differences between these concepts. However, it is their overlap that provides fruitful ways for biblical authors to use ritual impurity analogously to think through the concept of sin. It will suffice to make a few key observations that are particularly relevant for our future analyses since a full exploration of this topic cannot be undertaken here.[45]

(1) Whereas, except on the rare occasion of neglecting to bathe, ritual impurities have nothing to do with sin, moral impurity is caused by only three categories of sins. These are:

- Sexual sins (Lev 18: 6–30, esp. vv. 25, 27–28; 19:29)
- Worship of other gods (19:31; 20:1–3)
- Bloodshed (Num 35:33–34; cf. Ps 106:38–39)

(2) Unlike ritual impurity, moral impurity is not contagious, nor does it bar access to the sanctuary (cf. Num 5:11–31; Exod 21:14; cf. 1 Kgs 1:50–53; 2:28–30). Although the one who commits these sins is considered "impure" (*ṭāmēʾ*) (Lev 18:20, 23–25, 30; 19:31), "one need not bathe subsequent to direct or indirect contact with an idolater, a murderer, or an individual who committed sexual sin."[46] Moral impurity does not translate into ritual impu-

45. Many of these observations come from Klawans, *Purity, Sacrifice*, 55–56, and his *Impurity and Sin*, 26–31, though I present them slightly differently and offer my own additional observations, emphases, and slight corrections as noted.

46. Klawans, *Purity, Sacrifice*, 55.

rity. Hence the qualifier "moral" to distinguish this from "ritual" impurity, which is contagious and would prevent access to the sanctuary.

(3) Ritual impurity can always be dealt with through the proper rituals of purification and the sanctuary is purified with a purgation sacrifice, but *moral impurity has no sacrificial remedy*.

(4) One of the more obvious reasons for this is because the sins that produce moral impurity for the person and the sanctuary (Lev 20:3) also render the *land* "impure" (*ṭāmē*ʾ) (18:25, 27, 28; cf. 19:29; 20:22; Num 5:34) and "polluted" (*ḥ-n-f*) (Num 35:33) (cf. Gen 4:11–12; Deut 21:1–9; 24:1–4; Isa 24:5; Jer 2:7; 3:1–2, 9; 16:18 [*ḥillēl*, "profaned"]; Ezek 22:3, 4, 6, 12; 36:17–18; Ps 106:34–40). But atoning sacrifices are only ever said to purify sancta (e.g., Lev 16:16, 20, 33), which I will further detail below. Here I simply note that the purgation blood only decontaminates the object that receives the blood—nothing more—so the atoning sacrifices are impotent to purify both the sinner and the land itself.

(5) Since "the polluted land cannot be expiated [atoned] by ritual . . . the expulsion of its inhabitants is inevitable (18:24–29; 20:2)."[47] This is why moral impurity is a significant threat for Israel in Leviticus and Numbers (and the Prophets as we will soon discuss). The fact that atoning sacrifices have a limited decontaminating function can be easily observed in two cases.

First, Num 35:33 states "no atonement can be made for the land" that is made "impure" (35:33) or "polluted" (35:34).[48] Only exile of the commu-

47. Milgrom, *Leviticus 1–16*, 49; Milgrom, *Leviticus 17–22*, 1404, 1422, 1567, 1571–78 (esp. 1573).

48. It is confusing why Klawans includes "atonement" when he claims that "moral purity is achieved by punishment, atonement, or, best of all, by refraining from committing morally impure acts in the first place" (*Impurity and Sin*, 26; also verbatim in *Purity, Sacrifice*, 55). I suspect this owes to the polyvalent use of "atonement" flagged in the introduction, but nowhere does Klawans make his readers aware of a non-sacrificial meaning of "atonement" so this statement would suggest that sacrificial atonement could purify moral impurity. But Klawans later correctly observes that this is not possible, even on the Day of Atonement: "The Day of Atonement service involves the purgation of the altar and shrine [the holy place and holy of holies], which removes the stain left by sin upon the sanctuary (Lev. 16:11–19). . . . But these sacrifices do not appear to purify grave sinners, or the land upon which the grave sins were committed. Such sinners either live out their lives in a degraded state (like the guilty adulteress) or suffer capital punishment (like apprehended murderers). The land, it appears, likewise suffers permanent degradation" (*Impurity and Sin*, 30). Thus, I am not sure what Klawans means that "atonement" is one of the ways to deal with moral impurity earlier. Also, Klawans thinks the impurity of the land is a "permanent degradation," but as I show below, the land *can* be purified, according to Leviticus (albeit *apart from* the sacrificial atonement system).

nity or death of the offender purges the land (e.g., 35:31, 33; Lev 26:32–34, 43–44).

Second, there is a ritual prescribed in Deut 21:1–9 to purify the land from bloodguilt, but, importantly, this is only in the case of an *unsolved* murder. This is the ritual exception mentioned above. But this ritual proves that the Day of Atonement was never thought to address moral impurities like murder that pollute the land. If Day of Atonement was thought to deal with such sins, then unsolved murders would be ritually dealt with on *that* day. The need for a special ritual necessarily indicates that the author did not think the Day of Atonement had the capability to deal with bloodshed polluting the land. And this is for a good reason: the Day of Atonement cannot, by definition, deal with sins that pollute the land because atoning sacrifices simply do not have the capacity to purify land (Num 35:33).

This also explains why the ritual in Deut 21:1–9 is a *non-sacrificial* ritual. We know it is not a sacrifice because (a) it does not take place at the altar (and so nothing is turned into smoke and offered to God), (b) no priests are involved, and (c) the cow is given a *bloodless* death by breaking its neck (21:4; cf. Exod 13:13; 34:20), which is "nonsacrificial slaughter."[49]

But again, this purification ritual is an exceptional case for when the murderer is unknown. If the murderer is known, then they need to die (Num 35:31, 33) or the entire community is in danger of exile due to the polluted land (cf. Ezek 22:3, 4, 6, 12; 36:17–18; Ps 106:34–40). In any case, the fact that a non-sacrificial ritual is prescribed in Deut 21:1–9 proves that it is known in the Torah both that (a) sacrifices in general cannot purify the land and (b) this includes even the atoning sacrifices on the Day of Atonement. If the Day of Atonement cannot purify the land from unsolved murders how much less would it be able to do so for the other moral impurities when the culprit is known?

(6) Even though there are no atoning sacrificial remedies for moral impurity, according to Lev 18–26, the land heals after it vomits its inhabitants out (exile) (18:28; 20:22; 26:32–33, 44) and gets sufficient rest (26:34–35, 43).[50] Analogously to how time has a purifying role for ritual impurities, time similarly has a purifying role for moral impurities. Therefore, exile is not only the dreaded consequence of moral impurity polluting the land, but this *time* away from the land is also the ultimate purifying agent for not only Israel as a community (who also need to humble themselves and repent, Lev

49. Levinson, "Deuteronomy," 393; see also Tigay, *Deuteronomy*, 192; Sarna, *Exodus*, 67.

50. Similarly, Deut 32:43 says that only God can "atone" (*kipper*) the land. But this happens only after exile and quite apart from the sacrificial atonement system (cf. Ps 79 [esp. v. 9]).

26:40–43), but also the land itself.[51] After sufficient time has passed, then Israel will be able to inhabit the land once more (26:43–45).

CONCLUSION

As shown, the atonement system is anchored in Israel's ritual cosmology consisting of two binaries: holy and common, and pure and impure. This system aimed to keep what is holy, most particularly God's sacred dwelling place, either free from contact with what is impure or to decontaminate the sancta before too much impurity accumulated.

There are two types of impurity that we labeled "ritual" and "moral" to delineate the similarities and yet key differences across the uses of purity language in the Torah. On the one hand, ritual impurity has nothing to do with sins, but it is contagious. It can be removed from the body most often through a combination of time and water-washings and it can only be removed from sancta through atoning sacrifices. On the other hand, moral impurity is not contagious and cannot be removed through atoning sacrifices. This is because moral impurity polluted both the person and the land, and only sancta (holy objects in the dwelling place) can be decontaminated through atoning sacrifices.

These points are crucial for understanding the functions and limitations of atoning sacrifices and the so-called prophetic critique of sacrifice, to which we now turn.

51. Similarly, Milgrom states, "the pollution of the land is nonexpiable *culticly*, but is 'expiable' by Israel's exile. This is the basic message of [Lev] 26:40–45" (*Leviticus 17–22*, 1422).

4

Understanding Old Testament Sacrifice, Part 4

Atonement and the Prophets

RECALL THERE ARE TWO main categories for sacrifices (broadly speaking): "the categories of gift-offering-display and/or pollution removal."[1] Having dealt with the former, we turn now to the latter. I argue that "atonement" (*kipper*) has a relatively limited function: it only removes contamination from sancta (holy objects within the dwelling place) and only contamination caused by two sources, certain (ritual) impurities and certain (but not all) sins. The theses for this chapter are:

(1) Since the only things that can be decontaminated through *kipper* are sancta (holy objects in the dwelling place), not people and not the land, yet moral impurity pollutes both the *person* and the *land*, we need to recognize the inherent *limits* to the atoning functions of sacrifice (and the Day of Atonement in particular) set forth in the Torah. The Day of Atonement is not "the be-all and the end-all" solution to sin(s) many (especially Christians) have assumed it to be.

(2) Relatedly, forgiveness is associated with sacrificial atonement, but forgiveness is not reducible to sacrificial atonement. Forgiveness can and does happen completely apart from the atoning aspect of Israel's sacrificial system.

1. Smith, "Domestication," 197.

(3) The so-called "prophetic critique" of sacrifice is in line with the Torah's conception of the purpose and *limits* of sacrificial atonement. The prophets are not criticizing "the sacrificial system," they are keeping the community honest about the inherent limitations of what sacrifices can accomplish, which are expressed clearly in the Torah.

(4) The prophetic expectation of "restoration" when utilizing cultic imagery appeals not to some grand act of sacrificial atonement, but rather to a divine water-washing.

These latter two points (3 and 4) build on understanding the relationship and distinction between ritual and moral impurities from chapter 3 and that sacrificial atonement is never presented in any scripture text as a full solution to sins (1 and 2).

Although we have already dipped here and there into the notion of sacrificial atonement and the atoning sacrifices, everything up to this point has provided the framework to better ground a more concentrated discussion about these subjects. We can more fully answer these questions:

- What is the meaning and function of the *ḥaṭṭā ʾt* sacrifice?
- What does "atonement" (*kipper*) mean and do?
- Whom or what gets "atoned" by use of the *ḥaṭṭā ʾt*?
- What is the rationale for using blood?
- And finally, what is and what is not happening on the Day of Atonement?

Before diving directly into these, however, some brief comments regarding specific sacrifices are necessary.

THE TRIBUTE, BURNT, AND REPARATION OFFERINGS

The grain or "tribute" offering[2] is either offered as a necessary addition for the other types of sacrifices (Num 15:1–13), or as a substitute "purgation" (*ḥaṭṭā ʾt*) sacrifice (Lev 5:11–13).[3] It does not have an inherent atoning function unless it is specially serving as a substitute purgation sacrifice.

2. The word to designate the grain/cereal offering in Lev 2 is *minḥâ*, which simply means "tribute" or "gift" and does not have anything to do with grain in particular (though paying tribute to a king would often take the form of a gain payment).

3. I will explain this translation choice below.

Also, in chapter 2 we saw how the daily burnt offering (*tāmîd*) and otherwise regularly prescribed communal burnt offerings do not have an atoning function. But I also noted that Lev 1:4 says that burnt offerings offered by individuals and the burnt offerings on the Day of Decontamination/Atonement (16:24) do have an atoning function. However, since the burnt offering is not prescribed for situations of inadvertent sins by individuals (Lev 4:2–35; Num 15:27–29) it is hard to determine when it would have an atoning function for individuals. Even when it is prescribed as part of the final stage for major ritual impurities (e.g., 12:6–7; 14:19–20), the atoning function is only assigned (14:18, 19, 21) to the purgation sacrifice in that process (14:12–13, 19a, 21–22, 24–25, 28, 31a).[4] Perhaps when offering an individual well-being offering, since it was always offered together with a burnt offering, as noted in chapter 2, that burnt offering was initially (i.e., pre-Leviticus) thought to also have a sort of precautionary atoning function, which was eventually "replaced by the exclusive expiatory sacrifices, the *ḥaṭṭāʾt* and *ʾāšām*" in the Levitical system.[5] That is, "the reference to expiation in the exposition of the burnt-offering procedure (1:4) may reflect as much an early stage in the history of this offering as its mention in the Job story (Job 1:5; 42:8)," but this function faded away with the introduction of the atoning purgation and reparation offerings.[6] Whatever the case may be, outside of Lev 1:4 and 16:24, the only sacrifices that are given an atoning function are the purgation (*ḥaṭṭāʾt*) and reparation (*ʾāšām*) offerings.

The *ḥaṭṭāʾt* requires more detailed engagement, but we only need to make a few comments regarding the reparation offering. This is sometimes called the "guilt" offering because the word for it (*ʾāšām*) is generally translated as "guilt/to be guilty." With other scholars, however, I prefer the term "reparation" because *ʾāšām* more specifically carries the meaning "'to incur liability,' and '*ʾasham*' as a noun denotes the payment of damages (Num. 5.7–8; 1 Sam. 6.3–4, 8[, 17]."[7] It makes good sense, then, that in situations where monetary reparations are required that it would designate it as an *ʾāšām* since the wrongdoer has incurred a financial liability (Lev 5:14–26 [5:14—6:7 Eng.]).

4. Note the singular pronoun suffix "it" (*ô*) in the phrase "then he will offer *it*" (*wəhiqrîvô*) (Lev 12:7), which specifies that what makes "atonement" is not the burnt offering and purgation sacrifice together, but just the singular purgation sacrifice that was the last sacrifice mentioned in v. 6.

5. Milgrom, *Leviticus 1–16*, 153–54.

6. Milgrom, *Leviticus 1–16*, 176; see also 172–77.

7. Schwartz, "Leviticus," 205; see also Anderson, "Sacrifice," 880–81; Milgrom, *Leviticus 1–16*, 327–28, 339–45.

This is why the *ʾāšām* is the only animal offering that can be commuted into currency (Lev 5:15, 18, 25 [6:6 Eng.]).[8] The reparation offering has to do with paying back "restitution" with a 20 percent fine added on top (5:16, 24 [6:5 Eng.]; Num 5:7) when someone has either violated a sacred thing (5:15; e.g., a holy vessel, holy food from a well-being offering in their home, etc.) or scammed or stolen from somebody (5:21–25 [6:2–6 Eng.]; cf. Zacchaeus who goes way over this requirement in Luke 19:8, perhaps based on the fourfold restitution outlined in Exod 22:1 and 2 Sam 12:6). The wrongdoer can bring a ram or its monetary equivalent. The operative function here is money being repaid with interest; not the death of the offender.

Finally, if it is not commuted to a monetary value, then a literal sacrifice is made with a ram. But notably, there is no hand gesture for the reparation offering (7:1–7). This once again confirms that the hand gesture had nothing to do with transferring guilt or sins to the animal (let alone a substitutionary death) because if that were the case, then it surely would be required for *this* offering where specific premeditated sins of lying and deceit are flagged (5:21–22 [6:2–3 Eng.]).

What Is Meaning and Function of the *Ḥaṭṭāʾt*?

I have already been using my preferred translation for the *ḥaṭṭāʾt* offering: "purgation offering." From this vantage point I can explain that choice.

First, another option is to translate it "sin offering" because *ḥaṭṭāʾt* is also the word for the noun "sin," but we can now see why this is misleading since the *ḥaṭṭāʾt* offering is prescribed in situations where no sins have been committed, but rather when a major impurity needs to remedied: childbirth (Lev 12:6–8), scale disease (14:19, 22, 31), abnormal genital discharges (15:14–15, 29–30), and when the "holy" head of the Nazirite gets contaminated by corpse impurity by accident (Num 6:9–11). Therefore, calling this the "sin offering" is problematic contextually and it leads to other misunderstandings (such as priming readers to think of ritual impurities as sinful or the consequence of sinning).

Second, the *piel* construction of the root *ḥ-ṭ-ʾ* means "purify, purge" throughout the Hebrew Bible (e.g., Exod 29:36; Lev 8:15; 14:52; Num 8:21; 19:12, 13, 19, 20; 31:19; Ezek 43:20, 22, 23, 26; 45:18; 2 Chr 29:24; Ps 51:9 [v. 7 Eng.]).[9]

8. The only times when it cannot be commuted are the specific reparation offerings required for the scale-diseased person (Lev 14:12–14, 25) and the Nazirite who has accidentally contracted corpse impurity (Num 6:9–12).

9. See also Gilders, *Blood Ritual*, 29–32; Milgrom, *Leviticus 1–16*, 253–58; Feldman, *Story of Sacrifice*, 63n93; Levine, *In the Presence*, 101.

Therefore, since the *ḥaṭṭā ʾt* is prescribed both by situations in which only major ritual impurity involved as well as when inadvertent sins are involved (e.g., Lev 4:2; Num 15:27–29), a neutral yet functionally descriptive term is necessary. And since the name of the offering carries the verbal sense of "purge" or "purify" it ought to be translated as purgation/purification offering, which leaves open the matter of what situation it is being used for. In fact, Exod 30:10 in the LXX translates the *ḥaṭṭā' t* as *tou katharismou tōn hamartiōn*, "the purification of sins," the blood of which is used to purify the incense altar here. Some scholars, such as Milgrom and Feldman, likewise use "purification offering,"[10] but I am choosing "purgation" to help keep the rituals of bodily *purification* (which only ever require time and water-washing) separate from the sacrificial rituals that purge impurity—and, as we will now see, certain sins—from the sanctuary.[11] In either scenario, whether it be for major impurity or for an inadvertent sin, the function of the *ḥaṭṭā ʾt* is the purgation of sancta in the dwelling place; hence, "purgation offering/sacrifice."

Previously, I reiterated that the purgation sacrifice does not purge the offerer's body of impurity, but instead only the sanctuary from the offerer's impurity that traveled onto the sanctuary, and now we can detail why this is. Milgrom demonstrates how we can easily figure out what is being purged by means of a *ḥaṭṭā ʾt* by attending to *where its blood is applied*.

All throughout the Torah, the use of *ḥaṭṭā ʾt* blood "is confined to the sanctuary, but it is *never applied to a person*."[12] This means "that the *ḥaṭṭā ʾt* never purifies its offerer."[13] This is why I emphasized that the limited set of rituals wherein sacrificial blood is applied to persons never comes from the purgation sacrifice. In all those rituals (covenant inauguration, the initial consecration of the priests, scale-disease purification) the people were not being purged of impurities or sins (i.e., the person necessarily had to be pure from scale disease *before* even reaching the blood-ritual stages), but

10. Milgrom, "Sin-Offering or Purification-Offering," 237–39; Feldman, *Story of Sacrifice*, 63.

11. Milgrom also offers "purgation" as a viable option. See, e.g., Milgrom, "Israel's Sanctuary," 390.

12. Milgrom, "Israel's Sanctuary," 391; his emphasis.

13. Milgrom, "Israel's Sanctuary," 391. Similarly, Levine, *In the Presence*, 111. Against Milgrom, some have tried to argue that the purgation sacrifices also purge the sinner of a sin contamination. Cf. Zohar, "Repentance and Purification," 609–18. But these counter arguments are fallacious, as Milgrom and others have demonstrated in response. Cf. Milgrom, "The Modus Operandi of the *ḥaṭṭā ʾt*," 111–13; McLean, "The Interpretation of the Levitical Sin Offering and the Scapegoat," 345–56; McLean, "The Absence of an Atoning Sacrifice in Paul's Soteriology," 537. I will address and refute another argument against Milgrom's view below.

rather undergoing metaphysical transitions along the holy-common, pure-impure matrix via non-atoning sacrifices (or blood from a non-sacrifice in Lev 14:4–7).

The use of *ḥaṭṭāʾt* blood at the inauguration of the dwelling place and on the Day of Atonement illumines both the object of purgation and the use of purgation sacrifices for individual sins. At the inauguration we read:

> Moses took the blood [from the *ḥaṭṭāʾt* in 8:14] and put some on each of the horns of the altar with his finger, and purged [*wayəḥaṭṭēʾ*] the altar. Then he poured out the blood at the base of the altar. Thus he consecrated it [*wayəqaddəšhû*], to make atonement for it. (Lev 8:15)

And on the Day of Atonement:

> He shall sprinkle some of the blood [from the *ḥaṭṭāʾt* sacrifices in 16:3, 5–6, 11, 15, 18] on it with his finger seven times and purify it [*wəṭihărô*] and consecrate it [*wəqiddəšô*] from the impurities of the children of Israel. (16:19)

It is clear from these that the *ḥaṭṭāʾt* blood "is the purging element."[14] The Day of Atonement functions as a "reset button for the sanctuary, restoring the [dwelling place] to its original factory settings."[15] The inauguration of the dwelling place needed a purgation sacrifice to consecrate the altar and the Day of Atonement *re*consecrates it. The purgation sacrifices throughout the year, then, are small-scale iterations of these large-scale purgation rituals and consecrations.

As Milgrom explains:

> If not the offerer, what then is the object of the *ḥaṭṭāʾt* purgation? The above considerations lead but to one answer: that which receives the purgative blood, i.e., the sanctuary and its sancta. By daubing the altar with the *ḥaṭṭāʾt* blood or by bringing it inside the sanctuary (e.g., *Lev.* xvi, 14–19), the priest purges the most sacred objects and areas of the sanctuary on behalf of the person who caused their contamination by his physical impurity or inadvertent offense.[16]

Depending on who sinned, the blood from the purgation sacrifices when an individual commits an inadvertent sin is either only applied to the horns of the outer altar for sacrifices (4:25, 30, 34) or it is sprinkled on the veil

14. Milgrom, "Israel's Sanctuary," 391.
15. Baden, "The Purpose of Purification in Leviticus 16," 26.
16. Milgrom, "Israel's Sanctuary," 391.

separating the holy of holies and the holy place and then applied to the horns of the incense altar (4:5–7, 16–18). Since (a) only sancta receive purgation blood, (b) those who commit inadvertent sins are not called "impure," and neither, then, (c) are they supposed to let a certain amount of time to elapse or bathe before offering their purgation sacrifice (i.e., nothing like the process for major ritual impurities) nor (d) are they "contagious" the way a ritually impure person is. This means the only things contaminated by those sins are those things that are being physically purged by contact with the purgation blood: sancta, not people.

In the priestly conception, sins generate a contamination that gets attracted to the sanctuary similar to, yet distinct from, major ritual impurities.[17] The contamination from sins is never called an "impurity" (*ṭāmēʾ*) and "purification/be pure" (*ṭāhorâ/ṭāhēr*) is never said to result for the offerer after the purgation sacrifice for sins, while this is the ultimate effect after the purgation sacrifice for major impurities (12:7–8; 14:20). Rather, the contamination is just called "sins" (*ḥaṭṭōʾt*) for accidental sins and "transgressions" (*pišʿê*) for deliberate unrepentant sins (16:16, 21, 34).[18] What this means is that in the priestly imaginary, sin as a discrete act produces "sin" as a *substance* that contaminates the sanctuary (not the person). An act of sin generates "sin" as "an aerial miasma."[19] Baruch Schwartz clarifies:

> In the priestly conception, sins, once they have come into existence, behave *like* defilement. But . . . they do not metamorphose into defilement [i.e., what I have called "major ritual impurity"]; rather, they maintain their own essence and are attracted to the sanctuary, in a process distinct from though analogous to impurity, whence, like defilement they must be purged by the חטאת [*ḥaṭṭāʾt*]-ritual.[20]

In the priestly literature, then, sin itself is an aerial miasma. When people sin, it creates an invisible but very real contamination. Significantly, this contamination only gets attracted to holy places/objects. Milgrom likens this to a "magnetic attraction for the realm of the sacred."[21]

Again, we know that sin, as an aerial contamination, is only attracted to sancta by observing where the purgation blood is placed, namely to sancta.

17. Schwartz, "The Bearing of Sin," 4–7.

18. *Pešaʿ* is linked with deliberate acts of rebellion in passages such as 2 Kgs 3:5 and Ezek 2:38.

19. Milgrom, "Israel's Sanctuary," 392.

20. Schwartz, "The Bearing of Sin," 7; his emphasis.

21. Milgrom, "Israel's Sanctuary," 392.

But we can nuance this further. Not all sins contaminate equally.[22] When an individual layperson sins inadvertently (Lev 4:2, 22, 27; Num 15:27–29), they are required to offer a *ḥaṭṭāʾt* sacrifice and its blood is only placed on the horns of the outer altar (Lev 4:25, 30, 34). So then, the inadvertent sins of laypeople only contaminate the outer altar. But the sins of priests or of the whole assembly of Israel contaminate the inner incense altar in the holy place and the veil separating the holy of holies since the purgation blood is brought into the holy place and applied to these sancta (4:5–7, 16–18). And finally, the deliberate rebellious sins (*pišʿê*) (16:16, 21) of anyone penetrate right into the holy of holies; and these are only purged on the Day of Atonement when the high priest brings the blood of the purgation sacrifice into the holy of holies itself (16:11–17). As Milgrom summarizes, "In this way the graded purgations of the sanctuary lead to the conclusion that the severity of the sin or impurity varies in direct relation to the depth of its penetration into the sanctuary."[23]

Regular purgation sacrifices cannot purge deliberate sins (Num 15:30–31); only unintentional sins (15:27–29; Lev 4:2; 5:1–5). However, as Lev 5:21–22 (6:2–3 Eng.) evinces, willful sins such as stealing or scamming someone can be downgraded to atonable inadvertencies. Thus, "the repentance of sinners, through their remorse and confession, reduces their intentional sin to an inadvertence, thereby rendering it eligible for sacrificial expiation."[24] The purging of the deliberate transgressions (*pišʿê*) mentioned in 16:16, 21 are a communal "failsafe" of sorts for the contamination brought about by anyone in the community through their unrepented sins and ignored ritual impurities (both major ones and minor ones that transformed into major ones).

As we learned from the discussion on moral impurity, however, this failsafe cannot purge *all* sins. This is because *the purgation sacrifices have a limited scope*. They can *only* purge sancta. They can only purge sins off the outer altar, the inner incense altar, the veil, and the holy of holies. But the sins that produce a (moral) impurity on the land itself will remain. And, repentance is insufficient to downgrade sins that produce moral impurity. The impurity remains.

> [Leviticus] provides no countervailing measures for the polluted land. The land stores its defilement nonstop until it vomits out its inhabitants ([Lev 18] vv. 25, 28). Unlike [the] sanctuary, which can be purged of its pollution by the high priest's

22. Milgrom, "Israel's Sanctuary," 393–94; cf. Milgrom, *Leviticus 1–16*, 257–58.

23. Milgrom, *Leviticus 1–16*, 257.

24. Milgrom, *Leviticus*, 58; for the full argument, see *Leviticus 1–16*, 373–78.

> purification offerings (chaps. 4, 16), there is no purificatory rite . . . that the high priest can perform for the land.[25]

Hence, Ps 51 is a passionate prayer reckoning with the incapacity of sacrifices to address sexual immorality and murder and so the psalmist only has recourse to petition God to provide purification by divine fiat *apart from the sacrificial system*. This is because without God's extra-cultic purification, the only ways to remedy the moral impurity is (a) the death of the ones who produce the moral impurity (e.g., Lev 18:29; 20:2, 5–6, 9–18; Num 35:30–34) or (b) exile (Lev 18:25, 28; 20:22; 26:31–45).

That said, somewhat ideally speaking, barring the festering of moral impurity that has gone unaddressed, the individual purgation sacrifices and the annual special purgation sacrifices on the Day of Atonement will make it possible for God to dwell in the midst of people who keep contaminating the divine dwelling place, either through ritual impurity or sins (15:31; 16:16, 19).

At this point it is evident that this entire ritual framework has nothing to do with a "substitutionary death." Even more so than previously, it is evident that this concept is unintelligible within the Levitical cultic logic. When moral impurity results in "death" or being "cut off," *there simply is no sacrificial remedy* because sacrifices were never conceptualized as taking the place of the offerer's deserved death. That is an unwarranted assumption about Levitical sacrifice that too many smuggle into the text. I will discuss the rationale for using blood for these purgation rituals shortly, but for now it suffices to make it clear that the *ḥaṭṭāʾt* is a procedure that purges and/or consecrates sancta with the larger goal that God has a pure and holy space in which to dwell with Israel (Exod 25:8); nothing more.[26] God's desire is to dwell among Israel so long as they maintain a habitation-appropriate sacred place for God to dwell; hence the need for the atoning and consecrating sacrifices.

Finally, it is instructive that the *ḥaṭṭāʾt* is required at the inauguration of the dwelling place before it can even become the sort of thing (i.e., "holy") that the miasma of sin is attracted to (Exod 29:36–37; Lev 8:15). This means the inaugural purgation sacrifices are not even purging away impurities or sins. Rather, they are transforming common objects into holy ones. This transformation is called "consecration" or "sanctification." Before the altar is

25. Milgrom, *Leviticus 17–22*, 1567; cf. 1404, 1422, 1571–78.

26. In a sense, it may help to demystify this somewhat and realize that the priests are glorified janitors, butchers, cooks, and servers for God's holy dwelling place restaurant. The sacrifices that they administer either sanitize and disinfect the place, or they provide meals for the worshipers.

consecrated it is just a collection of "common" (i.e., not "holy") uncut rocks; it is not an altar in the true sense (at first). And because it is just a pile of rocks this means "sins" would not be attracted to it since sin only attaches itself to sancta. In order for it to become an altar, this pile of rocks needs to be consecrated/sanctified—made holy. The *ḥaṭṭāʾt* achieves this, not because "something needs to die as a substitute," but rather because the entire function of the *ḥaṭṭāʾt* is to consecrate (Exod 29:36–37 with Lev 8:15; 16:19); and its power to consecrate is the very reason it also has the power to purge away what threatens to profane it once it has been made holy.[27] It is the same power with two distinct effects depending on the condition of the object it is applied to. This is why anyone and anything that comes into contact with *ḥaṭṭāʾt* blood after it touches either of the altars gets consecrated, per Exod 29:37 and 30:26–29. Importantly, however, because that state of holiness is *undesired* at times, it is treated as an impurity that needs to be washed away (Lev 6:20–21 [Eng. 27–28]).

I have previously emphasized that *ḥaṭṭāʾt* blood is never applied to people, but to be more nuanced we should say that it is never *deliberately* applied to people as part of any ritual prescriptions. But it does get on other people and things *by accident*, as the instructions in Lev 6:20–21 (Eng. 27–28) assume. Nevertheless, because the *ḥaṭṭāʾt* has consecratory powers, these accidental contacts need to be mitigated through washings. When the altar gets contaminated by either impurities or sins after it has been consecrated, the *ḥaṭṭāʾt* is used to purge this new contamination and thereby maintain the sanctity of the altar because its only purpose is to consecrate and purge what it contacts. If it contacts the wrong things (human or object) by accident it still consecrates them because that is simply what the *ḥaṭṭāʾt* does. When it does this to the wrong things, that newly acquired yet undesired consecrated state needs to be remedied. This further corroborates the notion that the *ḥaṭṭāʾt* is not purging the offer because when *people* (even priests) get consecrated by contacting the *ḥaṭṭāʾt* that is considered undesirable, a ritual *faux pas* of sorts, that needs to be undone by washing (or destroying the object, if it is made of clay) (6:27–28).

It is evident, therefore, that the blood applications on sancta for individual sins do on a small scale what the purgation sacrifices accomplish on a large scale on the Day of Atonement for the entire dwelling place. By collocating Exod 29:36–37, Lev 6:27–28, 8:15, and 16:19, we realize that the *ḥaṭṭāʾt* has an inherent consecratory power (after it touches one of the altars per Exod 29:37 and 30:26–29) no matter what it contacts. What is

27. The initial consecration also requires the use of the sacred anointing oil (Exod 40:10 with Lev 8:10), but this is not used again on the Day of Atonement; just the *ḥaṭṭāʾt* offerings suffice to (re)consecrate the altar (16:19).

happening is that the contamination caused by inadvertent sins (Lev 4) or major ritual impurities (Lev 12; 14–15) is getting purged from these sancta while their full and total purgation and removal, especially for deliberate sins and neglect of ritual impurities, occurs on the Day of Atonement (16:16, 19).

Addressing Objections

Before transitioning to discussing *kipper* more directly, there is another misunderstanding regarding the *ḥaṭṭāʾt* that needs to be addressed now that we have laid sufficient groundwork in this and the previous chapter. We noted how the contamination from sin functions and is dealt with analogously with ritual impurities. Roy E. Gane agrees with this premise, but has objected to Milgrom and his followers' thesis that the *ḥaṭṭāʾt* is only used to purge sancta, not people, from the sin-contamination miasma (a thesis that I further defended above).[28]

Gane has argued that the *ḥaṭṭāʾt* also purges *the offerer* from sin-contamination that supposedly resides in the person's body. It is necessary to connect the dots from what was set forth above to Gane's own view since his argument has been taken up to buttress categorically wrong-headed monographs on Leviticus that work from the assumptions that sacrifice is about "substitutionary death" and that purgation sacrifices are meant to purge people from sin.[29] This is then taken to substantiate their doctrines of penal substitutionary atonement and specifically that Jesus is a *ḥaṭṭāʾt* sacrifice that purges sinners by dying in their stead. As we will see, even when Jesus is identified with the *ḥaṭṭāʾt* sacrifice on rare occasions in the NT, this is never construed as a substitutionary death,[30] and it keeps with the idea that the *ḥaṭṭāʾt* purges sancta (albeit heavenly sancta) (Heb 9:23–24), not people. The purgative functions that Jesus has for people are associated not with a *ḥaṭṭāʾt*, but rather with the ritual means of purifying bodies—i.e., water-washing—via baptism.

We will get to the NT in the following chapters, but here, drawing on the observations above, we can demonstrate that Gane's view is based on a mistaken understanding of what is happening with purifying ritual

28. Gane, *Cult and Character*, 106–43.

29. E.g., Morales, *Who Shall Ascend*; Sklar, *Leviticus*.

30. E.g., "I argued against the idea of seeing substitution as being central to sacrifice. . . . In none of the passages interpreting Christ's death as a sacrifice, do we see ideas of substitution incorporated. Saying Christ's death was a sacrifice does not entail saying that he died in our place" (Shauf, *Jesus the Sacrifice*, 173).

impurities and where the impurities are said to exist at various stages of ritual purification. This matters for the aims of this book since one of the results of this overall study is that the idea of penal substitutionary atonement has no exegetical basis in the Levitical sacrificial system. This also provides an opportunity to summarize the main points thus far by showing how all these concepts of im/purity, purification, and atonement relate.

Gane thinks the "residual ritual impurity"[31] that the *ḥaṭṭā ʾt* is said to purge in passages like Lev 14:19, 15:14–15, and 29–30 is impurity inhering in or on the person rather than the sanctuary.[32] Leviticus 15:31, the conclusion and summation of all the ritual purity regulations, however, says just the opposite. This passage explicitly says impurities cling to the sanctuary (cf. 16:16, 19). Gane is correct that the prefix *min* ought to be translated "from his/her impurity/discharge" in the above texts,[33] but he mistakenly assumes that this must mean that the impurity is existing *intrinsically*, in or on the person.

Gane claims that in 15:15, for instance, "when the priest effects purgation [his gloss for *kipper* in these verses] on his behalf from his discharge, the ritual impurity is removed from the individual himself."[34] But Gane nowhere justifies why "from" only and necessarily must mean that the impurity exists "in" or "on" the person at that point. He just makes assertions such as: "A physical ritual impurity . . . is a lingering state simply located in the body, 'from' which it must be removed."[35] In context Gane believes that the impurity is only removed from the body via a purgation offering. He appears to think that this is what "from" (*min*) necessarily must mean only because Milgrom chose to translate the above verses without using "from" and instead as "'for his discharge' and 'for her impure discharge.'"[36] From

31. Gane, *Cult and Character*, 116 (and used throughout).

32. My discussion here also answers Thomas Kazen's critique of Milgrom that "[t]here is a missing link in the reasoning" of Milgrom's "theory about airborne impurity" (*Issues of Impurity*, 57). He explains: "If the requirement to bring a sacrifice indicates that the discharging person has defiled the *sanctuary*, although without having been in direct contact with it, why does this sacrifice (Lev 15:14, 29) belong to the rites necessary for purifying the *person*?" (57).

33. Gane, *Cult and Character*, 117. See: m*iṭum ʾātô*, "from his impurity" (Lev 14:19); m*izôvô*, "from his discharge" (15:15), m*izôv tum ʾātāh*, "from her discharge of impurity" (15:30).

34. Gane, *Cult and Character*, 117.

35. Gane, *Cult and Character*, 127.

36. Gane, *Cult and Character*, 117; citing Milgrom in *Leviticus 1–16*, 902–3 (cf. 926) and *Leviticus 17–22*, 1291–92. He goes on to assert, "But taking מִן [*min*] the same way [i.e., as meaning 'from' rather than Milgrom's 'for'] in other contexts [4:26; 5:6, 10; 12:7; 14:19; 15:15, 30; 16:16, 30, 34; Num 6:11] would be devastating to his thesis that

here, Gane leaps from the *ḥaṭṭāʾt* for major ritual impurities to the ones for sins and concludes that since the *min* prefix is used there (cf. 4:26; 5:6, 10; 16:16, 30, 34) this must mean the *ḥaṭṭāʾt* is purging the sin contamination inhering in or on the person's body.[37]

Even putting aside the problem that Gane makes a lot of unwarranted assumptions about the prepositional prefix *min* ("from"), his view both misunderstands the multi-stage purification process for major ritual impurities discussed above as well as the explicit comments about the effects of *ḥaṭṭāʾt* blood. Essentially, although Gane is correct that "from" is the better translation in these passages dealing with ritual impurities (14:19, 15:15, 30; 16:16, 30) and sins (4:26; 5:6, 10; 16:16, 30, 34) and that there is an analogous relationship between sin and ritual impurity in Leviticus, he does not seem to realize that impurity can exist and *belong to* a person *extrinsically*. His writing assumes that when impurity belongs to someone that it can only be an intrinsic phenomenon. It can only be "theirs" if it is "located in the body."[38] This assumption is unwarranted and unsupported by any biblical text. Furthermore, the concept is also unknown in the Mishnah. Therefore, his application of ritual impurity purification to sin decontamination is categorically mistaken. He fundamentally misunderstands how ritual impurity "behaves" and is purified in stages.

Recall that the difference between a minor and a major impurity is that a minor impurity only exists on the person's body and this is why only the passing of time until sundown and a bath purifies the body. The impurity is largely removed by washing it off the body with water, and whatever "remains" is eliminated by the passing of time until sunset. The next morning, then, that person is no longer the source of defilement to things common or holy and they are free to access the sanctuary as normal. With major impurities, the need for a purgation sacrifice is introduced, not to purge the impurity away from the person's body, but rather because their impurity has somehow reached the *altar*, which is why the altar needs to be purged with a *ḥaṭṭāʾt*. A major impurity is so potent that it leeches *out from* the body and attaches itself to the altar. The *ḥaṭṭāʾt* is required in only these specific cases, then, because the ritual impurity now exists *outside* of the person's body. This shows us that some ritual impurities *only* reside in a person's body (minor impurities) and therefore do not require a *ḥaṭṭāʾt*, but some ritual impurities reside into *two* places, the person's body *and* the sanctuary

purification offerings always purge the sanctuary and its sancta rather than the offerer" (Gane, *Cult and Character*, 119).

37. Gane, *Cult and Character*, 123–43.

38. Gane, *Cult and Character*, 127.

(15:31; 16:16, 19) (major impurities). Hence the benefit of the heuristics "minor" and "major" to properly distinguish between these scenarios.

Recall, the *ḥaṭṭāʾt* is *the* ritual means of purging sancta to maintain its consecration (holiness). But the presence of the formerly impure person *at the sanctuary* is only possible *because their bodies no longer have the impurity on or in them since otherwise they would necessarily impart impurity to holy things.* As the Mishnah corroborates (e.g., m. Ṭ. Yom 2:1; 4:3; m. Zevaḥ. 2:1; 12:1; m. Ker. 2:1; m. Kelim 1:5; m. Neg. 14:3; m. ʿEd. 2:1; 5:1, 4), the only way to make sense out of the repeated declarations that people are "pure" at various stages of ritual purification for major impurities (e.g., Lev 12:6, 7, 8; 14:8, 9, 20; 15:13, 28) is that each proclamation is announcing that the person has transitioned one level up on a spectrum of ritual purity. At one stage of purification the person is pure enough to no longer impart impurity to common things, but is still impure enough to impart impurity to holy things (12:2–5; 14:8–9). At the next stage of purity (the penultimate stage) they no longer impart impurity to holy things (12:4–6; 14:9–11). This indicates that there cannot be any residual impurity *in or on the person when it is time for them to offer their purgation sacrifice*, otherwise they would still be barred from holy things as well as from accessing the sanctuary once again (e.g., 12:4).[39]

Contra Gane, what is clear from these passages is that their bodies are completely free of the impurity at the penultimate stage of "purity" just prior to being eligible to offer a *ḥaṭṭāʾt*. But just because their impurity no longer exists in or on them does not mean they are off the hook. They can only reach the ultimate stage of ritual purity once their impurity no longer exists. But until they offer the *ḥaṭṭāʾt* their impurity still exists on the sancta. Therefore, the final declaration of the person's purity status is not a tacit admission that their impurity has actually been existing in their bodies this whole time, as Gane assumes, but rather that *their* impurity *no longer exists anywhere* since its last remaining remnants have been eliminated from the altar. Though it is not sinful to contract a major ritual impurity, the onus is nevertheless on the person who contracts it to decontaminate the altar from their specific impurity that is clinging to it. Thus, the person is not a full participant in the community and its worship—i.e., they are not at the ultimate stage of purity—until every last vestige of *their* impurity has been purged *from the sanctuary*.

Moreover, since the combination of water and time is the only thing that removes ritual impurities from people, the *ḥaṭṭāʾt* must have a different function, especially since it is only required for a limited set of specific cases

39. Similarly, Milgrom, *Leviticus 1–16*, 849, 997.

of ritual impurity that are more severe. Their severity is specifically owing to the fact that the impurity did not stay located on the person, but leeched out from them and clung to the sanctuary as well (15:31). This is why a good way to capture what the priestly system is conveying is to think of impurity as an aerial miasma. But it is only in those situations where the impurity moves past the person and onto the sanctuary that a *ḥaṭṭā ʾt* is needed. If, as Gane believes, impurity resides *in the person* until a *ḥaṭṭā ʾt* purges it from their bodies, then there would be so such thing as impurities that resolve within a day after only taking a bath. This would mean any impure person would be a continual source of ritual contagion, transmitting impurity, if not to common things after their bath, then at least to any holy object (such as the meat from well-being sacrifice or something dedicated to be given to the sanctuary) they contacted until they got around to offering the *ḥaṭṭā ʾt* so that they no longer had any impurity within or on their body. (And those people they contact then become permanently impure as well until they offer their own *ḥaṭṭā ʾt*, and so on *ad infinitum*.)[40]

Again, even the bearer of major impurities can attain a level of purity such that they're no longer capable of transmitting secondary impurity, either to things common or holy (12:2, 4–6; 13:46 with 14:2, 7–8, 9; 15:13, 28), which the rabbinic teachings clearly recognize and address. They even draw upon this logic of the stages for major impurities to settle debates about the status of the *tevul yom* who only had a minor impurity (m. Parah 3:7–8; 8:7; 11:4–5). The reason that people at the penultimate stage of purity are no longer contagious to others, nor can they transmit impurity to sancta, and are thereby eligible to access the sanctuary (Lev 14:11) is *precisely because there is no longer any impurity lodged in their bodies.*

Gane does not explain—and his view *cannot* explain—why those who reach this penultimate stage of ritual purity are no longer contagious to holy things if, as he believes, they still have impurity "located in the body" the

40. If Gane is correct, no one would ever be able to eradicate their impurity fully from their body and thus, they would be contagious at least to holy things until they offered a *ḥaṭṭā ʾt*. But this would be an inherently unsustainable system because in order to be eligible to access the sanctuary the person cannot be capable of imparting their impurity to the sacred space of the sanctuary or their purgation offering. But so long as impurity is attached to the person's body, they will always at least contaminate what is holy (e.g., Lev 12:4; 14:8–9). It would also therefore be impossible to distinguish between "minor" and "major" impurities because they are all permanently clinging to the person, thereby necessarily rendering them continuously contagious to sacred things. On this framework almost everyone would be directly or indirectly rendered impure in short time span and they would never be able to reach the stage of their bodies being free from impurity so that they are no longer contagious to sacred things. Essentially, Gane's view generates a purity system that is unlivable.

entire time up to offering the purgation sacrifice.[41] But by attending to the claims made in 15:31, 16:16, and 19, we learn that the person's impurity still exists, but it exists *extrinsically* to them. It exists *on the sancta* until they eliminate it with a purgation sacrifice. Contra Gane, then, when the *ḥaṭṭāʾt* is offered for major ritual impurities, *the impurity necessarily has already ceased to exist on the person*. That is the plain meaning of the declarations that person becomes "pure" in several stages and especially at the penultimate stage in the process—and the rabbinic sages agree. Therefore, there is no "residual" impurity *on the person* as Gane asserts, which is why the person is no longer ritually contagious to things common or holy.

Moreover, we learn that water-washing is the way this penultimate stage of purity is achieved (14:7–8, 9; 15:13, 28).[42] This is the necessary stage of purity to reach before being able to *access* the sanctuary to offer a *ḥaṭṭāʾt*. The fact that no water-washings are prescribed for those who sin prior to them bringing their *ḥaṭṭāʾt* strongly suggests the Levitical system does not take the analogy of ritual impurity and the contamination of sin as a one-to-one correlation; but this one-to-one correlation is Gane's methodological working assumption (i.e., it is not argued, it is presumed as a premise). And this premise is unwarranted from the texts. According to these texts, the *only* way in which sins are like ritual impurities is that *both produce a contamination that can cling to sancta* and, therefore, they both share the *same ritual remedy* to remove these similar yet distinct contaminates from the sanctuary: the *ḥaṭṭāʾt*. But only one of these contaminates the person and none of the prescribed ways to remove contaminations from the body involve applying *ḥaṭṭāʾt* blood to the person.

Again, if the *ḥaṭṭāʾt* blood does come into contact with people, that is an *undesired* ritual effect that needs to remedied through *water-washing* (6:27–28; cf. 16:27–28). The need to wash after contacting a *ḥaṭṭāʾt* simultaneously proves (a) that the *ḥaṭṭāʾt*, though inherently consecrating, is only *meant* to consecrate sancta such that the accidental consecration of other things needs to be removed through washing, and (b) that water-washing is *the* way to purify *people/their bodies* from any undesired ritual state, be it contracting an impurity or accidental holiness.

However, Gane has a stronger point that deserves response. He offers Lev 12:7 as a text that proves that the *ḥaṭṭāʾt* itself effects the (ritual) purification of a person's body.[43] This text deals specifically with the purification

41. Gane, *Cult and Character*, 127.

42. This is why the rabbis apply the logic of these cases to the *tevul yom* who is also in a penultimate stage of purity from a minor impurity after bathing and prior to sundown (e.g., m. Ṭ. Yom).

43. Gane, *Cult and Character*, 115–20, 125–26.

of a mother after giving birth (a parturient). Here, as Gane rightly observes, the text specifically tethers offering the *ḥaṭṭāʾt* to effect atonement (*kipper*) with the result of ritual purity: "and she will be purified from [*min*] the flow of her blood." However, Gane's application of his conclusion regarding this instance—i.e., that "[i]t is logical that an offerer who receives כפר [*kipper*] 'from' a physical ritual impurity becomes pure 'from' that impurity"—to all other instances of ritual impurity, and thus for sins as well, is problematic.[44]

For one, Gane himself acknowledges that relating the situation in 12:7 to other instances such as the person healed from scale disease in 14:19 would only work "to the extent that these cases are similar."[45] But these circumstances are not as similar as they may appear at first. In the case of scale disease, the physical impurity has definitely gone away and no longer exists on the person's body (14:2). But in the case of childbirth the (potential) source of impurity, the lochial discharge, might literally still be flowing even after the prescribed time for offering the *ḥaṭṭāʾt*. The parturient is eligible to bring the *ḥaṭṭāʾt* after the fortieth day of giving birth to a male (12:2, 4, 6) or the eightieth day for female (12:5). Unlike abnormal genital discharges (15:28, 13), the parturient is *not* told to wait until the lochia *stops*. Rather, she is given a fixed timeframe.

It is well documented, however, that lochial discharge can last well past the fortieth day.[46] In one study at least 10 percent of the women experienced lochial discharge that lasted more than six weeks (forty-two days),[47] and in another the percentage was as high as 60 percent lasting more than six weeks.[48] In another, "a bleeding episode occurred at about 6–8 weeks postpartum in 26% of the breast-feeding women studied."[49] In yet another, 13 percent of women had lochia past sixty days.[50] In fact, researchers have observed lochia for up to ninety days, which is past the eighty-day timeframe

44. Gane, *Cult and Character*, 116.

45. Gane, *Cult and Character*, 115.

46. Visness, Kennedy, and Ramos, "The Duration and Character of Postpartum Bleeding among Breast-Feeding Women," 159–63; Oppenheimer et al., "The Duration of Lochia," 754–57; Khazardoost et al., "The Relationship between Ultrasonic Findings of Postpartum Uterus after Normal Vaginal Delivery and the Duration of Lochia Discharge," 187–93; Fletcher, Grotegut, and James, "Lochia Patterns among Normal Women," 1290–94.

47. Visness, Kennedy, and Ramos, "The Duration and Character of Postpartum Bleeding," 161.

48. Khazardoost et al., "The Relationship between Ultrasonic Findings of Postpartum Uterus after Normal Vaginal Delivery and the Duration of Lochia Discharge," 187.

49. Visness, Kennedy, and Ramos, "The Duration and Character of Postpartum Bleeding," 160.

50. Oppenheimer et al., "The Duration of Lochia," 755.

for a female child.[51] We can easily infer from this data that ancient Israelites surely knew from generations of experience that lochia can persist past the prescribed timeframes in Lev 12.

Knowing this, from a certain perspective it may seem odd that the prescriptions in Lev 12 stipulate strict timeframes rather than a flexible "*after the lochia stops*, wait seven days and take a bath" like it has for the genital discharges in Lev 15:13 and 28. Nevertheless, the text says what it says. If a mother gives birth to a male, for example, then on day forty she is declared eligible to access the sanctuary and offer a *ḥaṭṭāʾt* (12:6). This shows that being eligible to access the sanctuary and therefore, obviously, no longer barred from it and touching holy things per 12:4, is not contingent on the presence or absence of *lochial discharge* at all. Instead, it is all about the passing of the stipulated *time*. Hence, the parturient is barred from the sanctuary "until the days" (12:4), not "until the discharge stops." And this timeframe is contingent on the gender of the child, again not on anything having to do with the lochial discharge.

Therefore, the reason for the distinctive claim of 12:7 (that the sacrifice purifies her "from the flow of her blood") is almost certainly owing to the biological fact that it was well known that mothers can have lochial discharge for longer than forty (or even eighty) days. If 12:7 implies that the lochial blood is impure (which may not even be case as discussed shortly), then this is the only time the *ḥaṭṭāʾt* would have a preemptive purgative function. That is, the syntax of 12:7 makes it clear that even if the mother still has a literal lochial discharge, her *ḥaṭṭāʾt* offered on the prescribed day will nevertheless render her fully ritually pure. She can offer the required *ḥaṭṭāʾt* or any other sacrifice from this point on. In all other situations, the purgation sacrifice is always offered *after* the impurity has ceased being on the person. But in the case of childbirth it can purge *ahead* of time any impurity for the parturient who experiences a lochial discharge that persists beyond the stipulated timeframes for male and female children.

Because of these different circumstantial possibilities, therefore, 12:7 cannot be neatly transferred onto any other situation. In all other cases the source of impurity has definitely ceased, but in the case of childbirth, the mother may still have a genital discharge at the time of offering the purgation sacrifice. The parturient is purified "from her blood" that may or may not still be literally flowing out of her body, whereas the person who has healed from scale disease by the time they offer their *ḥaṭṭāʾt* necessarily cannot have any impurity inhering on their bodies per 14:2, 8, and 9. Thus, when we read about their ultimate stage of purity in 14:19–20, we know

51. Visness, Kennedy, and Ramos, "The Duration and Character of Postpartum Bleeding," 161; Fletcher, Grotegut, and James, "Lochia Patterns," 1291.

that this can only mean they are purified "from" their very own scale disease impurity that only existed extrinsically to them on the sancta since it most definitely was no longer in or on their body. The same is true for abnormal genital discharges. The impurity literally must be eliminated from the person entirely for a whole week before they are eligible to offer the *ḥaṭṭāʾt* (15:13–15, 28–30).

That said, Lev 12 never calls the parturient's discharge *impure* after the first stage of impurity.[52] In fact, on account of the status of impurity for the parturient being contingent solely on *time* rather than on the presence or absence of lochial discharge and because this discharge is explicitly called "the blood of purification" (12:4, 5), which is distinct from the discharge during the first stage of impurity likened to impure menstrual blood (12:2, 5), the rabbis reasoned that lochial discharge itself must actually be *pure* (m. Nid. 1:7; 10:7 with m. Ṭ. Yom 2:1 and 4:3; m. ʿEd. 5:1, 4).[53] That is, they conclude that "this blood does not impurify."[54] Thus, lochial blood during this second stage of purification can contact sacrificial food and it would not defile it (m. Nid. 10:7). The parturient *herself* is impure (capable of defiling things) during her first two stages of purification—with respect to common and holy things during the first stage just like a menstruant, but only impure with respect to holy things during the second stage (Lev 12:2, 4–5; cf. 15:19–24). During this second stage, the mother's impurity relative to sacred things does not affect the status of her lochial discharge because it is a nonsacral "common" thing. This is why even though her own lochia obviously has contact with her, she cannot defile it during the second stage. Theoretically, as others note, if the lochia got on sacrificial food it would *not* defile the sacred food.[55] The food would only become defiled if the parturient herself touched it. Therefore, the parturient's status changes solely on account of the requisite passing of *time* at each stage, not the presence or absence of lochial discharge, which Lev 12:4 together with v. 7 declares to be pure.

But when Lev 12 is first being legislated, the presence of *any* genital discharge might have caused the audience to become confused (especially in light of the regulations for discharges in Lev 15), perhaps thinking that the parturient would have to wait until all the lochial discharge has stopped (and perhaps wait a week after that, on analogy to 15:28–30) before offering

52. The first stage of impurity lasts seven days for a male child and fourteen days for a female child as is considered equivalent to menstrual impurity (12:2, 5).

53. The book of Jubilees confirms this understanding as well (3:1–14; see blood purity in vv. 8, 10–11, 12–14).

54. Cohen, "Tractate Eduyot," 659, cf. 662.

55. Cf. David Levine, "Tevul Yom," 924, 919–20; Cohen, "Tractate Eduyot," 659, 662.

the purgation sacrifice. But the wording in Lev 12 makes it clear that the *lochial blood itself is not a source of impurity*. The rabbis take this and the fact that it is called "the blood of purification" in Lev 12:4 and 5 as evidence that lochial discharge is distinct from all other genital discharges and is itself pure (cf. Jub. 3:10–11).

Put another way, on the basis of Lev 12, the rabbis don't think lochia past the fortieth or eightieth day would cause the parturient to delay offering the purgation sacrifice *because the legislation in Lev 12 implies that lochia itself is not defiling*. The lochial fluid does not cause impurity, only the parturient herself does during the forty or eighty days and her impurity lasts only for the *designated time period* precisely because it is not contingent on the lochial discharge itself. *That* determination *is* the point of Lev 12:4 and 7. The point of the wording is to make it clear to the audience that the presence of lochial discharge need not prevent the parturient from offering the requisite purgation sacrifice until it literally stops flowing.

Therefore, the rabbinic determination that lochial discharge is inherently pure and thus cannot transmit impurity even to sacral foods (m. Nid. 10:7 with m. Ṭ. Yom 2:1–2; cf. m. ʿEd. 5:1, 4) makes perfect sense from the exegesis of Lev 12. No one would know this if it were not for this specific legislation and wording in Lev 12:7 that makes it clear the parturient's ultimate stage of purification is not contingent on the stoppage of lochial flow.

All this means that Gane's extrapolation from 12:7 is fundamentally mistaken and wrongheaded. The point of that declaration is to make it clear that lochial blood itself is not defiling; this was not the cause of the parturient being impure. Rather, it was *the event of childbirth itself* that makes her impure, and only for the stipulated timeframe(s) at each stage. Moreover, once the parturient becomes eligible to offer the purgation sacrifice after the required passing of time, then she is at the penultimate stage of purity. This means she has become pure—there is no longer any impurity clinging to her body—such that she no longer defiles sacral food even if she is prevented, for whatever reason, from offering the required purgation sacrifice for some time yet (as discussed in the previous chapter).

Again, Gane makes his whole argument hinge on the fact that people are declared purified "from" their impurity rather than "for" their impurity (as Milgrom translates the *min* prefix). Gane is right that "from" is the better translation, yet he does not realize that "from" still works within Milgrom's framework. In fact, I think "from" strengths Milgrom's overall view. When a major impurity occurs and it comes time to offer the *ḥaṭṭāʾt* the person is purified "from" their very own impurity that caused the altar to be contaminated because now *all* of their impurity that they generated into the world has been purged, not only intrinsically from their body (through time and bathing), but also extrinsically from the sanctuary (through a purgation sacrifice). They were only able to access the sanctuary to offer the purgation sacrifice because their bodies were already purified in leveled increments. First, they attain a level of purity after the discharge or disease stops, then they gain another after a week has passed and a bath. At this point, their bodies are completely free from impurity, which is why they no longer transmit secondary impurity to anything (common or holy). Their impurity "from" their discharge or "from" their scale disease still exists though, but it exists extrinsically (on the altar), not intrinsically within their bodies.

Gane thinks that just because it is "his/her" impurity that this must mean it is "located in the body" still,[56] but this is an unwarranted supposition, as I have shown. All it has to mean is that the specific miasmic impurity belonging to someone still exists *somewhere*. Attending to where the purgation blood is applied reveals *where* the impurity still resides. It exists *on the altar*. But, it "belongs" to the person because they generated that particular impurity that is still left clinging to the altar. And we already know that the purgation sacrifice for an impurity cannot be purifying the person because if they still had impurity inhering to their bodies, then they would necessarily be contagious and transmit secondary impurity if not to common things, then at least to sancta (12:4; 14:8, 9).[57]

From here I can address a final objection raised by Gane. He claims, "[a]nyone who persists in arguing that the sanctuary or one of its components is purified will be constrained to admit that this interpretation requires assumption of an ellipsis," whereby passages like 12:7, 14:19, and 15:15, 30 ought to be read as (brackets are his, indicating the ellipses): "He

56. Gane, *Cult and Character*, 127.

57. I walked through these stages for scale disease purification in Lev 14 in chapter 2, but we see the same level of contagiousness in Lev 12 as well for the parturient (cf. m. Neg. 14:3, which also links together these two processes for a three-stage purification). For the first seven days (fourteen days if the child is female), the mother transmits secondary impurity to both common and holy things (12:2, 5). But after this point, during the second phase (thirty-three days for a male child, sixty-six for a female), she has gained one level of purity such that "she no longer communicates impurity to the nonsacred (to other humans or objects) at all. Thus she is permitted to resume relations with her husband in this second phase" (Schwartz, "Leviticus," 222). However, she is not at that necessary penultimate stage of purity since, according to 12:4, "she continues to contaminate sacred objects and the sanctuary, but only by direct contact, no longer from afar" (Schwartz, "Leviticus," 222). And from this context we can understand the claim of 12:7 being more of a reassurance, saying: "Do not worry if you still literally have any residual lochial discharge. You can still come to the sanctuary and offer the *ḥaṭṭāʾt* on the prescribed day. You do not need to delay your sacrifice until it stops. When you offer the *ḥaṭṭāʾt* and you are still having lochial discharge, the offering will purify you from your flow. No need to come back and offer another purgation sacrifice."

[i.e., the priest] shall purge [the altar] on behalf of the offerer (from his/her impurity)."[58] Fair enough. But he fails to realize he is hoist by his own petard since his interpretation *also requires an ellipsis*. On Gane's view, the passage should be read as: "from their impurity [still in/on their bodies]." In my view, following Milgrom while taking on board Gane's observation that the *min* prefix ought to be translated "from," the above passages ought to be read as: "from their impurity [that was clinging to altar]."

Both interpretations require an ellipsis, but, as demonstrated, my view has (1) a textual warrant since we are told where the impurities (and sins) reside (15:31; 16:16, 19). It is also supported (2) by close observation that the purgative function of the *ḥaṭṭā't* is restricted to what it *contacts* and (3) by that fact that its consecratory contact with people or objects besides sancta is ritually *problematic*. Further, (4) my view attends to the various stages of purification and what the status of a person at the penultimate stage entails (i.e., there is no longer any impurity on or within them because they are no longer capable of transmitting secondary impurity to either common or holy things), which (5) is corroborated by the rabbinic conclusions about this penultimate stage. Gane's view, however, is both anomalous (not found in either the Torah or the primary sources of early Judaism) and simply asserted on the assumption that "from" (*min*) somehow automatically hijacks the prepositions "in" and/or "on" along with it. Gane's view also ignores the actual use and practice of the *ḥaṭṭā't* blood rituals, and the carefully delineated stages of ritual purity with respect to addressing major ritual impurities. By not attending carefully to the successive stages of ritual purity in the multistep purification process from major ritual impurities, Gane misunderstands the final declaration of "purity" in all these cases, which therefore invalidates his argument that extrapolates from these cases of using a *ḥaṭṭā't* for ritual purification to the cases of using a *ḥaṭṭā't* for sins.

A person is not considered fully ritually pure, as we learned, until they are in "good standing," so to speak, with the sanctuary, which means being full participants in the regular rhythms of worship once again. They are only at a level of ritual purity of being *eligible* for reintegration prior to offering their *ḥaṭṭā't* since their *bodies* no longer have any impurity lodged in them. But they are not yet considered fully "pure" until they are *actually* reintegrated into the community's liturgical practices. And this cannot happen until all *their* impurity, which at the penultimate stage of purification only exists extrinsically to them on the sancta, has been eliminated. This is why the *ḥaṭṭā't* is the penultimate sacrifice and the burnt offering is the last one for major ritual impurities (14:19; 15:15, 30). The *ḥaṭṭā't* has removed the

58. Gane, *Cult and Character*, 122.

rest of the person's very own impurity (that at that stage was only existing extrinsically to the person on the sancta) and the burnt offering functions as their first "normal" sacrifice of worship after all their impurity has been purged and eliminated. The burnt offering thereby indicates that they are now fully restored to the rhythms and practices of the sanctuary. The burnt offering is a tangible sign-act of their recovered status as attaining the ultimate stage of purification; meaning, "able to resume regular practices of sacrificial worship."

Pulling the Threads Together for the *Ḥaṭṭā ʾt*

From the foregoing, it becomes apparent that the analogy between sin contamination and ritual impurity is limited to the major ritual impurities and the similar contaminating effect these both have upon sancta. Bringing a *ḥaṭṭā ʾt* for an inadvertent (or repentant) sin is analogous to the penultimate stage of ritual impurity. The person has no sin contamination on themselves—hence, no need for any time elapse or washing prior to offering the *ḥaṭṭā ʾt* or an analogous ritual—but the contamination produced by their own sinful act has clung to the sanctuary. For both major ritual impurities and sin contaminations, the priest is performing atonement *on the sancta* with the purgation sacrifice on the offerer's behalf with the end result that the offer is either rendered fully pure "from" their ritual impurities (12:7–8; 14:19–20; 15:15, 30; 16:16, 19) or "from" their sin-contamination (4:26; 5:6, 10; 16:16, 19, 34). If they do not offer the *ḥaṭṭā ʾt* then they still bear an obligation and responsibility to remove their contamination from the sanctuary, but at this point it transforms into a *peša ʿ*, a deliberate offensive act of disobedience, that contaminates all the way into the holy of holies. While this deliberate-sin-contamination (*peša ʿ*) will be taken care of for the community on the Day of Atonement (16:16, 21), the individual's *own liability* for causing a contamination and then neglecting to purge it remains and it is said they will bear the consequences (*ʿăwōnô*, "his iniquity") of this neglect (e.g., 5:1, 17; 7:18; 17:16; cf. Num 19:20).

In the priestly imagination, *ʿāwōn* is the full consequence(s) of allowing contamination to fester on the sanctuary and eventually means being cut off (for individuals) or exile (for the community) (e.g., 7:18–20; 18:25; 19:8; 20:17, 19; 22:16; 26:39–41, 43). By purging the sancta from impurity and sin-contamination, these consequences are avoided. The person is no longer "liable" since there is no longer anything contaminating the sanctuary. But if the person disregards their responsibility to purge their contamination (whether impurity or sin-contamination) from the sanctuary, even though the Day of Atonement purges it for the sake of the community, that individual person will nevertheless "bear their *ʿāwōn*" and be cut off.

In neither scenario, however, is the impurity or sin-contamination being purged from the offerer him- or herself. But the purgation rituals *release* the offerer from their *duty* to purge their contamination away from the sanctuary. For sins this is what "forgiveness" means (e.g., 4:20, 26, 31, 35) and for major ritual impurities this is what that final declaration of "purity" means (12:7–8; 14:19–20). It is intuitive that (even accidental) sinners need forgiveness, but major ritual impurities are not sins, which is why those who offer the required *ḥaṭṭāʾt* are not said to be "forgiven," but rather attain the full status of "pure." The only exception to this is when a major impurity started out as a minor impurity, in which case the offerer does need "forgiveness" (5:2–3 with vv. 10, 13; cf. 17:15–16), because of their neglect to take care of the impurity before it festered into a major one contaminating the sanctuary. But in both cases the sinner or the one who has recovered from a major impurity are duty bound to purge the sanctuary from their contamination; and if they do not, then they will eventually suffer the consequences (*ʿāwōn*).

The only thing being "removed" from the people, therefore, is not the contamination itself, but rather their *liability* to clean up the mess they made in God's dwelling place.

Although an imperfect analogy, it might help to think about this in terms of a dog owner's responsibilities in public. It is common to have fines for pet owners who fail to pick up their pet's excrement from public spaces. The excrement is the ritual impurity or sin contamination and the fine is the *ʿāwōn*. When their dog defecates, it "contaminates" the public place and this contamination "belongs" to the owner. It is "their" contamination and thus it is the owner's *responsibility* to remove it. Failure to do so results in a fine. When they remove it from the ground and dispose of it, the owner is released from their *responsibility* and they avoid the fine (the *ʿāwōn*). But, obviously, they are not removing the excrement from *themselves* even though removing the excrement is releasing them "from their contamination."

Or, imagine if someone else witnesses a pet owner not picking up the excrement and disposing of it and documents this omission. This witness then picks it up for them but also reports the incident to the authorities. The excrement is literally no longer there contaminating the public space, but the pet owner is still *liable* for their neglect and will "bear their iniquity [*ʿāwōn*]" and have to pay the fine.

This is like what is happening on the Day of Atonement. The contaminations from neglect are purged from the sanctuary, but the offenders are nevertheless still liable. But in all these cases, it does not make sense to imagine that the impurity, sin-contamination, or excrement is burrowed in the person just because the contamination "belongs" to them. Things can belong to people extrinsically and this is the case for sin-contamination, major ritual impurity (once the person reaches the penultimate level of ritual purity, of course), and pet excrement.

Now we can delve deeper into the notion of sacrificial atonement, which will strengthen the idea that atonement, by means of a purgation sacrifice, decontaminates sancta, not people.

What Does "Atonement" (*Kipper*) Mean and Do?

Milgrom's point that people are not being purged with a purgation sacrifice is further strengthened by observing how the purgation sacrifice is related to the act of "atonement" (*kipper*). This can be established from a few angles. For instance, Exod 30:10 specifies that it is the blood from a purgation sacrifice that effects atonement (hence their use in Lev 8:15 and 16:19) and since this blood is only ever applied to sancta, then this indicates that atonement only happens to sancta.

The Meaning of Kipper

It is worth lingering over the above point that Exod 30:10 already indicates that sacrificial atonement has something to do with *removing contaminations* from the sancta since *kipper* is accomplished with the blood of a purgation sacrifice. Scholars have long debated how the Hebrew root *k-p-r* is related to its conjugation in sacrificial contexts, in which it means "atone" in the sense of "purge" or "wipe away," and its use in economic contexts, where it means "ransom," or "the price of liberation."[59] Is there one basic concept informing two distinct meanings, or are these different conjugations "unrelated homographs"?[60] Just like we saw earlier, the same root letters in Hebrew can mean very different things. For example, the root *ḥ-ṭ-ʾ* can be used for the different nouns "sin" or "purgation," or the verbs "to sin" or "to purge/purify." English, obviously, uses different words for these distinct meanings. And, just as we would be led astray from what is being communicated if we always assumed that *ḥ-ṭ-ʾ* only means *one* of these meanings *all the time*, the same goes for *k-p-r*.

59. Milgrom, *Leviticus 1–16*, 255–26, 578, 1079–84; Levine, *In the Presence*, 56–77; Schwartz, "The Prohibitions Concerning the 'Eating' of Blood," 51–54; Gilders, *Blood Ritual*, 28–29, 135–39, 159–60, 164–78, 184; Feldman, *Story of Sacrifice*, 188–89.

60. Schwartz, "The Prohibitions," 54.

While we do not need to land on this issue firmly for the purposes of this project, the Greek Septuagint (LXX) is instructive. The LXX translations of the root *k-p-r* in the Torah use two different sets of words that coordinate to these different contexts, sacrificial versus financial.[61] In economic contexts where it means "ransom"/"price of liberation" the translators use the *lytron* word group (e.g., Exod 21:30; Num 35:31–32). But when it is used in a sacrificial context the translators use *exilaskomai*, "to atone"/"to expiate," or *hilasmos* "atonement"/"expiation" (e.g., Lev 4:20, 26, 31, 35; 25:9; Num 28:22, 30; 35:33[62]). This evinces that others have long understood at the very least that the root *k-p-r* usually requires different word groups when translated into another language.

Although these different uses and meanings are important—and this will be particularly relevant when it comes to analyzing key NT texts that speak about Jesus's death as a "ransom" (*lytron*) (Mark 10:45)—for the sake of argument here I will adopt Gilders's point that these distinct uses and meanings of the *k-p-r* root can nevertheless boil down to "a common base-meaning" such as "removal."[63] The genius of this is it "leave[s] open the question of what is removed and how."[64] Thus, when *k-p-r* denotes "ransom" what is being removed is the (potential) "danger of death" (Exod 21:29–30; Num 35:31–32) or "harm" (Exod 30:12, 15–16), or "the state of being enslaved" (Lev 19:20), etc., and the means of removal is a monetary payment. But when it denotes "atonement" what is being removed is "impurities and/or sin-contamination from the sanctuary" (16:16, 19, 34) and the means of removal is a purgation sacrifice, as Exod 30:10 states and as we observed above with the use of the *ḥaṭṭāʾt* for removing ritual impurities and sin-contaminations from the sanctuary.

61. English translations such as the NRSV and NASB usually follow suit and use "atone/ment" for sacrificial contexts and "ransom"/"redeem"/"redemption" in economic contexts.

62. Since land can be "redeemed" or "ransomed" in financial terms (Lev 25), the comment in Num 35:33 that "no *k-p-r* can be done for the blood that is shed on it" does not mean that "land is the type of thing that cannot be redeemed," but rather, that the "pollution" of blood (35:33) is the type of thing that cannot be "removed" or "wiped away," hence, "atoned." This is why the LXX translates v. 33 with *exilaskomai* rather than with *lytron*, which it used in vv. 31–33 when the referent was clearly to a monetary payment. Put another way, vv. 31–32 state that a ransom payment (*kōper*) cannot be made and v. 33 is stating that nothing besides the death of the murderer can remove or wipe away (*kipper*) the "pollution" of bloodshed from the land. The use of *k-p-r* in 35:33, then, carries the notion of "sacrificial atonement" rather than "ransom payment" and is saying that making an atoning sacrifice cannot purge the land of bloodshed.

63. Gilders, *Blood Ritual*, 29.

64. Gilders, *Blood Ritual*, 29.

This is why, as Feldman says, "The basic meaning of כפר [*kipper*] in the priestly narrative is 'to decontaminate' . . . [and] the use of this verb always signals the decontamination of the altar or some part of the tent of meeting."[65] Moreover, in sacrificial contexts, Gilders observes that since "*kipper* refers to the 'removal' of both impurity *and* the state of being common (*ḥōl*)" this means "*kipper* serves as a 'hypernym' for the other two verbs [purify and consecrate]."[66] The LXX translators of Exod 29:36–37 agree since they translate *kipper* there with *hagiazō*, "to sanctify/consecrate," apparently since prior to consecration, in alignment with what I argued above, there can be no ritual or sin contaminations on the altar that need to be removed. There is just a pile of rocks that need to be made holy. They are made holy by being "purified" (*ḥiṭṭē* ͗) with the *ḥaṭṭā* ͗*t* sacrifice. The *ḥaṭṭā* ͗*t* has inherent sanctifying powers, as we saw above. It consecrates whatever it touches and can thereby be used after the altar has been consecrated in other "rituals of removal" (atonement) to purge whatever contaminates it thereafter, which reconsecrates it. Therefore, as Gilders further explains, "when *kipper* refers to *ḥaṭṭaā* ͗*t* blood manipulations, I conclude that it [*kipper*] includes all of the specific effects that can be attributed to those ritual actions. It is the general term, the 'hypernym,' while verbs such as *ḥiṭṭē* ͗ (purify),[67] *ṭihar* (cleanse)[68] and *qiddēš* (consecrate) are more specific."[69]

In other words, we can think of *kipper* as "effecting removal" but *what* is being "removed" is not always the same thing. When *kipper* consecrates, the state of "commonness" is being removed. When *kipper* purifies, either ritual impurities or sin-contamination is being removed. As we will get to in detail shortly, the direct object of sacrificial *kipper* is always sancta; people are never the objects of *kipper*. This means that *kipper* is effecting the removal of certain states/contaminations *from the sancta*.

I have been using "atone/ment/ing" as a place holder for *kipper* for the most part up to this point, and some readers will have picked up that I have also already been using the words "remove(al)" and "decontaminate" to further gloss *kipper* in sacrificial contexts. From here on out, I will mostly avoid "atone/ment" and stick with "decontaminate" or use the transliteration

65. Feldman, *Story of Sacrifice*, 188.

66. Gilders, *Blood Ritual*, 137; his emphasis, my brackets.

67. I have been translating this as "purge" to provide an umbrella term for the purgative function of the *ḥaṭṭā* ͗*t* that is used to both purge ritual impurities and purge sin-contamination.

68. I have been translating this as "purify" again to try to provide more clarity within all these distinct Hebrew verbs since this verb is only used in the context of ritual impurities.

69. Gilders, *Blood Ritual*, 137.

kipper. For instance, I will refer to the Day of Atonement as the "Day of Decontamination" and to atoning sacrifices as "decontaminating sacrifices." I do this not only for variety, but also as an instructive defamiliarization technique.

The Object(s) of Kipper

The word *kipper* "can never have a personal direct object."[70] A direct object is the thing in a sentence that directly receives the action of the verb. For example, in the sentence, "He cleansed the floor," "he" is the subject, "cleansed" is the verb and "the floor" is the direct object because it receives the action of the verb. For the verb *kipper*, only literal objects, and more specifically, holy objects at the dwelling place that have become contaminated, can receive the decontaminating action of *kipper*.

How the process of decontamination relates to both holy objects and people differently is made apparent by the distinct grammatical constructions in the same verse speaking about the supreme act of *kipper* on Yom Kippur, "the Day of Decontamination." In Hebrew, direct objects are marked by the particle *ʾet* and Lev 16:33 makes it clear that only sancta get decontaminated:

> He shall decontaminate [*ʾet*] the holy sanctuary, and he shall decontaminate [*ʾet*] the tent of meeting and [*ʾet*] the altar, and he shall decontaminate for [*ʿal*] the priests and for [*ʿal*] all the people of the assembly.

Again, direct objects receive the action of the verb. This means the sanctuary, the altar, and the dwelling place as whole receive the action of *kipper*—blood is only being applied to these things and this means they are the only things getting atoned. People are related to the action of *kipper* differently, which is clear from the grammar throughout the priestly literature.[71]

The idea that *kipper* applied to sancta was well known and widespread in Second Temple Judaism. The author of Hebrews says that blood "purges"

70. Milgrom, "Sacrifices and Offerings, OT," 766; cf. "Israel's Sanctuary," 391; Levine, *In the Presence*, 64, 111.

71. See Baden, "The Purpose of Purification." Analyzing various prepositions in Leviticus gets complex and we do not need to delve into those details here. But when the syntactical analysis is complete, Baden's shows how there is a singular point being made in these passages through the use of distinct prepositions: the "object being purged is not the individual, not the offeror of the sacrifices or prayers, but the sanctuary . . . on behalf of Aaron and his household . . . and on behalf of the people" ("The Purpose of Purification," 20–21).

(*katharizō*) the objects of the physical dwelling place, which are "imitations" (*hypodeigmata*) of the sancta in the heavens, which then were purged upon Jesus's ascension to that heavenly and true dwelling place (Heb 9:22–24; cf. vv. 11–12).[72] Blood is the purgative element for both the earthly and heavenly sancta. Similarly, in the Mishnah, "Rabbi Meir says, 'the decontaminating effects [*k-p-r* root: *kappārāt*] of all the goats [used as *ḥaṭṭā ʾt* sacrifices referenced earlier] are [brought] for the same reason: for the impurity of the sanctuary and its sancta" (m. Šebu. 1:4).[73] And then two more times he repeats: "all of them [the *ḥaṭṭā ʾt* sacrifices] are brought to effect decontamination [*ləkappēr*] for the impurity of the sanctuary and its sancta" (1:4, 5). In *no* instance are *people themselves* being decontaminated. Rather, the sancta are being decontaminated with *ḥaṭṭā ʾt* sacrifices for the contaminations people *impart to the sanctuary*.

To return to our example sentence, if we expanded it to say, "He cleansed the floor for the children," we can better grasp what Lev 16:33 is saying. Just as it would be mistaken to interpret this sentence as "He cleansed the children," it is mistaken to take Lev 16:33 to mean that people themselves are being decontaminated. Rather, "He cleaned the floor for the children" means it is the floor that was cleaned, that "the children" were responsible for making the floor dirty, and that "he" took care of it and cleaned the floor on their behalf. The priests ("he") function in relation to the dwelling place ("the floor") and the Israelites ("the children") in a similar

72. Granted the comment, "Without the shedding of blood there is no forgiveness of sins" in Heb 9:22 is difficult, because at face value it is incorrect. As I've shown, forgiveness *can* and *does* happen apart from the sacrificial system and blood from a purgation sacrifice, let alone the shedding of human blood. This statement, however, is restricted to "the law" (9:22) and "purging" or "cleansing" the dwelling place and its sancta (9:21–23) from the contaminations clinging to it (from either ritual impurities or sins). But even with this limited scope in mind, the statement is still exaggerated because some things are cleansed *without* the shedding of blood, even in the law (e.g., water is used in Lev 6:19–20 [27–28 Eng.] and 16:26 to cleanse the holy priestly vestments and holy bronze vessels; fire and water is used in Num 31:22–23 for gold, silver, bronze, iron, tin, and lead vessels). Nevertheless, the author of Hebrews is likely aware of these exceptions because they hedge by saying that *"nearly"* or *"almost"* (*schedon*) all things are cleansed by blood (9:22). What the author of Hebrews is claiming is therefore not a totalizing generalization that forgiveness of any and all sins always requires blood (see my discussion in chapter 6, especially regarding Heb 10:18 and 26). Rather, the claim is restricted to what contaminates the dwelling place and its sancta. That is, since "*nearly* everything" (9:22) associated with the dwelling place and its sancta are purged by means of the blood from a purgation sacrifice (9:21–22), the heavenly counterparts have likewise been purged, but with an even greater ritual detergent: Jesus's life-blood (9:23–25).

73. My translation. Hebrew from Ms. Kaufmann. Hungarian Academy of Sciences, Budapest, Ms. A 50. Accessed through OakTree Software, Inc. (2009).

manner. Only the priests have access to the altar and the inner sancta of the dwelling place (e.g., Num 18:1–7). This means the Israelites are prevented from physically being able to decontaminate the contaminations (from sins or ritual impurities) they imparted on the altar. They do not have access to the objects that need purging, so they need someone else to do this for them. This is why the grammar always says that decontamination (*kipper*) takes place "for" (*ʿal*) them. This is the role of the priests, "to effect removal of the contaminations [*kipper*] on their behalf" (4:20, 26, 31, 35; 5:6, 10, 13, 16, 18, 26 [6:7 Eng.]; 10:17; 12:7, 8; 14:18–20, 31; 15:15, 30; 16:30, 33–34).

When the decontamination takes place, the individual (or all Israel on the Day of Decontamination) has fulfilled their responsibility to purge their impurities and/or sins from the sancta.[74] Bringing their *ḥaṭṭāʾt* to the priest is as much as a lay Israelite can do with respect to purging the sanctuary. They can just bring the cleaning supplies, but the priests have to be the ones who physically decontaminate the sancta since they are the only ones with access to them.

Combining the previous analogy to the pet owner one earlier, we can think of it like this: Some parents adopted a dog for their children who are learning to take on more and more responsibilities. The dog is considered the *children's* dog—this was what the children have been dreaming of and were promised would be *theirs* once they adopted a dog. But the parents always knew they would have to have a major role to play in taking care of it. For example, when they are out walking the dog in public spaces they teach their children about the importance of removing any of their dog's excrement. Once their dog defecates, they incur a liability (they become "guilty" [*ʾāšām*]) to remove the excrement from the public space and if they do not, then they would have to pay a fine ("bear their iniquity [*ʿāwōn*]") (cf. Lev 4:22, 27; 5:1–5, 17).

Let's imagine the parents also think the children are too young and perhaps too uncoordinated to handle the fecal matter directly—perhaps the parents do not want either the excrement to get on their children's fingers or clothes, or maybe they do not want their children to gag and vomit, or throw it at each other, etc. The parents know they have to be the ones to remove the excrement from the public space, but they want their children to have a share in the process. So they have the children be the ones to carry the waste baggies and hand sanitizer so that when the time comes to clean up the excrement, the children can bring the baggies to them and once the excrement has been placed in the bag and thrown away they can sanitize their hands. In this way, the children learn that *they* are responsible to

74. Milgrom, *Leviticus 1–16*, 256.

remove *their* (dog's) messes and that they are released from this obligation by bringing the decontamination supplies to their parents who physically carry out the process of removing the mess from the public space on their behalf.

This is basically what is depicted in Levitical sacrificial system of decontamination. We can supplement the last sentence of the previous paragraph in this way: The children (Israelites) learn that *they* are responsible to remove *their* messes (ritual impurities and/or sin-contaminations) and that they are released from this obligation by bringing the decontamination supplies (the *ḥaṭṭā ʾt*) to their parents (priests) who physically carry out the process of removing the mess (*kipper*) from the public space (the sanctuary) on their behalf.

Only sancta receive the action of *kipper*. Priests are engaging in this ritual process of contamination removal *for* those who contaminated it somehow (through a major impurity or an inadvertent sin), but *kipper* is not happening "to" or "on" those people.

Now, why is it that "blood" is "the purging element, the ritual detergent"?[75]

Blood Is Life

I discussed at length in chapter 1 how, as Moffitt states, "the death or slaughter of the [sacrificial] victim, while necessary to procure the blood, has no particular atoning significance in and of itself."[76] In chapter 1, I was primarily concerned to show how and why Levitical sacrifice was neither about *substitutionary* death nor about *death*. But why is blood necessary for rituals of contamination removal?

This all comes as a surprise to many I have taught, but Dennis J. McCarthy has shown how for Israel's geographical and cultural neighbors in western and eastern Mesopotamia, "the basic concept of sacrifice . . . for all their diversity, is remarkably unitary."[77] "Sacrifice is offering food to the gods, and *blood as such had no special, explicit part in it*."[78] Moreover, "ordinary Greek sacrifice did not bother about the blood."[79] However, blood was part of "the cult of the dead and the netherworld," but this means "blood

75. Milgrom, "Israel's Sanctuary," 391.

76. Moffitt, "Blood, Life, and Atonement," 219.

77. McCarthy, "Symbolism of Blood and Sacrifice," 168.

78. McCarthy, "Symbolism of Blood and Sacrifice," 168; my emphasis.

79. McCarthy, "Symbolism of Blood and Sacrifice," 170.

is connected with death, not life."[80] And when blood is put to ritual use (distinct from sacrifice *per se*) in places like Babylonia, "blood belongs to the gods of death, not life."[81]

In the Torah, by contrast, blood is consistently identified with the "life" of the creature and therefore people are banned from (a) consuming blood and (b) shedding blood (Gen 9:4–6; Lev 17:3–4, 10–11, 14; Deut 12:23–25). As McCarthy concludes, "the explicit claim that blood is life and so divine remains isolated to Israel."[82] I argued in chapter 1 how the priestly perspective on the ritual of proper sacrifices (right place, right blood rituals) and proper blood rituals when eating animals that cannot be sacrificed reconceptualizes the obvious death of the animal such that when carrying out these rituals, there is no guilt of "bloodshed." No matter what sacrifice is being offered—a well-being offering, burnt offering, purgation offering, reparation offering—*bloodshed* is not happening from this ritual point of view. But now we know that these sacrifices have various functions. Some are used in the rituals that remove contaminations from sancta, but some do not have this purpose at all. Here we can connect what was argued before regarding bloodshed and sacrifices to help us make sense of the use of blood in particular for the decontaminating sacrifices.

Whereas the other verses listed link the identification of blood and life to not eating blood and not shedding blood, Lev 17:11 specifically links this identification with the power of blood to effect removal (*kipper*) on the altar:

> For the life of the flesh is in the blood; and I have given it to you for making atonement [*ləkappēr*] for your lives *on the altar*; for, as life, it is the blood that makes atonement [*yəkappēr*]. (NRSV; my emphasis)

Before we discuss some important debates on this verse, we can already draw a few conclusions. Even though "the *general* explanation of sacrifice in terms of blood as life and so somehow divine would . . . be relatively late [in terms of the history of ancient civilizations] and specifically Israelite," it shows why blood became "a vehicle of divine purification and life."[83] Given that ritual impurity and sin-contamination defile the sanctuary because they are linked with the forces of death, it makes sense that the ritual means of purging these death-contaminations from sancta is going to be a substance

80. McCarthy, "Symbolism of Blood and Sacrifice," 170.

81. McCarthy, "Symbolism of Blood and Sacrifice," 172.

82. McCarthy, "Symbolism of Blood and Sacrifice," 174.

83. McCarthy, "Symbolism of Blood and Sacrifice," 176; his emphasis.

that becomes identified with "life." The power of life overwhelms the forces of death. If Israel's neighbors were aware of the Israelite use of blood it might have struck them as profoundly counterintuitive since for them blood was linked with death, as we saw, but the use of blood as a decontaminating detergent makes sense within the Levitical conceptual framework. Thus, when a person's ritual impurity or sin infects the sanctuary, they are responsible to bring the life-disinfectant to the priest who can then decontaminate the sancta on behalf of the person who cannot access the holy spaces and objects.

Now, there are few options for what this verse is claiming in particular with its use of *kipper*, but we can rule out "substitutionary death" since one of the main points of Israel's sacrificial system as a whole was to negate the idea that they were shedding blood and bringing death into the presence of God through ritual.[84] The logic of what is taking place in these decontamination rituals is not "something that bleeds needs to die or else the offender will bear the consequences," but rather, "we need something to purge this death contamination from God's holy dwelling place so that God does not abandon it—we need *life*." Recall, though, how if a person neglects their responsibility to purge away their contaminations, then they are held responsible (they will "bear their iniquity") for this failure even though the Day of Decontamination will purge it all away from the holy of holies. But it does not follow that bringing the "cleaning supplies" for the priests to carry out the rituals of removal means a substitutionary death is taking place. The point of the *ḥaṭṭāʾt* process for individuals was for them to take individual responsibility for their own contaminations on the sanctuary in some fashion, just like having children carry and provide bags and sanitizer for dealing with dog excrement gives them some measure of personal responsibility for removing their pet's excrement from public spaces.

Ironically, there is a type of "substitutionary" logic in Leviticus that is instructive. But it is not a substitution of animals dying instead of humans, but rather a substitution of birds for quadrupeds, or flour for birds and quadrupeds if the offerer is poor (Lev 5:5–13). If a person cannot afford a lamb or goat, they can instead offer two birds, but if they cannot afford (or catch) the birds, they can instead simply offer flour as a *ḥaṭṭāʾt* (5:11–13).[85] This proves that while the ideal ritual process of removing contaminations from the sancta would involve *the* symbol of pure life—blood—the process is more about *individuals* doing *their part* to maintain the sanctity of God's dwelling place so that the mere gesture of handing a handful of their flour

84. See also Milgrom, *Leviticus 17–22*, 1477.

85. For more on this passage, see Peres, "Bloodless 'Atonement.'"

to the priest suffices. Another way of putting it: the fact that it is even conceivable for Leviticus to claim that an offering of *grain* can be a legitimate *ḥaṭṭāʾt* necessarily excludes the theory that the *ḥaṭṭāʾt* is a substitutionary death, symbolically spilling the blood of the offerer, because this offering is literally bloodless.

The important point in the Levitical purgation process for ritual impurities and sins is that it is the individual's responsibility to clean up their "mess" and this is why they need to be personally responsible to bring the decontaminating "detergent" themselves. And they need to be the rightful *owners* of the ritual disinfectant. The fact that a mere handful of flour will do the job (5:11) if a person cannot afford to literally offer *ḥaṭṭāʾt* blood shows that this whole ritual process has more to do with simply, as parents might say to growing children, taking personal responsibility to clean up after themselves. Recall the single-hand-laying gesture discussion from chapter 1 where we learned it means "rightful ownership."[86] This is why "ownership" is key. The whole process depends on individual Israelites taking personal responsibility for their whole community's well-being by cleaning up their own "messes" that would cause God to abandon a desecrated dwelling place if left untreated. This is why one's *own* flour can substitute for animal blood.

Ideally, for the symbolic value, the cleansing agent should be pure life. The logic of requiring defect-free animal blood in Lev 22:19–25 is not the death of the animal. Rather, considering the rationale in Lev 17:11, their blood is a great symbol of pure life. Therefore, their blood "has the potential to be used on the altar for purification,"[87] as Feldman notes, "even if only some of it actually does."[88] This is why all animal blood needs to be handled in the proper ritual way—either on the altar or on the ground and covered (17:5–6, 11, 13–15)—otherwise it is treated as shedding blood (murder) (17:3–4). Surely if going about these blood rituals renders sacrifices as "not shedding blood" then it is illogical to suggest that the sacrifices is a substitution for shedding the offerer's blood. What is more, neither "ransom" nor "atonement sacrifice" can be made to substitute for someone who is worthy of death (Num 35:31–34). Therefore, the logic of decontaminating sacrifices is not "something that bleeds needs to *die*," but rather "we need a substance capable of *purging* the forces of death—we need pure *life*."

86. In chapter 1, we learned how the single-hand gesture means "this is *mine*, I rightfully *own* this," rather than "this is *me*, and it is *dying in my place*."

87. Feldman, *Story of Sacrifice*, 187.

88. Feldman, *Story of Sacrifice*, 186.

What Does Kipper *Mean in Leviticus 17:11?*

From this vantage point we can enter the debate on what precise meaning *kipper* has in Lev 17:11. Does it mean "ransom"[89] or "decontaminate"[90] or perhaps some combination of the two?[91] To begin, Feldman provides persuasive reasons to prefer "decontaminate":

> The basic meaning of כפר [*kipper*] in the priestly narrative is "to decontaminate." With very few exceptions, the use of this verb always signals the decontamination of the altar or some part of the tent of meeting.[92] The exact phrase לכפר על נפשתיכם [used in Lev 17:11] . . . [only occurs in Exod 30:15 and Num 31:50.] In both of these cases, the context makes it clear that a monetary offering is made in exchange for a human life. . . . In these two occurrences, כפר should be translated as "to ransom" and treated as a denominative piel verb from the root כֹּפֶר [*kōper*] (payment, ransom). It does not necessarily follow, however, that the same translation should be employed in Lev 17:11. The context of Exod 30 and Num 31 is markedly different than Lev 17:11. In both Exod 30 and Num 31, the context is monetary. . . . Lev 17:11 lacks the monetary context, and there is nowhere else in the Priestly Narrative where this monetary concept is imported into a sacrificial context. Rather than positing a unique occurrence of כפר in a sacrificial context meaning "ransom," it is simpler to suggest that כפר in Lev 17:11 means precisely what it means everywhere else in the Priestly Narrative: to decontaminate.[93]

Although I ultimately side with Feldman for "decontaminate," I want to show how even if "ransom" is meant, it nevertheless precludes a "substitutionary death" meaning.

For example, Milgrom holds that *kipper* means "ransom" just here in Lev 17:11,[94] but explicitly concludes, "the substitutionary theory of sacrifice,

89. Milgrom, *Leviticus 1–16*, 706–13; Milgrom, *Leviticus 17–22*, 1472–79; Schwartz, "The Prohibitions," 51–60.

90. Feldman, *Story of Sacrifice*, 188–98.

91. Gilders, *Blood Ritual*, 168–78.

92. Feldman has a footnote here that is worth citing: "When it does not refer to purification, the word is כֹּפֶר instead [*kōper*] of a piel form of כפר. See Gen 6:14, Exod 30:15–16; Num 31:50" (*Story of Sacrifice*, 188n133).

93. Feldman, *Story of Sacrifice*, 188–89.

94. But Milgrom thinks that *kipper* means "purify, purge" in the rest of the sacrificial contexts (*Leviticus 1–16*, 1079–84). I agree with his point, but, as noted earlier, in order to try to be more precise with the different Hebrew verbs being used in Leviticus, I

based largely on this verse and championed by so many in the scholarly world, must once and for all be rejected."[95] Essentially, Milgrom argues that *kipper* means "ransom" here in 17:11 because this verse is offered as a solution to the problem that killing an animal is shedding blood and thereby causes the person to become guilty of murder (17:3–4).[96] "Thus the function of the blood on the altar is to ransom the life of the one who offered it."[97] However, Milgrom also thinks 17:11 only applies to the well-being/eaten-sacrifices mentioned in 17:5, 7–8.[98] But, as he admits:

> Ostensibly, this conclusion faces two contradictions:
> 1. The *šĕlāmîm* is the one sacrifice that has no *kippûr* function.
> 2. No sacrifice can expiate a deliberate sin [e.g., Num 15:30–31], not to speak of a capital crime [e.g., 35:30–34]![99]

He then suggests that 17:11 "offers the remedy: the blood ransoms the offerer's life and clears him of the charge of murder."[100] Granted, though I follow Feldman against Milgrom, this is a viable reading of Lev 17. So, what would Milgrom's view mean for our purposes?

---

restrict "purge" for the *ḥaṭṭāʾt* sacrifices, "purify" for becoming pure from ritual impurities, and "decontaminate" for *kipper*.

95. Milgrom, *Leviticus 17–22*, 1477.

96. Milgrom, *Leviticus 17–22*, 1472–79.

97. Milgrom, *Leviticus 17–22*, 1474.

98. Milgrom, *Leviticus 17–22*, 1474–75. But Lev 17:8 also mentions burnt offerings so I do not agree with Milgrom's restrictions of 17:11 to the well-being sacrifices. Moreover, as Feldman notes in response to Milgrom: "The blood described in vv. 10–12 should be understood as the blood of any slaughtered animal, not just the blood of a well-being offering. While the first law in vv. 3–7 treat only the well-being offering, the second law in vv. 8–9 explants to treat both the well-being and the whole burnt offerings. This third law expands the topic even further to treat כל דם , all blood. The broader context, and the allusion to the original blood prohibition in Gen 9:4, suggests that the blood in question here is the blood of any animal, even if it is only the blood of some animals, offered in a certain way, that actually purifies the altar. . . . [I]t could be argued that all sacrifices (including the well-being offerings) are being attributed a purificatory function here. This would contradict Yahweh's earlier speeches, in which only the purification [what I call 'purgation'] and guilt [what I call 'reparation'] offerings had a purificatory function. There is a simple explanation for the assertion made in vv. 10–11, however. All blood has the potential to purify, even if only some of it actually does" (*Story of Sacrifice*, 186). To the latter point, this is why attending to the distinct blood manipulations (dashing, daubing, sprinkling, etc.) for distinct sacrifices matters. The non-decontaminating sacrifices have distinct blood rituals (cf. Josephus, *Ant.* 3.231, who notes that the purgation offering blood rites differs from the thanksgiving offering). This will be crucial when discussing Jesus's comments at the Lord's Supper.

99. Milgrom, *Leviticus 17–22*, 1474.

100. Milgrom, *Leviticus 17–22*, 1474.

First, we can take on board Milgrom's claim that the overall function of Lev 17 is to nullify the charge of murder without taking on board his views either that 17:11 is restricted to the well-being sacrifices or that *kipper* means "ransom" here.[101] The murder charge disappears no matter what, because Lev 17 as a whole is claiming that the necessary ending of an animal's life when it is used for any of the various sacrifices (e.g., burnt, well-being, purgation) means the sacrificial animal can be reconceptualized as a "sacrifice" rather than murder. And given this reconceptualization, this in turn means that there is no "bloodguilt" that needs "ransoming" anymore. From this ritualized point of view, if no "ransom" is needed because no blood has been *shed*, then it is very doubtful that *kipper* in 17:11 means "ransom" since a "ransom" would be otiose at that point. Instead, blood-as-life (not blood-as-[substitutionary]-death) has been placed on the altar as a "decontaminating" detergent. So Milgrom's point about nullifying the charge of murder can be folded into Feldman's argument that *kipper* means "decontamination" quite seamlessly.

That said, for the sake of argument, Lev 17:11 might be saying: "If you do not pay back this animal's life to me on the altar, then your life will be required of you, per Gen 9." But—and this is important—it would be illogical for 17:11 to be saying the animal is functioning as a substitutionary death for the offerer. All it would be saying on Milgrom's reading is something like:

> Killing an animal is murder and a capital crime, with one exception. The only exception is ritually killing an animal as a sacrifice and/or for food (either a clean animal for sacrifice or clean game for food) *if and only if its blood is ritually handled in the proper way at the proper place*. Blood equals "life" and the "life" of the animal needs to be returned ("paid back as a ransom") to God, either on the altar or on the ground and buried for animals that are ineligible for sacrifice.

Thus, for domesticated animals eligible for sacrifice, according to Lev 17:11 God is saying: "I have designated the altar as the depository for this payment. If you do not pay back the animal's life to me in this way and in this place, then your life will be required of you." For clean game that is hunted, Lev 17:13–16 says that God has designated the ground and dirt as the depository. The blood is only considered "paid back" in these scenarios if it goes on the ground and is then covered with dirt.

In other words, on Milgrom's reading of *kipper* as "ransom," the requirement for human life in Lev 17:11 cannot be *prior* to the sacrifice, but immediately *subsequent* to the act of killing an animal as sacrifice (or as

101. As argued in chapter 1 (and see footnote 98 just above).

food for vv. 13–16). At the moment of slaughter, "murder" and "bloodshed" technically took place (v. 4). The only way for it to be reconceptualized into a "non-murder" is if subsequently the animal's life (blood) is placed on the altar (or on the ground and covered with dirt for clean game). In this way the animal's *own* blood is the self-same "ransom" payment required for taking its life, but *only* if it is deposited in the right place so that it goes back to God.

In any other context, when an animal murder happens, then not only is the animal's blood *shed*, but the blood of the human who murdered it is also required by definition of being "bloodguilty."[102] Two bloodsheds occur in this scenario (first the animals, then the murder's). This is the "life for life" principle (cf. Exod 21:23; Lev 24:17–18; Deut 19:21). However, in the case of sacrifice (or hunting clean game), then only *one* bloodshed happens: the animal's just prior to being offered up as a sacrifice on the altar (or prior to its blood being poured on the ground and covered). If the animal's own blood is used as prescribed in Lev 17:11–13—either on the altar or on the ground and covered with dirt—then *this nullifies the need for the person's life to be forfeit*. The return of the animal's life to God has been accepted as a sufficient "ransom" payment.

Writing out the ideal sacrifice scenario in sequence will provide necessary clarity. I will use "legitimate sacrifice" to indicate that the blood is handled appropriately and at the right place. Again, the presupposition of Lev 17 is that by default killing an animal is murder (17:4).

Ideal legitimate sacrifice: An Israelite intends to offer a sacrifice of well-being to have a sacred meal (Lev 17:6, 8). An ethical problem emerges at the moment of slaughter because this is a technically a murder, which means this Israelite is bloodguilty and should die as well (17:4) (i.e., "life for life," 24:18; cf. Gen 9:5; Exod 21:23; Deut 19:21).[103] But God now ordains that so long as the animal's blood is placed on the altar, then this technically functions as the "ransom" payment for the one who just murdered the animal (17:11). The necessary "fine" for taking the animal's life, which is normally remitted by the murder's own life, is instead considered paid in full if the animal's life is simply paid/given back to God on the altar. This

102. Indirect responsibility for the death of another person's animal property needs to be appropriately compensated, but bloodguilt is not attributed to the person (Exod 21:33–36).

103. Again, non-Israelites would simply be responsible for the protocol in Gen 9:3–6, but Israelites are now subject to the framework in Lev 17. For Israelites, even if they refrained from consuming blood, if they eat meat by any other process, then they are considered guilty of murder for killing the animal and thus, God will "require" "[their] blood of [their] lives" (Gen 9:5). Similarly, Schwartz, "Leviticus," 236.

is the only way in which to "make peace" or "restitution" after killing an animal eligible for sacrifice (cf. 24:18, 21).

This is why understanding the transformative power of ritual from chapter 1 is crucial. The sacrificial blood rituals are for giving the animal's life-blood back to God where it belongs. It is a ritual rationale of "no harm, no foul" so to speak. Everything is back in its (ritual) place when the animal's life-blood is placed back where it belongs (to God). In other words, when all is said and done, if animal slaughter is done in this way *as a legitimate sacrifice*, then no "murder" actually happened and so the one who sacrificed the animal is not actually bloodguilty. "Murder" and "bloodguiltiness" has been completely nullified by the ritual prescriptions.

What is definitely not happening is a scenario in which the offerer's life is *already* required of them *prior* to offering the sacrifice and they are offering an animal as a substitutionary death in place of their own deserved death. The offerer's life is only technically required of them when they slaughter the animal about to be offered as a sacrifice. According to Lev 17, this bloodguilt is only abstractly and temporarily real, but is actually and ritually nonexistent because it is immediately nullified by proper blood rituals that re-place the animal's life in its proper place (back to God). This means Lev 17:1–12 is providing the behind-the-scenes ritual logic that justifies legitimate animal sacrifice by explaining why it is not considered a murder even though, according to Leviticus, the killing of animals by default is considered murder.

But now we are back to where we can take on board Milgrom's point that Lev 17 is all about nullifying the liability of being bloodguilty. But this also means this point actually renders the translation of *kipper* as "ransom" otiose since, ritually speaking, no blood is being shed. Thus, it is better to read Lev 17:11 as stating why blood is used as the ritual means of effecting removal of contaminates on the altar (i.e., as "decontaminate") because of its identification with life, the opposite of the forces of death that contaminate the sancta.

In any case, this overall point needs to be set forth and grasped because once it is, then it is apparent that Lev 17:11 is not saying: "If someone is liable to be put to death, then they can offer an animal sacrifice as substitutionary death that ransoms their life." Rather, it is explaining why even though all killings of animals are normally considered murder, and thereby under the "life for life" prescription, legitimate sacrifices are not considered murder because no blood is being shed according to the ritual conception. These events are ritually reconceptualized and recategorized. A murder occurs when a living being "takes" the life of another living being. And the reason offered in Lev 17:11 for why legitimate sacrifice is not murder is because the animal's life is not being "taken" since it is put back where it belongs (to God on the altar). The logic for why killing game for food is not murder is similar, though the depository to giving the animal's life back where it belongs changes (the ground and covered with dirt). In both cases, however, the ritual blood manipulations function so that the person is not liable for bloodshed.

In the end, all the elements that we have learned about come together here: the reason blood can be used to decontaminate sancta is because, as "life," blood can be used to overwhelm and thus purge "the forces of death" from the sanctuary so that it remains consecrated and therefore suitable for God's holy presence to remain in the dwelling place.

Understanding the Purpose of the Day of Decontamination

I pointed out above that not all sins contaminate the sanctuary equally. The individual purgation sacrifices can only be offered for inadvertent or repentant sins (e.g., Lev 4:2, 22, 27; 5:2–4, 15–18, 21–24 [6:2–5 Eng.]; Num 15:27–29) and the sin-contaminations from these only permeate the sanctuary up to the outer altar since this is where the *ḥaṭṭāʾt* blood is placed (Lev 4:25, 29, 34). Sins from the high priest or whole congregation of Israel, however, contaminate into the dwelling place proper since the *ḥaṭṭāʾt* blood is brought into the holy place and "daubed" (*nātan*) on the horns of the incense altar and "sprinkled" (*hizzâ*) before the veil separating the holy of holies from the holy place (4:5–7, 16–18).[104] Priests are not allowed to eat from any *ḥaṭṭāʾt* whose blood is carried into the holy place and beyond; the flesh from these animals needs to be burned outside the camp (not just outside the dwelling place) (6:30; 16:27). And finally, any deliberate unrepentant sin (*pešaʿ*), which would include intentionally neglecting to properly deal with minor and major ritual impurities, contaminates the holy of holies itself. These sins are purged from the sanctuary and then removed to the wilderness only once a year on the Day of Decontamination (15:31; 16:16, 21).

Thus, the purpose of the Day of Decontamination is straightforward, as Baden puts it: "The ritual of Leviticus 16 is a reset button for the sanctuary, restoring the Tabernacle to its original factory settings."[105] It accomplishes this especially by removing those contaminations left unaddressed by members of the community, so that God does not abandon the dwelling place.

104. Attending to the distinct verbs for specific blood manipulations and their attendant functions will be important later.

105. Baden, "The Purpose of Purification," 26.

Before outlining the various sacrifices and their important sequence on the Day of Decontamination we can immediately debunk another common misconception. No one is allowed into the holy of holies except for the high priest and he is only permitted to enter once a year on the Day of Decontamination (16:2, 29–34). Breaching these protocols means death (16:2). But it is often assumed by Christians that what keeps the high priest alive is that he enters the holy of holies with blood that is functioning as a "substitutionary death." Yet we know this cannot be what the blood is doing because according to 16:12–13, it is the *incense smoke* that the high priest brings into the holy of holies that *prevents him from dying*; not the purgation blood. The threat of death is announced in 16:2 and only brought up again in 16:12–13, but only in connection with bringing in incense smoke. Therefore, the blood from the purgation sacrifices that he brings in after (16:14–15) is used not to keep the high priest alive. Blood cannot be functioning as a "substitutionary death" here (or anywhere in Leviticus).

In addition to this ritual of incense, five animals are used (Lev 16:3, 5–6). One bull to serve as a purgation sacrifice for the priests (per Lev 4:1–12), two goats for the people, one of which serves as a purgation sacrifice (per 4:22) and one that is not sacrificed, but remains alive and is sent out of the camp and into the wilderness (16:20–22), and two rams for burnt offerings for the priests and people respectively offered at the very end (16:24–25).

There is a simplicity to the whole process that is easy to miss amid the details given in Lev 16. Feldman captures this wonderfully: "Much like someone who sweeps a multi-room home, the dirt is pushed from the innermost space to the outermost space before it is completely removed from the home."[106] This is the progression we see with respect to the dwelling place. At each stage "[t]he contamination is moved further and further from Yahweh."[107]

First the holy of holies is decontaminated (16:14–15), then the holy place (16:16–17), then the courtyard via the outer altar (16:18–19). After all the contaminations are removed from the sancta, everything is loaded onto the live goat and hauled away out of the camp and into the wilderness (16:20–22). As Feldman explains:

> When the goat carries this contamination, it carries them out of Yahweh's presence and to an area that is far enough removed that they can no longer have an effect on him. Just as a person afflicted with impurifying skin disease is sent beyond the borders

106. Feldman, *Story of Sacrifice*, 163.

107. Feldman, *Story of Sacrifice*, 163.

> of the camp so they do not affect Yahweh, this goat is similarly banished.[108]

And finally, now that the contaminations have been eliminated and the altar has been reconsecrated (16:19; cf. 8:15), the burnt offerings are made (16:24–25) to signal that the dwelling place has been "rebooted" (to use Baden's "factory reset" analogy from above). Just as the reconsecration of the altar reenacts the initial consecration in 8:15, the burnt offerings serve as reenactment of the same at sanctuary's inauguration (8:18–21; 9:12–14). The contaminations are gone, there is only the "pleasing aroma" from the burnt offerings there to attract God's continued presence.

Here we need to go into a little more detail. After the incense ritual in the holy of holies (16:12–13), the high priest decontaminates the holy of holies by "sprinkling" (*hizzâ*) the lid on the ark of the covenant and the space before the ark with the *ḥaṭṭāʾt* blood (16:14–15). He does this first with the purgation blood from the bull for himself and his sons (16:14) and then the same thing with the purgation blood from the goat for the people (16:15).

The next verse specifies what has been removed from the holy of holies by these rituals—"impurities" (*tumʾōt*) "willful sins" (*pišʿê*), and "inadvertent sins" (*ḥaṭṭōʾt*) (16:16)—but they have only been moved from the holy of holies and into the holy place.[109] Thus he needs to "effect decontamination in the holy place" (16:17; cf. 16:16); and these blood rituals for the holy place were already prescribed (4:1–21). This is why 16:16–17 does not repeat the instructions but only states that no other priest is allowed in there while the high priest is decontaminating the holy place.

By performing these rituals first in the holy of holies and then in the holy place, the high priest only "pushes the three different categories of contaminants [mentioned in 16:16] from the sanctuary into the courtyard. He then must do the same thing for the courtyard, which is what is described in Lev 16:18–19."[110] But when we read in v. 19 what the blood manipulations on the outer altar accomplish, we find out that only one of the above three contaminants have been purified: "impurities" (*tumʾōt*). What happened to the other two?

This is where the live goat comes in (16:20–22). It is not sacrificed. It is basically a walking dustpan that carries off the rest of the contaminations from 16:16 (that were not mentioned in 16:19) away from the sanctuary, plus one more thing. Leviticus 16:21 tells us that the goat is loaded up with

108. Feldman, *Story of Sacrifice*, 164.

109. On the meaning and distinctions of these categories of contaminants, see Feldman, *Story of Sacrifice*, 163–64.

110. Feldman, *Story of Sacrifice*, 163.

all of Israel's "iniquities" (*ʿăwōnōt*), "willful sins" (*pišʿê*), and "inadvertent sins" (*ḥaṭṭōʾt*), and carries them away into the wilderness.[111] Following Gane, I will call this the "tote-goat"[112] rather than the conventional "scapegoat" since (a) it best captures the function of the goat and (b) "scapegoat" now has all kinds of connotations that are foreign to its function in Lev 16. Four things are worth mentioning here with respect to the tote-goat.[113]

First, it is "Aaron's act of [double-]hand-laying and confession [that] serves to transfer the contamination caused by these sins and transgressions from the sanctuary to the goat."[114] This laying of "two hands" (16:21) is markedly different from the single-hand gesture that offerers do for some, but not all, of their sacrifices, as discussed in chapter 1. If it is the double-hand-laying gesture that serves as a transfer ritual, then the single-hand gesture must be functioning differently. And, as we concluded, it functions as a statement of rightly ownership ("this is mine").

Second, as Feldman observes:

> Unlike the contamination caused by unintentional sins, which can be eliminated by the blood of a purification offering, the contamination caused by intentional sins must be understood as permanent. It can be removed and relocated, moved from one space to another, but it cannot be eliminated entirely.[115]

Third, the tote-goat ritual is not about "curse transmission" in Leviticus, as others have claimed.[116] We will return to these when discussing a relevant

111. See further, Feldman, *Story of Sacrifice*, 163–64: "The term עון [*ʿāwōn*] appears a number of times, both in the context of intentional sins and in the context of unintentional sins that have not been recognized [e.g., Lev 5:1–5] and therefore no sacrifice has been brought for them. The term חטאת [*ḥaṭṭāʾt*] is used in numerous contexts throughout the Priestly Narrative and appears to be a more general term for unintentional sin. These three terms, then, serve to describe the whole range of sins in the Priestly Narrative, from unintentional sin that has been recognized (חטאת [*ḥaṭṭāʾt*]) to unintentional sin that has gone unrecognized or ignored (עון [*ʿāwōn*]) to intentional sin (פשע [*pešaʿ*])."

112. Gane, *Cult and Character*, 243.

113. I cannot get into the meaning of "Azazel" (Lev 16:8, 10) here. See Milgrom, *Leviticus 1–16*, 1071–79. All that matters for our purposes is that the goat is deposited beyond the boundaries of the camp to the wilderness.

114. Feldman, *Story of Sacrifice*, 164.

115. Feldman, *Story of Sacrifice*, 164.

116. E.g., Finlan, *The Background and Content of Paul's Cultic Atonement Metaphors*, 75–76. Granted, first-century Jewish teacher and philosopher Philo of Alexandria interpreted it in this way—he says the goat "carries . . . the curses [*komizonta tas . . . aras*]" (*Spec.* 1.188)—but this interpretation is unique to him. E.g., Josephus makes no mention of curses when he explains what is happening with the tote-goat (*Ant.* 3.241).

NT text, but "curse transmission" is manifestly *not* what the original rite was doing. The word "curse(s)" does not appear in Leviticus at all, let alone Lev 16. Rather, Israel's contaminations of "iniquities," "intentional sins," and "unintentional sins" are placed on the tote-goat to haul away (16:21–22). The tote-goat is the ritual dustpan for collecting these indestructible contaminants and disposing of them far enough away so that they no longer have a contaminating effect on God's dwelling place. We also know that the tote-goat is not loaded up with "curses" because curses are not a source of ritual impurity, but the priest who walks the goat out of the sanctuary, out of the camp, and into the wilderness becomes ritually impure and therefore needs to bathe before even entering the camp (16:26). This means the priest is temporarily as impure as someone with scale disease, an unnatural discharge, or corpse impurity because he is not allowed back into the camp until he has been purified (Num 5:2–3). But in this case the priest is purified immediately upon bathing and does not have to wait until evening (Lev 16:26). But if the tote-goat was carrying "curses," then it would not become the source of transmitting secondary ritual impurity.

Fourth, the tote-goat ritual is apotropaic (this would apply to the Day of Decontamination as a whole too). This is why Josephus calls the tote-goat an *apotropiasmos* (*Ant.* 3.241). The function of the tote-goat is to *preemptively* ward off dire conditions that would threaten the community if these contaminants were not removed and then located far enough away from the sanctuary to no longer be a source of contaminating it. Meaning, the Day of Decontamination only has a function when there is a *sanctuary* to be purged to ward off the threat of divine abandonment. But, crucially, it can only do this for contaminations that *can be* purged from the sanctuary.

As we now know, some sins have no ritual remedy since they not only pollute the sanctuary, but the person and the land as well. The Day of Decontamination can do nothing for these. Once the divine presence leaves, it is too late; no amount of tote-goating will bring it back. This is why the prophets only envision a divine washing and resurrection (e.g., Ezek 36:25, 29; Zech 13:1; 14:8), not a Day of Decontamination, to end the covenant curse of exile. The curse of exile is the culmination of the covenant curses (Deut 28:15–68; 29:22–28; 30:19; cf. Lev 26:14–45). If the tote-goat was a curse transmission ritual, then surely the "curse" of exile for moral impurity could either be averted by means of this ritual or cut short by engaging in some sort of grand tote-goat ritual while in exile. The fact that this is not even imaginable by prophets who are priests—such as Jeremiah, Ezekiel, and Zechariah—confirms both (a) that the tote-goat is not about curse transmission and (b) that it is only a viable ritual *before* exile, not afterwards, when the sanctuary has already been destroyed.

This brings us to our next topic: the limits of the Day of Decontamination.

Understanding the Limits of the Day of Decontamination

It is important to emphasize that the Day of Decontamination does not cover all the sins mentioned in Leviticus. What are left out are the sins that produce "moral impurity." I will return to these when discussing the prophets and their views on sacrifices, but here we need to recall how the need to create the heuristic category "moral impurity" is to group together sins that render the *land* itself "impure" (*ṭāmē* ʾ) (18:25, 27, 28; cf. 19:29; 20:22; Num 5:34) and "polluted" (*ḥ-n-f*) (Num 35:33) (cf. Gen 4:11–12; Deut 21:1–9; 24:1–4; Isa 24:5; Jer 2:7; 3:1–2, 9; 16:18 [*ḥillēl*, "profaned"]; Ezek 22:3, 4, 6, 12; 36:17–18; Ps 106:34–40). There is no monetary nor sacrificial remedy for these. Only exile of the community or death of the offender purges the land (e.g., Num 35:31, 33; Lev 26:32–34, 43–44; cf. Deut 32:43). If purgation sacrifices purged "sins" in general from whatever it contaminates (i.e., the person and the land), then there would be no sins belonging to the category of moral impurity since sacrifice *qua* sacrifice would be sufficient to purge anything. But the fact that there are sins that contaminate things beyond the scope and reach of *ḥaṭṭā* ʾ*t* sacrifices further proves that sacrifices were never about purging people in the first place.

Additionally, it is too often assumed that forgiveness of sins is reducible to sacrifices and thus, that the Day of Decontamination is the be-all and end-all solution to sins. For instance, Noami Janowitz asserts (but does not argue) that "the temple cult of animal sacrifice . . . was for them ['these priests'] the most . . . efficacious antidote to *everything* that ails human-divine interactions."[117] As should be apparent from our progress thus far, this is not true. The entire system of atonement (decontamination) is limited in what it solves, according to the Torah.

Also, forgiveness can and does happen apart from the *kipper* apparatus according to several texts. This is made clear in the Psalms (e.g., Ps 32, which Paul quotes in Rom 4:7–8; Pss 50:13–14; 51; 40:7–9 [vv. 6–8 Eng.], quoted in Heb 10:5–7; Pss 69:31–32 [vv. 30–31 Eng.]; 103, esp. vv. 3–4 10–14) and the prophets (e.g., 1 Sam 15:22–23; Isa 1:11; Hos 6:6, which Jesus quotes in Matt 9:13 and 12:7; Amos 5:21–24; Mic 6:6–8; Jer 6:20; 7:21–23). We can use King David's rape of Bathsheba and murder of Uriah as an example (2 Sam 11–12). There are no sacrifices available to rectify these grave sins. But just because there is no *kipper* sacrifice does not mean forgiveness is

117. Janowitz, "Rereading Sacrifice," 197; my emphasis.

impossible. This is the whole point of Ps 51 because *forgiveness is not reducible to sacrifice*. To be sure, no sacrifice can decontaminate the contamination David's grave sins caused, but nothing is beyond the capacity of God to deal with directly. This is why David pleads for God to directly "wash" and "purify" him "from his sin" (51:4 [v. 2 Eng.]), both "bloodshed" (51:16 [v. 14 Eng.]) and rape (51:2 [prescript in Eng.]).

Nevertheless, we need to understand the built-in *limited* function sacrificial *kipper* has. The purgation sacrifices are not Israel's *entire* "system of forgiveness." Instead, they are a way to keep God's dwelling place—a *specific* location—holy by decontaminating it from *certain* impurities and sins.

We already saw how Lev 1–16 restricts the direct objects of *kipper* to sancta. Hence, the Day of Decontamination can only atone for sins that contaminate the *sanctuary* and its sancta (16:33; cf. vv. 16, 19). The discussion of moral impurity in the later editorial half of Leviticus (Lev 17–26) makes the same point but from another angle.[118] It says that there are sins that can defile the *person* (18:20, 23–25, 30; 19:31) and *land* (18:25, 27, 28; cf. 19:29; 20:22; Num 5:34; 35:35)—and both objects are beyond the capacity and scope of what sacrifices can purge per Lev 1–16. Hence the dire warnings about avoiding these sins that produce moral impurity in order to avoid being spat out of the land in exile. The rationale is clear: if there are sins that pollute the land, then this must mean there is no ritual remedy, and not even the Day of Decontamination can remove the contaminations of these sins. And as we will soon see, the prophets agree. It does not matter which sources/texts are "first" for this point because they all agree and corroborate each other on these notions: (a) decontaminating sacrifices are inherently limited in what they address; therefore, (b) the sins that pollute beyond the scope of what purgation sacrifices can handle require another remedy altogether.

Moreover, other Second Temple Jewish sources agree with this. Rabbinic sources, for example, though slightly divergent from Leviticus in a few details, discuss the limits to what the Day of Decontamination can remedy (cf. m. Yoma 8:9; y. Yoma 8:7, 44c, 45b–c; b. Yoma 85b:7–8, 11; 86a:1, 7–8; y. Šebu. 1:6, 32c–33b).[119] Also, Jubilees repeatedly claims that there is no *kip-*

118. Leviticus 17–26 is often attributed to the "H" source (for "Holiness Code"), which is thought to be a later addition by priests influenced by Deuteronomy. See Knohl, *The Sanctuary of Silence*. This view has been taken up by other Pentateuch scholars such as Milgrom (*Leviticus 17–22*, 1319–67) and Baden (*The Composition of the Pentateuch*, 187–88).

119. According to Rabbi Simeon ben Judah in m. Šebu. 1:6, the tote-goat sent into the wilderness on the Day of Decontamination effects "atonement" (*kipper*) even for sins that would result in being "cut off" (divine punishment) or the "death penalty" (carried out by the community). If this means that the person's *own guilt/iniquity*

per remedy for sins that generate moral impurity (sins that pollute the land): see 7:20–39; 20:2–11; 21:1–25; 23:14–25; 36:1–17. The point is, the idea that the Day of Decontamination is the "ultimate antidote to everything that ails human-divine interactions"[120] has no basis in any biblical text and does not seem to be attested in other Second Temple Jewish literature, yet it keeps finding its way into biblical scholarship.

(*ʿāwōn*) is removed, then this would diverge from Lev 16, 18–26, the prophets, and the other rabbinic sayings cited above (e.g., y. Šebu.1:6, 32c–33b would curtail Rabbi Simeon's view by providing several qualifications in direct response to the seemingly extreme claims of m. Šebu 1:6). If this is indeed what was meant, then perhaps since Rabbi Simeon's view is from after the second temple's destruction, he was *expanding* the function of the Day of Decontamination to address any and all sins in anticipation of God's promised eschatological forgiveness from the prophets. However, it is more likely that Rabbi Simeon only intends to say that "[t]he *contamination of the Sanctuary* and its *sancta*" generated by that person's sin(s) "is removed by the Day of Atonement" no matter what the sin is, since this is how his saying is interpreted in Jerusalem Talmud (y. Šebu. 1:6, 32c–33b) rather than "the person's own guilt" is removed (Guggenheimer, *Tractates Ševuʿot and ʿAvodah Zarah*, 34n180). That is, y. Šebu. 1:6, 32c–33b is *clarifying* rather than correcting Rabbi Simeon's view in m. Šebu. 1:6. As noted earlier, the immediately preceding context for m. Šebu. 1:6 is that "the atoning/decontaminating effects [*k-p-r* root] of all the goats [used as *ḥaṭṭāʾt* sacrifices referenced earlier] are [brought] for the same reason: for the impurity [*tuməʾat*] of the sanctuary [*miqdāš*] and its sancta" (repeated three times in 1:4–5; my translation). Thus, Rabbi Simeon's mishnah in 1:6 is likely still limited to talking about the removal of impurity *from the sanctuary*. The point is that the Day of Decontamination eliminates all impurities and sin contaminations *from the sanctuary* regardless what type of sin it is (but this does not mean that the Day of Decontamination suddenly can remove moral impurities *from the land*). According to y. Šebu. 1:6, 32c–33b, the Day of Decontamination removes the impurities and sin contaminations from the sanctuary that for whatever reason were not dealt with by the person responsible for those impurities/sin contaminations (i.e., there were no witnesses to a murder, or a person recovered from scale disease forgot to bring their sacrifices for their third stage of purification), but the culpability/iniquity (*ʿāwōn*) remains on the person who was responsible for that mess that accumulated on the sanctuary. "The purpose of the sacrifice is to safeguard the integrity of the Sanctuary. Therefore it has to repair all infractions which cannot be repaired otherwise, i.e., intentional infractions that cannot be prosecuted (for lack of eye witnesses or prior warnings). Since severe unintentional infractions (those if intentional would be punished by Divine extirpation or judicial execution) require a sacrifice, the public offering does not absolve the sinner from his obligation; it only suspends the damaging influence on the Sanctuary" (Guggenheimer, *Tractates Ševuʿot and ʿAvodah*, 35n182). All of this confirms the conclusions reached earlier about the Day of Decontamination being a fail-safe for the purification of the sanctuary from unrepentant sins or ignored ritual impurities (major ones, or minor ones that transformed into major impurities) from anyone in the community. But this fail-safe has *a limited scope*. These atoning sacrifices can only purge sancta. And these rabbinic interpretations acknowledge these limits as well (esp. m. y. Šebu. 1:4–5).

120. Janowitz, "Rereading Sacrifice," 197.

Put another way, according to all these various perspectives (biblical and non-biblical) for the judgment of exile and the attendant destruction of the temple to be intelligible, this must mean that the *kipper* system has reached its *limits*, leaving exile as the *only* remedy available to the situation at hand. Accordingly, this also means that the people committed more heinous sins than the *kipper* system could handle/mitigate. Hence, the notion that there are certain sins that produce an impurity beyond the ordained scope and capacity of the *kipper* system to handle that will lead to exile.

As is clear from Second Temple Jewish texts, exile and the destruction of the temple (twice) was already a matter of theodicy crying out for explanation. The supposition that the Day of Decontamination is the remedy for any and all sins would exacerbate this problem since it essentially renders exile unintelligible, making God seem to revel in gratuitous punishments. Why is exile necessary if Israel carried out all the Day of Decontamination rituals (sacrifices, fasting, repentance, etc.)? But if the exile is addressing sins outside the scope of what the *kipper* system is ordained to handle, then whatever the other theological problems exile might generate, at least it makes sense from within the Torah's theology of *kipper*.

Ironically, Janowitz is correct to note that "[b]lood was their [the priests'] ultimate purifying agent."[121] But this is only one side of the coin. On the other side, Leviticus and Numbers also express that blood is equally *impotent* to purify *all* types of sins. This is the communal moral logic of Leviticus altogether. The sacrificial decontamination system falls short of Israel's potential needs, but this is a *known* and *intentional* gap in these priestly texts.

This is what Milgrom calls "the priestly doctrine of collective responsibility."[122] Everyone is responsible not only to purge their contaminations from the sanctuary, but to avoid polluting themselves and the *land* through moral impurity as well. This is because, as Klawans explains, "The moral defilements threaten not only the status of the individuals in question but also the land and in turn the sanctuary itself."[123] And recall that "[t]he purpose of the daily burnt offering . . . is to provide regular and constant pleasing odors to the Lord, so that the divine presence will continually remain in the sanctuary."[124] But the sins that produce moral impurity "undo what properly performed [burnt offering] sacrifice does. Sacrifice attracts

121. Janowitz, "Rereading Sacrifice," 197.

122. Milgrom, *Leviticus*, 32.

123. Klawans, *Purity, Sacrifice*, 71.

124. Klawans, *Purity, Sacrifice*, 72.

and maintains the divine presence; moral defilement resulting from grave sin repels the divine presence."[125]

There is only so much pollution the sanctuary can handle. And if the very land it rests on is polluted by grave sins, then God will abandon the dwelling place to destruction "and with its destruction, all the sinners will meet their doom."[126] The moral logic is that land can reach a point where it will no longer support the sanctuary because it is saturated with moral impurities that have gone unaddressed. The land will get sick and vomit its inhabitants out and, as shown above, this simultaneously serves as the consequence for these sins as well as the remedy for the community and the land.

It is as if the morally impure people pollute the land analogously to the way scale disease infects a house (Lev 14:33–53). The people themselves are like the disease on the land that needs to get washed away in exile. Recall that the processes of ritual purification for things like scale disease (whether on a person, textile, or house) do not physically heal and get rid of the disease. The disease must be gone before the ritual purification processes can begin. This is why I said the ritual purification is more of a "reinstatement" process. The person is reinstated into the regular worship of the community and the house is reinstated as a suitable domicile. Same with the land. There are no rituals that can get rid of or "heal" the pollution on it. The pollution needs to first go away (i.e., the death of the offender or community sent off into exile) and only then can it be reinstated after the appropriate amount of time has elapsed (e.g., 26:34–43). Therefore, it is *time* away from the land that is real ultimate purifying agent in Leviticus since that is what cleanses the land.

And in this way, we are beginning to see how aspects within the logic of ritual impurity are applied analogously to moral impurity. Just like time and water-washings purify people and objects from ritual impurity, time will ultimately purify people and the land from moral impurity according to Leviticus. The prophets also envision a divine water-washing, as noted.

But before getting there this brings us to Lev 16:30, which is an important instance where ritual impurity and sins are joined together.

Understanding Leviticus 16:30

What makes Lev 16:30 odd and worth special discussion is the apparent confusion of categories that have been kept carefully distinct up to this

125. Klawans, *Purity, Sacrifice*, 71.

126. Milgrom, *Leviticus*, 32.

point in Leviticus. We read: "For on this day, decontamination will be made on your behalf in order to purify [*ləṭahēr*] you from all of your sins. You shall be pure [*tiṭhārû*] before Yahweh."[127] As Feldman explains:

> The second clause presents a problem. . . . It claims that the decontamination is done in order to purify the Israelites from their sins. . . . The problem is the idea that the Israelites must be purified from their sins. This conflates two distinct categories in the ritual system: sin and impurity. An individual is purified from impurity and forgiven from sin. Sin can contaminate the sanctuary like impurity, but it is not the same thing as impurity, and its effect on an individual is different from its effect on the sanctuary. This distinction between these categories was maintained in the earlier part of the instructions for the tabernacle purification (Lev 16:2–28), yet collapses here.[128]

It is widely agreed that this verse has been added in later by the redactors of the Holiness Code (H).[129] From 16:1–28, God has been telling Moses what he needs to instruct Aaron. But there is a sudden break at 16:29. Now "Aaron" disappears and we only hear about the "anointed priest" (16:32) and rather than Moses being the addressee, now it is "you all" (16:29). But just because 16:30 is embedded in later tradition does not mean it can be safely ignored.

I think this verse provides a clue into the way the analogical relationship between ritual impurity and sins was developed. We already noted how Ps 51 seeks a direct divine remedy for David's moral impurities of murder and rape and draws from the remedies of ritual impurities to do so; hence, the pleas for God to "wash" and "purify" him (51:4, 9 [vv. 2, 7 Eng.]) and the mention of "hyssop" (51:9 [v. 7 Eng.]), which is used in scale disease purification. Notice, there is still no *sacrificial* remedy, since sacrifices were never thought to purge *people*. Rather, the rituals for purifying bodies from ritual impurities (washing, hyssop) are applied metaphorically to purify David's moral impurity. *God* must be the one who effects the "washing" though.

What this psalm is having David ask God to do for him regarding his moral impurity, and what we will see the prophets envisioning below, is an *extension* of the logic of what Lev 16:30 is claiming the Day of Decontamination does for people for those sins that are not in the moral impurity category.

127. Borrowing Feldman's translation (*Story of Sacrifice*, 166).

128. Feldman, *Story of Sacrifice*, 166.

129. Milgrom, *Leviticus 1–16*, 1056.

Two things are clear. First, for all the reasons already set forth, 16:30 cannot be talking about purifying people for sins that generate moral impurity. Second, it is apparent that the concept of ritual impurity was a useful and common way to think through the problem (certain) sins cause by analogy. We see this in the second half of Leviticus (18–26) with the category of moral impurity, and we see it too in the Prophets and the Psalms (e.g., Ps 51).

So then, just like there are minor and major ritual impurities, I think the best way to make sense of both the claim in 16:30 as well as the limits of the Day of Decontamination already discussed is to think about sins now in terms of "minor" and "major" moral impurity. What we have called "moral impurities" up to this point can be classified now as "major" moral impurities. The *major* moral impurities are the ones that pollute the *land* and so cannot be decontaminated through sacrificial *kipper*. But the claim of 16:30 implies that inadvertent sins[130] produce a similar moral impurity to that created by sexual immorality, false worship, and murder, except that *it can be purified* on the Day of Decontamination; hence "minor" moral impurity, since the impurity is delimited to the sanctuary and does not penetrate the land.

That is, we can infer that the H redactor of 16:30 is effectively subcategorizing moral impurity into "minor" and "major" moral impurity on analogy to how ritual impurity can be subcategorized into minor and major impurities. Major ritual impurity requires a purgation sacrifice whereas minor ritual impurities do not. Similarly, major moral impurity would be a way to distinguish between sins that have no *kipper* remedy from those that do (hence, minor moral impurity). If certain sins generate a moral impurity potent enough to pollute the land itself, not just the sanctuary—i.e., a "major" moral impurity—then it makes sense that the other sins generate a "minor" moral impurity that contaminates the sanctuary and therefore can be remedied through the rituals of removal (*kipper*) prescribed in Lev 4–6 and 16.

But, this purification from minor moral impurity is tethered to the individual personal responsibilities (fasting, not working) outlined in 16:29 that seem to directly effect this metaphorical purification of the person from their minor moral impurities.[131] However, in the same way that a person who

130. This would include previous intentional sins (not in the moral impurity category) that have been downgraded to inadvertencies through confessions and repentance, per Lev 5:21–23 (6:2–4 Eng.). For more on this notion, see Milgrom's section on "the priestly doctrine of repentance" (*Leviticus 1–16*, 372–78).

131. The *piel* verb of the root ʿ-*n*-*h*, "humble/afflict oneself," used in Lev 16:29, 31; 23:32 and Num 29:7 for the Day of Decontamination likely means to abstain from

has become penultimately "pure" once their bodies are free of any impurity but does not become declared fully "pure" until their impurity has been removed from the sanctuary, so too the rest from labor and fasting work together with the rituals of removal (both the purgation sacrifices and the tote-goat) to render the person "fully morally pure" (excluding, of course, major moral impurity). That is, what time and washing do for purifying the body from ritual impurity to get the person to a penultimate stage of ritual purity seems to be what rest and fasting does for purifying the person from minor moral impurity on the Day of Decontamination.[132] In the same way, then, the purgation sacrifices and the tote-goat remove the sins from the sanctuary to render the people fully pure from minor moral impurity just like the purgation sacrifices at the ultimate stage of purification remove the people's extrinsic ritual impurity from the sanctuary and thereby render the person fully ritually pure.

Therefore, it appears the claim in Lev 16:30 is that on the Day of Decontamination *minor* moral impurities caused by sins *other than* worshiping other gods, sexual immorality, and murder are not only removed from the sanctuary, but from the person too. This might be the idea that inspires the notion in the prophets and Ps 51 that *major* moral impurity can be eliminated from the person too, albeit only through a divine water-washing purification.

The analogical ritual logic seems to work like this: minor ritual impurity contaminates the person's body and major ritual impurity contaminates both the person's body and the sanctuary. Removing ritual impurity from one's body usually requires a combination of time and water-washing (though sometimes it goes away just by waiting until sundown). But removing it from the sanctuary requires a purgation sacrifice. Since inadvertent or repentant sins similarly contaminate the sanctuary and likewise require a purgation sacrifice to remove the contamination from the sanctuary, this implies sins might function on analogy to ritual impurity. So just like ritual impurity never adheres to the sanctuary apart from being mediated through a ritually impure person's body (i.e., ritual impurity does not "exist" on its own—it always comes into being via a human person and only then can it be transmitted to the sanctuary)[133]—this would mean that those sins that

---

eating (cf. Isa 58:3) and this is how it was understood by first-century Jews (e.g., Acts 27:9; cf. Josephus, *Ant.* 3.240). Cf. Milgrom, *Leviticus 1–16*, 1054–58, 1065–67.

132. "[S]ince the blood, the ritual detergent, cannot be applied directly to each Israelite as it is to the sanctuary, their fasting and abstaining from work serves to implicate them in the cleansing process" (Baden, "The Purpose of Purification," 22).

133. E.g., a carcass of an unclean animal will not automatically pollute the sanctuary. Only if a *person* touches it and then forgets (or refuses) to bathe that night will it

contaminate the sanctuary probably first contaminated the person's body in some way. And just like ritual impurity is removed from people's bodies apart from any purgation sacrifice (since purgation sacrifices, even for major ritual impurities, can only occur once the person themselves is purified through other ritual means), so too minor moral impurity is removed from the people apart from a purgation sacrifices, but through other rituals. Thus, similar to how ritual impurity is usually removed from the person through a combination of time and water, in 16:29–31 purification from minor moral impurity is effected by a combination of time and rituals (though no water). It takes a year (time) and a full day (time) of ritual fasting and resting to be purified from their "minor" sins.

Just like the ritual reset for scale disease discussed above reintegrates the person into the camp, their home, and finally into the liturgical sacrificial life of the community (this is "full" ritual purification), the Day of Decontamination is a ritual factory reset of the sanctuary *and* the community from minor moral impurity. Excluding major moral impurity, then, the purgation and removal rituals described in Lev 16:1–28 function to ritually reset the sanctuary back to its factory settings, and 16:29–30 provides instructions for the community so that they too can be "reset" to a state of moral purity (from all inadvertent or repentant sins not in the major moral impurity category). By abstaining from work and food for the whole day (time), they demonstrate repentance for any sins they failed to repent from and address from the previous year and thereby get a ritual reset back to their "factory settings"—"made pure" from minor moral impurity.

In terms of major moral impurity, however, exile does for the land with regards to removing major moral impurities what the purgation sacrifices do for the sanctuary with regards to removing major ritual impurities. This is how the Song of Moses in Deut 32 ends in v. 43, with a prediction that after the exile God will "purge (*kipper*) the land of his people" (LXX: "purify [*ekkathariei*] the land of his people"). And this happens without any recourse to sacrifices because sacrifices cannot decontaminate anything besides the sanctuary and its sancta. Once in exile, all that is left is to purify the people. And according to the prophets, along with other texts like Ps 51, this will be accomplished on analogy for purifying people from ritual impurities: by means of a (divine) water-washing.

To this we now turn.

---

be transmitted from the impure person to the sanctuary (Lev 11:24–28, 39–40; 15:31; 17:15–16).

THE PROPHETS ON MORAL IMPURITY, SACRIFICE, AND THE HOPE OF PURIFICATION

It is well known that the OT contains a lot of passages apparently critical of the sacrificial system, especially from the prophets.[134] A few notable passages suffice as exemplars:

> For I desire steadfast love and not sacrifice, the knowledge of God rather than burnt offerings. (Hos 6:6 NRSV)
>
> I hate, I despise your festivals, and I take no delight in your solemn assemblies. Even though you offer me your burnt offerings and grain offerings, I will not accept them; and the offerings of well-being of your fatted animals I will not look upon. Take away from me the noise of your songs; I will not listen to the melody of your harps. But let justice roll down like waters, and righteousness like an everflowing stream. Did you bring to me sacrifices and offerings the forty years in the wilderness, O house of Israel? (Amos 5:21–25 NRSV)
>
> Of what use to me is frankincense that comes from Sheba, or sweet cane from a distant land? Your burnt offerings are not acceptable, nor are your sacrifices pleasing to me. . . . For in the day that I brought your ancestors out of the land of Egypt, I did not speak to them or command them concerning burnt offerings and sacrifices. (Jer 6:20 and 7:22 NRSV)

This last one from Jer 7:22 may seem odd, but this same sentiment is found in places like Ps 40:7 (v. 6 Eng.) as well, where we read: "Eaten-sacrifice and grain offering you have not desired, . . . Burnt offering and purgation offering you have not required." Admittedly, passages like these are shocking. After all, up this point we have been analyzing all the commands concerning sacrifices, which were ostensibly given right after Israel left Egypt! But the point here is not to adjudicate whether Leviticus "happened" or not, but simply to mark that there are texts deeply critical of sacrifice in the OT. We already saw how Ps 51 is critical of sacrifice as well (e.g., Ps 51:18–19 [vv. 16–17 Eng.]) and more examples can be added (e.g., 1 Sam 15:22–23; Isa 1:11–15; 61:8; 66:3–5; Jer 14:12; Hos 8:13; 9:4–5; Mic 6:6–8; Pss 69:31–32 [vv. 30–31 Eng.]).

However, now that we know that one of the key criteria for legitimate sacrifice is that it requires "proper ownership of what is being offered"[135]

134. Klawans, *Purity, Sacrifice*, 75–100.

135. Klawans, *Purity, Sacrifice*, 85.

(recall the single-hand-laying gesture discussion from chapter 1) and appreciate the limits of *kipper*, we can better situate and understand these critiques of sacrifice.

Proper Ownership Is Impossible in a Morally Compromised Economy

As we learned in chapter 1, "[f]undamental to the proper working of [the sacrificial] system . . . is due ownership of what is offered. For how can a gift be a true expression of anything if what is given was stolen in the first place?"[136] This is why, as discussed above, a grain offering can be substituted for an animal purgation sacrifice (Lev 5:11–13) since blood is less important than ownership. The *kipper* ritual, at base, just requires that the person fulfill their personal obligation to purge the sancta, which is why this can happen if the person only has grain to offer. But offering an ill-gotten quadruped or bird to have "blood" would only make matters worse.

I agree with Klawans's arguments that we can frame the so-called prophetic critique of sacrifice as an extended meditation on what the notion of proper ownership entails. Klawans's main thesis is that "the prophets' 'rejection' of sacrifice was deeply connected to their belief that Israel was economically rotten to the core."[137]

That is, the prophets are not critical of sacrifice because it is "ritualistic" or "just symbolic" and Israel needs to move "beyond" sacrifice to something else.[138] As Klawans shows, "a number of the classic statements erroneously taken as 'rejections of sacrifice' are in context juxtaposed with expressions of concern over the economic exploitation of the poor (Amos 5:23 is preceded by Amos 5:10–11; Isa. 1:11–15 is followed by 1:17; Jer. 6:20 is preceded by 6:13)."[139] A basic premise of these prophetic critiques is that they "presume all to be guilty of—or at least culpable for—the crimes they find in their society."[140] "Who wasn't a thief in Amos's conception of things?" asks Klawans.[141]

136. Klawans, *Purity, Sacrifice*, 84.

137. Klawans, *Purity, Sacrifice*, 87.

138. See Klawans's critique of this common way of framing the prophetic critique (*Purity, Sacrifice*, 78–84).

139. Klawans, *Purity, Sacrifice*, 87.

140. Klawans, *Purity, Sacrifice*, 88.

141. Klawans, *Purity, Sacrifice*, 88.

Klawans's observations are significant, but he seems to be overlooking a crucial connection between these economic critiques and what we have been calling (major) moral impurity.

Economic Oppression Is a Form of Bloodshed

Recognizing how the prophets consistently tether the notion of bloodshed (murder) to economic exploitation serves to strengthen Klawans's overall point that the prophets are not critiquing sacrifice *per se*. But they are also doing more than merely saying the person "who has taken unjustly from the poor cannot properly *give* anything, and therefore the 'sacrifice' offered by such a person is anathema."[142]

First, recall that even in Leviticus major moral impurities can never be purged through *kipper* sacrifices. The Day of Decontamination cannot purge the moral impurity caused by worship of other gods, sexual immorality, and murder. Klawans highlights how in Jeremiah's temple discourse in 7:9–10, theft—which is more about economic exploitation on what we might call a societal or "systemic" level (cf. Jer 6:13, 20)—is juxtaposed with other sins in the moral impurity category (worship of other gods, sexual immorality, and murder).[143] He thus argues that "[t]he prophets' rejections of sacrifice are connected to their belief that economic transgressions render sacrificial offerings not just invalid but offensive."[144] That is, "[t]he prophet's attitude toward sin and its effects on the sanctuary reflects the notion of moral defilement, whereby grave sin—idolatry, sexual transgression, and bloodshed—defiles both the sanctuary and the land, leading to God's withdrawal from the sanctuary and Israel's exile from the land."[145] This is what is warned about by Jeremiah (Jer 12:7; 18:17; 22:5; 23:33, 39) and then what is narrated in Ezek 5–10.

The prophets agree that the land itself has become polluted due to moral impurities (murder, sexual immorality, idolatry) (e.g., Isa 24:5–6; Jer 2:7, 23; 3:1–2, 9; Ezek 7:23; 8:17; 9:9; 22:2–16, 24–31; 36:17–18; cf. Ps 106:38).[146] Klawans therefore concludes:

142. Klawans, *Purity, Sacrifice*, 87.

143. Klawans, *Purity, Sacrifice*, 91.

144. Klawans, *Purity, Sacrifice*, 91.

145. Klawans, *Purity, Sacrifice*, 92.

146. For these sins making the people and/or the temple impure, see Jer 7:30; 19:13; 32:34; Ezek 5:11; 20:7, 18, 31; 23:7, 30; 24:13; 37:23; 39:24; Hos 5:3; 6:10; Ps 106:39. See also "Ezekiel 22:1–16 comprises a list of Israel's violations of H prohibitions (drawn mainly from this chapter [Lev 18]) whose punishment is exile" (Milgrom, *Leviticus 17–22*, 1575).

> [I]n the presence of grave sin [i.e., major moral impurity], sacrifice is no longer adequate to the task of attracting and maintaining the divine presence among the people of Israel. . . . An important aspect of understanding the prophetic critique in general . . . is to appreciate that when the prophets speak of the futility of the temple or its cult, they are not necessarily criticizing ritual as much as they are evaluating the current state of Israel's relationship to God"[147]

I agree with this overall, but I think Klawans misses that the prophets are saying more than just (a) economic exploitation means all offerings are not properly owned and (b) Israel is guilty of other sins too and these are in the moral impurity category, hence, exile is coming.

The consistent prophetic message is that economic oppression *is itself a form of shedding blood*. Theft is murder on both an individual and societal scale. The prophets constantly link bloodshed with economic oppression (Mic 3:10–11 with 2:1–9; Isa 1:21–23; 5:7–8; Jer 7:9; 22:3, 13, 17–18 [cf. 2 Kgs 24:4 about Jehoiakim mentioned in Jer 22:18]; Hab 2:8–12; Nah 3:1; Ezek 22:12; 24:1–14, esp. vv. 6, 9). Take Micah, for example. When he finally concludes that Zion has been built "with blood" (3:10) he explains that this is due to economic oppression, bribery, and greed (3:11), and this also comes after a long list of other exploitative practices (2:1–9). This is more than mere juxtaposition. This is a meditation on what constitutes "bloodshed" and "murder." As Ezekiel puts it, "they take bribes, which is shedding blood" (22:12). As if that was not clear enough, we go on to read: "you take both advance interest and accrued interest, and make gain of your neighbors by extortion; and you have forgotten me, says the Lord God. See, I strike my hands together at the dishonest gain you have made, and at the blood that has been shed within you" (22:12–13 NRSV). The other prophets listed are doing the same things as Micah and Ezekiel. What the prophets are saying is that economic exploitation belongs to the moral impurities because it itself is a form of murder. All the various forms of theft have been "upgraded" to the level of moral impurities because it has enveloped the entire social framework and network for the distribution of land, its produce, and goods and services.

This is why I think the critique goes deeper than just "theft invalidates sacrifice because what is offered is not considered properly owned." When society is so polluted from moral impurity, the entire "system" of sacrifice is rendered ineffectual and only exile can be expected. But it is ineffectual for two distinct yet overlapping reasons. It is, first, ineffectual because what

147. Klawans, *Purity, Sacrifice*, 93.

is being offered is not properly owned. Nothing can be so in a society this rotten economically. But it is not saying that the temple and its sacrifices were *always* ineffectual. It is not as if the sacrificial system was considered inherently "ineffective" or "merely rituals." It is just that the corruption is so pervasive that the sacrifices themselves are considered invalid *now* due to these *particular reasons* (cf. the postexilic prophet Malachi's concerns in 1:6–14).

But second, the prophets are saying in concert that the sacrificial system is inherently incapable by design to deal with the kinds of sins the community is guilty of committing. This is because all sources agree that these sacrifices *could never* decontaminate for sins in the (major) moral impurity category. Sins that pollute the land are dangerous for this very reason. If the land that the temple is on is polluted, then God will abandon it and the temple will fall along with the people who will go into exile. The land can no longer support the temple when it is saturated with impurities. This is not a critique of the temple or sacrifices *per se*, but rather of moral impurity. And this message is consistent with the built-in limitations of the entire *kipper* system in the Torah. Again, it does not matter for our purposes which of these texts or their pre-canonical sources were written first or which were influenced by which. What matters is that there is a fundamental agreement about the limitations of sacrifices in the face of sins that produce moral impurity on the people and the land in all the sources.

Therefore, the so-called prophetic critique of sacrifices should actually be "the prophetic critique of sacrifices in a context of major moral impurity." Neither the Torah nor the prophets think the *kipper* system was ever intended or capable of dealing with sins that generate moral impurity. If the people think they can stave off disaster by offering more sacrifices, then *that thinking* is rebuked and we get statements about inefficacy of sacrifices. But this inefficacy is not about a *change* in efficacy. Rather, it is saying "these were *never* able to purge the land." The polemics against sacrifices are not against sacrifices themselves, but (a) against thinking *kipper* sacrifices could do more than the Torah actually says they can do and (b) presuming that the non-atoning burnt offerings and well-being sacrifices can somehow nullify the deleterious situation simply by throwing several feasts for God (e.g., Amos 5:21–25; Hos 8:13; 9:4–5; Mic 6:6–8; Isa 1:11; 66:3–4; Jer 6:20; 14:12).

The Prophetic Hope for Restoration

The prophets again testify in unison that restoration after exile is purely a gift of God. It is not contingent on the sacrificial system at all. It *cannot* be contingent on it because the solution to exile exceeds the scope of the sacrificial system by design. Exile is what happens when moral impurity reaches such an extent that the land itself can no longer sustain its impure inhabitants or the sanctuary. It is not just that the system of sacrificial purgation is no longer effective due to sacrificing ill-gotten offerings. Rather, what has been polluted (the people and the land) are beyond the purgative capacity of the decontaminating sacrifices, which also means the sacrifices that are supposed to be a tangible communion between God and the people (burnt offerings and well-being sacrifices) are nullified since the impurities have driven God away (Ezek 5–11; Jer 12:7; 18:17; 23:33, 39; 22:5). How can the system that was not even designed to deal with moral impurity suddenly be thought to be able to deal with it after all and/or still facilitate shared sacred meals?

This is why the prophets are not saying: "If only we can offer the biggest and greatest purgation sacrifice! . . . Maybe one day!" Rather, the passages that articulate the hope for Israel's restoration can be grouped into three types.

The first is to appeal to the fact that forgiveness has always been wider and deeper than the sacrificial system. God's forgiveness was always available via extra-sacrificial means (e.g., Pss 32; 51; 103; Isa 38:17), so the prophets are confident that God will have mercy and forgive Israel and restore them just because that is the kind of God that God is and this is the kind of thing God can do (e.g., Isa 43:25; 44:22; 55:7; Jer 50:20; Mic 7:18–19; Hos 14:2–7; cf. Zeph 3:15).

The second way is to speak about this extra-sacrificial divine forgiveness on analogy to the exodus (cf. Isa 11:16; 40:2–3; 43:14–21; 44:27; 48:20–21; 50:2; 51:10–11; 52:12; 58:8), only this new act of deliverance will surpass it (e.g., 43:18–19; 52:12 [cf. "haste" in Exod 12:11, 33; Deut 16:3]; Jer 16:14–15; 23:7–8; 31:32–33). And just as the first exodus culminated in establishing a covenant (cf. Exod 24:5–8; Jer 34:13), the prophets talk about the liberation from exile (again often related to their former liberation from Egypt, 30:3 with 2:6–7; 11:4; 32:21–22) together with establishing a "new covenant" (Jer 31:31–34; 33:6–8), (re)establishing God's "everlasting covenant" (Ezek 16:59–63), making "a covenant of peace" (34:25; 37:26) or affirming the "covenant of peace" (Isa 54:10), or simply making a "covenant" (59:21 together with 27:9).[148] It the establishment of the new covenant that indicates the needed forgiveness of sins that caused the exile has happened (Jer 31:34; 33:8). If any sacrifices are to be associated with this exodus-like deliverance, then they would specifically be the non-atoning well-being

148. Paul juxtaposes these two Isaianic passages in Rom 11:26–27.

sacrifices for the covenant inauguration and Passover, which marked the first exodus from Egypt. But these sacrifices would not be *facilitating* the restoration from exile, but rather *celebrating* God's deliverance of Israel from exile and then *ratifying* the (new) covenant relationship after the salvation took place.

This, along with the first point about forgiveness happening apart from the sacrificial system, is crucial. Too often, as we will soon see, NT scholars encounter a NT passage about "forgiveness" and assume this has something to do with *kipper*. And now we know why this is fundamentally mistaken. Not only can forgiveness happen apart from the sacrificial system, but the *kipper* sacrifices are inherently incapable of responding to sins in the major moral impurity category, which the prophets expand to include theft and economic exploitation. It makes perfect sense, then, that the prophetic hope is not predicated on the recovery of the sacrificial system at all. While Ezekiel, for instance, thinks that after Israel's restoration the temple will be rebuilt and everything will go "back to normal" again, the reinstitution of the sacrificial system is the *result* of God's forgiveness of Israel's grave sins, *not its cause* (37:26–28).

Finally, the third group of prophetic hope plays on the analogy of ritual and moral impurity. The prophets are confident in their hope that it is in and through exile, in line with Lev 26:31–45, that God will directly "purify" Israel from all their moral impurities (e.g., Jer 33:8; Ezek 22:15; 24:13; 36:17, 29, 33; 37:23; Mal 3:2–3). And sometimes this is depicted as a divine ritual water-washing precisely because it was bathing that purifies people from ritual impurities (Ezek 36:25; Isa 4:4; Zech 13:1–2; Ps 51:4, 9 [vv. 2, 7 Eng.]; cf. Isa 1:16). If actual water-washing purifies people from minor and major ritual impurities, then by analogy a divine water-washing would purify people from minor and major moral impurities.

In fact, Rabbi Aqiva's (50–135 AD) interpretation of Lev 16:30 recorded in the Mishnah connects these very points:

> R. Akiba said: Blessed are ye, O Israel. Before whom are ye made clean and who makes you clean [alluding to Lev 16:30 quoted just above]? Your Father in heaven; as it is written, *And I will sprinkle clean water upon you and ye shall be clean* [Ezek 36:25]. And again it says, *O Lord the hope* (mikweh) *of Israel* [Jer 17:13];—as the *Mikweh* cleanses the [ritually] unclean so does the Holy One, blessed be he, cleanse Israel. (m. Yoma 8:9)[149]

149. Translation from Danby, *The Mishnah*, 172; emphasis, parentheses, and italics his; brackets mine.

Rabbi Aqiva uses Jer 17:13 to interpret Ezek 36:25 by means of a wordplay with the word for "hope" (*miqweh*) in Jer 17:13. *Miqweh* usually means "hope" in the Hebrew Bible but in rabbinic Hebrew it comes to mean the "immersion pool" used to collect rain or river water for ritual purification baths.[150] Thus, he is interpreting Lev 16:30 exactly the way we have suggested above; that is, on analogy to purification from ritual impurities. We can see this, first, because he does not relate the purification in 16:30 to any of the *kipper* sacrifices on the Day of Decontamination, but rather to a type of *water-washing* since this is the ritual means of purifying people. Second, he is also following the prophets who expand on this analogical relationship between ritual and (minor) moral purity in Lev 16:30 by applying it to major moral impurity. That major moral purity is in view is made explicit in y. Yoma 8:7, 45c where Rabbi Aqiva's saying is related to idolatry. According to Rabbi Aqiva the smaller-scale claim in 16:30 that Israel can be purified from their sins that the Day of Decontamination can address (i.e., sins that are not in the major moral impurity category) points to the radical eschatological *moral* purification promised by the prophets. And by combining these three passages in this way we can see that Rabbi Aqiva takes it for granted that any purification of *people* would have to take place through a *water-washing* (not any sacrifice). The passage from Jer 17:13 even goes on to call God "the fountain [*miqôr*] of living waters [*mayîm hayyîm*]," which is the most potent ritual purification agent for humans (cf. Lev 14:5–6, 50–52; 15:13; Num 19:17; Jer 2:13; m. Mikq. 1:8).

Therefore, Rabbi Aqiva's interpretation confirms the interpretation of Lev 16:30 above as well as the point here regarding the prophets and moral impurity. Purification of any kind—ritual or moral—for humans will be facilitated through some sort of (i.e., even metaphorical/spiritual) water-washing. For purification from the moral impurities that sent Israel into exile, this will require a divine washing of sorts (Ezek 36:25), being immersed in the divine Spirit (36:26–27; cf. 37:5, 9–10, 14).

This is crucial to note since this explains why no prophet is hoping for or envisioning a grand purgation sacrifice as the solution to moral impurity. This makes sense since it is inconceivable within the framework set forth in the Torah with regards to these grave sins. The fact that the prophets express their hope for restoration completely apart from *kipper* sacrifices affirms that it was taken for granted that the purgation sacrifices were only ever meant to decontaminate the sanctuary, not people. Especially in exile, then, when there is no sanctuary, a purgation sacrifice does not even make

150. Miller, "Tractate Yoma," 627. This may also be due to "hope" and "fountain" in Jer 17:13 sharing three Hebrew characters. Compare *miqweh* (מקוה) and *miqôr* (מקור).

sense because it is neither possible to offer one nor is there a sanctuary that is being contaminated. The sanctuary has already been destroyed. What is needed is a divine reconstitution or "resurrection" of the people, which is another way that Ezekiel envisions the restoration from exile (37:23). And it is only *after* the divine washing and forgiveness of Israel's moral impurities takes place that Ezekiel can imagine a new temple appearing and being consecrated for the recommencement of regular sacrifices.

The sacrificial system is simply never conceived of as the solution to Israel's most dire needs—neither in Leviticus nor in the prophets.

CONCLUSION

Previously I demonstrated how Torah's sacrificial and purity system is focused on keeping what is holy free from contact with what is impure. Here I traced how there are inherent limitations to the atoning functions of sacrifice, as only sancta (holy objects in the dwelling place) can be decontaminated through atonement, not people or the land. Moreover, I highlighted how forgiveness is associated with sacrificial atonement, but it is not reducible to it, and can happen completely apart from the *kipper* system. From these observations I was able to clarify the so-called prophetic critique of sacrifice. The prophets are not criticizing the sacrificial system *per se*, but rather emphasizing its limitations—the same limitations I stressed were inherent to the *kipper* system in relation to moral impurity—and they announce a future forgiveness of sins that will be accomplished by God apart from the *kipper* system that will bring about the much needed moral purification.

From here we can examine how various NT texts present and comprehend Jesus within this framework.

5

Lamb of the Free

Jesus, Purity, and Non-Atoning Sacrifices

Now that we have completed the heavy lifting and ground clearing of both debunking common misconceptions and understanding the overall logic and functions of various sacrifices in the OT, we can delve into the NT passages that use sacrificial imagery to understand the saving significance of Jesus's death. We will see that Jesus's death is most often related to non-*kipper* well-being sacrifices. And since we now know how ritual purity goes hand in hand with sacrifice, we ought to first survey Jesus in relation to ritual and moral purity before getting to the non-*kipper* sacrificial texts. Thus, the theses I will argue here are:

(1) According to the Gospels, Jesus's life and ministry operated entirely consistent with and within OT purity laws and concern for the sanctuary.

(2) Jesus was a source of contagious holiness that nullified the sources of the major ritual impurities as well as moral impurity.

(3) Thus, Jesus was not anti-purity and he was not rejecting the temple *per se*.

(4) Jesus's appropriation of the prophetic critique of sacrifice fits entirely within the framework of the grave consequences of moral impurity. That is, like the prophets, Jesus is not critiquing sacrifice *per se*, but rather moral impurity, which will cause another exile and the destruction of the sanctuary.

(5) But, his followers will be able to experience the moral purification he offers.

(6) The only sacrificial interpretation of Jesus's death that is attributed to Jesus himself occurs at the Lord's Supper. At this meal Jesus combines two communal well-being sacrifices, the Passover and a covenant-inauguration ceremony, to explain the importance of his death. There are several other NT texts that reiterate these claims. However, the notion of *kipper* is not used in any of these accounts, despite some attempts to read that into the descriptions.

Throughout these discussions an important theme will emerge that will only be reinforced in each subsequent chapter. The NT appropriates sacrificial imagery (both non-atoning and atoning) to Jesus not only to make certain claims about the saving significance of Jesus, but also to encourage a certain pattern of life for Jesus's followers that is best described as "participatory." These sacrificial interpretations are not about Jesus dying a "substitutionary death." They are about helping followers of Jesus understand that they are called to follow Jesus precisely in the sense that they imitate and unite with Jesus's cruciform (cross-shaped) life that culminated in his crucifixion. Jesus himself made this clear (e.g., Mark 8:34–38; 10:38–39). Living a cruciform life is the way to participate and share in Jesus's death and thereby share also in his resurrection (e.g., Phil 2:5–11; 3:10–11).

JESUS OVERCOMES THE FORCES OF DEATH

Contrary to common interpretations, Matthew Thiessen has persuasively shown that "[t]he Jesus of the Gospels does not reject the system of ritual purity or abandon all concern for ritual purity; rather, Jesus systematically roots out the sources of ritual impurities when he encounters them."[1] The Synoptic Gospels (Matthew, Mark, and Luke) narrate Jesus encountering and healing someone suffering from each category of major ritual impurity mentioned in Num 5:2–3. In fact, in Mark, Jesus heals the ritually impure in the same order that they appear in Num 5:2–3.[2] Jesus heals a man with

1. Thiessen, *Forces of Death*, 149. For examples of scholars who think Jesus rejects the purity system, see ibid., 1–5. Also, Kazen highlights how Jesus's complaint "that the Pharisees are like unmarked graves" that people walk over unaware (Luke 11:44, cf. Matt 23:27–28) "could be taken to indicate that Jesus acknowledged corpse impurity and worked with a basic purity paradigm like any Jew in the Second Temple period" (*Issues of Impurity*, 133).

2. Thiessen, *Forces of Death*, 177.

scale disease (Mark 1:40–45; Matt 8:2–4; Luke 5:12–14);[3] then he heals a women with an abnormal genital discharge (Mark 5:25–34; Matt 9:20–22; Luke 8:43–48); and then he touches and raises the corpse of a twelve-year-old girl (Mark 5:21–24, 35–43; Matt 9:18–19, 23–26; Luke 8:41–42, 49–56).[4]

Moreover, by the time of Jesus, similar to how the prophets expand on the notion of moral impurity, views of ritual and moral impurity expanded beyond what we find in the Torah (or the Prophets).[5] Thus, the Synoptic Gospels also depict Jesus as one with power to expel demonic impurity, which is similar to yet distinct from ritual impurity (i.e., having an impure spirit did not make the person ritually impure and touching someone with an impure spirit would neither "transfer" the spirit to that person nor render them ritually impure). While I am not going to discuss Jesus's exorcisms here, I raise these observations to emphasize how the Gospels present Jesus as being capable overcoming *all* the sources of impurity—the forces of death.[6]

Ultimately, the Gospels claim that Jesus is the kind of being, and has the type of "holy" life (cf. Mark 1:24; Luke 1:35; 4:34; John 6:69; Acts 3:14; 4:27), that necessarily overwhelms not only the *forces* of death, but *death* itself, by means of his own resurrection (2:27, 31–32; cf. Heb 7:16). As Thiessen expresses it, "This dramatic story culminates in Jesus facing off with death itself in his crucifixion, taking ritual impurity into his very own body, only once again and with finality to come out victorious when Israel's God raises him from the dead."[7] That is, the resurrection can be understood within the framework of the purity system as the ultimate purification from death.[8]

However, these observations can still be construed as Jesus *rejecting* the temple purification system as if his healings (not to mention his declarations of forgiveness of sins) *circumvented* the temple and the priesthood. After all, didn't Jesus prophesy the temple's destruction (e.g., Mark 13)? Doesn't this mean he rejected the temple and the attendant purification protocols?

3. Other instances of healing scale disease are found in Matt 8:2; 11:5; Luke 7:22; 17:12–19). And Jesus presumably healed Simon (not Simon Peter), who had scale disease at some point (Matt 26:6; Mark 14:3).

4. And Matthew, Luke, and John add more stories of Jesus raising the dead (cf. Matt 27:50–53; Luke 7:11–17; John 11:1–46). Cf. Thiessen, *Forces of Death*, 97–122.

5. See, e.g., Klawans, *Impurity and Sin*.

6. For understanding demonic impurity in the Gospels in relation to the Hebrew Bible, the wider ancient Near East, Second Temple Jewish traditions, and the Greco-Roman contexts, see Thiessen, *Forces of Death*, 123–48.

7. Thiessen, *Forces of Death*, 179.

8. Shively, "Purification of the Body," 62–89.

Addressing this question adequately is why we needed to detail the appropriate ritual purification protocols previously as well as properly situate the prophetic critiques of sacrifice as critiques of moral impurity, which the sacrificial system was always incapable of addressing. Next I highlight how the sayings and actions of Jesus regarding the temple in the Gospels align with both the Torah and the Prophets.[9]

Jesus and the Protocols for Ritual Impurity

Jesus's first encounter with a ritually impure person in the Synoptic Gospels is a man with scale disease, whom he heals (Mark 1:40–45; Matt 8:2–4; Luke 5:12–14). In each account, after he heals the man's skin, Jesus instructs him: "Go, show yourself to the priest, and offer for your cleansing what Moses commanded, as a testimony to them" (Mark 1:44 NRSV; cf. Matt 8:4; Luke 5:14). This direction makes perfect sense due to the multistep process for ritual purification for scale disease in Lev 14.

Remember that the ritual purification process is only applicable once the person has *already* been healed from their scale disease (Lev 14:2). The ritual purifications (the time lapse, washings, shaving, blood sprinklings, getting anointed with oil, offering reparation, purgation, and burnt sacrifices) do not remove the *physical* disease from the person, but rather the invisible miasmic and aerial ritual impurity so that they stop transmitting secondary impurity to other people and things (common and holy). All Jesus has done is bring the man into the physical condition required at the very start of the ritual purification process in Lev 14:2. Jesus heals the *scale disease*, and thus "destroys the impurity-creating condition,"[10] but he has not actually dealt with the *ritual impurity itself* on the person and on the temple. That is the function of the ritual purification steps in Lev 14 that need to be administered by a priest. Jesus has dealt with the *source* of the ritual impurity and this healing has done nothing to circumvent the protocols of Lev 14. Jesus's comment that the man needs to go follow the protocols of Lev 14 confirm their necessity.

Also, this instruction necessarily means that Jesus did not usurp the role of the priests. Jesus does not issue a declaration that the man is now "pure" because even that is specifically and only "the priestly prerogative,"

9. I cannot address the topic of Jesus and the food purity laws here, but Thiessen has convincingly shown how Jesus is not actually overthrowing the Levitical food laws in Mark 7 (*Forces of Death*, 187–95). See also Williams, "The Stomach Purifies All Foods," forthcoming.

10. Thiessen, *Forces of Death*, 61.

according to Lev 14 (cf. m. Neg. 3:1).[11] The unanimous testimony from these Gospel accounts, therefore, is that "Jesus intends for the man to fulfill the laws pertaining to *lepra* impurity because he thinks that they remain valid and significant."[12]

Besides summary statements where we read that Jesus healed those with scale disease, noted above, the only other account directly narrating Jesus healing scale disease is in Luke 17:12–19. Here Jesus heals ten people of their scale disease and Luke records an abbreviated form of Jesus's instructions to the first man he healed in 5:14: "Go and show yourselves to the priests" (17:14). Luke thereby emphasizes Jesus's continued alignment with and insistence on following the purity protocols in Leviticus.

Granted, when Jesus encounters another major ritual impurity with the woman who was healed of her irregular genital discharge there are other protocols (waiting seven days, bathing, and then offering a purgation sacrifice) that need to be done, and there is no statement from Jesus telling her to do these things (Mark 5:25–34; Matt 9:20–22; Luke 8:43–48; cf. Lev 15:25–30). I don't think the absence is significant, however, as there is no reason to think that Jesus suddenly changed his mind.

Rather, the very first account of Jesus encountering a major ritual impurity narratively frames and informs all of Jesus's other interactions with ritually impure people. Jesus has already explicitly expressed his commitment to the ritual purification protocols in Leviticus involving the priests, sacrifices, and the temple. Also, unlike the case for a person who has been healed of scale disease, the woman does not need to right away "go show herself to a priest." Priests do not declare a discharger "pure" the way they need to with someone with scale disease (at several stages). For genital-discharge impurity the need for a priest is only at the moment of offering the purgation sacrifice, which is the regular role of a priest facilitating all the sacrifices. Readers familiar with the Levitical protocols would presume that the woman would follow these and offer her required purgation sacrifice whenever she visits the temple in Jerusalem next.

Nevertheless, attending to Jesus's respect and commitment to the role of the priests and the need for the ritual purification protocols involving them and the temple (Mark 1:44, Matt 8:4; Luke 5:14; 17:14) is instructive. It demonstrates that the Gospels were keenly aware of when something eclipses Jesus's rather obvious *non-priestly* status. Instead of presenting a Jesus that circumvents either the priests or the temple system more broadly, they depict Jesus as fulfilling his ministry in line with the Torah's procedures

11. Thiessen, *Forces of Death*, 60.

12. Thiessen, *Forces of Death*, 61.

for ritual purification. That is, *the Gospels portray Jesus affirming the temple's efficacy for dealing with ritual impurity.*[13]

Jesus and Handwashing

There is a point of controversy, however, between Jesus and some of his contemporaries that needs to be addressed before moving on since some have mistaken this to prove that Jesus did not care about ritual purity. This is the notion of handwashing prior to eating (e.g., Matt 15:2; Mark 7:3; Luke 11:38).[14] Washing hands is only mentioned in the Torah as part of the ritual purification for a man with an abnormal genital discharge (Lev 15:11). If he touches another person and had not washed his hands then that other person would become impure until they take a bath, wash their clothes, and wait until sundown. And, as flagged previously, according to the Torah, the only time eating in a state of ritual purity was required is when the person is consuming a well-being sacrifice (7:20–21). It was perfectly fine to eat any common thing while ritually impure, let alone without ritually handwashing.[15] However, it became customary for *some* (not all) Jews to eat *all* meals in a state of ritual purity as if they were eating a sacrificial meal. This is what Klawans calls "the 'templization' . . . and the 'sacrificialization' of . . . food practices."[16] Klawans further explains:

> Purity is first and foremost the prerequisite for entry to the temple. As such, the maintenance of ritual purity beyond the temple

13. This also shows that for all the grand claims the Gospels are making about Jesus, they do not present Jesus as someone who can take upon himself Levitical priestly prerogatives as if he is thought to be a priest himself. As we will soon see, though, Hebrews claims Jesus is a priest according to the order of Melchizedek (not according to the Levitical/Aaronic order). Although it can be tempting to read the conclusions of Hebrews back into other texts, this would conflate two different priesthoods (Melchizedek's and Aaron's). In any case, Jesus's unwillingness to take upon himself any Levitical priestly prerogatives during his ministry indicates how mistaken that would be.

14. Luke uses the verb for "immerse" (*baptizō*), which might refer to ritual bathing rather than just handwashing. It also may just be a way that "immersing" one's hands into the water was a microcosm of immersing one's entire body in a ritual bath. Mark also refers to this group as completing a full water immersion (*baptizō*) (7:4) in addition to handwashing (7:2), but only when the person has come from a crowded public space (perhaps given the likelihood of bumping into someone who was ritually impure would be quite high). In any case, whether Luke and Mark are referring to full body immersions or not, the point I am making would still stand. Neither handwashing nor a full immersion in a bath is required to eat regular meals in the Torah.

15. Sanders, *Jesus and Judaism*, 265.

16. Klawans, *Purity, Sacrifice*, 201.

> is evidence of the effort to "templize" other aspects of religious life. Moreover, what is "templized" or "sacrificialized" here are those aspects of daily life—particularly prayer and eating—that were already conceptually related to temple worship.[17]

And thus, some "adopted the practice of eating even common food in a state of purity"[18] as if they were eating a well-being sacrifice at the temple.[19] This is a meta-level ritualization of ritual purity. Therefore, handwashing, which was only required for one sort of ritual impurity in Leviticus, became a microcosm of full ritual immersion in a bath by immersing one's hands in water. It became the way for those who wanted to "templize" their meals to enact the protocols for ritual purity on a smaller (and thus more practical) scale for everyday life. It is noteworthy that while the "Rabbis eventually made handwashing 'normative', . . . before 70 the common people did not accept the practice" and "it was limited to a small group" (cf. m. Ber. 8:1–2).[20]

Therefore, *Jesus's lack of handwashing means nothing more than that he does not think every meal should be eaten as if it were a sacred sacrificial meal.* Like most Jews of his time, he did not extrapolate the requirement to be ritually pure to eat a sacrificial meal at the temple beyond literally eating a sacrifice at the temple. This is why Jesus is careful to distinguish between the "commandment of God" (i.e., the commands in the Torah) and what had become a customary practice (i.e., "tradition," Matt 15:3; Mark 7:8) for his opponents from the "expansionist groups."[21] From everything observed thus far, however, we can plausibly infer that Jesus and his disciples would have all been ritually pure for eating the Passover/Lord's Supper since this was an actual sacrificial meal.

Furthermore, Jesus's comments about the (inadequate) Pharisaic practice of purifying cups and dishes (Matt 23:25–26; Luke 11:39–40) evince that Jesus was concerned with the protocols for ritual purity. But more than this, Jesus's comments reveal that he thought the Pharisees were *too lenient* in their purification protocols. Here Jesus sides with the more stringent position held by the Sadducees and the Qumran authors.[22] So even though Jesus rejects the expansionist custom of handwashing before eating common meals, this in no way indicates he completely disregarded ritual purity. If anything, it demonstrates Jesus's commitment to a more "literalist"

17. Klawans, *Purity, Sacrifice*, 201.

18. Sanders, *Jesus and Judaism*, 186.

19. Cf. Fishbane, *Judaism*, 110.

20. Sanders, *Jesus and Judaism*, 186.

21. This phrase comes from Kazen, *Issues of Impurity*, 115.

22. Furstenberg, "Controlling Impurity," esp. 190–94.

interpretation of the Torah since "[t]his notion [of handwashing for common meals] is completely unknown in the Torah and in other halakhic systems,"[23] while the washing of cups and dishes is rather straightforwardly addressed (Lev 6:21 [Eng. v. 28]; 11:32–33; 15:12; Num 31:23).

Nevertheless, since (a) by neglecting ritual handwashing for eating common meals Jesus is not rejecting ritual purity *per se*, (b) he participates in debates about proper ritual purity protocols, and (c) he affirms the efficacy of the priests and sacrificial system with respect to major ritual impurities, as discussed above, how are we to understand his criticisms of sacrifice and his prophecy that the temple is doomed to destruction?

Jesus and the Protocols for Moral Impurity

In short, just like Jesus is portrayed as operating within the protocols for ritual impurity, he is likewise depicted as operating within the prophetic protocols for moral impurity. *This is precisely why he believes the temple will be destroyed.* And this is also why, perhaps surprisingly at first mention, his declarations of forgiveness cannot be construed as "anti-temple." I will start with the latter of these.

Jesus as the Agent of Moral Purification

Jesus's declarations of forgiveness of sins need to be understood within the context of John the Immerser's ministry, which itself is framed in the Gospels as the penultimate fulfillment of the prophetic hope for Israel's restoration (Matt 3:2–3; Mark 1:2–3; Luke 3:3–6; John 1:23).[24] Without getting into historical reconstruction debates, our goal here is simply to observe how the Gospels portray John the Immerser and his relation to Jesus.[25]

But first, recall from the end of chapter 4 that the prophetic hope for forgiveness was *always* an extra-temple and extra-sacrificial divine act. This is because the sins Israel needed forgiveness for were grave sins of moral impurity—which the prophets had expanded to include economic exploitation, considered tantamount to murder—and *these have no sacrificial remedy*. Hence, it was these moral impurities that sent Israel into exile, according

23. Furstenberg, "Controlling Impurity," 194n87.

24. Similarly, Thiessen, *Forces of Death*, 21–23. Also, I am following Thiessen's use of "Immerser" rather than "Baptist" as a helpful defamiliarization strategy to remind us that John's water immersion activity was connected to ritual purification.

25. For inquiries into the historical John the Immerser, see Taylor, *The Immerser*; Marcus, *John the Baptist*.

to the prophets (and warned about in Lev 18–26). Remember also that the two images the prophets used to talk about this time of forgiveness of sins was (a) a new act of divine deliverance patterned after the exodus, which thereby comes with a (re)new(ed) covenant, and (b) a divine water-washing.

The Gospels claim that John is announcing that this time is near and that he has come as a forerunner to prepare the way for the one who will bring about the real purificatory washing by immersing people in the Holy Spirit (Matt 3:11–12; Mark 1:7–8; Luke 3:16–17; John 1:33). John's water immersion in a river is a prophetic symbolic action for this greater washing to come.[26]

While the Gospels identify John as the "voice in the wilderness" from Isa 40:3 (Matt 3:2–3; Mark 1:2–3; Luke 3:3–6; John 1:23),[27] John's activity and message lines up especially well with the promise of moral purification in Ezek 36:25–27.[28] Water-washing for ritual purification was self-administered, but Ezekiel says the people will be washed *by God* rather than washing themselves (contrasting with Isa 1:16). Also, Ezekiel correlates this divine washing with purification from moral impurities (36:17–19, 29, 33). Likewise, John's ministry is described in terms of water purification (done *to* the people; not self-administered), forgiveness of sins, and ultimate immersion in the Holy Spirit. Granted, Ezekiel does not use the language of "forgiveness" but rather of purifying moral impurity, but "forgiveness" is a major theme in Isaiah (and Jeremiah), as noted previously.[29]

The Gospels' description of John combining the various ways the prophets envision Israel's hope for restoration therefore makes sense. The needed "forgiveness of sins" must happen through some sort of "washing"/"immersion" not through a *kipper* sacrifice because (a) the sacrificial system cannot address the grave sins that need forgiveness and (b) this is also just what the prophets have proclaimed (which is consistent with the way ritual and moral purity are related yet distinct in the Torah). Put another way, the "forgiveness of sins" John is announcing is *not* made on analogy to sacrifice, but rather to water-washing. This observation aligns with both

26. John's symbolic action is like Isaiah walking around naked (Isa 20:2–3), Jeremiah breaking a pot (Jer 18–19) or burying a belt (13:1–11), or Ezekiel laying on his sides and cooking bread over animal excrement (Ezek 4:1–17), enacting Israel's exile by taking baggage and digging a hole through the city wall (12:1–28), or being silent and not mourning the death of his wife (24:15–27).

27. And this portion of Isaiah is riddled with exodus-like themes for the return from exile: e.g., 43:14–21; 44:27; 48:20–21; 50:2; 51:10–11; 58:8.

28. Josephus interprets John's immersion in terms of purity (*Ant.* 18.117). For how the Gospels depict John's immersion in relation to other Second Temple notions of ritual and moral purity, see Klawans, *Impurity and Sin*, 138–43.

29. E.g., Isa 27:9; 43:25; 44:22; 55:7; Jer 31:31–34; 33:6–8; 50:20.

the limitations of the *kipper* system and the prophetic expectations of forgiveness depicted *as* moral purification via washing, not sacrifice. Therefore, any interpretations or theologies that trade on the premise that "forgiveness of sins" necessarily evokes the concepts of "sacrifice" let alone "atonement" are not only reductive and simplistic, they are also incorrect because the premise itself is unwarranted.

Moreover, running water—that is, water that flows, as in rivers or wadis—is "a potent ritual detergent."[30] This makes sense since it is called "*living* water" and thereby has the power to purify (cf. Lev 14:5–6, 50–52; 15:13; Num 19:17; Jer 2:13; 17:13). The powers of life can nullify and thus purify the impure forces of death. And, according to the rabbinic tradition, living water cannot become ritually impure (m. Mikq. 1:4–8). It cannot contract ritual impurity from anything that contacts it. Rather, like fire (Num 31:23; Mal 3:2–3), it purifies whatever it touches. Therefore, John's use of living water for purification and forgiveness of moral impurities means he is using "the strongest form of water purificant available to humans."[31]

But while going about this ministry, John is simultaneously announcing that someone else is coming after him who will immerse the people in the most potent purificatory detergent possible: the Holy Spirit.[32] This aligns with how Rabbi Aqiva links Ezek 36:25 with Jer 17:13 (m. Yoma 8:9) to say that God will purify Israel with "waters" (Ezek 36:25) that are in fact God himself since God is Israel's "hope/*miqweh*" (Jer 17:13), "a fountain of living waters" (17:13; cf. 2:13). Thus, the divine Spirit (Ezek 36:26–27) is the ultimate "waters" for moral purification. Hence John's insistence on an even greater immersion to come from someone else.

This relates to Ezekiel's claim that the purification will not be self-administered (contra Isa 1:16), but rather it will be a third party, God, who washes Israel and puts the divine Spirit in them. A unique feature of John's activity is that he immerses others. John is not telling the people to immerse themselves in the river (e.g., Elisha telling Naaman to immerse himself in the Jordan to heal his scale disease, 2 Kgs 5:1–14). By John insisting that the people are be washed rather than wash themselves, he is allowing the people to anticipate the experience of the divine immersion to come where God washes and purifies them.

The Gospels thereby frame John's immersion ministry with the most powerful *natural* purification agent for humans as a proleptic sign of the greater immersion Jesus himself will administer with *the* most potent

30. Thiessen, *Forces of Death*, 23.

31. Thiessen, *Forces of Death*, 23.

32. Thiessen, *Forces of Death*, 23.

supernatural purification: an immersion in the divine Spirit.[33] I agree with Klawans that "John's baptism worked as a ritual of moral purification," but only in the sense that it was a ritualized *anticipation* of the real moral purification to come through Jesus by the Spirit.[34]

As far as the Gospels' accounts are concerned, John did not think his immersion actually purified the people from their sins of moral impurity. As Thiessen notes, "he expresses the expectation that one will come soon who will wash with a newly available pneumatic detergent to perform a full purification."[35] This one to come is Jesus. He is the promised divine source of moral purification. And the Gospels make the case for this on analogy to how Jesus is able to overcome the forces of ritual impurity.

This moral purification is not due to Jesus's *death per se*, though this is part of it, but more because of *who* he is as the source of contagious holy purification. Jesus's death-and-resurrection is still part of this whole framework because it proves he can not only purify scale disease,[36] for instance, but also his life is the kind of life that cannot be held down by death. *His life nullifies death itself.* The point is: just as it is the nature of

33. Matthew and Luke have John saying that Jesus will immerse people "in the Holy Spirit and fire." While some might want to relate fire only to notions of judgment, I agree with Thiessen "that John connects fire to the *pneuma* [Spirit] because both have the ability to purify" (*Forces of Death*, 23n8) like in Num 31:23. However, Mal 3:2–3 combines the notions of purification and judgment. This is one of the passages quoted by Mark in relation to John (1:2). In other words, this is a false choice. Divine purification from moral impurity can happen *through* divine judgment.

34. Klawans, *Impurity and Sin*, 143. There are a few problems with Klawans full quote, however. He says, "John's baptism worked as a ritual of moral purification, effecting atonement by purifying individuals from moral defilement" (*Impurity and Sin*, 143). One issue is that Klawans evinces the problematic slippage with the word "atonement" here. We know he does not mean "atonement" in the sense of sacrificial *kipper* because he explicitly notes earlier how atonement in this sense is not possible for moral impurities (30–31). Therefore, his use here must mean "forgiveness of sins" or similar. Secondly, however, Klawans might be correct that the historical John the Immerser thought his water immersion effected moral purification. But the Gospels frame John and his immersion differently—as a proleptic enactment of the actual moral purification to come by someone else (Jesus). Historically accurate or not, the Gospels portray John as talking about his own ministry (a) within the framework of moral purification, but also (b) in *penultimate* terms since he is depicted as a forerunner to Jesus's ministry of *actual* moral purification. This is what matters for our present purposes.

35. Thiessen, *Forces of Death*, 23.

36. To clarify: The healing is the first purification (*ṭāhŏrâ*) that has to happen prior to priestly involvement (Lev 14:2). The priests are involved in the *subsequent* stages of purification.

Jesus's very being that purifies ritual impurities that contact Jesus, it is Jesus's very being that makes him "powerful enough to remove moral impurities."[37]

We can see this from how the Gospels portray Jesus as a potent source of holiness and purification. In every encounter, when Jesus touches the impure, he does not contract secondary impurity as expected. As we saw, normally, contact with the ritually impure transmits secondary impurity to the other person. But the opposite happens when impurity contacts Jesus: *purity* gets transmitted to the impure person. These impure persons get brought into the first level of purity, only needing to go through their specific multistep protocol for their full ritual purification outlined in Lev 14–15 (cf. Mark 1:42–44; Matt 8:4; Luke 5:14; 17:14).

This means Jesus is like "living waters" that cannot contract impurity (cf. m. Miqw. 1:8). But since these people also leave the encounter with Jesus in the first stage of ritual purity, the physical source of their impurity having been healed, this means that Jesus is greater than physical living waters. Even though living waters cannot become ritually impure (even if a scale disease person went in them), ritual immersions are required *after* the physical source of the impurity is healed. The living waters do not (normally) heal the physical impurities themselves.[38] Therefore, Jesus's ability to not only remain pure, but also to heal them from their physical impurity, indicates that he is indeed the one to come that John announced.

Jesus's very being is purifying because he is "the holy one of God" (Mark 1:24; Luke 4:34; John 6:69; cf. Luke 1:35; Acts 2:27; 3:14; 4:27; 13:35), the locus of the Holy—i.e., sanctifying—Spirit (Matt 3:16; Mark 1:10; Luke 3:22; John 1:32). As Thiessen observes:

> Mark's title for Jesus, the holy one of God, parallels Leviticus 21:23 LXX, which refers to the tabernacle as *to hagion tou theou*, which is the neuter form of Mark's title for Jesus—*ho hagios tou theou*. . . . Mark's Gospel portrays Jesus's holiness removing the conditions that give rise to ritual impurities in others. Contact with Jesus, the holy one of God, causes a discharge of holiness to surge out of Jesus—a holiness that overpowers the source of impurity in the one touching Jesus.[39]

37. Thiessen, *Forces of Death*, 178.

38. I say "normally" because of the story of Elisha instructing Naaman to immerse himself in the Jordan river to heal his scale disease (2 Kgs 5:1–14). But this was a miracle. Immersing in rivers was not thought to be a regular cure for scale disease. This was specific to Elisha and Naaman.

39. Thiessen, *Forces of Death*, 92.

Whereas the Levitical system only dealt with these major ritual impurities once they went away by whatever means that happened, Jesus *causes* these impurities to vanish. He has the power to attack these impurities at their source due to the very nature of his being as the walking sanctuary. His very flesh is like another mobile dwelling place (cf. John 1:14), except that it cannot be defiled; it can only purify.

Whereas the instructions for ritual impurity in the Torah are *defensive* against impurity, Jesus goes on the *offensive*. Just like the *kipper* system has built-in limitations, as Thiessen explains:

> They [the functions of the purity system and the role of the priests] had a divinely ordained limitation: they could not and were never meant to wipe out death itself or cure *lepra* or address the human condition that results in various genital discharges. The temple could not eradicate the *sources* of ritual impurity, but it could eliminate the *aftereffects* once those sources of impurity left a person's body. . . . [This] is a recognition of what the texts like Leviticus and Numbers claim about the efficacy of the temple and its rites; they were inherently and divinely intended to have limitations.[40]

What the Gospels are demonstrating through their narrations of Jesus's encounters with the severely ritually impure (along with his other healings, of course) is that "Israel's God has unleashed a force of holiness in the world that goes on the offensive against impurity."[41] By calling Jesus "the holy one of God" (Mark 1:24; Luke 4:34; John 6:69) and then showing how "a holy power emanates out of Jesus's body and can overcome all sources of impurity" the Gospels declare that Jesus "embodies God's holiness let loose on earth."[42]

The same logic is the reason for Jesus's power and authority to forgive sins. This is exactly what the Gospels say John was preparing the people for: the arrival of God's means of moral purification, the forgiveness of the grave sins that sent Israel into exile. This is why Jesus appeals to his miracles—including eradicating major ritual impurities such as scale disease and rising the dead—as proof for John while he is in prison that he (Jesus) is indeed the one to come who will bring about the expected moral purification as well (Matt 11:2–6; Luke 7:18–23). If he can remove the *sources* of major ritual impurities themselves, then he is the "coming one" who can affect moral purification, the forgiveness of sins.

40. Thiessen, *Forces of Death*, 180.

41. Thiessen, *Forces of Death*, 180.

42. Thiessen, *Forces of Death*, 180.

This is the same rationale at work when Jesus declares forgiveness of sins. The physical healing for the man who was paralyzed is the proof Jesus offers that he can forgive sins and that the man's sins were indeed forgiven (Mark 2:5–12). As Thiessen notes, "Perhaps Mark's Jesus alludes to a belief that we later find preserved in the Talmud: 'A sick person does not arise from his sickness until all his sins are forgiven' (Babylonian Talmud, *Nedarim* 41a)."[43]

Consider the narrative context thus far in Mark. First, John comes immersing people in living water as the promised forerunner for the greater moral purification, the forgiveness of sins, that is to come through Jesus by means of an immersion in the Holy Spirit (1:1–8). Then, Jesus is filled with the Holy Spirit, begins his ministry, and gathers a few followers (1:9–20). Jesus is called "the holy one of God" and drives out an "impure spirit" from a person and then heals many more people from illnesses and their demonic impurities (1:21–39). The next major scene is when Jesus heals a man who has the major ritual impurity scale disease and then instructs him to follow through on all the ritual purification protocols from Lev 14 (1:40–45). The narrative is quickly connecting these dots, showing that Jesus is indeed the one who will bring about the moral purification John announced would soon come since Jesus has been purifying all these other ailments. And in the very next scene Jesus is explicitly talking about the "forgiveness of sins" (2:1–12), "the removal of moral impurities,"[44] all of which links back to John's proclamation in 1:4–8.

Furthermore, there is another clue in this scene that the forgiveness Jesus is declaring has to do with moral impurity. He says "the Son of Man has authority to forgive sins *on the land*" (*exousian echei ho huios tou anthrōpou aphienai hamartias epi tēs gēs*) (Mark 2:10).[45] The wording is very similar to Lev 25:10 LXX where it says that on the year of Jubilee they are to "proclaim release upon the land" (*diaboēsete aphesin epi tēs gēs*).[46] The year of Jubilee in Leviticus has to do with resetting the land back to its original family clan inheritors, but this notion gets taken up in Isa 61:1–2 to describe what

43. Thiessen, *Forces of Death*, 179n4.

44. Thiessen, *Forces of Death*, 179.

45. Mark's word order differs from Matthew and Luke's. Mark has *aphienai hamartias epi tēs gēs*, "to forgive sins on the land," which may indicate that Jesus can forgive sins that impact the *land* (moral impurities). But Matthew and Luke have *exousian echei ho huios tou anthrōpou epi tēs gēs aphienai hamartias*, "the Son of Man has authority on the land to forgive sins" (Matt 9:6; Luke 5:24). They put "on the land" ahead of "to forgive sins," which makes "on the land" seem to modify where Jesus's *authority* is (his authority is "on the land/earth").

46. My thanks to Logan Williams for pointing out the connections between these texts. See also his article, "Melchizedek, the Son of Man, and Eschatological Jubilee."

will happen when Israel gets restored from exile to their own land (cf. Luke 4:18–19; 11QMelch). And these restoration hopes are expressed in terms of the forgiveness of sins in the prophets as we have seen. Thus, while the notion of forgiveness of sins has already been framed in Mark in terms of the promised moral purification to come from the prophets, perhaps the comment in 2:10 is a further indication of that motif if it is saying that Jesus can forgive what the temple and even the Day of Decontamination cannot: sins that impact the *land* (i.e., moral impurity).

In any case, Jesus's declarations of forgiveness are explicitly linked with moral impurity when they are directed to "the sinners" Jesus encounters. As Sanders has argued, this is not about the doctrine of universal sinfulness or the like; rather, it means "'the wicked', and it refers to those who sinned willfully and heinously and who did not repent."[47] That is, when we read about Jesus and "the sinners" we ought to be thinking about this in terms of moral impurity because these are the sins that have no *kipper* remedy (cf. Num 15:30–31). Thus, when Jesus tells the morally impure woman in Luke 7:48 that her sins are forgiven, he is declaring his power to purify *moral* impurity (Luke 7:36–50, see esp. vv. 37, 39, 47–50), not that there is in fact a hitherto unknown super-duper *kipper* sacrifice available. Just as Jesus "removes the sources of ritual impurity" by virtue of his very being as the enfleshed sacred dwelling place of God, "he also removes moral impurities or sins, explicitly forgiving [them]."[48] It is Jesus's own *person*, as a living holy place, not his death *per se*, that overwhelms the forces of death in full, thereby being the permanent source of holiness that can purify both ritual and moral impurities.

Now, obviously, Jesus's own death is part of this entire program of moral purification, but it is framed as the culmination of what Jesus was always already capable of doing by virtue of his own supreme holiness. "The Gospel writers portray Jesus first destroying impurities that he encounters, then giving his disciples the power and authority to do what he does, and then personally entering into the source of all impurity: death."[49] From this perspective, Jesus's death is significant precisely because when Jesus encountered death itself, he overcame it. As Peter in Acts later says, "God raised him up, releasing him from the agony of death because *it was impossible for him to be conquered by it*" (Acts 2:24). That is, Jesus was resurrected because he has the type of holy life that necessarily overwhelms not only the

47. Sanders, *Jesus and Judaism*, 174–211, here 177.

48. Thiessen, *Forces of Death*, 178.

49. Thiessen, *Forces of Death*, 184.

forces of death that generate ritual impurity, but *death itself*, the consequence of moral impurity (2:22–24, 27, 31–32; cf. Heb 7:16).

This is why in another speech in Acts the proclamation of the "forgiveness of sins" (Acts 13:38) is explicitly linked to the logic of his resurrection (13:34–39; note the "therefore" [*oun*] in v. 38). Just as the paralytic walking out of the house healed proved that Jesus has authority to forgive sins, to effect purification for sins defiling the land, Jesus walking out of the tomb proves it all the more. When Jesus defeats death itself, he is victorious over both the source of ritual impurity and the consequences of sins, especially grave sins that produce moral impurity and lead to covenant death (e.g., Ezek 37). This is the meaning of his signs and works of power that Jesus relayed to the messengers from John (Matt 11:2–6; Luke 7:18–23). This is the very prophetic purification—ritual and moral—that John was expecting to happen in and through Jesus. Thus, as Thiessen further explains,

> By inserting a new, mobile, and powerfully contagious force of holiness into the world in the person of Jesus, Israel's God has signaled the very coming of the kingdom—a kingdom of holiness and life that throughout the mission of Jesus overwhelms the forces and sources of impurity and death, be they pneumatic, ritual, or moral.[50]

This will be celebrated and memorialized through a ritual intimating a thanksgiving well-being offering (the Lord's Supper discussed below), but it is not Jesus's death as a *sacrifice* that brings all this purification about. It is Jesus's death *qua death* (as contact with death itself), *qua covenant* death (as the temple's destruction *in nuce*), as the ultimate consequence of the forces of death, that exhausts the powers of death, terminates it, and ultimately overcomes it by not being held down by it. Jesus did not see decay; he has an indestructible holy life and thus he was raised (Acts 2:24, 27, 31; 13:35; cf. Heb 7:16). It is because of his resurrection that he is the agent of the prophesied moral purification (Acts 13:34–39) that John was announcing as imminent. The Lord's Supper—as a ritual intimation of the communal thanksgiving well-being sacrifices of Passover and a covenant inauguration/renewal—*memorializes* that victory over the forces of impurity and *celebrates* it, but it does not bring it about.

That is, there is a difference between the meaning of Jesus's death *qua* "death," and the meaning of Jesus *qua* "sacrifice." The NT authors express the saving significance of Jesus in a variety of ways, but when it comes to Jesus's death as *death*, they do not use sacrificial imagery since, as we

50. Thiessen, *Forces of Death*, 179.

learned, sacrifice is not about the concept of death.[51] Sacrificial imagery is used for expressing other meanings of Jesus's entire life (and resurrection and ascension).

The point here is that Jesus's death and resurrection are comprehended within the framework of moral purification and that *this is distinct from thinking about Jesus in terms of sacrificial imagery*. When Jesus's death is framed as a sacrificial event in the Gospels, during the Lord's Supper, it is viewed as the sacrificial meal of celebration for the end of the curse brought about by Israel's moral impurity and the ratification of the new covenant. Jesus-as-sacrifice is not the saving event itself from this angle, but rather, like the first Passover, the proleptic ritual celebration of the deliverance immediately about to take place.

Jesus's *death* is saving only insofar as it is seen in tandem with the resurrection, whereby just as when Jesus encountered major ritual impurities he vanquished them and was not affected by them, so too the resurrection is proof that (a) when Jesus encountered death itself he vanquished it and therefore (b) he is the promised agent of moral purification: the one who is able to forgive the most heinous of sins that drag the entire community and the land into the covenant curse of death.

But if Jesus is the agent of moral purification, what are we to make of his criticisms of sacrifice and his prophecy that the temple will be destroyed again?

Jesus, the Destruction of the Temple, and the Logic of Moral Impurity

In short, Jesus announces the inevitable destruction of the temple (Matt 23:37–24: Mark 13; Luke 13:34–35; 19:41–44; 21:1–38) because he is operating within the logic of the prophetic protocols for moral impurity. As already set forth, when moral impurities saturate the land (Lev 18–25), then God will abandon the sanctuary, leaving it doomed to destruction (Jer 12:7; 18:17; 22:5; 23:33, 39; Ezek 7–10). Jesus's Jeremiah-like temple-destruction discourse (cf. Jer 7) is not because he thinks the temple is inherently "ineffective." It is that the sacrificial system *could never* atone for sins in the "moral impurity" category: idolatry, sexual immorality, and murder (which the prophets expanded to include economic exploitation). And this is because these sins pollute the land itself, but the *kipper* system can only purge impurity from the *sanctuary*.

51. See Eberhart, "Characteristics," 59, quoted in chapter 1 footnote 60. See also Moffitt, "It Is Not Finished," 164n19.

This is why Jesus's affirmation of sacrifices for dealing with major ritual impurities (e.g., Mark 1:44) is not in conflict with his prophecy of the temple's looming destruction on account of moral impurity. As we learned, the system of decontaminating sacrifices necessarily cannot deal with moral impurities that pollute the land, and this limitation is *by God-ordained design*.

According to Luke 19:42, Jesus thinks this catastrophe could have been avoided if (perhaps most of) the community repented and listened to him (i.e., received moral purification). But by the time he arrives in Jerusalem for what would be his last Passover, he is convinced the temple will be destroyed and the people will be driven out from the land once again (19:41–44; 21:1–38; cf. Mark 13). This is why immediately upon his entry into Jerusalem "he made a demonstration which prophetically symbolized the coming event," namely, "the destruction of the temple[,] and carried out an action symbolic of its destruction by demonstrating against the performance of the sacrifices."[52] But, in light of the foregoing, we can affirm Sanders's conclusion that this cannot be interpreted as though Jesus "was opposed to the temple sacrifices which God commanded to Israel."[53] Jesus "intended, rather, to indicate that the end was at hand and that the temple would be destroyed."[54] Moreover, comprehending Jesus's prophetic symbolic action in the temple not as critical of temple sacrifices *per se* "has the additional advantage of making sense of the acceptance of temple worship by the early apostles (Acts 2.46; 3.1; 21.26). They did not think that Jesus had considered it impure, but only that the days of the present temple were numbered."[55]

Also, Jesus's belief that the temple will be soon destroyed seems to be ultimately anchored in his conviction that he will be murdered. At the Lord's Supper Jesus described his death as his "blood" (*haima*) being "poured out" (*ekchunnō*) (Matt 26:28; Mark 14:24; Luke 22:20). The combination of *ekchunnō* and *haima* only appears in six verses in the NT. Half of these clearly refer to murder—pouring out innocent blood (Matt 23:35 [cf. 23:29–34]; Luke 11:50 [cf. vv. 49, 51; 13:34–35]; Acts 22:20)—and the other half are in these Lord's Supper pericopes. Thus, Jesus's death is specifically indexed as a murder and Jesus says that the reason God has abandoned the

52. Sanders, *Jesus and Judaism*, 75, cf. 61–76.

53. Sanders, *Jesus and Judaism*, 75.

54. Sanders, *Jesus and Judaism*, 75.

55. Sanders, *Jesus and Judaism*, 76. See also Paul's positive comments about the temple liturgy of sacrifices in Rom 9:4 and Klawans, *Purity, Sacrifice*, 217–22.

temple to destruction is because of all the innocent bloodshed (i.e., accumulation of a moral impurity) (Matt 23:30–39; Luke 11:50–51; 13:34–35).[56]

Also, Jesus's teachings have been calling out other moral impurities up this point and, like the prophets, he expands what belongs in the categories of moral impurity (Mark 7:20–23; Matt 15:18–20; cf. 23:27–28). For example, murder includes hatred (Matt 5:21–22), idolatry includes ordering one's life by Mammon (6:24; Luke 16:13; contrast with 11:41 where charity purifies), sexuality immorality includes lust and divorce (Matt 5:27–32; Mark 10:10–12; Luke 16:18).

The temple's destruction might have been avoided (Luke 19:42), but the murder of Jesus, pouring out his innocent blood, seals the temple's fate, just as the murders of the prophets Zechariah and Uriah sealed the first temple's fate (cf. Matt 23:35; Luke 11:51; 2 Chr 24:20–21; Jer 26; esp. vv. 15, 20–23 with 2 Kgs 24:3–5 and Jer 22:3, 17–18; see also Ezek 24:1–14). Jesus is convinced he is going to be murdered just as these other innocent prophets were (especially John the Immerser, see Matt 17:12–13) and this is necessary for understanding why he is persuaded the temple is going to be destroyed. Murder is morally defiling and, as Jesus sees it, his death is "the last straw" so to speak.

Therefore, claiming that the land is saturated with innocent bloodshed and thus will be destroyed because the divine presence has vacated it (Matt 23:30–38; Luke 13:34–35) is not a critique of the *temple*; it is a critique of a *morally impure community*. The destruction of the temple is simply the expected outworking of unaddressed moral impurity per the Torah and the prophets.

In this way, Jesus's (a) affirmation of the sacrifices to deal with ritual impurity and then (b) a prophetic announcement of the temple's destruction are not "in tension" with each other. Jesus has not changed his mind about the efficacy of the sacrificial system. *It works for what it was always intended to address, but it obviously cannot work for what it was never meant to address.* And according to Matthew, Jesus affirms God's actual dwelling in the temple (Matt 23:21) and he believes the altar functions to sanctify whatever touches it (Matt 23:19), just like Exod 29:37 and 30:29 say. But, as anyone who reads the words on the scrolls of the Torah would realize, Jesus knows that the sacrificial system was never meant to deal with the moral impurity generated by grave sins. This explains why he believes God will abandon the temple to destruction—it is due to the accumulation of moral impurity, per the logic of the Torah's teaching on moral impurity and the

56. Similarly, Moffitt, "Righteous Bloodshed," 299–320.

logic of prophets announcing the destruction of the first temple (13:31–38; Luke 13:34–35; cf. Jer 12:7; 18:17; 22:5; 23:33, 39; Ezek 7–10).

Moreover, Jesus's appropriation of Hosea's supposed critique of sacrifice—"I desire mercy, and not sacrifice" (Matt 9:13; 12:6–7; cf. Hos 6:6)—is not in conflict with his affirmation of sacrifices elsewhere (e.g., Matt 5:23–24; 8:4; cf. Mark 1:44; Luke 5:14; 17:14). This is because Jesus first makes this comment in the context of calling Matthew the tax collector and then having a party at his house with his other wealthy tax collector buddies and hoodlums, i.e., "sinners" (Matt 9:9–10). As mentioned above, "sinners" are the heinously "wicked," those guilty of moral impurity. Since the prohibition on usury among fellow Israelites is in the "holiness code" in Leviticus (25:36–38; cf. Exod 22:25; Deut 23:19–20) and the prophets extend the moral impurity of murder to include economic exploitation, Sanders is correct that this is why "'tax collectors' and 'sinners' go together in several passages in the Gospels."[57] That is, tax collectors are morally impure persons due to their economic oppression, which is tantamount to murder. It was Jesus's welcome of these morally impure people that caused the Pharisees in Matthew's scene to criticize him (Matt 9:11). And this is when we get Jesus's response that quotes from Hosea:

> Those who are well have no need of a physician, but those who are sick. Go and learn what this means, "I desire mercy, not sacrifice." For I have come to call not the righteous but sinners. (9:12–13 NRSV)

As we saw in the section on the so-called prophetic critique of sacrifice, the prophets are providing a critique of moral impurity that recognizes the God-ordained built-in limitations for what sacrifices are for.

Therefore, Jesus is not critiquing the system of sacrifices itself, but rather making it clear that his mission is to be the agent of the moral purification of the wicked, which necessarily requires a solution *beyond the built-in capacity* of the temple system to address. And Jesus is saying that this requires, first of all, the merciful welcome of the wicked. Later he reminds his interlocutors of his quote from Hosea (12:6–7) and makes the more startling and explicit claim that this extra-temple moral purification is happening through him, which is "greater than the temple" (12:6; cf. vv. 41–42). But again, recognizing that the promised restoration and attendant moral purification is "greater than" or beyond the God-ordained scope of what the temple is all about it *not* a critique of the temple.[58] It cannot be a criticism

57. Sanders, *Jesus and Judaism*, 177–78.

58. This coheres with the notions of eschatological forgiveness in the Dead Sea Scrolls. Two texts feature either a heavenly (11QMelch II, 7–8) or earthly (TLevi 18=4Q541 9) intermediary who will bring about "atonement" (*kipper*) apart from

sacrifices or other cultic rituals (Baumgarten, "Messianic Forgiveness," 539–41). And two other texts specify that an eschatological priestly Messiah "will atone for their sin *better than* meal and sin [purgation] offerings" (CD XIV, 18–19=4Q266 10 I, 12–13) or "will atone for iniquitous guilt and for sinful unfaithfulness and as good will for the earth *better than* the flesh of burnt-offerings and the fat of sacrifices" (1QS IX, 4) (Baumgarten, "Messianic Forgiveness," 541; my italics). While some have restored the text of CD XIV, 19 as having the preposition "*bet* [ב] . . . before מנחה וחטאת, thus yielding the sense through 'meal and sin offerings,'" this supposition "raises the question as to why the coming of the Messiah is needed for the bringing of regular atonement sacrifices" (541). Moreover, "in Genizah MS A, the curvature of the base of the letter after עונם fits a *mem* [מ] rather than a *bet*" (541). Also, the parallel of CD XIV, 19 with 1QS IX, 4 confirms this since the *mem* (מ) is plainly there (מבשר עולות ומחלבי זבח) and "'better than' . . . is preferable as a more commonly used connotation of מן [*min*]" (541). All the texts that mention messianic atonement (*kipper*) from Qumran agree that it "will be available without the need for ritual sacrifice" (542). Therefore, "The Messiah of Aaron and Israel, that is of the total eschatological community, would with his coming atone for any sins resulting from the previously imperfect knowledge of the Law. He would do so not through ritual sacrifice, מנחה וחטת ['grain offerings and purgation offerings'], but through his illuminational presence as the embodiment of divine good will for the earth" (544). While these texts use the root *k-p-r* and the Gospel accounts do not, it is clear the "atonement" in these texts is more about how the *effects* or *results* of sacrificial atonement are eclipsed by a different sort of "atonement" that is accomplished apart from sacrifice/cultic rituals by the appropriate messianic figure. To use an imperfect analogy: In the evolution of transportation some sort of boat was required to traverse oceans to get to other continents. Boats are limited since they can only work on water and cannot be used to travel on land. But then a whole new mode of transportation that fulfills yet also transcends the limitations of the old way appeared with the invention of airplanes. Airplanes accomplish the same result as boats (transoceanic transportation) but do so much faster and they are even used to travel across, or rather, over land. Obviously, an airplane is not a boat and it is because it is *not* a boat that it is able to be a mode of transportation that is "better than" boats. So too, atoning sacrifices ("boats") were one way of accomplishing *kipper* ("transportation"), but they are limited. These texts from Qumran evince a hope when a new mode of *kipper* ("transportation") will be available that happens apart from sacrifices ("boats") but rather through "the divinely anointed redeemer" (Baumgarten, "Messianic Forgiveness," 542) who accomplishes an alternative mode of *kipper* ("transportation") through his person/presence ("airplane") that is *better than* the former way of *kipper* through sacrifices.

If Jesus is being linked up with this type of expectation in the Gospels, then this would only mean he can bring about this eschatological situation by virtue of *his person*, not his cultic activities. This is what "greater than the temple" (Matt 12:6) means. Just like it is nonsense to conflate airplanes and boats simply because they are both modes of *transportation* in contexts that depend on their *differences* that allows for comparison such that airplanes are deemed superior, it is irresponsible to reduce all modes of *kipper* or forgiveness into sacrificial atonement. That is like insisting on calling airplanes "boats" simply because airplanes can traverse oceans like boats can. But as Baumgarten observes, "The claim that כפר על always refers to ritual expiation is contradicted by the occasional usage in both biblical and Qumran Hebrew of this phrase for divine forgiveness" ("Messianic Forgiveness," 540; he cites Jer 18:23; CD IV, 10; 4Q221 IV, 4). But again, none of the Gospels use the language of "atonement" (this only appears in 1 John and Hebrews). In any case, whatever atoning sacrifices could accomplish (e.g.,

because it is simply honoring and taking seriously what the scriptures have set forth regarding its capabilities, functions, and God-ordained limitations. The *kipper* sacrifices can only remove ritual impurities and a limited set of sin-contamination from the temple, but Jesus can effectuate the greater purification promised by the prophets. Jesus can purify grave moral impurity. But this is *not* anchored in nor analogized to the *kipper* system, but rather in the prophetic promise of the *divine water-washing of the Spirit.*

This is the framework within which we need to interpret Jesus's other comment (found only in Matthew's account of the Lord's Supper) about the effects of his death, that it will result in "the forgiveness of sins" (26:28).[59] This alludes to when an angel reveals to Joseph that Mary will name her son "Jesus" and he will "save his people from their sins" (2:21). It is common for scholars to read "forgiveness of sins" and automatically think that has to do with "the Day of Atonement in Leviticus 16 (plus perhaps the atoning sacrifices more generally [e.g., Lev 4:1—6:7])."[60] But as already noted, the notion of "forgiveness of sins" as it is framed in the prophetic hope for Israel's restoration and within John's immersion ministry is not about sacrificial *kipper*. It is all about moral purification, the forgiveness of the sins that caused the destruction of the kingdoms of Israel and Judah. And these sins are understood as the sins of moral impurity that polluted the land itself. Therefore, the forgiveness of these sins cannot be related to the limited notion of forgiveness for the sins that merely produce a contamination on the sanctuary.

This is why a lot of space detailed these interrelated concepts earlier. Now we can easily dismiss such interpretations because sacrificial *kipper* absolutely cannot be seen as the solution to Israel's needs regarding these sins, just like Leviticus (chapters 18–26) and Numbers (35:31–34) already made clear. This is also why the sacrificial imagery that is present in all the Lord's Supper accounts draws from the non-atoning well-being sacrifices: Passover (Matt 26:17–19; Mark 14:12, 14, 16; Luke 22:7–8, 11, 13, 15)[61] and the covenant-inauguration sacrifice (Matt 28:28; Mark 14:24; Luke 22:20; 1 Cor 11:25).

---

forgiveness of [certain] sins), Jesus can also accomplish *and then some* precisely because he is *not* an atoning sacrifice, and he is even "greater than the temple" itself (Matt 12:6).

59. See also the previous footnote 58.

60. Gorman, *The Death of the Messiah*, 15; similarly, Shauf, *Jesus the Sacrifice*, 123.

61. John does not have a Last Supper account, but when he reports Jesus's teaching about his flesh as bread and his blood as drink (6:51–56) this is framed within a Passover context (6:4). Similarly, before Paul reminds the Corinthians about Jesus's words at the Last Supper he already has said Jesus is the Paschal lamb that has been sacrificed (5:7).

We will return to these sacrifices shortly below, but here it suffices to note a few points. (1) These sacrifices have no atoning functions. And this is reinforced by the obvious fact that the Lord's Supper is *eaten*. Sacrifices eaten by laity can never be from the *kipper* sacrifices. (2) It would have been *very confusing* (to say the least) for Jesus at a literal Passover meal, which is a type of thanksgiving well-being sacrifice, to further "sacrificialize" what he wants his disciples to then *consume* as a *kipper* sacrifice, let alone one of the purgation sacrifices on the Day of Decontamination, which *not even the high priest ate from*. Besides what was burned on the altar, the rest of the flesh and carcasses of the animals were burned outside the camp (16:27; cf. 4:11–12, 21; 6:30).[62]

(3) More importantly for the present discussion, these are the very sacrifices that would be associated with the beginning of Israel's exodus-like restoration from exile. This is their ultimate Passover celebration, a sacred meal in thanksgiving for God delivering them from the curses of the covenant, the consequences of their moral impurity. Like the first exodus, this deliverance is then marked by establishing a covenant that uses the well-being sacrifice so that the people partake from the sacred meal. Therefore, "forgiveness of sins" in Matt 26:28 is to be linked with the new covenant in Jeremiah (31:31–34; 33:8),[63] the affirmation of God's eternal covenant in Ezekiel (16:59–63) and making "a covenant of peace" (34:25; 37:26; cf. Isa 54:10), simply making a "covenant" (Isa 27:9 together with 59:21),[64] or even just the promise that God will eventually forgive Israel's sins by divine fiat (e.g., Isa 43:25; 44:22; 55:7; Jer 50:20; Mic 7:18–19; Hos 14:2–7; cf. Zeph 3:15). The moral purification the prophets announce, which many envision as a divine water-washing and immersion in the sanctifying Spirit, is inextricably bound together with the idea of the forgiveness of the sins that generated the moral impurity (Ezek 22:15; 24:13; 36:25–27, 29, 33; 37:23; Isa 4:4; Zech 13:1–2; Ps 51:4, 9 [vv. 2, 7 Eng.]; Jer 33:8; Mal 3:2–33).

This further strengthens points 1–2. Making Jesus's comment about "forgiveness" relate to *kipper* sacrifices is superfluous since now we can see that the new/eternal covenant (of peace) from prophetic contexts makes the most immediate sense, given Jesus's use of "covenant." And this was always expected to be a forgiveness that was granted by God *apart from kipper sacrifices*, especially since these—by God-ordained design—could

62. *Pace* Shauf, who thinks "Jesus' death as a covenant sacrifice takes on an additional role, that of the [purgation] or guilt offering (*hattat* or *asham*)" simply because "forgiveness" is mentioned in Matt 26:28 (*Jesus the Sacrifice*, 123).

63. Shauf and I agree on this point (*Jesus the Sacrifice*, 123) though I disagree that "forgiveness" is also then related to the *kipper* sacrifices.

64. Paul juxtaposes these two Isaiah passages in Rom 11:27.

not address the sins that needed to be forgiven. Trying to then link Jesus's comment about "forgiveness" to *kipper* sacrifices is further incoherent since Jesus's comments are all happening through a *meal* and offerers (priest or lay) could never eat from the atoning sacrifices offered to decontaminate their sins.

From several angles, then, interpretations that attempt to find *kipper* associations simply do not work. It is only possible to make such an association by (a) ignoring the differences in function between the well-being sacrifices and the *kipper* sacrifices in terms of consumption as well as (b) ignoring the built-in limits to what *kipper* sacrifices address, and (c) failing to appreciate the unanimous prophetic hope that conceptualizes the promised restoration as a divine moral purification, which functions *on analogy to ritual purification* (i.e., the means of purification is a combination of time and water) and does not analogize from the *kipper* system in general nor the Day of Decontamination in particular.

Furthermore, while we do not need to outline the details here, to see how Jesus's death *qua* death relates to moral purification we need to note that the Gospels construe Jesus's death as the embodiment of Jerusalem's judgment as they narrate Jesus's arrest, trials, and crucifixion. The same things and signs that Jesus prophesies are going to attend the fall of Jerusalem, happen *in nuce* to Jesus during his arrest, trials, and crucifixion.[65] Jesus's death is like Ezekiel's laying down to share in and identify with Israel and Judah's covenant curse (Ezek 4:4–6). Ezekiel is not a "substitute" since Israel and Judah still experience exile. He is "place-sharing" and enacting both their curse and eventual restoration. So too with Jesus. His death is the destruction of the Jerusalem *in nuce* and his resurrection is the ultimate restoration to come *in nuce*. Like Ezekiel, Jesus does not suffer as a substitute, but as a prophetic *place-sharer*. Since his death is his proleptic experience of Jerusalem's looming destruction, his resurrection therefore signals Israel's resurrection and thus, their restoration—the forgiveness of their grave sins (Ezek 37).

And now we have come full circle with Jesus's mission to be the agent of moral purification. But this is not because Jesus's death is a *sacrifice* (let alone a *kipper* sacrifice), but rather because by *experiencing actual death* Jesus is able to make *direct contact* with the consequences of moral impurity

65. See, e.g., the chart outlining the parallels between Jesus's prophecy of Jerusalem and the temple's destruction in Mark 13 and the narration of Jesus's passion beginning immediately afterwards in Mark 14–15 in Achtemeier, Green, and Thompson, *Introducing the New Testament*, 139. Matthew and Luke do this similarly as well, but John makes the link between Jesus's death and the temple's destruction more direct and succinct in 2:19–22.

and exhaust them—evidenced by his resurrection from the dead—on analogy to how he is able to make direct contact with ritual impurity and thereby heal it by the contagious holiness of his very being.

Put another way, it is only because Jesus's death has this particular significance of *sharing in* the death of Jerusalem as the consequences for moral impurity, that Jesus's resurrection means anything for Israel (let alone the world) (cf. Acts 3:26; 4:2; 26:6–8, 22–23). Jesus takes the judgment that he announces for the temple upon himself as one so united with Israel that their destiny becomes his and vice versa.

Just like we have already established, when Jesus contacts ritual impurities, he purifies them. As the Gospels present Jesus's teaching, activity, and eventual explanation of his death at the Lord's Supper, it is clear that Jesus believes he can only bring the moral purification Israel needs by making contact with the deepest consequences of moral impurity—touching death and experiencing God's abandonment of the temple in himself (compare Matt 27:46 [par. Mark 15:34] with Matt 23:38 [par. Luke 13:35]; cf. Lev 26:31–33; Jer 12:7; 18:17; 22:5; 23:33, 39; Ezek 7–10)—and then defeating that death in his resurrection. Jesus decides he must endure the prophesied destruction of Jerusalem ahead of time to pioneer the way through death into the promised resurrection life (e.g., Ezek 37). Therefore, from this perspective, the resurrection is about purification, both ritual and moral.[66]

It is also worth pausing to note that Jesus repeatedly tells his disciples that they are called to follow him along the same way (Matt 10:38; 16:24; 20:22–23; Mark 8:34; 10:38–39; Luke 9:23; 14:27; John 12:24–26; 13:16–17, 36; 15:18, 20; 16:1–4; 21:18–22). This conception of Jesus's death is not a substitution from any angle. Jesus did not die "instead of" Jerusalem, since it is still going to be destroyed. Jesus did not die "instead of" the disciples, who will still brought to trial and some of them killed. Jesus goes the way of Jerusalem's destruction on the cross and Jesus's disciples follow the way of the cross as they pick up their own. This is about *solidarity*, not substitution. According to the Gospels, Jesus is not dying *instead* of anyone, let alone his disciples, but rather, *ahead* of them. He is the one who pioneers the way through death and into indestructible resurrection life, moral purification, the forgiveness of sins, and the establishment of the new eschatological covenant.

66. Similarly, Shively, "Purification of the Body"; cf. Moffitt, "It Is Not Finished," 164n19: "By virtue of his resurrection the morally pure Jesus . . . now has ritually pure humanity."

THE LORD'S SUPPER AND COMMUNAL WELL-BEING SACRIFICES

I have already stated throughout this study that the primary sacrificial associations in the NT to Jesus's death are the non-atoning well-being sacrifices of Passover and the covenant-making ceremony. This much is easily recognizable given that Jesus's words at the Last Supper explaining his imminent death happen while eating a Passover meal (Matt 26:17–19; Mark 14:12, 14, 16; Luke 22:7–8, 11, 13, 15) and he says he is inaugurating the promised (re)new(ed) covenant (Matt 26:28; Mark 14:24; Luke 22:20; 1 Cor 11:25).[67] But sometimes what is indeed obvious and right there in front of us goes either unnoticed or underappreciated. Hence, Michael Gorman's expression of shock:

> However, the fact that there is no theory or model of the atonement called "covenant," "covenant-renewal," "new-covenant," or something very similar is, or should be, rather surprising. These terms refer, after all, to a biblical image connected to Jesus' death—originating, it appears, with Jesus himself at his Last Supper—and the source of the term "the New Testament."[68]

In the introduction I have already addressed how uses of "atonement" as Gorman uses here are potentially problematic. But Gorman is right to call our attention to "the obvious," especially when, as here, scholarship oddly revolves around "the absence of the obvious."[69] I am carrying this notion forward and highlighting what is also rather "obvious" regarding the various sacrificial imagery applied to Jesus, yet has similarly been overlooked.

The Lord's Supper is essentially a "sacrificialized" (to borrow Klawans's terminology) ritual laid *on top* of a ritual that just *is* a non-atoning sacrifice (the Passover). Jesus isolates two elements from this sacrificial meal (wine and unleavened bread) and links them to his imminent murder as

67. I use "(re)new(ed) covenant" since Jeremiah is the only one who calls it "new" among the prophets (Jer 31:31–34; 33:6–8), whereas Ezekiel uses both "everlasting covenant" (Ezek 16:59–63) and "covenant of peace" (34:25; 37:26), and Isaiah uses "covenant" (Isa 59:21) and "covenant of peace" (54:10). Moreover, only Luke (22:20), Paul (1 Cor 11:25; 2 Cor 3:6), and the author of Hebrews (8:8; 9:15) use "new covenant." Matthew and Mark simply say "covenant" (Matt 26:28; Mark 14:24). Whether a new covenant-making ceremony or a covenant-renewal ceremony, the sacrifices to celebrate either event would be the well-being sacrifices, as discussed previously (Exod 24:3–8; Deut 27:4–8; Josh 8:30–35; 2 Chr 15:10–15; 29:30–36; 30:1–27; 33:16; Ps 50:5).

68. Gorman, *Death of the Messiah*, 1. Later he says again "how odd it is that there is no 'new-covenant' model of the atonement" (133).

69. Gorman, *Death of the Messiah*, 133.

a way of memorializing the salvation his death (and resurrection) will obtain. In short, the Lord's Supper is a ritualization of an existing ritual. Just like handwashing was a way for some Jewish contemporaries to "templize"/"sacrificialize" ordinary meals, ritually transforming common meals into quasi-sacred meals and their table into an altar of sorts, so too with the Lord's Supper. It is not *literally* a sacrificial meal thereafter (the Corinthians sure aren't traveling to Jerusalem each week to eat a well-being sacrifice together), but it is intelligible as a meal partaken of "as if" it was a well-being sacrifice.

In fact, the ritual purity regulations for partaking in such meals are also appropriated by Paul. But rather than instituting, say, ritual handwashing, Paul *analogizes* this in terms of *moral* purity. Thus, in 1 Cor 5 he talks about keeping the feast of Passover with Jesus as the Paschal lamb in *moral* purity terms (5:6–13). And this also explains his comments about eating the Lord's Supper "in a worthily manner" later on (11:26–34). It is because he knows the Lord's Supper is a sacrificialization of the eaten well-being sacrifices that he plays on the warnings in Leviticus about eating these in the wrong manner and being "cut off" as a result (Lev 7:18–21; 19:5–8; 22:3–7, 29–30). But Paul's appeal is not to intimate ritual purity before eating, but rather to ensure that everyone is looking out for the interests and nutritional needs of their neighbor (1 Cor 11:21–22, 33–34). We cannot get into these instructions more here, but it suffices for our purposes to realize that Paul's instructions and warnings here in 1 Cor 5 and 11 are intelligible precisely because he is thinking of Jesus in terms of the non-atoning well-being sacrifices and their attendant regulations in Leviticus.

Nevertheless, when Jesus's death is celebrated by a meta-"sacrificialization" of well-being offerings that are *eaten*, this then excludes any "atoning" function in these texts. No one is permitted to eat a purgation sacrifice that decontaminates *their sin* (neither priest nor lay). There are no exceptions to this. Knowing this, it is rather easy to see that the Lord's Supper categorically cannot have any *kipper* function.[70] We have already shown how even Matthew's lone inclusion of the notion of "forgiveness" cannot be plausibly interpreted within the framework of *kipper*. Rather, it belongs within the context of the prophetic hope for Israel's restoration, which will take the form of a moral purification—which *kipper* sacrifices are inherently incapable of effecting—and the establishment of the (re)new(ed) covenant.

It bears repeating that not only is it *possible* in general for "forgiveness of sins" to happen outside of the atoning sacrificial system, but that

70. Had Gorman been aware of the various sacrifices, their distinct functions, and what is eaten, then perhaps he would have included this point as another instance of "the absence of the obvious" in NT scholarship (cf. *Death of the Messiah*, 133; cf. 1).

the *prophetic expectation* within which the NT authors explicitly situate the meaning of Jesus's entire ministry is *necessarily* a forgiveness that must occur *apart from the atoning sacrificial system* because the sins that need forgiveness are *moral* impurities. And this is also why when the prophets draw upon Levitical concepts, they do so on analogy to *bodily* purification from the *ritual* impurities, which only require a combination of sufficient time lapse and a water-washing. As we saw, the time lapse is the exile and the water-washing is the immersion in God's sanctifying Spirit. Neither of these are "sacrificial," let alone sacrificial *kipper*. This explains why water immersion is such a primary rite in John's, Jesus's, and Jesus's followers' ministries. This was a movement that conceived of "forgiveness" as moral purification on analogy to ritual purification, not *kipper*.

Therefore, when something like "forgiveness" is mentioned, it is exegetically irresponsible to simply equate this with *kipper* since we now know the notion of forgiveness as it relates to the sacrificial system is extremely limited in scope. When analyzing any NT text about the saving significance of Jesus we need to understand that there are other frameworks besides "sacrifice" and "sacrificial *kipper*" within which the authors might be trying to express the benefits Jesus brings and/or the meaning of his death in particular.

Sacrificial atonement—*kipper*—*is* activated in a few NT texts, but I hope to show how once we have developed sufficient knowledge about the Levitical system and the prophetic expectations (and the reception of these things in the first century) it becomes rather obvious to know when this is happening. Thus, since Matthew's construal of "forgiveness" is *not* related to the limited notion of forgiveness in Leviticus for atonable sins, then this means the function Jesus's death has, according to Matthew, is something *other than* the *kipper* sacrifices.

Moreover, "the only sacrificial interpretation of Jesus' death that is attributed to Jesus himself"[71] is that it inaugurates the promised (re)new(ed) covenant and is combined with Passover. This best explains why relating Jesus to *kipper* is rare in the NT. It is only directly stated in Hebrews and 1 John.[72] This idea is an *expansion* on the original meaning and function of Jesus's death, which drew upon communal non-atoning well-being sacrifices, which celebrate and mark occasions of divine deliverance and were not linked to *kipper* in any fashion—and the author of Hebrews acknowledges this, as we will see in chapter 6.

71. Shauf, *Jesus the Sacrifice*, 116. See also Gorman, *Death of the Messiah*, 1.

72. Cf. Shauf, *Jesus the Sacrifice*, 104. Shauf thinks there are "indirect references" to atoning sacrifices, but I will argue both here and in the next chapter why these are unlikely and need to be interpreted within another framework.

Since it is clear now *that* the Lord's Supper is linked with the communal non-atoning well-being sacrifices for Passover and a covenant-inauguration/renewal ceremony, here I will discuss more about how the function of these relates to Jesus's mission of moral purification as well as address one other way some scholars have thought the Lord's Supper includes the notion of *kipper*. Then I will discuss other NT texts apart from the Lord's Supper account that likewise associate Jesus with either the Passover and/or a covenant-making sacrifice.

The Lord's Supper Celebrates Moral Purification, Not *Kipper*

Combining the covenant sacrifice with Passover by deliberately staging his words of institution at a Passover meal "is the only sacrificial interpretation of Jesus' death that is attributed to Jesus himself."[73] For good reason then, "it is the most widespread interpretation of Jesus' death as a sacrifice in the New Testament," which arguably renders it "the most important, the most foundational, interpretation of Jesus' death as a sacrifice in the New Testament."[74] Since all texts that discuss the Last Supper combine both the Passover and the covenant-inauguration sacrifice I will treat the concept as a whole rather than give special attention to each pericope.[75]

Both events, Passover and the initial covenant inauguration, are related to God's liberation of Israel from Egypt.[76] The Passover marks the beginning of Israel's journey, and the covenant inauguration marks its climax—sealing the covenant bond between God and Israel, which then immediately results in constructing the dwelling place and establishing their ongoing sacrificial worship there.[77]

It makes good sense, then, that as the prophets draw upon the paradigm of the exodus to depict Israel's restoration from exile and proclaim the

73. Shauf, *Jesus the Sacrifice*, 116.

74. Shauf, *Jesus the Sacrifice*, 116.

75. Technically, Paul's account of the Lord's Supper in 1 Cor 11:23–26 does not mention the Passover context, but Paul makes a direct reference to Jesus as the Paschal lamb earlier in 5:7.

76. This will be important when analyzing passages in chapter 7 that some have mistaken to be about sacrifice when they are merely referring to the *event* of liberation itself, not its sacrificialized memoralization.

77. Worshiping through sacrifice was the stated goal of the exodus journey from the beginning (Exod 5:1–3, 8, 17; 8:8, 25–29; 10:24–26). See also Shauf, *Jesus the Sacrifice*, 142: "The covenant sacrifice in Exodus is the culmination of the story line [sic] of which the Passover sacrifice is an early high point, the force that starts the Israelites on the road toward the Sinai ceremony."

hope of (re)new(ed) covenant so Jesus would institute a ritual that unambiguously tethers the climax of his mission—his crucifixion—to the communal well-being sacrifices that memorialize the first exodus. Recall that remembrance or memorialization of God's prior acts of deliverance is one of the main purposes for well-being sacrifices (e.g., Num 10:10; Exod 12:14)—and Luke and Paul both state this explicitly (Luke 22:19; 1 Cor 11:24–25).

While it may be tempting to read "blood of the covenant" (Mark 14:24; Matt 26:28) or "new covenant in my blood" (Luke 22:20; 1 Cor 11:25) and link this with *kipper*, recall that this is the phrase used at the covenant-inauguration ceremony in Exod 24:8. And as Shauf observes, "the covenant ceremony of Exodus 24 says nothing about forgiveness of sins and contains no other language of atonement—it is . . . about establishing a relationship between God and Israel."[78] I already argued why the mere mention of "forgiveness" (only in Matthew's account) is both insufficient to establish a link with *kipper* and why its meaning has to be interpreted within another framework altogether. Since many of the prophetic expectations of the (re)new(ed) covenant include the notion of forgiveness of the sins that produce moral impurity (e.g., Jer 31:31–34; 33:8; Ezek 16:59–63), this means the establishment of the (re)new(ed) covenant entails and signifies that God has granted this promised forgiveness from these sins apart from any *kipper* sacrifice. The establishment of the (re)new(ed) covenant is the celebration and proof that God's forgiveness *has already happened*. Thus, Matthew's inclusion of "forgiveness" is perfectly intelligible apart from the *kipper* sacrifices, which could never address such sins anyway.

Moreover, as we saw when discussing the blood-sprinkling upon the people in Exod 24:8, this was all about effecting a metaphysical transition and no blood from an atoning purgation offering was used. Therefore, "just as the blood of the sacrificed animals was used to seal the covenant between the Israelites and God in the Exodus" and was sprinkled on the people to index and mark the transition of the people into this covenant relationship with God, so too, "Jesus' death is thus the sacrifice that seals the covenant between his followers and God."[79] Since the Lord's Supper is a meta-ritual sacrificialization alluding to this covenant-inauguration ceremony in the middle of a Passover meal, the wine that links with Jesus's blood was not literally sprinkled on the disciples. Rather, they drank it just like they would drink the wine from which a portion was used as the drink offerings that accompany

78. Shauf, *Jesus the Sacrifice*, 123. Note also that "blood of the covenant" occurs in Zech 9:11 too. As Shauf observes, "Zech 9:11, itself drawing on the Exodus 24 ceremony, states that God's covenant with the people is the reason for their ultimate liberation" (*Jesus the Sacrifice*, 122).

79. Shauf, *Jesus the Sacrifice*, 118.

all sacrifices, per Num 15:1–13. And Paul expresses the significance of this sacrificialization by noting that drinking from "the cup of blessing" is "a participation [*koinōnia*] in the blood of Christ" (1 Cor 10:16), which he then links to the "new covenant" (11:25). At each eating and drinking of the Lord's Supper followers of Jesus "remember" (11:24–25; cf. Num 10:10) the establishment of the new covenant and their share and participation in it. Each Lord's Supper is a sacrificialized "new covenant renewal" celebration akin to the covenant renewal celebrations in the OT where the whole community partook from the well-being sacrifices together.

Further, Paul takes this "shared meal" aspect and uses it to reinforce what we might call his "ethics" whereby followers of Jesus are to comprehend the cross as the norm for the pattern of life in Christ. Thus, the Lord's Supper, which memorializes Jesus's death by means of two communal well-being offerings, makes sense of the believer's very real participation and union with Jesus's death as a pattern of life since these are the only sacrifices in the OT the offerer has a share in themselves. It is no wonder the well-being sacrifice is the dominant sacrifice used to make sense of Jesus's death for a movement that understood itself as the body of the crucified Lord (1 Cor 10:16–17; 12:12–13), called to follow Jesus to the cross and participate in his death (e.g., Phil 3:10; 2 Cor 4:10–11; cf. Mark 8:34–38; 10:38–39; 1 Pet 2:21).

And this is why we need to be careful to distinguish between the meaning and function attributed to Jesus's death as a *death* versus the meaning of Jesus as a *sacrifice*. These are *not equivalent*, but the very nature of ascribing various types of meaning to one event—the crucifixion of Jesus by Romans—means the associations are going to require subtlety and nuance. When viewed from the perspective of the ethical shape impressed upon Jesus's followers, his death is the pattern for the form of life they are to inhabit and cultivate among one another.[80] Similarly, when viewed from the perspective of moral purification, Jesus's death is saving because it is by Jesus's direct *contact* with death itself while having the type of life that cannot be held down by death to decay (cf. Acts 2:24–32; 13:35–37) that made it possible for him to "swallow up death" and emerge "victorious" over it (1 Cor 15:54) and thereby able to effect the moral purification from grave sins (e.g., Acts 13:33–39), the very sins the law of Moses itself says there is no sacrificial or ritual remedy for, as explained in previous chapters (13:39). But when Jesus's death is viewed from the perspective of these well-being sacrifices, these memorialize his victory over all sins and death by means of a shared sacrificialized meal drawing upon Passover and the

80. See Gorman, *Inhabiting the Cruciform God*. Cf. Shauf, *Jesus the Sacrifice*, 143.

covenant-inauguration ceremony. The emphasis on the *sacrificial* aspect is not about what *causes* the saving event, but how that divine deliverance is *remembered*, *commemorated*, and *celebrated*.

Obviously, the institution of the Lord's Supper by Jesus happened before that final victory took place by his resurrection, but this is no different than the way the first Passover was presented in Exod 12 before the actual exodus out of Egypt happened. Thus, both the first Passover and Jesus's institution of the Lord's Supper are proleptic anticipations of a full deliverance that is imminent. But importantly, both are also celebrating a deliverance that has *already started*. Israel's deliverance from the first nine plagues anticipate the full deliverance from Egypt to come just as Jesus's miracles healing ritual impurities—the forces of death—and restoring people's bodies to health (even after some have died), declaring forgiveness, all anticipate the full deliverance from death, the full moral purification, to come.

Some, however, think these accounts not only combine the non-atoning sacrifices that mark these events, but also the *kipper* sacrifices due to Matthew's inclusion of the idea of "forgiveness."[81] Now, the combination of the Passover and the covenant inauguration/renewal makes sense since (a) they are both communal non-atoning well-being sacrifices that are *eaten* by the people and (b) they function as a tandem bookending the exodus journey from leaving Egypt to arriving at Sinai. But the idea that these eaten non-atoning sacrifices are then further combined with atoning sacrifices that absolutely *cannot be eaten* by their beneficiaries (cf. Heb 13:10–11) is suspect from the start.

A sacrifice is *either* eaten *or* not, depending on its function in relation to the offerer. Since the Lord's Supper is explicitly indexed along with two types of sacrifices that are eaten and Jesus's followers are to continue eating this sacrificialized meal together as a way to "remember" (a function only associated with the well-being sacrifices), then this ritual *has* to be about sacrificializing non-atoning well-being sacrifices since these are the only ones beneficiaries *eat*. To smuggle in an atoning function to this eaten ritual would introduce a fundamental incompatibility in practice since the atoning sacrifices cannot be eaten by their beneficiaries. Further, there is no "gap" needing to be filled that renders the non-atoning well-being sacrifices insufficient for comprehending the meaning and function of the Lord's Supper. Adding in the notion of "atonement" only *generates* (several) problems for making sense of it, thereby obscuring the rather intelligible sense it makes when comprehended in light the non-atoning well-being sacrifices (Passover and a covenant inauguration/renewal).

81. E.g., Gorman, *Death of the Messiah*, 15; Shauf, *Jesus the Sacrifice*, 118, 123.

Moreover, it has puzzled scholars as to why Hebrews makes no mention of the Lord's Supper, especially since Jesus is linked to Melchizedek there and Melchizedek is associated with providing bread and wine to Abraham in the only canonical narrative about him (Gen 14:18). Understanding the various sacrificial distinctions in terms of function and practice (i.e., eaten and non-eaten), however, easily accounts for why this is. Since Hebrews is interested in associating Jesus with *kipper*, Melchizedek is only activated as a way to establish Jesus's *priesthood* as *distinct* from Aaron's. But it would be confusing (and unhelpful to their main argument) to press in on the Lord's Supper in this teaching context because (a) it draws upon sacrifices that have nothing to do with atonement and (b) this was a *meal*. But *fasting*, not *feasting*, is associated with atonement, so highlighting the links between Jesus and Melchizedek that center on *eating* would actually detract from the main point about how Jesus is effecting *kipper* in the heavenly dwelling place, and therefore whose flesh needs to be "burned outside the camp" (Heb 13:11)—definitely *not eaten* (13:10).[82] Best then to leave out the ritual about Jesus that involves *eating*, which is in fact left out of Hebrews.

Further, as several Hebrews scholars note, the author of Hebrews acknowledges that their claims about Jesus's priesthood in the order of Melchizedek and heavenly *kipper* are teachings that go beyond the basic "first teaching about Christ" (6:1; cf. 5:10—6:2).[83] If Jesus's priesthood and *kipper* had been right there embedded in the institution of the Lord's Supper by Jesus himself this whole time, then why would the author of Hebrews miss this? Why wouldn't they base any aspect of their teaching relating Jesus to either a heavenly priesthood and/or to *kipper* on *Jesus's own teaching* about the meaning and function of his death in the Lord's Supper? In other words, if the Lord's Supper indeed includes the notion of *kipper*, then we cannot explain why the author of Hebrews is so transparent and apologetic that their teachings go beyond "the basic teaching about Christ" (6:1 NRSV), nor why they not only do not base any of their *kipper* theology on Jesus's institution of the Lord's Supper, but also fail to even hint at the Lord's Supper altogether. Therefore, I think it best we take the author of Hebrews at their word—what they are setting forth is theologically mature "advanced teaching" that goes beyond the elementary "milk" that is first taught as part of the gospel (5:12; 6:1).[84] And when we follow the evidence in the Lord's Supper, which only

82. I will discuss this important section of Hebrews from two different angles in the following chapter.

83. Lane, *Hebrews 1–8*, 125–27, 133–36, 139–40; Johnson, *Hebrews*, 155–56, 160; Cockerill, *Hebrews*, 259, 262, 267, 465.

84. Cockerill, *Hebrews*, 262, 267, 465; cf. Lane, *Hebrews 1–8*, 135, 140. This same line of reasoning similarly means that whatever "Christ died for our sins" means in

features eaten well-being sacrifices, we can rather securely conclude that *the Lord's Supper has nothing to do with kipper.*

To be clear, this is not to say that it is contradictory to think about the theological and/or saving significance of Jesus in both atoning and non-atoning ways. This is entirely possible without there being any tensions. But it is to say that the *self-same ritual* that involves *eating* cannot simultaneously be activating sacrifices that *can never be eaten* by their beneficiaries. To think that Jesus and his early Jewish followers would make that kind of contradictory juxtaposition would be a textbook example of special pleading. The sacrificial associations for the ritual of the Lord's Supper are best thought of as being restricted to the sacrifices that are *eaten* by their beneficiaries. The fact that this has the best explanatory power for why when Hebrews wants to examine how Jesus might be related to the *kipper* system it does so *apart* from any link to the Lord's Supper only strengthens that conclusion all the more.

Addressing an Important Objection

At this point, there is a detail in Matthew's Lord's Supper account that needs to be addressed, especially since it demonstrates the important payoff for learning the intricacies of the Levitical sacrificial system from previous chapters.

Paul M. Hoskins has argued that Matthew includes the atoning purgation sacrifices from Leviticus in his distinct Lord's Supper pericope.[85] Hoskins believes that "the combination of blood, poured out, for the sinner, and for the forgiveness of sins is a strong combination of elements that are unique to Lev 4:1–5:13 and Matt 26:28."[86] A lot rests particularly on Matthew's inclusion of "forgiveness" and the phrase "poured out" (all of the Synoptic Gospels use the verb "poured out" [*ekchunnō*] in relation to Jesus's blood).[87] I demonstrated above why *ekchunnō* is an explicit way to indicate that Jesus's death is a *murder*, and here I will show why that argument holds up and why it is unlikely to be referring to the purgation sacrifices in Leviticus.

1 Cor 15:3, it is near certain that it cannot be related to *kipper*, otherwise the author of Hebrews would not think their teaching progresses from the first teaching of Jesus. "Christ died for our sins" is embedded in a tradition preserved in 1 Cor 15:3–7 that Paul says is part of the "first" (*prōtos*) teachings when proclaiming "the gospel" (15:1).

85. Hoskins, "Neglected Allusion," 231–42.

86. Hoskins, "Neglected Allusion," 233.

87. Paul's account of the Lord's Supper is the only one lacking this verb (1 Cor 11:23–25).

While Hoskins does not deny that "pouring out blood . . . can refer to killing someone" and affirms that this phrase means that Jesus's "blood was poured out by means of a violent death," he also thinks Matthew is combining this with the purgation offering in LXX Leviticus since "[t]he sin [purgation] offering is the only offering who blood is 'poured out' (ἐκχέω + αἷμα)."[88] He is correct that the purgation sacrifice is the only one that refers to this particular blood manipulation in Leviticus, but he is arguably wrong to think Matthew is combining these two notions of "poured out" (murder and purgation sacrifice) for three reasons.

First, his appeal to the mention of "forgiveness" is problematic for all the reasons elucidated thus far. Matthew's inclusion of forgiveness cannot be reasonably understood within the general framework of *kipper* or the purgation sacrifices in particular. Thus, the mention of "forgiveness" cannot be used as evidence that "poured out" is a reference to the purgation sacrifices. In fact, given how "forgiveness" has been framed from the beginning of Matthew as the fulfillment of the prophetic hope for Israel's restoration via moral purification, the presence of "forgiveness" here suggests the precise opposite: i.e., whatever Jesus is linking his death to in the Lord's Supper, it is beyond the realm and scope of the *kipper* system since it is effecting the promised forgiveness for the types of sins that the *kipper* system cannot address.

Second, Hoskins appeals to the broad "thematic connection" that mere "sacrifice" is present: "the language of sacrifice is already explicit in 'blood of the covenant,' and the verse occurs in a Passover context."[89] It appears he is implying that if any mention of a sacrifice is present, then that increases the likelihood that *any* or *all* sacrifices are meant to be understood, regardless of their distinct functions and protocols. But the presence of these two sacrificial contexts (Passover and covenant inauguration) militate *against* any notion of that a *kipper* sacrifice is involved since these are *non-atoning well-being sacrifices* that are eaten, but no one is permitted to eat from purgation sacrifices offered for their sins. This why attention to all the details of the sacrificial system matter. Ironically, it is the presence of *well-being sacrifices* in this "thematic" context that pushes against Hoskins's reading.

Third, and most significantly, although Hoskins is correct that *ekchunnō/ekcheō*[90] ("poured out," translating the Hebrew word *šāfak*) is only used in LXX Leviticus for the purgation sacrifices (Lev 4:7, 18, 25,

88. Hoskins, "Neglected Allusion," 235.

89. Hoskins, "Neglected Allusion," 233.

90. The LXX uses the variant spelling *ekcheō*.

30, 34), this evidence is significantly misunderstood and misconstrued.[91] Hoskins does not attend to the specific types of blood manipulation and their attendant functions. Merely noting that this verb is present in the context of a purgation sacrifice tells us nothing about the *meaning* and *function* of this specific action.

In a cultic context "pouring out" (Greek: *ekcheō*, Hebrew: *šāfak*) is a ritual of "disposal" for *unused* blood.[92] It has no atoning function or significance. As we saw previously, the blood that functions to purge the sancta is what is "daubed" on the horns of the altars (inner or outer, depending) and "sprinkled" on the veil separated the holy place from the holy of holies. Those are the purgative blood manipulations. But, "the remaining blood is poured out at the base of the sacrificial altar in the court, that is, drained onto the ground *since it is not a sacrifice*."[93] The verbs used in these passages (*ekcheō* and *šāfak*) only refer to whatever is *discarded* in the only other rituals in Leviticus in which they are used (cf. 14:41; 17:13). Thus, as Milgrom notes, "The verb . . . indicates a noncultic [and, therefore, a non-sacrificial] act" and only indicates that the remaining blood from a purgation sacrifice is "discarded blood."[94] So "poured out" blood in a sacrificial context *literally has no atoning significance or function*. It is simply cultic *waste*. It is the unused leftovers that have no cultic use and just need to be disposed of in a careful manner since it is still *blood*.[95]

The fact that this "poured out" blood has no decontaminating significance or function is explicit in the Mishnah (m. Zebaḥ. 5:1–3). The rabbis imagine a scenario in which this step does not happen and state twice that "he [the priest] would pour the remnants of the blood on the western base of the outer altar. If he did not apply it, he did not disqualify it [i.e., disqualify the sacrifice from its decontaminating function]" (5:1, 2).[96] This is because the decontaminating functions were understood to be when the blood was placed on the horns of either one of the altars or sprinkled on the veil. If *these* steps were to be left out, then that would invalidate the decontamination rite (once again this is twice repeated): "Omission of any of these applications invalidates [the decontaminating function]" (5:1, 2; cf. 4:2: "it does not atone").

91. Shauf makes the same point as Hoskins, but independently, based on this observation (*Jesus the Sacrifice*, 118; cf. 132), so my comments here apply to Shauf as well.

92. Milgrom, *Leviticus 1–16*, 238–39; Gilders, *Blood Ritual*, 15, 23.

93. Schwartz, "Leviticus," 202–3; my emphasis.

94. Milgrom, *Leviticus 1–16*, 238.

95. Cf. Feldman, *Story of Sacrifice*, 190, 190n143.

96. Translations from Cohen, "Tractate Zevahim," 20, 21.

Therefore, if Matthew intends an allusion to Lev 4 by using "poured out," then it is extremely odd that he associates Jesus's blood with the left-over blood that is *discarded* and literally *has no atoning function or significance.* Had Matthew intended to associate his blood with the effective blood manipulations of the purgation sacrifice, then he could have used one of the verbs in Leviticus LXX that actually have purgative functions: *epitithēmi*, "place on," the LXX translation for "daub/place" (*nātan*) in Lev 4:7, 18, 25, 30, 34; or *prosrainō*, "sprinkle toward," or *hrainō*, "sprinkle," the LXX translations for "sprinkle" (*hizzâ*) in Lev 4:6 and 17, respectively.

But even this counterfactual is unlikely since Matthew is specifically referring to the "blood of the covenant," which does not feature any purgation sacrifices. And, not only is the "blood of the covenant" from non-atoning sacrifices, when it gets "spattered" on the people in Exod 24:8, this passage uses different verbs in both Hebrew (*zāraq*) and Greek (*kataskedannumi*) than when purgation-blood is "sprinkled" (Hebrew: *hizzâ*; Greek: *prosrainō/hrainō*) on the veil throughout Lev 4.

This is why attending to the details of all these distinct sacrifices with distinct functions and distinct attendant blood manipulation rituals is crucial. Otherwise, interpreters are at the mercy of their own surface-level connections that are merely apparent, but lack a coherent rationale upon a more patient interrogation. Therefore, rather than seeing a double meaning for "poured out" in the Lord's Supper, the evidence marshalled by Hoskins is actually evidence *against* his view.

It is best to understand "poured out" in the Lord's Supper only as a reference to Jesus's imminent murder. This combination of *ecchunnō* and *haima* is only used six NT passages: half are in Lord's Supper pericopes (Matt 26:28; Mark 14:24; Luke 22:20); the other half all refer to murder, pouring out innocent blood (Matt 23:35 [cf. 23:29–34]; Luke 11:50 [cf. vv. 49, 51; 13:34–35]; Acts 22:20). Further, the variation of *ecchunnō*, *ekcheō*, is used with *haima* in only four NT texts: two clearly refer to murder (Rom 3:15; Rev 16:6) and two are images conveying death (16:3, 4).[97] Since the combination of *ecchunnō* and *haima* only appear in the Synoptic Gospels (including Acts as part of Luke-Acts) and only refers to murder, the use of it in the Lord's Supper therefore appears to be making an intentional link between the murder of the prophets and Jesus's death as a murder.

97. See also *ekcheō* and *haima* in the LXX outside of Leviticus where it means murder: Gen 9:6; 37:22; Lev 17:4; Num 35:33; Deut 19:10; 21:7; 1 Sam 25:31; 1 Kgs 2:31; 2 Kgs 21:16; 24:4; 1 Chr 22:8; 28:3; 2 Chr 36:5d; 1 Macc 1:37; 7:17; 2 Macc 1:8; Ps 13:3 (MT 14:3); Ps 78:3; 78:19 (MT 79:10); 105:38 (MT 106:38); Prov 1:16; 6:17; Sir 28:11; 34:22; Wis 8:20; Pss. Sol. 8:20; Hos 2:15; Joel 4:19 (MT 3:19); Zeph 1:17; Isa 59:7; Jer 7:6; 22:3, 17; Lam 4:13; Ezek 16:38; 18:10; 22:3, 4, 6, 9, 12, 27; cf. 24:7; 35:6.

And the value of construing Jesus's execution as a *murder* is not just that "poured out" is not alluding to Leviticus, but more about how Jesus's death can plausibly be understood by others at the time as a *justified* (lawful) capital punishment carried out by the Roman authorities. That would have been the default position for many people at the time. This is just like when someone is killed by police there are many whose first reaction is "what law did they break/crime did they commit to deserve that?" while others protest "this was actually a murder." In an effort to combat the idea that being crucified by the Roman authorities is a justified capital punishment, the Synoptic Gospels narrate how Jesus's execution should be understood as a murder (of an innocent/righteous person no less).

But more than this, if there is a sort of double meaning going on, this notion that Jesus is murdered is intentionally and directly associating him with the murders of other prophets. And framing Jesus's death in this way is necessary for understanding why Jesus is convinced the temple is going to be destroyed. As discussed above, murder is morally defiling and Jesus's death is the "last straw." There is no going back, all the innocent blood "poured out" will be required of Jesus's "generation" (i.e., this is why the temple will be destroyed) (Matt 23:35; Luke 11:50–51).

And there is still yet another function. It is not that Jerusalem is being randomly "punished" for murdering Jesus. It is that the moral impurity for shedding innocent blood has reached the tipping point. As noted earlier, since the temple is going to be destroyed, Jesus becomes convinced he must die in solidarity with that coming destruction, experience its death *in nuce*. In this way his resurrection signals Jerusalem's resurrection. The message of the Gospels is that God is paradoxically turning what is the final nail in Jerusalem's coffin for the accumulation of moral impurity—the murder of Jesus—as the very means by which to unleash God's holy death-defeating Spirit upon Jerusalem and thus the whole world. When Jesus dies, his Spirit goes forth (John 19:20; Matt 27:50; cf, Mark 15:37; Luke 23:46; Paul in 1 Cor 15 and 2 Cor 3). Thiessen expresses this rather well as it relates to Matthew 27:50–53 in particular:

> What is most shocking about this portrayal is that at the very moment that the forces of impurity seem to have finally beaten Jesus, at the precise instant that Jesus becomes a corpse and presumably a source of corpse contamination, holy power emanates out of him and into the abode of death—tombs—to snatch away bodies who were themselves sources of ritual impurity. Whereas corpses usually emit some miasma of impurity, Jesus's corpse appears to emit a miasma of holy power that selectively revivifies long-dead saints. This holy discharge is wide-ranging,

> traveling from Jesus's corpse at Golgotha to and through Jerusalem. It is also unspeakably powerful, reaching deep into the bowels of death to give life to those who have been long dead. Matthew narrates in dramatic fashion how Jesus's crucifixion is ultimately a victory over death itself.[98]

Bringing this back to the institution of the Lord's Supper, Jesus is saying:

> My murder, rather than just being yet another innocent murder of a prophet, will turn out to be the event that delivers Israel (and thus the world) from the covenant curses of exile. My murder is for the sake of that promised moral purification, the forgiveness of their grave sins, including my murder. This is why we can celebrate this event by relating them to these thanksgiving well-being sacrifices. I am inaugurating and sealing the New Covenant.

It should go without saying that this only makes sense in light of the resurrection. The two are a tandem. Jesus's death has this function because it is construed as the destruction of the temple *in nuce* and thus his resurrection signals the resurrection of Israel (and the nations) after experiencing the curses of the covenant for grave sins.

But this does not mean that either the Passover or the covenant-inaugurating sacrifice being activated at the Lord's Supper *themselves* are suddenly taking on a "forgiveness" or a *kipper* function. Rather, they are, like all other well-being sacrifices (especially the thanksgiving sacrifice), memorializing and celebrating an act of divine liberation. And these events of divine deliverance were not accomplished *via* a well-being sacrifice. Rather, they are *commemorated* and *memorialized* by these sacrificial feasts. In this case, it is celebrating, albeit proleptically the first time with Jesus, the fact that God has already forgiven/released Israel from their grave sins. And this promised forgiveness of the grave sins that produced the exile is never analogized as the forgiveness that comes after a *kipper* sacrifice. Rather, the promised forgiveness is simply something God promises to do (apart from the *kipper* system) when the time comes (Isa 40:1; Jer 31:31–34; 33:5–8); and it is likened to moral purification by divine washing with God's Spirit (Ezek 34:25–29, 33; Zech 13:1).

The Lord's Supper, therefore, celebrates that God has fulfilled the covenant promise to bring an end to the covenant curses for Israel's sins (i.e., forgiveness) by Jesus's direct contact with Israel's covenant death. But

98. Thiessen, *Forces of Death*, 111.

it is not Jesus-as-well-being-sacrifice that accomplishes this. Rather, this happens through Jesus's *actual death* (and resurrection). The Lord's Supper "remembers" this event via a sacrificialized ritual meal. As Shauf says, "The Romans killed Jesus in a ritual of execution, but the Christian ritual of the Lord's Supper transforms the meaning of Jesus' death for the celebrants from execution to sacrifice."[99] It is Jesus's-death-as-execution that brings about the deliverance, but it is Jesus-as-well-being-sacrifice that celebrates that salvation wrought by his death *qua* death.

Addressing Another Objection: Jesus as Atoning Scapegoat in Matthew?

Hans M. Moscicke has recently argued that the Day of Atonement is present in Matthew.[100] Moscicke's argument fails to convince for at least two reasons: (1) he does not recognize—and therefore does not address—how introducing the Day of Atonement generates category mistakes vis-à-vis the non-atoning well-being sacrifices that are being explicitly activated in this gospel and (2) although he addresses the notion of innocent blood, he does not seem to recognize the real force of this motif upon the narrative.[101]

Regarding this latter point, Moscicke thinks there is "a correspondence between Pilate and the high priest of Lev 16" when the former "presents[s] the two prisoners [Jesus and Barabbas] to the crowd at the same time" and he then links Pilate's hand *washing* (Matt 27:24–25) with the high priest's double-hand-*laying* ritual in Lev 16:21.[102]

First, this link immediately strains credulity. There is no hand washing involved in the double-hand-laying ritual in Lev 16:21. Moscicke says "the evangelist . . . transform[s] the hand-leaning rite of Lev 16:21 into a hand-washing rite that is functionally equivalent to the former."[103] However, to use Moscicke's own words responding to another argument almost immediately prior to this: "This interpretation seems far too subtle to be taken

99. Shauf, *Jesus the Sacrifice*, 129.

100. Moscicke, "Jesus, Barabbas," 125–53. As noted in the article, others have argued a similar thesis. I limit my response with respect to Moscicke here (a) because of space, (b) it is the most recent attempt to find the Day of Atonement in the passion narrative, and (c) my reasons for rejecting Moscicke's view would also apply to other iterations of this overall argument.

101. See my argument above and Moffitt, "Righteous Bloodshed."

102. Moscicke, "Jesus, Barabbas," 139 and 142, respectively.

103. Moscicke, "Jesus, Barabbas," 142.

seriously."[104] Second, Pilate washing his hands in the context of explicitly talking about bloodguilt is remarkably similar to the hand-washing ritual in Deut 21:6–8.[105] Moscicke swiftly dismisses this by begging the question: "once Matt 27:24–25 is read properly within Matthew's Yom Kippur typology, it becomes unnecessary to posit an allusion to Deut 21."[106] This, however, is the very issue that needs to be argued. The allusion to Deut 21 is the evidence that Matthew's passion narrative is activating the themes of shedding innocent blood, as argued above, not the Day of Decontamination. Moscicke is overreading Matthew's passion narrative by pushing aside evidence to the contrary and asserting the very thesis that needs to be proven.

But Matthew comprehends Jesus's death *apart* from the *kipper* system and links it with two non-*kipper* well-being sacrifices. Given the explicit activation of innocent blood motif both in the passion narrative (Matt 27:4, 6, 24–25; cf. 27:19), the Lord's Supper as argued above (26:28), and in Jesus's predictions about the temple's destruction (23:30–36), if Pilate corresponds to anyone in the Torah, it makes more sense that Pilate is playing the role of the leader of a city who "happens upon" a murder and needs to enact a ritual of innocence (Deut 21:1–9). That is, Matthew does not want his readers to only blame Rome, even though it is obvious that *Rome* is the material cause of Jesus's death since *they crucify* Jesus. Matthew also blames "this generation" (Matt 23:35–36; cf. 27:25) as partakers in the actual efficient cause of Jesus's death. (The final cause would be God's plan of salvation for his people, 1:20–21.) And this notion, that "this generation" shares blame (importantly, not "all Jews"—Matthew limits the blame to the specific crowd present before Pilate and the priestly leadership more specifically), is more about theodicy than polemic: If Jesus is the Messiah, why didn't he stop the temple from being destroyed? Why is Israel scattered again? The answer is that, according to the Torah and the prophets (cf. 2 Kgs 21:16; 24:3–4), bloodguilt only has a few options to be dealt with since it generates moral impurity: the death of the murderer, or exile/destruction of the temple. *There is no sacrificial remedy to moral impurity*, which further weakens the notion that Matthew is trying to allude to the Day of Decontamination to solve this problem.

To support his point, however, Moscicke claims that "the two etiologies of Yom Kippur contained in Jub. 5:17–18 [cf. 7:23, 25] and 34:10–19" have to do with "atonement for corporate bloodguilt."[107] While it is true that

104. Moscicke, "Jesus, Barabbas," 141n72.

105. Moscicke, "Jesus, Barabbas," 141.

106. Moscicke, "Jesus, Barabbas," 142.

107. Moscicke, "Jesus, Barabbas," 143, 144, respectively.

shedding innocent blood is linked with the cause of the flood (Jub. 7:23, 25), which is the basis for the etiology in 5:17–18, the connection to Joseph in 34:10–19 is not about bloodguilt, but rather tells the audience that the Day of Atonement "is for mourning" and "function[s] as a memorial of the incident of Joseph's brothers' selling him into slavery and deceiving Jacob about his fate."[108] Thus, neither of these etiologies are claiming that the Day of Decontamination actually atones for bloodguilt.

In fact, Jubilees repeatedly says there is no *kipper* remedy for bloodguilt nor for any of the other sins that generate moral impurity (i.e., sins that pollute the land): see 7:20–39 (vv. 28–29, 33 are about bloodshed in particular); 20:2–11; 21:1–25 (vv. 19–20 are about bloodshed in particular); 36:1–17.[109] Additionally, Jubilees cites Num 35:33 (Jub. 7:33 and 21:19; cf. Num 35:31 and Jub. 21:20), which makes it clear that it is not departing from the framework for dealing with moral impurity in the Torah, especially when it comes to shedding innocent blood. Further, Jub. 23:14–25 outlines the consequences for polluting the land with moral impurity (23:14).[110] In sum, the land needs to be destroyed (23:18) and the people exiled (23:22)—which accords with what the Torah and the Prophets say needs to happen with regard to moral impurity, as we observed earlier. It is only after all this happens that the land will be purified, and the people will be purified solely by divine agency at the proper *time*/Jubilee (i.e., not by a *kipper* sacrifice) (cf. 23:26–31; 1:7–25 [esp. v. 23]; 50:3–5).[111] For all the varieties of interpretations of the Day of Decontamination in Second Temple Judaism, I do not know of any that advances the idea that grave sins that produce moral impurity are atoned by any *kipper sacrifice*, even the ones offered on the Day of Decontamination.

108. Gilders, "The Day of Atonement in the Dead Sea Scrolls," 65.

109. Cf. VanderKam, *Jubilees*, 347–48, 642, 685, 1197–98.

110. Cf. VanderKam, *Jubilees*, 685.

111. Jubilees 50:3–5 makes it clear that moral impurity is remedied through *time*, specifically the time of Jubilee. Leviticus 25:9 says the Jubilee is announced on the Day of Decontamination. This makes sense since, as discussed above, that day is ritual factory reset/restart for the temple and the Jubilee is factory reset/restart for the land and society (all land goes back, debts forgiven, etc.). But this doesn't suddenly grant new meaning to the *sacrifices* on the Day of Decontamination. Their function is still limited to their God-ordained function. What purifies the land and the people (Jub. 50:3–5; 1:23) is what *God* does via the passing of *time*, which is analogous to how time is crucial in the ritual purification process. Put another way, it's the "*day*" in Day of Decontamination that effects moral purification: it's simply the "time" when this great act of moral purification, a factory reset for the community, takes place. The *kipper* sacrifices themselves on that day cannot be the means by which this moral purification happens. Cf. VanderKam, *Jubilees*, 1197–98.

Therefore, what Matthew seems to be doing is giving a particular covenantal answer to the problem of yet another temple destruction ("exile")—a problem made more pressing when claiming the Messiah has already come—by making the case that Jesus was an innocent man, which means his crucifixion generates moral impurity and leads to exile (e.g., Num 35:33–34; 2 Kgs 21:10–16; 24:1–4; Jer 7:6).

So then, if I may be tongue in cheek, "once Matthew is read properly within [the framework of moral impurity, both its causes and consequences,] it becomes unnecessary to posit an allusion to [Yom Kippur]."[112] Thinking the *kipper* system is relevant to these concerns is a category mistake since *kipper* sacrifices can do nothing for moral impurity. But, thankfully, Jesus's life, death, and resurrection can. As noted above, Jesus's death is paradoxically part of the very means by which he saves his people from all their grave sins.

OTHER REFERENCES IN THE NEW TESTAMENT TO PASSOVER OR COVENANT INAUGURATION

The two non-atoning well-being sacrifices activated in the Lord's Supper appear elsewhere in the NT. I want to use the following as case studies to demonstrate how to apply what we learned about the various sacrificial and ritual procedures to comprehend these texts.[113] And just like before, though these are all talking about Jesus in sacrificial terms, I show why I do not think the notion of *kipper* is present in these texts, despite what others have concluded.

112. Moscicke, "Jesus, Barabbas," 142.

113. Hebrews also reiterates Jesus as a covenant-making sacrifice (9:15–20; 10:29; 12:24; 13:20), but because this is a major *premise* for the author's explanation of Jesus in terms of atonement, I will postpone further discussion of Hebrews for the next chapter. Also, the covenant-making sacrifice is likely being referred to in Ephesians (esp. 2:12–13, 18; 3:12), but I cannot address that in depth here (see Shauf, *Jesus the Sacrifice*, 130–33). Although Shauf concludes that *kipper* is also being activated, my arguments below against the inclusion of *kipper* for other texts would equally apply to these in Ephesians (*mutatis mutandis*). Also, my comments on ransom/redemption below under the subsection "Revelation 1:5, 5:6–10, 7:14–15, and 1 Peter 1:3, 18–19" are, *mutatis mutandis*, applicable to Eph 1:7 too (see especially footnote 146). For more of my own conclusions on Eph 2, see my article "*Tertium Genus* or Dyadic Unity?," 31–51.

John 6:47–56

I begin with John 6:47–56 since, although set in a different context, this is the closest John comes to anything like Jesus's words at the Lord's Supper.[114] Also, this discourse takes place near Passover in 6:4, so it is likely that Jesus's words in 6:47–56 are linking him to the unleavened bread of Passover (as well as the wilderness manna, of course).

The point here is simple: since all this discourse in John 6 focused on eating and drinking, this precludes an atoning significance. As Shauf explains, "The echo of the Last Supper also suggests an allusion to the covenant sacrifice, even if somewhat distant. Finally, v. 56 says that 'those who eat my flesh and drink my blood abide in me, and I in them.' This sounds like the kind of communion associated with the *shelamim*, the offering of well-being."[115]

John 1:29, 36

John the Immerser's identification of Jesus as "the lamb of God, who takes away the sins of the world" (1:29; cf. v. 36) is well known and used in many denominational liturgies. Before getting to the phrase "takes away the sins of the world," we need to recognize that the "lamb" image is "rooted in the Passover lamb imagery [that is also] prominent in John's crucifixion account."[116] John explicitly construes Jesus as the Passover lamb (19:14, 31, 36; cf. Exod 12:46; Num 9:12). In fact, he deviates from the timeline in the Synoptics to drive home this very point. Who has the "history" right is immaterial. The timing of Jesus's death serves to reinforce Jesus's identification with the Passover lamb. The Synoptics have the Lord's Supper occurring on Passover and Jesus being crucified the following day. In John, however, Jesus is crucified the day before the Passover, "the day of preparation" (19:14, 31), which is when all of the Passover lambs were sacrificed at the temple. Further, Jesus's death sentence occurs at noon (19:14), which is around the time of day the paschal lambs were being sacrificed.[117] Therefore, "lamb of God" is primarily about Jesus as the ultimate Passover lamb.

114. Shauf, *Jesus the Sacrifice*, 164.

115. Shauf, *Jesus the Sacrifice*, 164.

116. Shauf, *Jesus the Sacrifice*, 139.

117. Although "no ancient source unequivocally locates this sacrifice of Passover lambs at noon," they agree that it started sometime after late morning, after the daily burnt offering (Thompson, *John*, 389–90, here 389).

As we have discussed, and Marianne Meye Thompson explains, "the Passover lambs . . . were not killed to atone for sin or to purge uncleanness."[118] So then what are we to make of the phrase in 1:29 that Jesus "takes away the sins of the world"? Shauf thinks this is sufficient "to see a connection to the atoning sacrifices."[119] This is despite acknowledging "lambs were not commonly used in atoning sacrifices at all."[120] But "commonly" is misleading because male lambs were *never* used for purgation sacrifices in the OT.[121] In any case, Shauf is so convinced that "takes away sins" is related to atonement that he at first entertains the idea that "the appellation of Jesus as the 'Lamb of God who takes away the sin of the world' would seem unlikely to refer to the Passover lamb, because the Passover lamb was not an atoning sacrifice."[122] That is, because he knows Passover has nothing to do with atonement, but he presumes "taking away sins" *has* to be about atonement, then he thinks that "lamb" might not be referring to the Passover lamb after all. But since he equally acknowledges that John is definitely identifying Jesus as the Passover lamb throughout the narrative, he concludes that John must be combining atonement and Passover in 1:29 even though "identifying Jesus as a sacrificial lamb and as atoning for sin is not the most natural of pairs" for all the reasons just mentioned.[123]

However, the presumption that "takes away sins" is related to sacrificial atonement (*kipper*) is unlikely for two main reasons. For one, male lambs are never used for any purgation (*ḥaṭṭāʾt*) sacrifice, as noted above. Thus, it would be odd for John to call Jesus a *male lamb* if he was hoping people would associate that with a "purgation sacrifice." If John wanted to link Jesus with the purgation sacrifices or the Day of Decontamination, then he should have used "the bull and/or goats of God."

Two, the verb for "takes away" is *airō*. And *airō* with *hamartia* ("sin") does not occur in the LXX. But this same root verb with a prefix *apo*, "away from," does. In the six passages where *hamartia* is the direct object of *aphaireō* only one of them is used in a sacrificial context (Lev 10:17). All other instances are all about God forgiving sins *apart from the sacrificial system* (Exod 34:7, 9; Num 14:18; Isa 27:9; Sir 47:11). But Lev 10:17 is difficult

118. Thompson, *John*, 47; cf. 47n15.

119. Shauf, *Jesus the Sacrifice*, 138.

120. Shauf, *Jesus the Sacrifice*, 137.

121. Bulls are used as purgation sacrifices for priests (Lev 4:1–12; 16:3) or the whole congregation (4:13–21). Male goats are used for leaders (4:22–26). And a female goat or lamb can be used for individuals (4:27–35). On the Day of Decontamination the purgation sacrifice for the people is a male goat (16:5, 9).

122. Shauf, *Jesus the Sacrifice*, 137.

123. Shauf, *Jesus the Sacrifice*, 137.

to use as an interpretive anchor for John 1:29 because it comes on the lips of Moses in a dispute with Aaron and Aaron is the one who wins the argument (Lev 10:19–20).[124] The saying also does not relate to the ritual blood manipulations, but rather to the priests *eating* from purgation sacrifices offered for *other people's* sins (priests cannot eat from a purgation sacrifice for their own sins per Lev 4:1–12; 6:22–23 [Eng. vv. 29–30]). I think this, combined with in incongruity of Passover and atonement (or even just male lambs and atonement), is a sufficient amount of incompatibility to dismiss this as a viable option, especially when the other instances of "takes away sins" fit the claims in the Gospel of John seamlessly and do not generate other interpretive difficulties.[125] To neglect these in favor of Lev 10:17 is special pleading to smuggle in a sacrificial connotation when all other cues point away from this.

In the other Torah passages, the phrase "takes away sin(s)" are all about God removing Israel's sins, i.e., putting up with their disobedience, after they leave Egypt (Exod 34:7, 9; Num 14:18 [notice v. 19 "from Egypt until now"]). Right after the relationship between God and Israel is established—celebrated with the Passover and sealed in the covenant-making ceremony—Israel worships the golden calf at the foot of Sinai (Exod 32). This is the context of the first use of this phrase, which anchors Moses's hope that God will listen to his prayer for Israel and God will take away their grave sin of idolatry (34:7, 9).

Then after they depart Sinai, the people start complaining and rebelling right away and continually (Num 11–21 contains seven episodes of this).[126] Numbers 14:18 occurs in middle of these episodes and it becomes apparent that "taking away sins" becomes a necessary thing for God to do if the people are not going to be totally abandoned or destroyed in the wilderness. But, importantly, this "taking away of sins" in both Num 14 and Exod 34 happens quite apart from the sacrificial system. This is just the prerogative of God because there are no atoning sacrificial remedies for these deliberates acts of rebellion (hence the notice in 15:30–31). If Israel is to have any hope in the face of such sins, they are completely at the mercy of God.

124. Feldman, *Story of Sacrifice*, 118–20.

125. The implausibility of linking John 1:29 with Lev 10:17 is plain because it would have to mean that Jesus takes away the people's sins by *eating* a purgation sacrifice somehow. But as it is, John never narrates Jesus eating anything (cf. 4:31–34) unless the "they" in 21:15 includes Jesus. (My thanks to Paul Sloan for alerting me to this.) But this post-resurrection fish fry is a far cry from Jesus eating a sacrifice of any kind. In any case, the only eating John links with saving significance is when Jesus is the one being eaten in John 6.

126. See Num 11:1–4; 12:1; 14:1–2; 16:1–3; 16:41; 20:3; 21:5.

And these wilderness stories give reason for future generations to have hope in God since "taking away sins" is revealed to Moses as part of the divine character—this is the kind of God YHWH is (Exod 34:7, 9). This is exactly what Moses appeals to when he petitions God to do this very thing in spite of Israel's repeated rebellions in Exod 34:8–9 and Num 14:17–19.

Moreover, this phrasing is spoken about as the divine prerogative in the only other Greek texts outside the Torah that use this phrase: Isa 27:9; Sir 47:11. Sirach 47:11 says, "the Lord took away his [David's] sins and raised his horn forever." This is clearly referring to David's grave sins of rape and murder and thus is a comment about the divine prerogative to forgive sins of moral impurity. It may also be alluding to Ps 51, which states clearly that only God can purify David from these moral impurities since nothing in the sacrificial system can. Isaiah 27:9 (LXX) says that the "blessing" God will grant "Jacob" is the end of their exile, which is when God will "take away his sin." It then goes on to talk about the abolition of idolatry and other altars in the same verse. Again, what we see is that "taking away sin" is something God alone can do because it refers to removing sins of moral impurity, which the sacrificial system is impotent to handle (by built-in design).

This meaning fits seamlessly with what the Gospel of John has claimed about Jesus up to 1:29 and then goes on to develop to the end of the narrative. The prologue has already established that Jesus is the embodiment of God (1:1–18) and thus ascribing to him the divine prerogative to "take away sins" apart from the sacrificial system makes sense. John the Immerser's declaration is made immediately after he is being questioned about his role in Israel's promised restoration (is John the Messiah, or Elijah, or the Prophet, or someone else?—1:19–25). His comment that Jesus is the one who will "take away the sins of the world" in this context is most likely a direct reference to Isa 27:9, which is expanded out for all the world. What Israel was looking forward to for God to do for them (quite apart from the sacrificial system) is happening through Jesus, and it will benefit the entire cosmos.

The statement that Jesus is "the lamb of God, who takes away the sins of the world" (1:29) is likely combining two separate identity claims. That is, the phrase "takes away the sins of the world" is not *because* Jesus is the "lamb of God." As we noted, lambs are never used to "take away sins" in any purgation sacrifice. Rather, Jesus is the "lamb of God" *and* he is the one "who takes away sins." Jesus is the "lamb of God" because he is the ultimate Passover lamb. And Jesus is the one "who takes away the sins of the world" because he is also the embodiment of God (1:1–18) and thus can carry out this divine prerogative. While these are separate identity claims and highlight different nuances of Jesus's mission in John, they are nonetheless intelligibly related.

The larger point of John 1:29 is to combine these distinct identity claims as having one and the same personal referent: namely, "Jesus," this most unlikely of candidates who comes from Nazareth (1:45–46). John 1:29 is a declaration that Jesus of Nazareth is both the liberator of a new exodus for the entire cosmos (i.e., the ultimate Passover lamb) and, as the embodiment of God, the one who will "take away the sins of the cosmos." These notions of a cosmic exodus, Passover lamb, and taking away sins go together precisely because "taking away sins" is a way of talking about what the promised exodus-like restoration would entail (Isa 27:9; cf. Jer 31:34). But, again, this is not because Passover suddenly brings about the forgiveness of sins, but rather that it marks, celebrates, and commemorates that cosmic-exodus-restoration event of forgiveness with a sacred feast.

All this being said, I want to also leave room for the possibility that "lamb of God" might also be referring to the daily burnt offerings, the *tāmîd*. Recall that these use a male lamb, but they are non-atoning sacrifices. As Shauf notes, "Given the importance of the Tamid, and of the well-known use of lambs in the Tamid, it also seems reasonable to see in the lamb appellation the idea that Jesus is now the most important expression of the people's relationship to God."[127] Combining the Passover with the *tāmîd* is more likely than combining it with the purgation sacrifices since both the Passover and *tāmîd* use male lambs and both are non-atoning sacrifices. Since we learned how the *tāmîd* visualized God's continual presence to "meet with" and "dwell among" Israel (Exod 29:42–46), this would also align with what John is claiming about the significance of Jesus himself without generating the problems that combining "lamb of God" with purgation sacrifices does. Jesus would be understood as the fullness of the *tāmîd*, the very incarnation of God's dwelling with humanity (1:1–18, esp. v. 14: *eskēnōsen*, "he tabernacled/dwelt/tented").

Therefore, while I think the Passover is the primary referent for "lamb of God" in John 1:29 and 36, this does not preclude a double reference to the *tāmîd* as well. The only thing precluded is an atoning connotation because it grates against the non-atoning functions of these sacrifices and does not factor in the non-sacrificial meaning of the phrase "takes away sins," which is the divine prerogative when dealing with grave sins and the promise linked with the exodus-like restoration.

127. Shauf, *Jesus the Sacrifice*, 138.

Revelation 1:5, 5:6–10, 7:14–15, and 1 Peter 1:3, 18–19

Both Revelation and 1 Peter draw upon Jesus as the Passover lamb in similar ways. But before we look at that, Rev 7:15–15 provides a good opportunity to see how Jesus's "blood" can be conceptualized as other cultic liquids or viscous substances besides merely "blood." Importantly, the use of "blood" itself does not automatically signal that "sacrifice" is in view. More often than not, "blood" (*haima*) simply indicates a "violent death" in the LXX and the NT.[128] Only specific context cues will alert the reader to interpret "blood" within a sacrificial register.[129] And, if it is in a sacrificial register, then we would need to determine what kind of sacrificial blood is being specified (e.g., it could be the blood of a well-being sacrifice or a purgation sacrifice, etc.). The mention of Jesus's blood can therefore refer only to his violent death, or it can be sacrificial blood, or it can be conceptualized as other cultic substances, such as oil and water. I argue that Rev 7:14 depicts Jesus's blood as the water, oil, and (non-atoning) ordination blood applied to the priests for their consecration in the Torah. And, as I argued earlier, there is a difference between the meaning of Jesus's death *qua* death and the meaning of Jesus conveyed with sacrificial imagery.

In Rev 7:9 John sees "a great crowd . . . from every nation and [all] tribes and peoples and languages." Then we read that the people in this great crowd "have washed their robes and made them white in the blood of the lamb" (7:14). According to Shauf, "Jesus' death here is being pictured as an atoning sacrifice."[130] His warrants for this are the washings in Isa 1:18, in which washing and forgiveness are linked, and the garment change for Joshua the high priest in Zech 3:3–5, in which a change of his priestly garments

128. E.g., Gen 9:6; Num 35:33; Deut 19:10, 13; 21:7–9; 27:25; 1 Sam 19:5; 25:26, 31; 2 Sam 3:28; 4:11; 1 Kgs 2:5, 31–32; 2 Kgs 21:16; 24:4; 1 Chr 22:8; 28:3; 2 Chr 36:5d; Esth 16:5; Pss 13:3 (MT 14:3); 78:3, 10 (MT 79: 3, 10); 93:21 (MT 94:21); 105:38 (MT 106:38); Isa 59:7; Jer 2:34; 7:6; 19:4; 22:3, 17; 33:15 (MT 26:15); Lam 4:13; Ezek 16:38; 18:10; 22:3, 4, 6, 9, 12, 27; 23:45; 24:7; 35:6; Prov 1:11, 16; 6:17; Joel 4:19 (MT 3:19); Jonah 1:14; Sir 28:11; 34:22; Wis 8:20; 1 Macc 1:37; 2 Macc 1:8; Matt 23:30, 35; 26:28; 27:4, 24, 25; Luke 11:50–51; 22:20; Acts 5:28; 18:6; 22:20; Rom 3:15; Rev 16:3–4, 6.

129. E.g., I do not think there are contextual indications that would signal readers to interpret the reference to "blood" in Col 1:20 within a sacrificial register. If anything, the mention of the "cross" serves to index Jesus's death as a state-sanctioned *political lynching*. It refers to the violence of crucifixion *per se*. But the larger claim of Colossians is that what appears like a straightforward capital punishment for non-Roman insurrectionists and slaves was actually God's public triumph in and through Jesus Christ over these powers (2:14–15). Paradoxically, crucifixion as the enactment of the state's capacity for ultimate *exclusion* turns out to be the means of God's ultimate *inclusion* by which God has "reconciled all things to himself . . . things in heaven and on earth" (1:20).

130. Shauf, *Jesus the Sacrifice*, 140.

and forgiveness are linked. But neither of these feature an atoning sacrifice of any kind and thus Shauf's conclusion is a *non sequitur*. Isaiah 1:18 is in a context that names the *incapacity of any sacrifices* to deal with Israel's grave sins (cf. 1:13–15). I am not denying that these passages might be part of the scriptural contextual matrix of Rev 7:14, however. I am only pointing out why these cannot be used in support of Jesus's blood here as atoning since these passages feature no such blood. Shauf is conflating the very notion of "forgiveness" with "atonement," which is one of the core misunderstandings I flagged earlier. Both passages are about the possibility of God's forgiveness outside of the sacrificial system.[131]

If Rev 7:14 is not about an atoning sacrifice, then what is going on with this image of "washing" in "blood"? Jesus's blood is doing triple duty here. First, "wash" (*plynō*) signals that Jesus's blood is conceptualized as *water*. And there are multiple allusions to the ritual use of water going on here. (1) This is an allusion to when all of Israel was commanded to "wash" their garments before the theophany at Sinai (Exod 19:10, 14—the LXX uses *plynō* here).[132] The great crowd is located in the heavenly temple "before the throne of God" in the next verse (Rev 7:15) so it is rather straightforward that John is drawing upon the requirement in Exod 19:10 to have one's garments washed to be in God's presence. (2) Washing garments is part of several ritual purification procedures, which makes sense since ritual purity is all about being in the appropriate state to access the sacred dwelling place where God's presence is and washing garments was the initial requirement at Sinai.[133] (3) Washing garments was part of the ritual purification for the Levites at their installation and dedication to serve at the dwelling place (Num 8:7, 21). Although the Aaronic priests are Levites, the rest of the

131. In fact, the language in the LXX of Zech 3:4 that God "has taken away [*aphēka*] your [Joshua's] lawless deeds [*anomias*]" is similar to the passages discussed above about how God "takes away sins" apart from atoning sacrifices discussed above. Both phrases are based on God's revelation to Moses about his character in Exod 34:6–7. God describes himself as the one who "takes away" (*aphaireō*) both "lawlessness" (*anomia*) and "sins" (*hamartia*) as well as "injustice" (*adikia*) (34:7). Again, this is about the divine prerogative to forgive all kinds of sins apart from the sacrificial system, which explains why Moses does not offer an atoning sacrifice, but rather immediately petitions God to do just this for Israel after their grave sin of idolatry with the golden calf (34:9) and again after Israel's repeated rebellions in Num 14:11–19 (esp. vv. 18–19).

132. Fee, *Revelation*, 114. Shauf dismisses this option in favor of "an atoning sacrifice" with no justification other than fallacious appeals to Isa 1:18 and Zech 3:3–5 (*Jesus the Sacrifice*, 140). Again, my critique is not that Isa 1:18 and Zech 3:3–5 cannot be part of the allusive background to Rev 7:14, but rather that even if they are they actually work *against* the idea that "atonement" is being activated. In any case, the allusion to Exod 19:10 and 14 is straightforward.

133. Lev 11:25, 28, 40; 13:6, 34, 55–56, 58; 14:8–9, 47; 15:5–8, 10–11, 13, 17, 21–22, 27; 16:26, 28; 17:15–16; Num 19:7–8, 10, 19, 21; 31:24.

Levites are not *priests*. They have clearly delineated tasks from the priests (e.g., 1:47–54; 8:5–22, 18:1–32). They are just dwelling-place workers or, more specifically, they are the sanctuary guards that make sure no one encroaches onto sacred space unlawfully. From all of these we can see that having washed clothes indicates that the great crowd is in the right state of ritual purity to be in God's presence and to serve God like Levites. But there is still more going on.

Revelation 7:15 provides cues that Jesus's blood is also being conceptualized as the ordination blood and oil that consecrated the *priestly* garments in Exod 29:21 and Lev 8:30.[134] That is, the great crowd is not only like the whole congregation of Israel who washed before Sinai or the Levites who were washed for their installation as sanctuary guards, but they are in fact also priests. In Rev 7:15 we read that the great crowd is not only "before the throne of God," but they also "serve him day and night in his temple." While this would include the service the Levites offer to God, John has already informed his audience that Jesus has made his followers "priests" (1:6; 5:10; cf. 20:6).[135] And as we discussed previously, part of the priestly consecration and ordination ceremony was sprinkling the blood of the ordination ram along with the consecration oil on their garments (Exod 29:21; Lev 8:30).[136] Future priests do not go through this ceremony; they just inherit the consecrated garments. That is, the garments make the priest. Putting on these consecrated garments functions as their ordination into the priesthood (Exod 29:29; 40:14–15; cf. Num 20:26, 28). Therefore, in addition to Jesus's blood being conceptualized as water, it is also functioning as the consecrating substances of oil and blood that are applied to the priestly garments. The description of garments washed in blood indicate that those in the great crowd are not only before the throne of God, but also serving as priests. And because these are *priestly* garments we can infer that Jesus's blood is being depicted as both the consecrating *oil* and the consecrating *blood* that sanctifies the priestly garments.

134. Similarly, Eberhart, "Characteristics," 51–52.

135. It is worth noting how the claim in 22:4 that God's servants will "see his face and his Name is on their foreheads" is likely an allusion to the gold plate that the high priest is to wear on his forehead which says, "holy to YHWH" (Exod 28:36–38). Besides Moses, who saw and spoke to YHWH "face to face" (33:11; Num 12:8; cf. 7:89), only the high priest ever had direct access to the holy of holies (Lev 16:2; cf. Exod 25:22; 30:6, 36). In this way, Rev 22:4 indexes the faithful through this description as those who see God's face as high priests who have access to God's presence in the holy of holies and have the divine Name on their foreheads.

136. Water-washings were also part of the ordination ceremony (Exod 29:4; 30:19–21; 40:12, 31–32; Lev 8:6).

And this consecrating blood does not come from an atoning sacrifice. Recall that the ordination blood comes from a well-being offering that the priests ate from (Exod 29:19–20, 28; Lev 8:22–23, 28, 30–31). So while there is no doubt that Jesus's blood is in a sacrificial register here, it is non-atoning well-being ordination blood. It is bringing about a metaphysical transition for these people from all the various nations and consecrating them to the priesthood of God's heavenly temple, which will eventually come down and fill the entire earth (Rev 21:2–3, 22; cf. 22:3).

Again, "blood" does not always have a sacrificial or ritual meaning. It can just "be a synonym for 'death,' or more precisely for 'murder,'"[137] but its use in Rev 7:14–15 has several cues that indicate both ritual and sacrificial images are being activated. Thus, 7:14–15 is instructive because it shows how Jesus's blood can be conceptualized to function as a variety of different cultic liquids: water, oil, and non-atoning blood, which will be important for discussions in chapter 6. We turn now to see how it is also conceptualized in Revelation and 1 Peter as money in relation to the Passover lamb.

Notice first that Jesus as the "lamb" in Revelation is primarily rooted in Passover. The first mention of Jesus as the lamb is linked with a quotation from Exod 19:5–6 (Rev 5:6, 9–10).[138] As Craig Keener comments, "in Revelation, the lamb is a Passover lamb that delivers God's people from the plagues (cf. 5:6, 9; 7:1–8, 17)" just like the first Passover was a celebration of Israel being delivered from the tenth plague (and all the previous ones).[139] In addition to deliverance from plagues, "God's formation of a people through the sacrifice of Christ parallels God's formation of Israel through the Passover events" recounted in Exod 19:5–6.[140] That is, the particular use of the Passover motif is to emphasize the Christ-event as an act of liberation, a cosmic exodus. Jesus has formed a *people* who are "purchased" out from all the nations just like God formed Israel into a people by "ransoming" them from Egypt (Deut 7:8; 13:5). This is why Richard Bauckham refers to this as an "eschatological exodus" since this idea of "ransoming" or "purchasing" Israel back from exile was linked with the promise of an exodus-like liberation (e.g., Isa 35:9; 41:14; 43:1, 14; 44:22–24; 51:11; 52:3; 62:12; 63:9; Jer 15:21; 27:34; 38:11; Zech 10:8; Mic 4:10).[141] But the Passover feast itself is not what redeemed Israel from Egypt the first time nor what will facilitate the new exodus-like deliverance. Rather, as discussed, the Passover feast

137. Eberhart, "Characteristics," 58.

138. Shauf, *Jesus the Sacrifice*, 139–40.

139. Keener, *The Gospel of John*, 1:452; cf. 1:454.

140. Shauf, *Jesus the Sacrifice*, 140.

141. Bauckham, *Book of Revelation*, 70.

celebrates the prior act of divine liberation, and by Jesus's day was also a proleptic anticipation of the eschatological exodus. But the sacrificial feast itself is not the saving event; it commemorates the old event while looking forward to the new one.

As Bauckham goes on to explain, "Revelation treats the blood of the lamb as the price of redemption," but "this really goes beyond the role which the blood of the Passover Lamb played in the exodus."[142] This is because John has shifted the function of Jesus's death from being like the Passover lamb itself to the *redemption*-event which that sacrificial feast memorialized; namely, liberation from slavery. Slaves are normally freed when the price of liberation (ransom) has been paid to their master. For John, Jesus's blood is like the currency that pays the ransom.

This same idea is made in 1 Pet 1:18–19. Like John the Seer, Peter also claims that Jesus's "blood, like an unblemished lamb" (1:19) functions as the currency for "redeeming" the people (1:18). Peter then goes on to quote from Exod 19:5–6 (1 Pet 2:5, 9–10), just like Revelation did. The connection to Passover is further strengthened since this section of 1 Peter begins in 1:13 ("gird up the loins of your mind") with an allusion to the Passover instructions in Exod 12:11 to eat with "girded loins."[143] Thus, 1 Pet 1:18–19 is bookended with Passover and exodus references.

These are good examples that show how just because "blood" is mentioned and there are sacrificial context cues does not mean the reference to "blood" is necessarily to be understood purely within a sacrificial register. First, since the Passover lamb is not a purgation sacrifice we know that, if anything, this is non-atoning blood. Second, in both Revelation and 1 Peter Jesus's blood is a *currency*. In 1 Peter it is specifically compared to "silver and gold" that "redeems" (*lytroō*) (1:18). In Revelation it "purchases" (*agorazō*) people "out from every tribe, tongue, people, and nation" (5:9; cf. 14:3, 4) and earlier, it "frees" (*lyō*) people from their sins (1:5). Since neither of these is a function of any sacrificial blood (these verbs are never used in the LXX regarding any sacrifice) we know that both John and Peter are doing something *in addition* to the sacrificial imagery of Passover. They are going outside of a strict sacrificial register and moving into an economic one.

These verbs are all used in slavery contexts and the blurring of these categories makes sense when we keep in mind what the Passover was commemorating: Israel's redemption from slavery. Rather than ransoming people from literal slavery like Israel from Egypt, Jesus is ransoming people from their slavery to sin (Rev 1:5) and from the "worthless way of

142. Bauckham, *Book of Revelation*, 71.

143. Shauf, *Jesus the Sacrifice*, 144.

life handed down by your ancestors" (1 Pet 1:18). All the nations become "Egypts" here, enslaving everyone under their offensive and destructive patterns of life. But Jesus has freed them and formed them into a new people,[144] a kingdom and priests (Rev 5:10; 1 Pet 2:5, 9; both quoting Exod 19:6) with a new way of life, patterned after Jesus, specifically his suffering and death (cf. 1 Pet 2:21–25; 3:8–9; 4:13, 16, 19; Rev 3:21; 5:6; 11:7–12; 12:11; 13:7–10; 14:12–13; 15:2).

But, this idea of Jesus's blood as a currency cannot be taken too far. Especially when we keep the scriptural exodus in mind, we realize that the use of "ransom" was never "literal," even for the first exodus. Neither Pharaoh, nor Egypt, nor their gods were paid a ransom for Israel's liberation. God just freed them. The use of "ransom" language, then, especially as it relates to exodus motifs, was never intended to convey that God paid some entity a ransom of any kind. That is, when we read, "I will deliver you from slavery and I will ransom [*lytrōsomai*] you by a raised arm and great judgment" (Exod 6:6 LXX; cf. Deut 7:8; 13:15; Mic 6:4; Hos 7:13), it would be foolish to think God is paying some entity a ransom. Rather, it just means that *what a literal ransom effects—freedom from slavery—God will do, but quite apart from paying anyone off*. When salvation is conveyed with the economic metaphor of ransom in the OT it is based on the exodus[145] and should not be pushed beyond the point that God brings about a change in status for those who were once slaves/in exile and now are freed and therefore belong to God. In fact, Isa 52:3 declares directly: "and you will be ransomed without money."

Therefore, just like no one would conceptualize the redemption God accomplished in the exodus as God paying someone off, it is inappropriate to do the same with "ransom" sayings in Revelation and 1 Peter—and in the whole NT for that matter[146]—since these are all based on God's promise to

144. It seems likely that the comment in 1 Pet 1:2 that the believers have been "sprinkled with his [Jesus's] blood" is a reference to the blood of the covenant ceremony in Exod 24:8 (Shauf, *Jesus the Sacrifice*, 133–34). Thus, "In picturing the audience having come into relationship with God as a new exodus, Christ's death is viewed as both the initiation and the completion of the process, the Passover lamb and the covenant sacrifice" (145).

145. See the passages from Isaiah noted above.

146. E.g., Eph 1:7 and Col 1:13–14 (cf. Exod 6:6; Deut 7:8; 13:15; Isa 1:27; 44:22; 47:4; 59:20; Pss 103:3–4, 10–14; 130:8 [129:8 LXX]); Titus 2:14 (this strongly echoes Exod 19:5, 10, 14; 23:22; Deut 7:6; 14:2; 26:18); 1 Cor 6:20 (no sacrificial connotations, just economic); 7:23 (no sacrificial connotations, just economic); Mark 10:45 and Matt 20:28 (these will be discussed further in chapter 7). It is also worth pointing out that the mention of "blood" with "redemption" and "forgiveness" in Eph 1:7 is most likely linked with the prophetic promise of a new covenant of peace (cf. 2:12 and "peace" in 2:17, quoting from Isa 57:19; see also "covenant of peace" in Isa 54:10 and the promise

recapitulate the first exodus. All it means is that those who were in some sort of bondage (to sins, to their worthless inherited patterns of life, to the devil, to their own passions, etc.) have now been freed by Jesus. Jesus ransomed them and they now belong to him. Yes, it "cost" Jesus his life, or as Paul says Jesus "emptied himself . . . to the point of death, even death on a cross" (Phil 2:7–8).[147] But to ask, "Who was paid?" is an exercise in missing the point, especially since that question is already unintelligible regarding the first exodus.

Yet many Christians have both asked and answered this question and have proposed various payees who received the payment of Jesus's blood. Some have said Jesus paid off the devil (e.g., Origen, *Commentary on Matthew* 16:8; Gregory of Nyssa, *Great Catechism* 21–23) and others think Jesus paid off God the Father (e.g., Gregory of Nazianzus, *Orations* 45.22; John Damascene, *Concerning the Orthodox Faith* 3.27).[148] Both are unwarranted and overlook the fact that the first exodus is the paradigm for divine "ransom." Therefore, just as no one thinks that when God ransomed Israel from Egypt (or was to repeat this type of salvation in a new exodus from the nations) either Egypt, or the nations, or God himself were being "paid off," so too we should not think that the use of "ransom" imagery in the NT is conveying that Jesus's blood "paid off" anything or anyone.

---

of a "covenant" in 59:21 together with 27:9, which Paul collocates in Rom 11:26–27). That is, if "blood" has a sacrificial connotation in Eph 1:7, it is the non-atoning covenant ratification blood of the new covenant, which signals that the post-exile era of forgiveness of sins has arrived, as discussed earlier. This is strengthened by the mention of Jesus as "an offering and sacrifice" that produces a "fragrant aroma" (5:2), which, as discussed in chapter 2, is both (a) the way the non-atoning burnt and well-being offerings are characterized and (b) these are the sacrifices used for covenant inaugurations and renewals (e.g., Exod 24:5, 11).

147. In the same way the "cost" that Jesus talks about in Luke for following him is not about a literal or spiritual payment to be made to an entity, but rather about the personal toll being his follower will have upon oneself (Luke 14:27–33), the "price of liberation" (ransom) may also convey the personal impact Jesus was willing to endure to heal human beings (something he was more than willing to *give* because of his love), but this is *not* a transactional payment. No one is receiving the ransom money. The ransom sayings underscore a key *result* of what Jesus accomplished: where we were once enslaved, we are now set free and belong to Jesus. All of this, though, is based on the prophetic hope for another exodus-like deliverance, so the language of "ransom" ought to be interpreted within that framework. And since the two sacrificial feasts marking Israel's ransom from slavery were the Passover and the covenant inauguration, it makes sense both that Jesus also tethered the meaning and purpose of his life, death, and resurrection to these two communal well-being sacrifices, and that these would become the meditative staring points for further reflection by the NT authors on the saving significance of Jesus's death and resurrection (e.g., see 1 Pet 1:3–4; 2:21–22).

148. Primary source references from Marcus, *Mark 8–16*, 757.

Additionally, every parable Jesus tells to teach about forgiveness in economic terms utilizes the motif of debt remission/forgiveness, not debt satisfaction (Luke 4:19; 7:40–50; Matt 18:21–35). In no instance does someone else pay off the "debt" for someone else. And the prayer Jesus teaches his followers is also only about debt forgiveness (Luke 11:4; Matt 6:12). The notion that "Jesus paid my debt" to God or the devil lacks any scriptural basis and contradicts Jesus's own teachings. This notion that Jesus's blood is paid out to some entity comes from taking "ransom" language too rigidly and by not recognizing how "ransom" is anchored in the exodus tradition, which makes the very idea of there being any payees nonsensical.

CONCLUSION

The institution of the Lord's Supper conveys the earliest and only explanation of how Jesus's death factors into his mission. And early followers of Jesus unanimously ascribed this elucidation to Jesus himself. We have discovered that the only sacrifices Jesus himself associated his death with are two communal well-being sacrifices—Passover and covenant-inauguration/renewal. These are the foundational sacrificial feast celebrations of Israel's liberation from slavery in Egypt and formation into a covenant people of God. The theme of "forgiveness of sins" in the NT is anchored in the prophetic texts that promise a specific sort of forgiveness of sins: Israel's release from the consequences of moral impurity (exile as covenant death, e.g., Ezek 37), which will be celebrated as a new exodus (hence Passover) and establishing/re-affirming God's (re)new(ed) covenant (exile as covenant death, e.g., Ezek 37).

Neither the Jesus-as-Passover lamb nor Jesus-as-blood-of-the-(re)new(ed)-covenant *effects* this forgiveness. Rather, these sacrificial feasts are sacrificialized in the Lord's Supper to commemorate that the promised forgiveness of sins has already happened apart from any "sacrifice" (atoning or non-atoning). Jesus was literally offering this forgiveness prior to his death because the forgiveness he offers springs from the fact that "the time is fulfilled" (Mark 1:15)—it is the *time* of God's promised forgiveness—and that he is God's "mobile, and powerfully contagious force of holiness in the world . . . that overwhelms the forces and sources of impurity and death, be they pneumatic, ritual, or moral."[149] The Lord's Supper takes the bread and wine from a literal Passover meal and further ritualizes the sacrificial ritual of Passover. That is, the Lord's Supper is a sacrificialization of (unleavened) bread and wine that makes them a thanksgiving well-being sacrifice that

149. Thiessen, *Forces of Death*, 179.

doubles as both a Passover (e.g., 1 Cor 5:7–8) and covenant-inauguration meta-ritual meal (e.g., 1 Cor 11:23–26).

Moreover, we saw that "ransom"/"redemption" is bound up with the liberative eschatological-/cosmic-exodus motif. When those like John the Seer or the author of 1 Peter combine the notion of Jesus as a Passover lamb with Jesus's blood as the currency for a ransom, they are merely joining together what the Passover commemorates—the (cosmic) exodus—and the prophetic metaphor for the divine act of accomplishing that event. That is, this combination is not suddenly saying that Passover lamb's blood *qua* sacrificial blood is the means by which the (cosmic) exodus happened—i.e., that the blood was a "ransom payment" to some entity. They are just borrowing from the language of the prophetic hope to make the point that those who were once enslaved (and this enslavement itself is variously depicted) have now been set free by Jesus. Jesus is the lamb of the free.

Therefore, just as Israel was not ransomed from Egypt with any sort of payment let alone *by* sacrifice,[150] so too the "ransom" of the second exodus would not come about by a payout to any entity (Isa 52:3). This is the theological framework within which the various "ransom" and "purchased" statements in the NT need to be comprehended. The ideas of Passover and (re)new(ed) covenant are tightly linked with the notion of "ransom," but those sacrifices do not *bring about* the ransom, but rather *celebrate* that ransom-event since that is the function of well-being sacrifices in general and these two in particular from the first exodus. Further, "ransom" is just an image to talk about the freedom and deliverance Jesus—the ultimate Passover lamb—accomplished. It is a way to talk about the significance of Jesus from multiple angles. Jesus himself in his literal contact with and then victory over death—the consequences of moral impurity swallowing up both people and Jerusalem—freed the cosmos from death. Jesus brought about a cosmic exodus, a cosmic liberation, a cosmic ransom. But Jesus's death was not actually "paid" to anyone or anything.

Further, the consistent witness throughout the NT is that people are purified as they contact the risen Jesus, or rather, as Jesus contacts them by touching them with his Spirit (e.g., John 15:3; 17:17–19; 20:21–23; 1 Cor 6:11;[151] Rom 8:9–11). This union with Jesus is described as co-crucifixion (Rom 6:3–6; Gal 2:20), co-cross bearing (Mark 8:34–35), and co-suffering

150. But they memorialized their liberation through a non-atoning commemorative well-being sacrifice.

151. Note the language of "washing" (*apolouō*) here since this is about moral purification from the sins listed in 6:9–10 on analogy to bodily ritual purification (just the like prophets envision).

with Jesus (Mark 10:38–39; Phil 3:10; Rom 8:17; 2 Cor 1:5; 2 Tim 2:12; Heb 13:11–13).

This is what the participatory nature of the well-being sacrifices make possible and intelligible. This is why Paul says eating the sacrificialized Lord's Supper is "participation" (*koinōnia*) in Jesus's shed blood and broken body (1 Cor 10:16–17). But more than this, the Lord's Supper unites all partakers to each other:

> The cup of blessing that we bless, is it not a sharing [*koinōnia*] in the blood of Christ? The bread that we break, is it not a sharing [*koinōnia*] in the body of Christ? Because there is one bread, we who are many are *one body*, for we all partake of the one bread. Consider the people of Israel; are not those who eat the sacrifices partners [*koinōnoi*] in the altar? (1 Cor 10:16–18)

We know we are dealing with the non-*kipper* sacrifices because Paul is talking about sacrifices which are *eaten* by the people.[152]

Paul's point is that eating sacrifices binds one with the deity and to the other worshipers for better or for worse (10:20–21). And Paul's use of *koinōnia* elsewhere shows how he thinks about this as all believers sharing in Christ's sufferings and becoming conformed to the likeness of Jesus's death together (e.g., 2 Cor 1:5, 7; Phil 3:10; cf. Col 1:24). He says something similar in 2 Cor 4:7–12 where he talks about his life as a living narration of the life and death of Jesus. Basically, to the extent to which believers are living narrations of Jesus's death, they are having *koinōnia* with Christ Crucified. A cross-shaped, cruciform pattern of life is the theological result of Paul's well-being sacrificial imagery.

Since eating well-being sacrifices binds us with the deity, it is by partaking of the well-being offering that is Jesus's body that we become made participants in his broken body and shed blood and made members of the new covenant. It is by this that we become "living [well-being] sacrifices," ourselves (Rom 12:1). This makes sense for why Paul calls himself a drink offering (Phil 2:17), which accompanied sacrificial feasts (Num 15:1–13). And he says the Philippians' gift can be thought of as the smoke arising from the well-being sacrifices that pleases God (Phil 4:18), just Jesus was (Eph 5:1–2).[153]

152. And if there was any doubt about this, he actually quotes from Exod 32:6 earlier in 10:7, which is about the Israelites eating well-being sacrifices in the presence of the Golden Calf.

153. Shauf's comments on this verse are insightful: "The unique aspect of this reference is that, rather than Christ's death being presented as atoning, as initiating a new exodus, or as a covenant sacrifice, it is presented as a gift that pleases God. The point is not that God enjoyed his death but that his death was an act of self-giving love and

Paul's letters make explicit what is narratively presented in the Gospels via the Lord's Supper. That is, eating the sacrificialized Lord's Supper binds one to Jesus and thereby to the cross where his body was broken and his blood shed (e.g., Mark 8:31–35; 10:38–45; cf. John 6:48–58; 12:23–26; 13:36; 21:18–19). The well-being sacrifices are key to understanding the way NT authors, and especially Paul, conceive of the relationship between Jesus and the church, which Paul calls Jesus's body (1 Cor 12:12–13, 27; Rom 12:5; cf. Eph 1:23; 4:12; 5:30; Col 1:18, 24, 2:19). The participatory nature of the well-being sacrifices allow Paul a way to make sense of believer's very real participation and union with Jesus's death (and resurrection) because these are the only sacrifices the offerer eats and so has a share in themselves. It makes perfect sense for a movement that saw itself as the body of the Crucified Lord and called to share in his sufferings to draw on the well-being sacrifices activated in the Lord's Supper when seeking to comprehend Jesus's death.

Therefore, if Jesus is a well-being sacrifice and his followers sacrificially partake of his body and blood and thereby become members of and sharers in his body—a new covenant people united to the ultimate Passover lamb who also seals the new covenant in his blood—then as Jesus's body, they also become a collective "living well-being sacrifice" (Rom 12:1) and living narrations of Jesus's cruciform pattern of life.

---

for that reason pleasing to God. . . . This interpretation of Christ's death as a sacrifice . . . views Christ's sacrificial death not as a unique, eschaton-defining event but as an exemplary act, a model to be followed" (*Jesus the Sacrifice*, 168).

6

Jesus, Purgation Sacrifices, and the Day of Decontamination

THERE ARE ONLY TWO NT books that explicitly articulate the significance of Jesus in relation to the atoning purgation sacrifices and the Day of Decontamination: 1 John and Hebrews. 1 John is brief, but direct, while "Hebrews provides us with the most elaborate and detailed such interpretation [of Jesus as an atoning sacrifice]."[1] Here I argue:

(1) Atonement theology is not part of the gospel message. Rather, it is a theological innovation based on prior "ingredients" from the gospel.

(2) In both 1 John and Hebrews, Jesus's blood is conceptualized as various cultic "liquids" (e.g., water, blood from atoning sacrifices, and blood from non-atoning sacrifices). And, especially in Hebrews, we can see that Jesus fulfills the entirety of the Levitical sacrificial and purity systems.

(3) In Hebrews, both Jesus's high priesthood and his association with the *kipper* system is *predicated* on Jesus's relation to the non-*kipper* covenant-making sacrifices.

(4) The *kipper* system is activated in Hebrews to claim that Jesus accomplished a cosmic decontamination of the heavenly sanctuary.

(5) The author of Hebrews pushes this further and makes the bolder claims that to be a follower of Jesus is (a) to become co-high priests with him and (b) to suffer for Jesus's sake is to become part of the same

1. Shauf, *Jesus the Sacrifice*, 147.

purgation sacrifice Jesus offered. Once again, the concept of "participation" rather than "substitution" best conveys what is being described in these texts.

ATONEMENT THEOLOGY IS NOT PART OF THE GOSPEL

Without a doubt the atoning sacrifices are applied to Jesus in 1 John and Hebrews. The Greek word for atonement is *hilasmos*. It is only used twice in the NT: 1 John 2:2 and 4:10. In the LXX the verb *exilaskomai* is used throughout to translate *kipper*, but this verb is never used in the NT. However, an alternative form of the verb without the prefix, *hilaskomai*, is used, though only twice (Luke 18:13 and Heb 2:17). The use of *hilaskomai* in Luke 18:13 does not have to do with an atoning sacrificial offering and thus no translation of the NT uses a word associated with atonement here. In this verse it is a petition for God to "be merciful." The use of *hilaskomai* in Heb 2:17, however, clearly carries the sense of atonement. Jesus is called a "merciful and faithful high priest" who "decontaminates [*hilaskesthai*] the sins of the people." Although Hebrews does not use either *hilasmos* or *hilaskomai* later in the letter, it is clear, as we will see, that the author is associating Jesus with the Day of Decontamination in Heb 9–10 as well.

Since the fact *that* 1 John and Hebrews associate Jesus with the *kipper* system is thus easily established, most of the discussion in this chapter focuses on how even when Jesus is identified with the atoning sacrifices this is neither about "substitutionary death" nor was it thought of as part of the gospel message proper. Rather, relating Jesus to the *kipper* system is acknowledged as a theologically advanced teaching. Hebrews and 1 John are baking a *new* theological dish based on *prior common "ingredients"* (e.g., Jesus's resurrection, subsequent ascension to the right hand of God, and his mission to effect moral purification).

This is made explicit in Hebrews. The author acknowledges how *kipper* theology is for the theologically "mature" (Heb 5:10—6:3). Everything that follows *substantiates* the claims made earlier about Jesus as high priest and the *kipper* he provides (cf. 1:3; 2:17; 3:1; 4:14–15; 5:5, 9–10).[2] The transi-

2. Given that I have received pushback on this in other venues, Lane's observations bear this out and are worth quoting: "Three aspects of this subject were announced thematically in the description of Jesus' exaltation in 5:9–10. What was entailed in the declaration that Jesus 'was made perfect' occupies the central place in the exposition and receives the fullest development (8:1—9:28). This unit is framed by two other sections that provide commentary on the significance of designating Jesus as 'a high priest like Melchizedek' (7:1–28) and as 'the source of eternal salvation' (10:1–18)" (Lane,

tion from the claim in 5:10 to 5:11 reveals that all this priestly talk about Jesus in 7:1—10:18 is "advanced teaching."[3] This is the "solid food," not the basic "milk" mentioned in 6:1–2, which is for the "mature."[4] The author acknowledges that the exegetical and theological moves that need to be made to comprehend Jesus in terms of a high priestly *kipper* ministry cannot be taken for granted. It takes a lot of work to substantiate, which is what the rest of the letter is aimed at doing. One obvious yet major hurdle is Jesus's descent from Judah, not Levi (nor Aaron more specifically) (7:13–14; cf. 8:4). This is one reason that explains why Jesus-as-high-priest was not part of the basic proclamation of the gospel about Christ, but a later development, "prob[ing] the deeper implications of Christian commitment."[5]

Moreover, Jesus-as-*kipper*-sacrifice is conceptually at odds with Jesus-as-non-*kipper*-well-being sacrifice(s), which is what is reinforced repeatedly by *eating* the Lord's Supper. Thinking about Jesus-as-high-priest and/or Jesus-as-*kipper*-sacrifice, which cannot be eaten, logically needs to be grounded in something *other* than a ritual that memorializes Jesus through non-atoning communal well-being sacrifices, which are eaten. And this is exactly what we find in Hebrews; namely, a sacrificial atonement theology of Jesus constructed independently from (a) the basics of the gospel proclamation and (b) the Lord's Supper.

This accounts for why it is, as scholars note, "that Hebrews does not betray any indication of literary dependence on the Gospels."[6] This absence of literary dependence on the Gospels does not necessarily indicate so much the author's actual ignorance of the Gospels (or a Lord's Supper tradition),

Hebrews 1–8, 125). Further, "The writer clearly enunciated his intention to discuss the subject announced in 5:9–10, since he states, 'On this subject we have many things to say.' . . . The end of the preliminary remarks is indicated by the declaration that Jesus has become 'a high priest forever, like Melchizedek' (6:20). That affirmation constitutes a second announcement of one aspect of the subject (5:10), which is developed systematically in 7:1–28 . . ." (125–26). Also, the use of "τετελειωμένον, 'has been made perfect,' [in 7:28] is assigned the final position in the sentence for emphasis. It repeats the announcement of the subject in 5:9, καὶ τελειωθείς, 'and once made perfect,' and provides the point of transition to the central section of the exposition (8:1—9:28)" (126). Finally, "Once again, [in 9:28] the crucial term σωτηρίαν, 'salvation,' is assigned the final, emphatic position. It calls to mind the statement in 5:9 that Jesus 'has become the source of eternal salvation to all who obey him.' The final clause in 9:28 repeats the announcement of the subject in 5:9 and marks the point of transition to the third section of the exposition, which is devoted to that aspect (10:1–18)" (127).

3. Cockerill, *Hebrews*, 262, 267; cf. Lane, *Hebrews*, 135 ("advanced exposition"), 140 ("advanced instruction provided in 7:1—10:18").

4. Similarly, Cockerill, *Hebrews*, 259; cf. 262, 267.

5. Lane, *Hebrews 1–8*, 136; cf. 140.

6. Joseph, "'In the Days of His Flesh,'" 209.

but rather is one way of getting at the observation that the points the author is trying to make are not a repackaging of either (a) the views in the Gospels or (b) the Lord's Supper more specifically. The author surely believes their new teachings relating Jesus to *kipper* are *consistent with* the "confession" (cf. *homologia*, 3:1; 4:14; 10:23), but they present their views as unashamedly *mature* and *advanced* teachings (5:10—6:3).

Put slightly differently, for an author that is clearly "in the know" about basic Christian proclamations and traditions (e.g., 1:2–4; 5:7, 12; 6:1–2), the fact that they do not make use of something as foundational as the Lord's Supper is best explained by the simple notion that they did not think the points they were wanting to make are to be found in these traditions. The author of Hebrews is not repeating old doctrines; they are teaching new things *based on* "the basic teaching about Christ" (6:1).

The gospel speeches in Acts confirm this. Not a single speech associates Jesus with *kipper*.[7] Therefore, all students of the NT need to recognize that (a) no gospel speech in Acts relates Jesus to the *kipper* system; (b) Hebrews neither grounds its *kipper* theology in the Lord's Supper nor something like the early kerygma in 1 Cor 15:3–8; and (c) Hebrews acknowledges that Jesus-as-high-priest-according-to-the-order-of-Melchizedek-who-effects-(heavenly)-*kipper* is a "mature" teaching, not part of the basics of the gospel (Heb 5:12; 6:1).[8]

7. The closest moment comes on the lips of Paul in a speech delivered to people who are already followers of Jesus (the elders of Ephesus) and thus is not in a gospel speech. Paul says the elders are called "to shepherd the church of God, which he procured [*periepoiēsato*] through his own blood." Some have thought that the mention of "blood" in Acts 20:28 is about atonement. There are several problems with this, but the most obvious is the fact that this is based on the fallacy that assumes "blood" equals "sacrifice" and then the further misunderstanding that "sacrifice" equals "atonement." One of the aims of this book thus far has been to uncouple these kinds of fallacious equations. The verb used here (*peripoieō*) is *not a sacrificial verb*. This verb is never found in sacrificial contexts. So this verb already tells us that we are not within a sacrificial framework. Rather, it communicates that we are either in an economic register (i.e., "purchased," "obtained," "acquired") or one having to do with safety (i.e., "keeps safe"); hence my translation of "procure," which blends these two together (LSJ, s.v. περιποιέω). This is why no English translations use "atonement" words here. The claim in this verse is only that acquiring (and protecting) the church came at a cost. It cost Jesus his life. In any case, even if for argument's sake someone could prove that the "blood" in 20:28 was a reference to atonement—which it most definitely is not—it *is not in an evangelistic speech*. This comment is made by Paul to mature Christians (elders). And relegating atonement theology to mature Christian teaching is exactly what Hebrews explicitly marks it as.

8. See also Stökl, "Yom Kippur," 363–64: "The idea of introducing a non-Levitical high priesthood according to the order of Melkizedeq is a *novum* . . . , otherwise the author would not have had to waste so many words on the midrash on Melkizedeq." This is "the *specialissima* of *Hebrews*," especially "the high priest sacrificing himself, . . .

In other words, *kipper theology should not be confused with the gospel itself.* The author of Hebrews emphasizes this immediately before launching into their explanation of Jesus's high priesthood and work of atonement. Either they were greatly mistaken, and *kipper* really was part of the Lord's Supper and/or the basic gospel proclamation, or they are correct and these earlier comments about sin and forgiveness were not associated with *kipper* from the beginning, as I have argued.

Admittedly, the author of 1 John talks about Jesus and *kipper* as if this was already a known teaching for his audience. Given the explicit evidence from Hebrews and the indirect evidence from Acts, I suspect that 1 John was influenced by the *kipper* and priesthood Christology in Hebrews, but it could also very well be the case that the author drew similar conclusions independently.[9] In any case, the presence of *kipper* theology in 1 John, especially given its later date relative to most of the rest of the NT texts, is not a problem for the thesis that *kipper* was not part of the *initial* message about Christ, but rather was a later development in early Christian thought, meditating on the multivalent meaning that key claims about Jesus (e.g., his ascension) might generate.

KIPPER IN 1 JOHN

First John applies the language of sacrificial atonement to Jesus straightforwardly. Twice John declares that Jesus is "the decontamination (*hilasmos*) for our sins" (1 John 2:2; cf. 4:10). Knowing all the sacrificial information established so far helps us figure out what John *is not saying*. John isn't saying that Jesus was a substitutionary death. We know this because that is not

bringing his own blood into the adytum [holy of holies]. . . . [O]therwise the author . . . would not have had to explain these ideas in such a detailed way—they are new to his readers" (363).

However, Stökl also thinks there may have been a non-Melchizedekian "high priesthood Christology prior to and independent of *Hebrews*" based on a typology of "Jesus/Joshua ben Jozedeq" the high priest in Zech 3 (364). The problem with this hypothesis is that the only references making this connection postdate Hebrews (Justin Martyr, the Epistle of Barnabas, and Rev 1:13—if indeed this alludes to Zech 3, rather than Dan 10:5–6). It is difficult to see, then, how these can be used as evidence for a high priesthood Christology *prior* to Hebrews. It could just as well be that Hebrews influenced and inspired these later authors to find more high priesthood links with Jesus. Whatever the case may be, I agree with Stökl that linking Jesus with Melchizedek, and then with *kipper* is unique to Hebrews in the NT.

9. And regardless of when scholars date either Hebrews or 1 John (i.e., pre- or post-70 CE), they tend to date 1 John later. Jonathan Bernier compiles the various dating views from NT scholars in a helpful chart in *Rethinking the Dates of the New Testament*, 4. For Bernier's own dates see 118 and 195.

how any sacrifices function. The question we ought to be asking is, "What holy objects or spaces are contaminated by our sins and therefore are the things being purged by Jesus?" But 1 John does not say. It seems the answer to this was taken for granted. But answering what sancta are being decontaminated by Jesus is the very question that Hebrews spends so much of its time developing. Before delving into Hebrews, five observations from 1 John are worth highlighting.

(1) The first time John tells us that Jesus is "the decontamination for our sins" he adds a surprising qualifier: "and not simply for our sins, but also the sins of all the cosmos" (2:2). John goes out of his way to make it clear that Jesus's work of *kipper* extends well beyond the Jesus-community. Just like the Day of Decontamination purged the sins and impurities on the sanctuary regardless of how many people "believed" in the ritual, John is saying the purgative power of Jesus is not contingent on anything else, let alone anyone's "belief" in that effectiveness. Jesus simply decontaminates *everyone's* sins. Period. Attempts to wriggle out of the universal implications of this comment not only grate against the "plain sense" of the words on the page, but they go against John's attempt to not be misunderstood on *this specific point*. Had John not offered this expansive qualifier, it would be possible to think he meant that Jesus is "the decontaminating sacrifice for our sins [*only*]." Without falling down a rabbit hole, it needs to be said that the fact that John goes out of his way to make it clear that Jesus's work of *kipper* is "not simply for our sins, but also the sins of all the cosmos" means anyone wishing to delimit the scope of beneficiaries is ignoring John's intentional effort to not let his audience think about Jesus in terms of a "limited atonement" (let the reader understand).

(2) Although interpreters can fixate about whether *hilasmos* should be translated "expiate" or "propitiate," as Shauf argues, "since God is the one making the ἱλασμός available, it makes little sense to translate with a sense of propitiation."[10] Levitical sacrifice was not about appeasing the wrath of God, but about keeping God's sanctuary regularly decontaminated. True, God's absence from the sanctuary would result in exile, but that is an indirect consequence of God no longer being there to "meet with" Israel and bless them (Exod 29:42–46; 20:24). The atoning sacrifices are ritual detergents, not substitutionary death penalties. The sacrificial animals are neither suffering nor dying in place of the offerer. Therefore, to the extent that Jesus-as-*hilasmos* is based on the sacrificial system in the Torah this cannot be framed as either a substitutionary death or substitutionary suffering. The only claim is that Jesus can effect the same purgation that the purgation

10. Shauf, *Jesus the Sacrifice*, 154.

sacrifices did, but on a greater scale. Moreover, 1 John itself repeatedly relates both Jesus's death and Jesus-as-*hilasmos* to revealing God's "love" (3:16–18; 4:7–12), but *wrath is never mentioned.* "Wrath" has to be smuggled into the word *hilasmos,* a move that lacks warrant both with respect to Leviticus and to 1 John. This notion simply must be rejected for anyone wishing to stick to the way the words run on the pages of these texts.

Moreover, it is not even clear that 1 John 2:2 is claiming anything about Jesus's *death* specifically. This is only assumed because of the mistaken view (debunked in chapter 1) that OT sacrifice finds any meaning in the *death* of the sacrificial animal. The claim in 2:2 is based on the personal *presence* of Jesus before the Father (2:1). I will touch on this point again below, but the point here is that since sacrificial decontamination is accomplished by conveying "life" (i.e., blood, cf. Lev 17:11, 14) *in the presence of God* in the holy of holies, then Jesus-as-*hilasmos* may be owing to the fact of the kind of life Jesus *is* and that this life is present before God. The *kipper*-function of Jesus would be due to his *personal* resurrected and ascended *presence* before God, not to his *death* itself.

(3) As Shauf further observes, John's use of "cleanse"/"purify" (*katharizō*) in 1:7 (cf. 1:9) is a clear parallel to the claim about the Day of Decontamination in Lev 16:30 LXX:[11]

1 John 1:7 *katharizei hēmas apo pasēs hamartias*

Lev 16:30 *katharisai hymas apo pasōn tōn hamartiōn hymōn*

Just because there is a link to the Day of Decontamination does not mean that Jesus is being conceptualized in terms of an atoning sacrifice here, however. Jesus's work is accomplishing all of what happens on the *Day* of Decontamination, which includes more than the mere purgation sacrifices.

As discussed, Lev 16:30 is the only time in Leviticus that ritual impurity is used as an analogy for moral impurity. I suggested using "minor" and "major" moral impurity to distinguish between sins that do not contaminate the land (minor) and those grave sins that do pollute the land (major). Moreover, 16:29 implies that it is not the *purgation sacrifices* offered that purify the people, but rather the passing of *time* (each year), their own fasting, and cessation from labor.

Also, the prophets (especially Ezekiel and Jeremiah) expand on this notion of the possibility of moral purification and envision God purifying people from the major moral impurities. As we saw, this is what Rabbi Aqiva picked up on in his interpretation of Lev 16:30 in m. Yoma 8:9. Recall that he appeals to both Ezek 36:25 and Jer 17:13 to say that the cleansing will

11. Shauf, *Jesus the Sacrifice*, 153.

come from the promised water-washing done by God. In other words, the moral purification from *minor* moral impurities on the Day of Decontamination (Lev 16:30) is taken as a harbinger of the eschatological purification from *major* moral impurity promised by the prophets. 1 John 1:7 is thus claiming that this eschatological purification event has happened in Jesus.

What is important is Rabbi Aqiva does not relate the purification in 16:30 to any of the *kipper* sacrifices on the Day of Decontamination, but rather to a type of *water-washing* since this is the ritual means of purifying *people*. Purification of any kind—ritual or moral—for humans will be facilitated through some sort of water-washing. This explains why Rabbi Aqiva takes it for granted that any purification of *people*, which is what Lev 16:30 claims is happening, must take place through a *water-washing*, not via any purgation sacrifice. The claim in Lev 16:30 is not taken to mean that the purgation sacrifices function to purify people after all, but rather that some *other* means of purification for people is available. The other means of this sort of purification in Leviticus is the combination of time and water-washing. And since this is exactly what the prophets proclaim about moral purification—that it will take the shape of a divine water-washing—the links between Lev 16:30, Ezek 36:25, and Jer 17:13 (let alone all the other prophetic texts that envision a divine washing noted previously) that Rabbi Aqiva sees are "obvious" to him. But apart from a thorough understanding of ritual and moral purification (and the limited role purgation sacrifices have as only purging *sancta*) Rabbi Aqiva's interpretation may seem less than "obvious" to some.

Essentially, the comments in both Lev 16:30 and 1 John 1:7 require some sort of gap filling. Neither of these texts explicitly says if the purification of people is brought about by a purgation sacrifice and neither text denies this. However, linking the notion of purification of people to purgation sacrifices has little to no evidential warrant, whereas linking the purification to the promised divine water-washings is the only exegetically warranted—and thus logical—conclusion given the protocols of ritual impurities, the way ritual impurity is analogous to moral impurity, and the prophetic promises of moral purification only being envisioned in terms of washings, not purgation sacrifices of any kind. In other words, Rabbi Aqiva's interpretation of Lev 16:30 is preferable because it coheres with all of these purification protocols and the way moral purification is analogous to ritual purification.

What this means for 1 John is that Jesus's "blood" in 1:7 is probably not being conceptualized as *blood*, but rather as *water*. Just like Jesus's blood in Rev 7:14 was water and oil (and ordination-blood), the function Jesus's blood has in 1 John 1:7—purification of people—is the function water has and this is the substance the prophets use to talk about the necessary moral purification to come. This would explain the emphasis on "water" alongside "blood" in 5:6 and 5:8 (cf. John 19:34). Jesus blood *qua* blood is his death, and when John wants to convey the moral purification his death accomplishes then it is not Jesus's blood-as-death, but Jesus's blood-as-*water* that accomplishes this.

Whether written by the same hand or not, scholars agree that the author of 1 John knew the Gospel of John.[12] The claim in 1 John 1:7 (together with 5:5–12) appears to be an interpretation of John 7:38 in light of Jesus's death (19:34) and giving of the Spirit after his resurrection (20:22). Jesus declares, "just as the scripture said" those who believe in him will have "rivers from their belly flow with living water" (7:38), which is then specified in terms of the "Spirit" (7:39). This collocation of water and Spirit is exactly what scriptures like Ezek 36:25–27 promise (cf. Isa 44:3). And remember that "living water" is not capable of becoming ritually impure no matter what contacts it. It is a perpetual source of ritual purity. Jesus's death (blood and water, 19:34) and the giving of the Spirit to dwell in his followers (20:22; cf. 14:16–17; 16:7, 13) together are the purifying "living water" (7:38–39) continually present in the person. Therefore, the comment in 1 John 1:7 appears to be thinking about Jesus's "blood" not in terms of sacrificial blood, but in terms of purifying living *waters* understood as an image of the indwelling Spirit (3:24; 4:13; 5:5–8), which is tantamount to Jesus's very "life" (5:11–12) and "God" "abiding" in believers (3:34; 4:12–13, 15–16 cf. 2:6, 24, 27–28; 3:14–15).

As a result, 1 John 1:7 may also then be a poetic reference to baptism since "water" is what purifies *people* from ritual impurities and it is what the prophets use to metaphorically depict moral purification. If so, this would mean the use of "blood" is referring both to Jesus's *death*—which is when Jesus's "gave over his Spirit" (19:30; cf. "released his Spirit," Matt 27:50)—and the effect of *moral purification* that results from *water* immersion *into his death*. Earlier traditions already associated baptism with sharing in Jesus's death (e.g., Rom 6:3–11; Mark 10:38–39; Col 3:12) and there are also texts that explicitly draw upon the water-washing purification aspect of baptism (e.g., 1 Pet 3:21; Titus 3:5; 1 Cor 6:11 with 12:13).[13]

In this light, it may be significant that in the Gospel of John Jesus says his "word" (*logos*) makes his disciples "pure" (*katharos*) (15:3; cf. 13:10) and "consecrates" or "sanctifies" them (*hagiazō*, 17:17) and 1 John begins with

12. E.g., Méndez, "Did the Johannine Community Exist?"

13. Cf. "the mystery of purity . . . is closely associated with the mystery of baptism in the early church" (Furstenberg, "Controlling Impurity," 175n33).

reference to "the word (*logou*) of life" (1:1).[14] And, immediately after talking about purification in 1 John 1:7 and 9 there is another reference to the "word" (*logos*, 1:10). In this context, having "his word in us" in 1:10 seems to be how we experience the purification talked about in 1:7 and 9 (cf. John 15:3).

Thus, it is unlikely that 1 John 1:7 is associating purification to blood *qua blood* since the idea of purification is not linked with blood *per se* in any other text and the Johannine literature has particular emphasis on the purifying function of both the "word" and "water." Hence, 1 John 1:7 seems to be activating the *liquid* quality of blood on analogy to a purifying water-washing.

If this is the case, then the claim of 1 John 1:7 is conveying something like this: "The blood of Jesus purifies us of all sin because just as water-washing purifies, then much more will the blood of Jesus—the purest 'water'—wash us and purify us of all unrighteousness in baptism since baptism is what unites us to Jesus's death." This would explain why 1 John 1:7 is phrased in a way that alludes to Lev 16:30 and it evokes the prophetic expectation of moral purification, which is said to come through a divine washing. If this is correct, the reference to "blood" here is *not* to be understood as declaring (without precedent) that sacrificial atoning blood is *applied to people* for their purification, but to play on the viscous nature of blood to evoke water baptism. In this way, "blood" functions to anchor the promised moral purification in a *union* with Jesus's *death*, but its viscous quality evokes the purifying "waters" of baptism, which themselves are understood as the promised divine waters from the prophets and are associated with the divine "pouring out" of the Spirit like water (Ezek 36:25–27; Isa 32:15; 44:3; Joel 3:1 [2:28 Eng.]), which is the very thing Johannine literature emphasizes (cf. 1 John 5:6–8; John 7:38–39; 19:30, 34).

(4) The phrasing in 1 John 1:9 (*katharisē hēmas apo pasēs adikias*, "he would purify us from all injustice") parallels 1:7 (*katharizei hēmas apo pasēs hamartias*, "it purifies us from all sin"). But the phrasing in 1:9 is a slight modification of the promises God makes to the exiles of Judah and Israel in Jer 40:8 LXX (33:8 MT): *kathariō autous apo pasōn tōn adikiōn autōn* ("I will purify them from all their acts of injustice").[15] Crucially, this promise of moral purification comes by divine fiat, not a ritual of *kipper*. Moreover, within Jeremiah, this promise is linked with the establishment of the new covenant greater than the first exodus (31:32), which is what occasions

14. This same notion is in Eph 5:26: "in order to sanctify (*hagiasē*) her, by purifying (*katharisas*) her by the washing of water with the word (*hrēmati*)."

15. Raymond E. Brown, *The Epistles of John*, 200.

God's "forgiveness" of their "iniquity" and "not remembering" their grave "sins" in the MT (31:34) or, in the LXX, God's "mercy" on their "acts of injustice" and "not remembering" their "sins" (38:34). And this seems to be the exact connection being made in 1 John 1:9 since "he is faithful and just in order to forgive us our sins"—which corresponds to Jer 38:34 LXX (31:34 MT)—immediately precedes "and purify us from all injustice"—which corresponds to Jer 40:8 (33:8 MT).

The association in Jeremiah of the promised forgiveness of and moral purification from the sins that brought the kingdoms of Israel and Judah into their respective exiles with the new covenant and the greater exodus motif once again reinforces the contention that neither of these notions—forgiveness and purification—are automatically related to the *kipper* system. 1 John 1:9 is explicitly drawing upon this prophetic promise for forgiveness and moral purification that will come apart from the *kipper* system. Neither Jer 31:34 (38:34 LXX) nor 33:8 (40:8 LXX) even draw upon the *kipper* system *analogously* to anchor their point. It is all related to the promise of bringing the people out of exile and establishing a new covenant, and the only sacrifices associated with these two events are non-atoning sacrifices: a covenant inauguration/renewal and Passover.

This strengthens the point being made for (3) above because it means that the allusion to Lev 16:30 in 1 John 1:7 is less likely to be about associating Jesus's blood with *kipper*-blood, but rather to the fullness of what Lev 16:30 was pointing to: namely, major moral purification that is never said to come about via atoning sacrifices but always through some other means (time, fasting, rest, a divine water-washing, divine fiat, etc.). Put another way, the allusion to the Day of Decontamination is more to the *Day* of Decontamination—which results in moral purification from "minor" moral impurity through the passing of time (each year), fasting, and rest, as argued earlier—rather than to the *atoning sacrifices* that occur on that day. Obviously, Jesus *is* associated with these atoning sacrifices as well in 1 John (2:2; 4:10), but these are distinct claims that differ from what is being declared in 1:7 and 1:9.

The logic of these distinctions seems to follow the narrative plot of the exodus and promised restoration as an exodus-like deliverance. First, Israel is liberated from slavery (celebrated with a non-atoning well-being sacrificial meal), then God established a covenant with them (sealed with non-atoning sacrifices), and then the dwelling place is established for God to continually dwell with Israel and also to provide various ways to deal with the people's subsequent impurities and sin contaminations (except for sins in the moral impurity category) by means of the atoning sacrifices. The accumulation of moral impurity caused the land to vomit Israel out, sending them into exile, but God promised through prophets like Jeremiah and Ezekiel to restore Israel from exile and establish a new covenant. This is what "forgiveness" in the postexilic context means. It means the forgiveness of the grave sins that caused the exile, which is nothing other than moral purification from "major" moral impurity. In 1 John, Jesus is declared to be the one who brings the promised forgiveness and moral purification (1:7, 9). Now that this has happened—the promised grand purification/forgiveness has come—it makes sense for there to be a way of dealing with any subsequent sins on analogy to the dwelling place that makes use of the *kipper* system. And this is exactly what 1 John is claiming in 2:1–2 (and then repeats in 4:10). Jesus is both the *beginning* of the promised restoration, which happens apart from the *kipper* system, as well as the *guarantor* of the continuation of the promised new covenant by being the personal means of decontamination (*hilasmos*) for the sins of the whole cosmos because he serves as a continual "intercessor" for us before the Father.

All this anticipates what will be key for understanding how Hebrews speaks about Jesus in relation to *kipper*; namely, that Jesus's *kipper*-function is due to his personal resurrected and ascended presence before God, not to his death *per se*. But before turning to Hebrews there is one more point to be made.

(5) The practical payoff of all this *kipper* and purification with water in 1 John is grounding the ethical character of the community as *participants* in Jesus's death.[16] John does not talk about Jesus's death as something Jesus did so that others do not have to, but rather as something others can unite with and actively participate in. Thus, John instructs his readers that they are to "also walk in the same way just as he [Jesus] walked" (1 John 2:6) and to love others in the same way God loved us (4:7, 11). Further, since "he laid down his life for us, we also are obligated to lay down our lives for our siblings" (3:16; cf. 4:21). And John does not just mean this in the sense of "be willing to die to benefit someone else," but to share the means of survival and life with those in need (3:17). Living in this way is living a life of love (3:16, 18), and failure to do this is a life of hatred (3:14–15; cf. 4:20; 2:9, 11). The juxtaposition of 3:15 and 3:17 means that John, like the prophets and Jesus, equates the various forms of economic oppression and hatred to "murder."[17]

16. Similarly, Shauf, *Jesus the Sacrifice*, 155.

17. And since murder is in the category of moral impurity, perhaps this is what the mysterious phrase "sin unto death" (5:16) means: those sins that generate moral impurity and have no sacrificial *kipper* remedy since the only "solution" is the death of the offender/exile. This would be distinguished from those sins "not unto death" (5:16–17) that are able to be addressed by a *kipper* sacrifice (cf. 2:2; 4:10; 1:7–9).

Simply put, it is a mistake to think that the love of God is something merely private to individuals. To walk just as Jesus walked means to love *as* God loves. This love "puts shoes on" and "walks" toward others according to the pattern set by Jesus's death (3:16; 4:9–10). This is limitless and self-emptying love that extends to all the *cosmos*, even to enemies in darkness (2:2; 4:10; cf. Rom 5:5–11).

At the end of the day (or letter) John has made it inexcusable to think either (a) that Jesus's death was substitutionary or (b) that the "love of God" does not have social significance. Jesus's blood can have some unique functions when conceptualized as water or as *kipper*-blood, but Jesus's death itself is specifically what those who love God will intentionally pattern their "walk" of life after. Jesus's death is not a substitutionary reality; it is a *participatory* reality. Or rather, it reveals how the reality of true life *is* participation in Jesus Christ, specifically his death.

KIPPER IN HEBREWS

The author of Hebrews is unequivocal that Jesus has atoning significance (Heb 1:3 [cf. *tou katharismou tōn hamartiōn* in Exod 30:10 LXX]; 2:17; 7:26–27; 9:1—10:18).[18] More than this, Jesus also achieves what water, oil, and blood from the non-atoning sacrifices (covenant making and binding, priestly ordination/consecration) and atoning sacrifices (decontamination of sancta) all do, only more so and permanently (9:12–14, 21–24; 10:10–11, 14, 19, 22, 29; 13:12). Hebrews also reiterates how Jesus's death is a non-atoning covenant-making sacrifice (9:15–20; 10:29; 12:24; 13:20; cf. 10:16–17) and says that it is through Jesus that believers themselves can "continually offer up [non-atoning] thanksgiving/praise sacrifices" (13:15). Thus, according to Hebrews, Jesus accomplishes all the benefits of the entire Levitical system, from both atoning and non-atoning sacrifices as well as

18. Hebrews seems to attribute atoning significance to the daily burnt offerings (*tāmîd*) in 7:27 and 10:11. As discussed, in the Torah, the *tāmîd* does not have an atoning function (cf. Shauf, *Jesus the Sacrifice*, 52–53, 77, 137). Either "[t]he author may simply have erred here" (Johnson, *Hebrews*, 195), or they just share a view developed in the Second Temple period only attested in Jub. 6:14 and 50:11 that the *tāmîd* is atoning (Moffitt, "Jesus as Interceding High Priest," 550n5; Shauf, *Jesus the Sacrifice*, 76–77). It could also be that Hebrews is only referring to the daily burnt offerings "in the week preceding the Day of Atonement" rather than the *tāmîd* itself (Johnson, *Hebrews*, 195) (cf. Lev 16:24 where the burnt offerings on the Day of Decontamination are said to have an atoning function). It does not matter which of these (or some other solution) is correct for our purposes since my claim is that, in Hebrews, Jesus is associated with the full spectrum of sacrifices and functions of the Levitical system.

moral purification, which is ultimately a figural "shadow of the good things to come" (i.e., Christ and his work) (10:1; cf. 8:5).

For our purposes, it is important to see how Jesus as a non-atoning, covenant-making sacrifice is a key premise for the author's explanation of Jesus in terms of decontamination. According to the author, the change in covenant signals a change in priesthood and vice versa (cf. 7:11–12, 22; 8:6–7). Thus, Hebrews can "advance" theological mediation on the meaning of Jesus within an atoning register precisely by attending to implications of Jesus *as a non-atoning covenant-making well-being sacrifice.* If Jesus's death inaugurated the new covenant (9:15–20; 10:16–17), then this means a "perfect" way to God—into the actual holy of holies in the heavens—has been opened up (9:7–8; 10:19–22) by means of a new order of priesthood (7:11—8:2), which also means a decontamination of that heavenly temple must have taken place as well (9:23–24).

Moreover, just as I argued earlier regarding other NT passages, Hebrews also tethers the notion of forgiveness of sins, not to Jesus-as-*kipper*, but to the establishment of the new covenant (10:16–18, quoting Jer 31:33–34).[19] Hebrews thinks within the covenant framework and therefore knows that the sins that led to the exile and the need for a new covenant cannot be forgiven via a *kipper* sacrifice (cf. Heb 9:15). There is no *kipper* sacrifice available for these sins that produced moral impurity. This is what I take the meaning of 10:18 ("and where there is forgiveness of these things, a purgation offering [*peri hamartias*] is no longer [available]") to be.[20] The near verbatim repetition just a few sentences below in 10:26 supports this reading.[21] In 10:26 the author is drawing upon Num 15:30–31, which says that the purgation sacrifice is only for unintentional sins (cf. Heb 9:7), which means there is no *kipper* sacrifice for deliberate transgressions (see chapter 4). Not only is the syntax almost the same between Heb 10:18 and 26, but the sins being referred to in Jeremiah and thus in Heb 10:18 are also the same types of sins for which Num 15:30–31 declares there is no purgation sacrifice available. These sins are framed in the prophets both as intentional and as sins that generate moral impurity on the land (idolatry, murder [and exploitation], sexual immorality). Hence the need for a total restart: a new covenant. Therefore, the claim in Heb 10:16–18 is that these sins that led

19. "With the new covenant comes the promise of 'forgiveness'" (Buchanan, *To the Hebrews*, 166).

20. I take the *peri hamartias* to be a reference to the LXX's translation for the purgation sacrifice in Lev 4 and elsewhere.

21. Hebrews 10:18: *ouketi prosphora peri hamartias*. Hebrews 10:26: *ouketi peri hamartiōn apoleipetai thysia*. The words *phrosphora* ("offering") and *thysia* ("sacrifice") are synonymous.

to the exile (cf. 9:15) simply need to be forgiven by God and the proof that they have been forgiven would be the establishment of the new covenant as Jeremiah promised. Jesus has inaugurated the new covenant; ergo, these sins have been forgiven.

This "forgiveness" also means that moral purification has taken place since this is what was promised by the prophets announcing a new covenant (cf. Jer 31:31–34; 33:8; Ezek 16:59–63; 34:25; 36:29, 33; 37:23, 36). That is, moral purification will come about apart from the *kipper* system since it comes about as a result of a divine washing in the Spirit upon the establishment of the new covenant. Jesus's once-for-all and unrepeatable obedient life dealt with the sins that caused the exile because it was his life (culminating and sealed in his faithful death) that established the promised new covenant (9:15–20, esp. v. 15; 10:16–17).[22] This is what is repeated in 10:29. Jesus's life-blood is "the blood of the covenant" and it is this event—the inauguration of the new covenant—that is made possible by Jesus's obedient life that deals with the grave sins (per 10:16–18) and therefore accomplishes moral purification (9:14; 10:22; cf. 10:1–2).

Some link the notion that there is no longer a purgation offering in 10:18 to the "once for all" aspect in 10:10, 12, 14, meaning something like: "There is no longer a need to offer more purgation sacrifices because Jesus was the final once-for-all purgation sacrifice."[23] While the "once for all" aspect is obviously there and important, the context for these is a quotation of LXX Ps 39:7–9 (Eng. 40:6–8), which says *God does not desire purgation sacrifices* nor any of the other ones (Heb 10:6, 8). Instead, it is *obedience* to God's will that matters (10:7, 9). That is, the claim in 10:18 is not saying: "Purgation sacrifices are necessary to deal with these grave sins, but the problem is that they only have a mere temporary effect and thus need to keep being offered. But since Jesus himself is the ultimate one-off purgation sacrifice we no longer need any more purgation sacrifices." No. The point being made is the purgation sacrifices were *always* impotent to deal with grave sins and they were never intended to be a means of moral purification, just as we detailed in chapters 3 and 4. Another remedy outside of the purgation sacrifices needs to be sought for these sins. According to Hebrews, God revealed this in LXX Ps 39. What this means is Jesus's *obedience* to God's will (i.e., his "life") constitutes his "offering" (10:10). Jesus's obedient human life is what is "once for all" (10:10). Jesus's death is the culmination of a full life of obedience (5:7–9; cf. 2:9, 14–15; Phil 2:5–8), but the focus is on Jesus's whole embodied life doing God's will (hence, *sōma*, "body," Heb 5:5,

22. Cockerill, *Hebrews*, 459.

23. E.g., Cockerill, *Hebrews*, 458–59; Lane, *Hebrews 9–13*, 269, 271.

10).[24] This is what is conceptualized as better than any of the sacrifices from LXX Ps 39. And while Jesus's obedient life is conceptualized as a "sacrifice" (10:12) and "offering" (10:10, 14) that takes place "in behalf of sins" (*hyper harmartiōn*) (10:14), this sacrifice is *not* conceptualized here as "a purgation offering" (*peri hamartias*), which is used in 10:6, 8, and 18. Rather, the "offering"/"sacrifice" that Jesus is being analogized to in 10:10, 12, 14 is *the non-atoning covenant-inauguration sacrifices*, which is confirmed by the quotation of Jeremiah's new-covenant passage in 10:16–17 and then reinforced in 10:29—all of which is returning to the point made in 9:15–20.

The point of Heb 10:1–15, then, just as discussed in chapters 3 and 4, is that none of these sacrifices were ever meant to be able to purify the *worshiper* from grave sins. It would not make sense for the author of Hebrews to say, "these sacrifices cannot purify by their God-ordained design (cf. 10:8), but I nevertheless want to assert that Jesus-as-purgation-sacrifice just does this." Why analogize Jesus to a specific cultic ritual that *cannot* address the problem at hand? That comparison would be unintelligible, especially when there are plenty of other cultic analogies to draw upon, along with the prophetic promises. (And drawing on these other cultic analogies and prophetic promises is precisely what Hebrews does when making links between Jesus and the entirety of the Levitical system along with presenting him as the fulfillment of the prophetic hope.)

That said, the point in 9:12 and 22–28 is that Jesus does for the heavenly sanctuary what the purgation sacrifices do for the earthly sanctuary: namely, they grant the high priest access to the holy of holies and decontaminate the sancta (cf. 9:7, 23–25). Then the author pivots in 10:1 to return to the claim in 9:13–14 that Jesus's own life-blood is also capable of purifying people on analogy to the ritual detergents used in the purification process for corpse impurity (ash-water)[25] and perhaps scale disease as well (water, non-sacrificial bird blood mixed with water, the blood from a guilt offering, and oil) (cf. 9:13–14; Num 19; Lev 14). This is why the emphasis in Heb 9:14 is on purification from "*dead* works." The main analogy is dealing with corpse impurity by sprinkling the purgative ash-water. And, it is also plausibly alluding to the promised washing in the divine "Spirit" (Ezek 36:25–27) that resurrects Israel and Judah from their covenant death due to the sins committed under the first covenant (37:1–23; Heb 9:13–15). Jesus bringing about the promised moral purification is where the argument from 10:1–18 is leading, which is made clear in 10:19–22. In sum, the author relegates Jesus-as-*kipper* to purging the (heavenly) sanctuary (9:12, 22–28; 10:19),

24. Cf. Johnson, *Hebrews*, 251, 253; Moffitt, "Blood, Life, and Atonement," 220–21.

25. Johnson, *Hebrews*, 237; Cockerill, *Hebrews*, 396.

but also attributes to Jesus the power to purify *people*, which, in addition to some other elements discussed shortly, draws upon the various *water-washings* in the purity system and the prophetic hope for moral purification (9:14; 10:22).

In short, Jesus is analogized to *distinct* cultic functions. And although these distinct functions are related, they ought not be conflated.[26] As noted briefly above, one of the major claims overall in Hebrews is that Jesus's life (blood) fulfills all the aspects of the sacrificial (both atoning and non-atoning) *and* purity systems, but does so on the heavenly plane. Thus, in one passage Jesus's life-blood is likened to *kipper*-blood and in another it is likened to water, ash-water, and, as we will soon see, to priestly consecrating blood from the non-*kipper* ordination sacrifice (a type of well-being offering). By recognizing how the significance of Jesus's life-blood is conceptualized on analogy to various cultic "liquids" it becomes easier to discern the flow of thought from 9:11—10:22.

I will further support and nuance some of these specific claims made here, but the basic reasoning from 9:11—10:22 seems to be this: since Jesus's own life-blood is his means of accessing the heavenly sanctuary (9:11–12)—i.e., this is what qualifies him for the high priesthood in the order of Melchizedek (7:15–16, 23—8:2)—*it is therefore the most potent purifying and consecrating element in the cosmos*. This is the main point from which all the others are derived. Because of its potency, it can bring about moral purification on analogy to the non-*kipper* ritual purification elements (9:13–14). It is also for this reason what can establish the promised new covenant (9:15–20) as well as decontaminate and consecrate the heavenly sanctuary (9:21–28). The former relates Jesus's life-blood to the non-*kipper* covenant-making sacrifices and the latter to the *kipper* function of the purgation sacrifices. Then the author wants to return to the point about moral purification from 9:14, but before he gets there in 10:22 he makes it clear from three pieces of scriptural evidence that the Torah's prescriptions could never and were never intended to be the means of moral purification (10:1–18). The first piece of scriptural evidence is implicit. Had these sacrifices been able to effect (minor *and* major) moral purification, then they would not have to be offered continually (10:1–4). The *continual* nature of the offerings witnesses that something greater was yet to come (cf. 7:11, 19; 8:7–8).

26. While Shauf rightly notices that both the non-atoning covenant-making sacrifices as well as the atoning sacrifices are activated in Hebrews, he nevertheless conflates the categories by thinking that forgiveness and the purification of the people are both necessarily alluding to the atoning sacrifices (*Jesus the Sacrifice*, 147–52).

The author finds confirmation for this by the second piece of scriptural evidence: a Davidic psalm that plainly states that God does not desire purgation sacrifices, but rather obedience to the divine will (10:5–14). This is what Jesus offers, *his entire embodied obedient life* (cf. 5:7–9). And because Jesus's obedient life just *is* the sort of life that necessarily has access to the true and most holy heavenly sanctuary (9:12, 21–28; cf. 7:16), this means his life is potent enough to consecrate the faithful (10:10, 14). We learn from 10:19–22 that this consecration is to the order of *high priests* because it grants the faithful direct and perpetual *access to "the holy of holies"* (10:19; cf. 4:16).[27] True, the author does not call believers "high priests," but since only high priests are fit to access the holy of holies (9:7, 25), the access believers have to the innermost sancta necessarily indexes them as high priests.[28] This would cohere with Second Temple Jewish texts such as Sir 50, which depicts the high priest as the embodiment of ideal humanity, the *telos* of what being human is about: being crowned with divine glory and honor as they worship in the presence of God (cf. Sir 50:11–13; Ps 8:6–9 [Eng. vv. 5–8]; Heb 2:5–10).[29] The goal of the Son's work is to "bring many children to glory" (2:10), which, in the present age, is represented in the high priest (cf. 9:7–10). Their lone access to the holy of holies was an indication of a larger access for the "many" (2:10) yet to be "disclosed" (9:8). This is exactly what Jesus's work revealed and "inaugurated" (10:20). The claim is that Jesus has "consecrated" believers (cf. 2:11; 10:10, 14) such that they are brought

27. Although Moffitt does not make the connection that this access is indicative of a high priestly status, he agrees that 10:19 is referring to "the holy of holies where the presence of God dwells" (*Atonement and the Logic of Resurrection*, 282). English translations of 10:19 such as "the holy place" (NASB) or "the sanctuary" (NRSV) obscures the Greek *tēn . . . tōn hagiōn* ("the [holy] of holies"), which is the same phrase used in 9:8 where there is no doubt from the context it refers to the holy of holies (cf. 9:6–7).

28. Gilders notes how in Leviticus the status-distinction between the laity, priests, and the high priest is indexed in terms of levels of "access" within the sanctuary (Gilders, *Blood Ritual*, 118–19). "[W]e become aware of who holds high status by noting who enters the Tent of Meeting" (119). The high priest is the only one with "special access" to enter the holy of holies "into the presence of Yahweh inside his abode, whereas ordinary priests act only in the external sphere [of the sanctuary]" (118). Thus, "the special access of the anointed priest is a function of his special status" and the converse, "the special access of the anointed priest enacts his special status" (118). Hebrews operates with the same status index (9:7, 25), which is why the author uses Jesus's ascension to the right hand of God to indicate that he is a high priest (7:15–8:2). Therefore, believers's access to the holy of holies (10:19; 4:16) indicates that they are high priests as well. At the very least, if "high priests" sounds too scandalous, "Christ 'has perfected' those 'being made holy,'" which means he is "making [them] capable of entrance into God's presence," something up till now was only possible for the high priest once a year (Cockerill, *Hebrews*, 466; cf. 451–52).

29. Crispin Fletcher-Louis, "Ben Sira 50," 89–111, esp. 105–7.

to their human *telos* ("perfection," 10:1, 14) and "glory" (2:7, 9–10), which is depicted as being able to be and worship where the Aaronic high priest is once a year, only now continually (4:16; 6:19–20; 9:7, 25; 10:19, 22).

The author's third piece of scriptural evidence is the new-covenant passage from Jeremiah. Here it says that the establishment of the new covenant itself is the forgiveness of grave sins that is also the purification of the heart (i.e., moral purification) (10:16–18, cf. 22; 9:14–15). Since Jesus has both decontaminated the heavenly sanctuary and brought about moral purification of the people (by analogizing his life-blood to the respective distinct cultic elements) the author brings these two points together in 10:19–22 to exhort the people to "draw near" (10:22) to the heavenly "holy of holies" (10:19). This is possible because the heavenly holy of holies has been purified and the people have been granted access since they have been purified through a divine water-washing (10:22) that restored them from death to life (9:14–15) and have also been consecrated as (high) priests (10:10, 14, cf. 29).[30]

Therefore, in Heb 9–10 Jesus is related to both *kipper* and non-*kipper* sacrifices as well as to cultic and divine water. Jesus's power to decontaminate the heavenly holy of holies is linked with the purgation sacrifices (9:23–26). But Jesus's power to forgive grave sins (i.e., effect moral purification) is linked with the non-*kipper* covenant-making sacrifices (9:15–20; 10:16–18, 29), the purification ash-water for corpse impurity, and to the promised washing in the divine "Spirit" that resurrects the people from covenant death (cf. 9:14; 10:22; and Ezek 36:25–27; 37:1–14, 23). The link is not made to the *kipper* purgation sacrifices here since the *kipper* purgation sacrifices cannot deal with these and the prophets link forgiveness/moral purification with the establishment of the new covenant. Additionally, Jesus's power to consecrate the people (10:10, 14) can only be linked with the non-*kipper* covenant-making sacrifices from Exod 24:4–8 (cf. Heb 10:29; 9:19–20) as well as the priestly ordination sacrifice (a type of well-being sacrifice as discussed in chapter 2, Exod 29:19–28) since no *kipper* sacrifices have this function.[31]

30. For a similar argument that Hebrews "envisioned its readers doing priestly acts" such as "go[ing] into the holy place, through the veil (10:19–20)," see Peeler, "If Sons, Then Priests," esp. 95–96, 101–5 (here, 95).

31. Recall from chapter 2 how when non-*ḥaṭṭāʾt* blood is applied to people, its function is to index that a metaphysical transition up the holiness spectrum has taken place. This happens in three situations: the consecration of priests (the person goes from lay to holy priest), the covenant-inauguration ceremony (Israel becomes a kingdom of priests relative to the other nations), and finally at two different stages in the purification process for scale disease (the person goes from the walking dead outside the camp to having access to the camp and then is restored to the sanctuary at the final stage).

It is important to realize Hebrews does not conflate everything about the saving significance of Jesus with the atoning purgation sacrifices. The author does not think Jesus's atoning significance suddenly forgives the sins the Torah says cannot be remedied by a purgation sacrifice. This is the whole point of the warning in 10:26–27. Here the author says the exact opposite of, "Jesus has provided a means of sacrificial *atonement* even for the sins the Torah excluded from sacrificial atonement." No. There can be "forgiveness" of these sins (10:18), but this forgiveness does *not* come by means of an atoning purgation sacrifice (cf. 10:6, 8, 18). It comes because God has *decided* to forgive and to establish a new covenant (9:15; 10:16–18). Anyone thereafter who commits either willful sins (10:26) or sins that generate moral impurity (e.g., sexual immorality in 13:4) is solely at the mercy of God's judgment (10:27; 13:4). These claims only make sense if the author thinks about Jesus-as-*kipper* within the *limited* framework of atonement discussed previously (i.e., sacrificial atonement is not "the be-all and the end-all" for dealing with sins in the Bible).

Hasty equations of the notions of forgiveness, sacrifice, and atonement obscure the message these ancient writers were attempting to get across. Even when an author plainly associates Jesus with the *kipper* system, as in Hebrews, this means something quite different from what is often supposed. Atonement in Hebrews has nothing to do with Jesus as a substitutionary death. It has nothing to do with satisfying God's wrath. It has nothing to do with *forgiving* the types of sins that seem to matter most for Hebrews (ending the exile and establishing the new covenant).[32]

32. Lest I be misunderstood, Jesus *is* the means of *forgiveness* for these "sins under the first covenant" (9:15), but this is on account of Jesus's obedient life and death as establishing the new covenant (9:15–22, see "forgiveness" in v. 22; 10:16–18), which uses non-*atoning* sacrifices, not on account of Jesus-as-*kipper*. In fact, the author uses "redemption" (*apolytrōsis*) in 9:15, which evokes the Passover event (celebrated with the non-atoning thanksgiving well-being sacrifice) that is the prophetic paradigm for salvation from the covenant death of exile, as discussed in previous chapters. As discussed earlier, the Passover and the covenant inauguration are closely connected sacrificial ceremonies, neither of which have anything to do with *kipper*, especially since the dwelling place had not yet been erected and consecrated. In Hebrews, the devil takes the place of Pharaoh as the enslaver from whom Jesus liberates the people (2:14–15). Therefore, the sacrificial element Jesus is analogized to with "redemption" in 9:15 has nothing to do with *kipper* since Passover has nothing to do with sacrificial atonement (similarly, Moffitt, "It Is Not Finished," 165). Jesus-as-non-*kipper*-sacrifice brings about a new Passover redemption and forgiveness as he also establishes the new covenant, while Jesus-as-*kipper* decontaminates the heavenly sanctuary so that the new-covenant people—who have been consecrated as a community of high priests by Jesus-as-non-*kipper*-ordination-blood(/oil)—have unlimited and continual access to the holy of holies.

Rather, as I will argue in more detail just below, atonement in Hebrews has to do with (a) decontaminating the "true" (8:2; 9:24) and "perfect" (9:11) sanctuary in the heavens (9:21–25) as well as, on the basis of receiving a priestly consecration (10:10, 14), (b) granting believers the same access to God the Levitical high priest has once a year, but continually and without the need to keep decontaminating the place (10:19–22; 6:19–20; 4:16; 7:7:24—8:2; 9:25–26). Finally, (c) Jesus's solidarity with Abraham's seed (2:9–18) enables their participation with Jesus as co-purgation sacrifices (13:10–13).

Participatory Atonement in Hebrews

To be sure, those final two claims are startling, especially the latter since I have only argued for the first one. But both points are crucial for realizing that once again we have a NT text that understands Jesus's death, not as substitutionary, but rather as a participatory reality. Jesus's death makes possible our own. Borrowing the author's words to make a distinct yet related point, Jesus is a "forerunner" (6:20) such that he does not die *instead of* us, but rather *ahead* of us. Far from establishing something like penal substitutionary atonement, the atonement theology of Hebrews is in service of one of the most vigorous articulations of *participation* and *solidarity* with Christ in the NT. In short, whatever is going on with Jesus's death in Hebrews, the author thinks it is something at the very least we ought to pattern ourselves after, if not the *reality* within which our own sufferings and death gain their sense. Jesus's death is not something we avoid as if he died "in our place" or "instead of us." To support and develop this, more from point (a) above needs filling out.

Again, what is being decontaminated by Jesus-as-*kipper* is heavenly sancta (9:23–24) on analogy to the Levitical *kipper* system that decontaminated the "sanctuary" and its sacred "objects" (9:21–22, 25). But is it Jesus's *death* itself or something else that purges the heavenly sanctuary?

As discussed in chapter 1, Levitical sacrifice is not about "death," but is rather a means of conveying "life" (blood) in God's presence (Lev 17:11, 14; cf. Gen 9:4; Deut 12:23). The death of the sacrificial animal has no ritual function or meaning. The various blood manipulations, depending on the specific sacrifice, have different functions that convey distinct meanings (i.e., the different manipulations and meanings for purgation versus well-being sacrifices), but what matters for any sacrifice is the act of placing the life-blood on the various sancta (i.e., bringing this "life" into the presence of God at various levels). Moffitt has convincingly argued in various contexts that Jesus is a means of atonement in Hebrews, not so much because of his *death*, but rather because Jesus's resurrected and ascended "indestructible life" (7:16) is bodily present in the heavenly holy of holies.[33] If one premise to argue that Jesus has the capacity to atone is because he established the new covenant, as argued above, then another equally if not more important premise is Jesus's *resurrection* and subsequent *ascension* to the presence of God. *This* is what grounds his high priesthood (7:15–28), his power to establish the new covenant (9:11–20), and his capacity to decontaminate the heavenly sanctuary (9:23–26).

Therefore, as Moffitt elucidates, although "references to Jesus' blood in Hebrews are assumed to be self-evident references to Jesus' death," "the writer is unlikely to have conflated Jesus' atoning work with the crucifixion."[34] This is because "[j]ust as Yom Kippur does not focus on the slaughter of the victim, but the presentation of its blood—that is, its life—before God, so also the author of Hebrews thinks in terms of the presentation of Jesus' indestructible life before God as the central act that effects atonement."[35] In every passage that either talks about Jesus's high priesthood or his power to decontaminate sancta, the author is explicit that this is happening in the heavenly sanctuary (e.g., 4:14; 6:19–20; 7:26; 8:1–2; 9:11–12, 23–26; 10:19).[36] Indeed, the author admits that "if he [Jesus] were on earth, he would not even be a priest at all, because there are those who offer gifts according to the Torah" (8:4). This means both Jesus's priesthood and atoning work can only occur, and be possible, in the heavenly sanctuary. Jesus's crucifixion, which happened on earth, therefore cannot be when Jesus was appointed high priest nor when he effected atonement. And, "the language of 'blood' in this larger [sacrificial] conception would probably not function for the writer as a metaphor for Jesus' death (as if one would ever bring death into God's presence), but for his life."[37] Further, recall how in general, the act of killing the sacrificial victim has no cultic meaning; only the subsequent presentation of its blood into the various sacred precincts on the appropriate sancta did.[38] In other words, Jesus is not presenting God with a dead body, but rather his "indestructible life" (7:16). Therefore, "the blood language in

33. Moffitt, *Atonement and the Logic of Resurrection*, 198–200, 220–29, 257–85; Moffitt, "Blood, Life, and Atonement," 218–22; Moffitt, "It Is Not Finished," 168–70, 173.

34. Moffitt, "Blood, Life, and Atonement," 214, 220 respectively.

35. Moffitt, "Blood, Life, and Atonement," 212.

36. Cf. Moffitt, *Atonement and the Logic of Resurrection*, 220–29.

37. Moffitt, "Blood, Life, and Atonement," 220.

38. Moffitt, "Blood, Life, and Atonement," 220; cf. Eberhart, "Characteristics," 58–59, 63.

Hebrews likely functions as a metonymy for Jesus' life, not for his death."[39] Of course, Jesus's crucifixion is part of his "life."[40] It is specifically in Jesus's death that we understand the full perfection of his life lived in total obedience to the will of God (5:7–9; 10:5–9). But the point is that Hebrews frames Jesus in relation to *kipper*, not on the basis of his *death*, but rather on the basis of his *resurrected and ascended bodily life in the presence of God* since this is how and where the atoning actions take place.[41]

39. Moffitt, "Blood, Life, and Atonement," 221.

40. Cf. Eberhart, "Characteristics," 61–62, 61n48; Joseph, "'In the Days of His Flesh,'" 22–24.

41. The fact that one of the key premises for Hebrew's atonement theology is the ascension does not mean every confession in the NT about Jesus's ascension is either inherently or likely about heavenly *kipper*. *Pace* Moffitt, who argues that Acts depicts Jesus's ascension within a high priestly and atonement framework ("Atonement at the Right Hand"). To be clear, Moffitt does not argue that the ascension *alone* is sufficient to establish a reference to *kipper*, but the corroborating evidence alongside the ascension that he marshals generates several problems. Moffitt argues that the presence of "forgiveness and purification (i.e., key elements of sacrificial atonement)," which are then linked to "Jesus' departure from the earth and elevation to God's right hand" (553) means that "Jesus must have done something that effected sacrificial atonement on their behalf" (566). That "something" is being present at God's right hand, which is where the sacrificial blood from the purgation sacrifices offered on the Day of Decontamination is brought to in the holy of holies (562, 566). There is no doubt that this is the logic of Hebrews, as Moffitt has argued elsewhere (*Atonement and the Logic of Resurrection*). But Moffitt is reading the Christology of Hebrews back into Acts, which only shares some key premises with Hebrews (such as the ascension) that the author of Hebrews builds upon to make their own unique claims about Jesus and his relationship to the entire sacrificial and purity system in the Torah. Moffitt is correct that forgiveness and purification can be related to the *kipper* system. But, as we already saw, (a) forgiveness can and does happen apart from the *kipper* system, (b) the forgiveness that Luke-Acts is talking about is this sort of extra-sacrificial forgiveness because it is all about forgiving the grave sins that produce moral impurity that led to Israel and Judah's exiles (cf. Acts 13:23–24, 38–39; Isa 40:1–2; Jer 31:34; Luke 1:76–77; 3:3–6; 24:46–47; Acts 2:38–39). And, (c) this forgiveness is likened to a moral purification that is accomplished not by means of a *kipper* sacrifice, but rather through a divine water-washing and reception of the divine Spirit in Ezek 36:25–33 (cf. 37:14, 23; 39:29; Isa 44:3; 32:15; Joel 3:1–2 [2:28–29 Eng.]). This is exactly what Acts is linking forgiveness and purification to via baptism (cf. Acts 2:33, 38–39; 10:43–48; 11:16–18; 13:23–24; 15:8–9). Moffitt claims that "the outpouring of the gift of the Spirit upon Gentiles implies that these Gentiles have been purified and are therefore able to be recipients of this gift" ("Atonement at the Right Hand," 560). This implication more specifically is that this ostensible pre-reception-of-the-Spirit-purification was accomplished because "Jesus actually made some kind of sacrifice that purified the people to the point that they could be recipients of God's own Holy Spirit" (562). However, there are several mistakes with this gap-filling.

(1) The *kipper* system cannot purify people from major moral impurity, which is exactly what the people, both Jew and gentile, are liable for (Acts 3:13, 15, 19; 5:28, 30; 7:52; 13:38–39; 14:15; 15:20; 17:16, 23–31; 18:19, 26). (2) When a *kipper* sacrifice is required for the final stage in the purification process for a major ritual impurity, the

kipper sacrifice is purging the *sanctuary* of the person's impurity that up till that point was existing extrinsically to the person on the altar. To be at this stage in the process, the person's body must already be pure. The *kipper* sacrifice is not removing any impurity from them. (3) A combination of time and water is what purifies *people*, which is why the promised solution to the peoples' moral impurity is envisioned *on analogy to ritual purification* requiring time and water (a water-washing of God's Spirit). (4) Acts does not imply that people need to be made pure *first* (i.e., as a condition of receiving the Holy Spirit) because it specifically claims that receiving the gift of the outpouring (water imagery) of the Spirit is *precisely what purifies them* (Acts 11:16; 15:8–9; 22:16). That is, the Holy Spirit *is the purgative element* (which is attested in other places as well, e.g., 1 Cor 6:11; Titus 3:5). And that event of moral purification is given a ritual enactment in water-washing (baptism).

Moffitt is solving (via gap-filling) a problem that does not exist. There is no basis for supposing some sort of pre-reception-of-the-Spirit-purification that Jesus-as-an-atoning-sacrifice needs to bring about somehow. Even if someone wanted to reason on analogy to the consecration of Israel at Sinai prior to receiving the law, this purification did not make use of *kipper*, but rather water-washings (and abstaining from sexual intercourse, which would render the person ritually impure) (Exod 19:10, 14–15). Further, the notion that Jesus-as-an-atoning-sacrifice *could* bring about such a state does not line up with how *kipper* sacrifices are incorporated into the ritual purification process, from major ritual impurities anyway. More importantly, Moffitt does not account for how "forgiveness of sins, repentance and [moral] purification" ("Atonement at the Right Hand," 549; cf. 552–53) are the things the prophets promise God will do *apart* from the *kipper* system and apart from *analogy* to the *kipper* system. Rather, these things happen on analogy to the *purity* system and specifically the purgative element of water (and time—the time of exile). And this is the exact framework Luke-Acts draws upon to frame both John the Immerser's and Jesus's ministries and to show how reception of the Spirit (ritually enacted through baptism) works to bring these things about. Crucially, not even physical water immersion is the precondition for receiving the Spirit (Acts 10:44–48). This confirms that *the Spirit* just *is* the purifying agent. Nowhere is it implied that a lesser level of purity is needed prior to receiving the Spirit. What Acts is teaching is that Jesus's ascension to God's right hand is key because it is from there that Jesus can send the Spirit (2:33–36). And sending the Spirit is crucial because the Spirit is *the very means of moral purification* (11:16; 15:8–9), which itself is the grounds for being able to repent (5:31; 11:16–18; cf. Ezek 36:25–33 [esp. v. 31, where repentance follows from being washed in the Spirit, cf. 20:41–44]; 37:14, 23). Those who receive the Spirit cannot be pure prior to receiving the Spirit since it is the very act of pouring out of the Spirit that washes them clean, just as "promised" (Acts 2:33).

Finally, the ascension is specifically linked with *David* and the theme of enthronement (i.e., royal not priestly connotations) (2:33–36). This is one of the main obstacles that the author of Hebrews knows they need to overcome to convince their audience that Jesus is not only royal but also a (high) priest (Heb 7:13–14; 8:4). Therefore, the author of Acts has no reason to predicate or imply either anything priestly about Jesus or more specifically that Jesus effects *kipper* and/or offers himself as *kipper* sacrifice. This is because forgiveness of (grave) sins that the Torah could not address (cf. Acts 13:38–39), repentance, and moral purification all happen through Jesus by means of him *washing* the people clean with the most potent agent of purification possible: immersing them in God's Holy Spirit, just as the prophets promised (Luke 3:16; Acts 1:5; 11:16). Acts does not construe the "problem" such that either Jesus-as-*kipper*-sacrifice or Jesus-as-priest is the (implied) "solution." Everything in Acts makes sense quite apart from either of

This means Jesus isn't so much a high priest and an atoning sacrificial victim so much as that *his person is the type of indestructible life that does not require a sacrifice of any sort to obtain access through the veil to the direct presence of God* (7:16, 27; 6:19–20; 9:12, 25–26)! Hebrews 10:5–9 seems to intentionally frame Jesus's sacrificial function as *not being like a sacrificial victim*, but rather just being the sort of human whose perfect obedience makes it so that he just *is* the kind of life and body that is fit to be in the holy of holies. This is what makes his life-blood more potent than anything else.

To be sure, Jesus is depicted as a sacrificial victim as well (13:11–12). But this passage frames Jesus's suffering and death as what happens to the carcasses of sacrificial animals *after* their blood has been presented by the high priest in the holy of holies on the Day of Decontamination (13:12; cf. Lev 16:27; 4:12, 21; 6:23 [Eng. v. 30]). This passage confirms Moffitt's argument against the traditional understanding that the moment of atonement was "on the cross—the place where he [Jesus] offered himself, where his blood was shed, and where his body was offered."[42] Rather, "The atoning effect of the blood . . . is . . . connected with the high priest's act of carrying the blood into the holy of holies (13:11)."[43] Additionally, what is significant for our purposes is that the burning of the carcass outside the camp is the *final* ritual action in the multistep process of the *kipper* sacrifices on the Day of Decontamination. I will discuss this passage to make a different point just below, but whatever else is going on here, it is important that Jesus's crucifixion "outside the gate" (Heb 13:12) is *not* correlated with the initial sacrificial slaughter of the animal *prior* to all the blood manipulations in the sanctuary. That is, Jesus's crucifixion is neither framed as the moment of atonement nor as the moment of slaughter as the precondition for acquiring the animal's blood.[44]

---

these claims. In fact, it is these very claims that generate theological problems that need solving, as Hebrews evinces.

42. Moffitt, *Atonement and the Logic of Resurrection*, 229.

43. Moffitt, *Atonement and the Logic of Resurrection*, 277.

44. Contra Eberhart, "Characteristics," 52: "The death of Jesus is the precondition for the availability of his blood" (cf. 59). Moffitt also makes the same observation: "Instead of highlighting the correlation of Jesus' crucifixion outside Jerusalem with the moment of the slaughter of the victim, he links it with the final act of the Yom Kippur ritual—the disposal of the victim's body 'outside the camp.' . . . A careful mapping of Jesus' suffering onto the moment of the slaughter of Yom Kippur is simply not what the author is about here" (*Atonement and the Logic of Resurrection*, 277). Linking Jesus's death to the corpse disposal outside the camp just won't allow for a neat one-to-one correspondence between Jesus's death, resurrection, and ascension and the sequence of sacrificial atonement as Eberhart seems to suppose.

Since Jesus's crucifixion literally precedes his resurrection and ascension, the sacrificial sequence is going to be a bit garbled no matter what. How does the final ritual act (burning of the carcass, which equates to the crucifixion) take place *before* the atoning action (bringing the life-blood into the sanctuary, which equates to the resurrection and ascension)? While the answer is hard to determine, associating the crucifixion to the burning of the carcass *after* the atoning manipulations have occurred only reinforces the idea that it is Jesus's *full obedient life* that correlates to atonement, not his death. Since his death correlates to carcass disposal after atonement has taken place, then this implies that it happens "after" the means of atonement have been obtained; namely, his total obedient life. *After* that life-blood that has the power to atone has been obtained—living a full human life from birth to death—then the "body" can be "burned" (=crucified) outside the camp/city (13:11–12). If we wanted to try to keep with the sacrificial sequence, then perhaps it is the incarnation (2:14) that correlates to the moment of slaughter since the incarnation is the precondition for procuring Jesus's obedient life-blood. This is speculative, of course, because no matter what, the sacrificial sequence is jumbled since the presentation of that obedient life in the heavenly holy of holies *necessarily* happens after the crucifixion.

However anyone who wants to parse the sacrificial sequence out, what is said in 13:11–12 reveals that Hebrews does *not* associate Jesus's crucifixion with either the initial moment of slaughter or to the moment of atonement, but rather with burning the carcass outside the camp *after the atonement has taken place*. This rules out any neat sequence that positions Jesus's death as corresponding to the slaughter so that Jesus's presentation in the holy of holies would align smoothly with the Levitical sacrificial sequence.

Whatever the reason for the author tethering Jesus's crucifixion to the ritual carcass disposal, this also further strengthens the case made in chapter 1 that sacrificial slaughter is not about death or suffering. When the author of Hebrews wants to press in on the fact that Jesus suffered and died, they chose to correlate that with the carcass disposal that happens after all the atoning work has been completed.

All this significantly undermines any notion of penal substitutionary atonement because it exposes how this framework is mistaken in each one of its terms. Levitical atonement is not about a substitutionary death. Nor is the sacrificial animal being punished in place of the offerer. No. The work of atonement (restricted to decontaminating the heavenly sanctuary, 9:23–26) itself is aligned with Jesus's *living* entry into the holy of holies where he presents "himself," his "life-blood" (13:11–12; 6:19–20; 7:24—8:1–2; 9:11–12, 14, 23–26).

From this vantage point we can further uncover problems inherent to penal substitutionary atonement, by observing how the atonement theology in Hebrews is embedded within a theology of participation. The author conceives of our union with Jesus to be so tight that believers are indexed as co-purgation offerings with him as they "bear his reproach" through cruciform suffering (13:10–13).

To see how this makes sense within the conceptual imaginary of Hebrews, we need to understand the implications of the incarnation. Among other things, the Son's incarnation in a body like ours (2:14)—experiencing temptations, sufferings (2:17–18), and weakness (5:2), and even "tasting death" (2:9–10) and then being resurrected to indestructible life (7:16, 24–25; 13:20)—is what makes moral purification of humanity possible. And this culminates in our purification from death itself: resurrection (6:2; 11:19, 35). Thus, Jesus first participates in the full human condition, and it is this *contact* Jesus makes with humanity that purifies and consecrates them. It is because of his *incarnation*, Jesus contacting each aspect of human existence with all its attendant temptations, weaknesses, and sufferings, that he can purge the human body itself with his pure indestructible life (9:14; 10:22; cf. 10:2).[45]

The Son's participation in human likeness (incarnation) also grounds and enables *humanity's* participation in the Son's high priesthood and sufferings. Once the body, heart, and conscience are purged and then consecrated (2:11; 10:10, 14, 29), this enables believers to *share* in Jesus's high priesthood and to do what no one other than the anointed Aaronic high priest (and now Jesus himself, of course) has been able to do before (cf. 9:7, 25): enter the holy of holies itself (10:19; 4:16). But this time, rather than it being limited to once a year (9:7, 25), this can be an ongoing continual thing since believers have a unique fellowship with God through Jesus (10:19–22; 4:16).[46] Moreover, although the atoning work of decontaminating the heavenly sanctuary does not need to be repeated (cf. 7:26; 9:12, 28; 10:10, 12, 14), the people need continual "intercession" (7:25 cf. 1 John 2:1–2 discussed above). Both Jesus's decontaminating of the heavenly sanctuary and his continual intercession are possible because Jesus is "always living" (Heb 7:25) in

45. Again, this purification of body and heart is made on analogy to ritual purification whose main purgative element is water. Hebrews says our "conscience" (*syneidēsis*, 9:14, 10:22) and heart (*kardia*) are "sprinkled" on analogy to corpse impurity ash-water (9:13–14; 10:22) and our bodies (*sōma*) "washed with pure water" (10:22). Jesus-as-*kipper* is restricted to decontaminating the heavenly sancta from its sin-contaminations (9:23–26).

46. This is similar to Moses's continual face-to-face encounters with God in Exod 33:7–11, but this was not happening in the holy of holies, but rather in another tent "outside the camp" (33:7).

the holy of holies, thereby making it *impossible* for it to ever get defiled again and making it *possible* to intercede for "those who draw near to God" (7:25).

While much more can be said about Jesus's intercession,[47] the point I want to emphasize is that Jesus's high priesthood and entry into the holy of holies beyond the second veil of the heavenly dwelling place functions as a "forerunner" of our own entrance into the holy holies after him (6:19–20; 10:19, 22; 4:16). Therefore, as it turns out, Jesus's high priesthood is not substitutionary. Rather, it is something we are enabled to participate in because it grants us access to the heavenly holy of holies, which it seems Jesus will be bringing with him when he returns (9:28; 10:34, 37; 11:10, 16; 12:22, 27–28; 13:14).[48]

The theme of participation does not stop there. The author conceives of our union with Jesus to be so strong and close that just as Jesus was associated with the purgation offerings on the Day of Decontamination,[49] *so are we*, according to Heb 13:11–13. Recall that any purgation offering whose blood is brought into the holy place needs to be burned (Lev 6:23 [Eng. v. 30]; 4:12, 21; 16:27). This is what Heb 13:11 is reminding readers about to support the preceding claim that there are certain purgation sacrifices that the priests cannot eat (13:10). This prohibition on eating the sacrifice is especially pertinent for the purgation offerings on the Day of Decontamination because their blood is not only brought into the holy place, but into the holy of holies as well (13:11; cf. Lev 16:14–15).[50] Having a share in the altar is normally indexed by eating part of what is offered on it (e.g., 1 Cor 10:18) and the claim being made in Heb 13:10 is that believers have a share in the purgation sacrifices that even the priests cannot eat from. But this share does not come through *eating*, but rather through *cruciform suffering*—"bearing his [Jesus's] reproach" (13:13). This is made possible because believers have been "consecrated through his [Jesus's] blood" (13:12). This not only makes their suffering "holy," it also indexes it as belonging to the very nature of Jesus-as-purgation-offering. This is because just as Jesus's

47. For a fuller discussion of this aspect, see Moffitt, "It Is Not Finished," 167–73.

48. Since in 9:28 and 10:37 "the author does not say that Jesus will bring his people to himself . . . through the heavens to where he is, but rather that Jesus will appear again to be present with his people who are waiting for him" it seems likely that the author envisions Jesus bringing the heavenly sanctuary, "the heavenly Jerusalem" and "Mount Zion" (12:22), with him (Moffitt, "It Is Not Finished," 170–71).

49. The purgation sacrifices are explicitly in view because of the use of *peri hamartias* in 13:11, which is the LXX's translation of the *ḥaṭṭā ʾt* sacrifice in Leviticus.

50. And this is why the author does not and cannot tether the idea of Jesus-as-*kipper* with the Lord's Supper since the Lord's Supper is not a purgation sacrifice and it is, obviously, *eaten*. For another argument that Hebrews is not drawing upon the Lord's Supper, see Lane, *Hebrews*, 538–39.

"suffer[ing] outside the gate" (13:12) is equated with being "burned outside the camp" (3:11), so too, then, is the suffering of Jesus's followers who are "bearing his [Jesus's] reproach" "outside the camp" (13:13) thereby equated with being "burned outside the camp" (3:11). Associating both Jesus's and believers' suffering with the final act of disposing the carcasses from the Day of Decontamination purgation sacrifices indicates that believers are being conceptualized as co-purgation sacrifices with Jesus.[51] Only purgation sacrifices need to be "burned outside the camp" (13:11) and this is what their suffering is identified as. Believers are so intimately connected with Jesus that their suffering "belongs" to Jesus—it is "*his* reproach." Their suffering is his suffering. This is as clear of a statement of total solidarity and participation as it is profound.

The connection between Jesus's "reproach" and cruciform suffering is plain in the only other passage where "reproach" (*oneidismos*) is related to Jesus in Hebrews, where Moses's choice to "endure suffering with the people of God" (11:25) is equated with "the reproach of Christ" (11:26).[52] Bearing Jesus's reproach means suffering like and with him. Therefore, to cover a potential counterargument, it will not do to say that "bearing the reproach of Jesus" means believers are linked to the priest who *carries* the carcass outside the camp. This is because (a) believers are exhorted to go out to where Jesus is in 13:13, which means they are not "carrying" him anywhere, and (b) 11:25–26 makes clear that Jesus's "reproach" is *suffering* (in solidarity with the oppressed). The crucial point is more than just that believers somehow identify with Christ's sufferings in their own sufferings, but that this suffering is indexed, not only for Jesus but also for those he consecrates (13:12–13), as being "burned outside the camp" as a purgation sacrifice (13:11). Since purgation sacrifice carcasses, not the priests, are burned, this means believers cannot be indexed as anything other than the purgation sacrifices.

The reasoning behind the consecration of the people and then their identification with Jesus-as-purgation-sacrifice is probably based on the principle set forth in Exodus that whatever touches the altar becomes holy (Exod 29:37; 30:28–29; cf. Matt 23:19). This would draw together a few things Hebrews has already established, which would be appropriate since

51. Although they do not make the link to believers as being identified with Jesus-as-purgation-sacrifice, many note that the overall point of "bearing Jesus's reproach" is identifying and sharing in Jesus's suffering and death (Cockerill, *Hebrews*, 697, 701–3; Lane, *Hebrews*, 543–44; Johnson, *Hebrews*, 349).

52. Cf. Johnson, *Hebrews*, 349; Lane, *Hebrews*, 544; Cockerill, *Hebrews*, 703. The only other use of *oneidismos* is in Heb 10:33 and refers to the general abuses suffered by the community.

Heb 13:10–13 is part of the authors concluding remarks. Here is what we know so far:

(a) The heavenly sanctuary is equipped with the same spaces and objects for the dwelling place, which would include both the altar for animal sacrifices and the incense altar (8:1–5; 9:2–5, 23–24).

(b) Because Jesus has decontaminated the heavenly sanctuary (9:11–12, 23–26) then purified (9:13–14; 10:22) and consecrated believers as high priests (10:10, 14), they have access to all the spaces and objects in the heavenly sanctuary (10:19–20; 6:19–20; 4:16).

(c) Believers somehow "have an altar" (13:10) that is specifically being framed with reference to the purgation sacrifices (*peri hamartias*) offered on the Day of Decontamination (13:11). This means the author is anchoring believers's possession of this altar via sacrifices that cannot be eaten by the priests since they are burned outside the camp instead (13:11).

(d) Therefore, whatever "have an altar" entails, it must mean their connection to it cannot be mediated through *eating*. This excludes the Lord's Supper, and it definitely excludes the idea that the author is saying believers are somehow able to eat from purgation sacrifices that not even the high priest was able to eat from.

(e) Jesus's life-blood has consecrated the believers such that their suffering is now indexed as belonging to Jesus's crucifixion and as the burning of purgation sacrifices outside the camp on the Day of Decontamination (13:12–13). Not all "consecrations" have the same function. Prior to this, the consecration of believers referred to a *priestly* consecration that made them fit to access the heavenly sanctuary. Here it refers to consecrating an *animal* as a sacrifice and, therefore, *holy* (cf. Matt 23:19; Exod 29:37).

The principle of whatever touches the altar becomes consecrated (Exod 29:37) would thread these points together. Because of their access to the heavenly sanctuary as co-high priests, believers have contacted the heavenly altar that itself was consecrated and purified by Jesus's living presence ("blood"). This contact with the altar and Jesus's life-blood now makes them a holy sacrifice. But this is not just any sacrifice here because it is specifically indexed as the purgation sacrifices that are not eaten since they are burned outside the camp on the Day of Decontamination instead (Heb 13:11–13). Since Jesus's suffering (13:12) is indexed as being "burned outside the camp" (13:11), then our suffering, which is equated with bearing Christ's "reproach" (11:25–26; 13:13), is likewise being indexed as being "burned outside the camp." Therefore, the claim "we have an altar" in 13:10 is saying that believers have contact with Jesus's life-blood on the heavenly altar, which has consecrated them so that they must be burned outside the camp with and like Jesus as a co-purgation sacrifice, which implies they were likewise offered on the heavenly altar.

The priests involved in the purgation sacrifices on the Day of Decontamination surely *benefit* from these sacrifices, but they do not have a "share in the altar" since they "have no right to eat" from those sacrifices (Heb 13:10; cf. 1 Cor 10:18) since the meat is burned (13:11). The spectacular claim being made in 13:10–13 is that believers are uniquely connected to the altar—they "have an altar" (13:10)—vis-à-vis the atoning sacrifices, not because they can eat from them after all, but rather *precisely because they have become consecrated as co-purgation sacrifices* as they have been touched by both Jesus's blood and the heavenly altar. This is quite a radical way to conceptualize suffering for Christ! Suffering has already been a repeated theme (cf. 11:25–26, 36–38; 12:2–4; 10:32–39; 2:10, 14, 17–18). Here in 13:10–13, the author expresses the meaning of Jesus's atoning work as making it possible for others to participate in his suffering-as-a-purgation-sacrifice.

I do not think the author is meaning to say that the suffering of believers on analogy to the burning of purgation sacrifices is additive. These are not multiple individual purgation sacrifices stacking up on Jesus's purgation sacrifice. Rather, the sufferings of Jesus's followers are being conceptualized as sharing in the *same single* purgation sacrifice that Jesus is/offers. Their suffering is a sharing in and identification with *Jesus's* reproach.

What this means is that Hebrews has a *participatory* atonement theology, not a substitutionary atonement theology. While indexing believers as fellow purgation sacrifices is no doubt a radical claim, other NT texts conceptualize believers as sacrifices as well (e.g., Phil 2:17; 4:18; 2 Cor 2:14–15; Rom 12:1). Revelation 6:9, for instance, communicates this vividly. Here, as Craig Keener comments, "the lamb in union with . . . the martyrs" is similarly so close that "the martyrs are portrayed as sacrifices beneath the altar."[53] Moreover, the overall point that Hebrews makes aligns with other comments about sharing in the singular suffering and death of Christ in the NT (e.g., Phil 3:10; Gal 2:20; 6:14; Rom 6:3–6; Col 1:24; Mark 10:38–39; 2 Cor 4:10–12; 1 Cor 10:16). What is clear in Hebrews, though, is that Jesus's death is not an act of substitution. The audience is not supposed to look at

53. Keener, *Gospel of John*, 1:454. Given the link between Jesus as the Passover lamb in 5:6–10 and no mention of nor allusion to atonement in Revelation, it seems the martyrs are being associated with either the Passover specifically or the well-being offerings in general.

Jesus's sufferings and death and think: "Phew! Jesus did all of that instead of me!" Rather, they are "to look upon Jesus, the author and perfector of faithfulness" (12:2) and thereby pattern their lives after the crucifixion, bearing his reproach, realizing that Jesus suffered and died *ahead* of them rather than *instead* of them (12:2–4; 10:32–39; 11:25–26, 36–38). Jesus's suffering and death is what *determines* what faithfulness and obedience mean (5:8; 10:7, 9) while the wilderness generation provides the antitype (3:18–19; 4:2–3, 6, 11). In any case, Jesus is not a "substitute" because he is the "forerunner" all the way down (6:19–20). The concept of substitution is categorically incorrect and misleading because it not only obscures the message, it also logically precludes the message of identifying with Jesus's suffering and death.

Also, Jesus's death is described as an act of *solidarity* with mortal humanity in 2:14–18 (cf. 5:7–9). The author of Hebrews says that Jesus's death and subsequent vindication by God in resurrection liberates believers from "the fear of death" (2:15) and thus from the one "who has the power of death, that is, the devil" (2:14). The only person wielding death in Hebrews is the devil. To think that Jesus is dying a substitutionary death to appease God is to put God in the place of the devil, according to Hebrews. Yes, sin leads to death, but God is cast as the rescuer and deliverer; the one who purges death with indestructible life; not the enslaver who gives out death as his wages (to borrow Paul's phrasing in Rom 6:23).

What we have in Hebrews, then, is the notion of double participation. First the Son of God participates in the full experience of humanity by even tasting death so that, second, humanity is enabled to participate in his death and resurrection to indestructible life.

CONCLUSION

We have established that although 1 John and Hebrews both apply the language of sacrificial atonement to Jesus, this does not mean that they view Jesus as a substitutionary death or that atonement is a central aspect of the gospel message. Instead, the authors of these texts are making innovative theologies based on the preexisting "ingredients" of Jesus's resurrection, ascension, and mission to effect moral purification. Hebrews acknowledges that its teaching on Jesus as a high priest who provides atonement for the heavenly sanctuary and who consecrates his followers as both co-high priests and co-purgation sacrifices is intended for the theologically "mature."

Further, both 1 John and Hebrews analogize Jesus's blood to various cultic "liquids," though this is more apparent in Hebrews. Hebrews is making the argument that Jesus's life-blood serves as a sacrifice that fulfills the functions of both *kipper* and non-kipper sacrifices in the Levitical system. According to the author, Jesus is a non-kipper covenant-making sacrifice, and he also has atoning significance and can accomplish the purification of the heavenly sanctuary. Just as we saw from the Gospels, the author also links the forgiveness of sins and moral purification with the establishment of the new covenant, rather than with the *kipper* system. In fact, the author grounds Jesus's capacity to bring about atonement in the non-atoning sacrifice that establishes the new covenant. Once again, we see how Jesus's association with the non-atoning sacrifices are primary. It is what makes these other theological moves possible.

Overall, Hebrews is emphasizing the all-encompassing nature of Jesus's resurrected "indestructible life" (Heb 7:16) and his ability to fulfill the functions of the entire Levitical system, rather than only linking it to the *kipper* system. The potency of Jesus's indestructible life is what allows it to be understood on analogy to the various aspects and "liquids" of the Torah's sacrificial and purity systems. Jesus's life-blood decontaminates sancta on analogy to the *kipper* blood of purgation sacrifices. Jesus's life-blood inaugurates the new covenant on analogy to the non-*kipper* blood from covenant-making sacrifices. Jesus's life-blood consecrates people on analogy to the non-*kipper* blood of ordination sacrifices (and perhaps ordination oil too) as well as to the consecratory function of the covenant-making ceremony. Jesus's life-blood effects moral purification on analogy to the purgative ash-water for corpse impurity and as such simply *is* the promised washing in the divine Spirit.

Moreover, according to Hebrews, Jesus not only decontaminates the heavenly sanctuary, his consecrating life-blood also grants believers access to God in the holy of holies, indexing them as co-high priests, and enables them to participate with Jesus as co-purgation sacrifices enveloped in the same single purgation sacrifice Jesus is and offers. This understanding of atonement (in the sense of *kipper*) is not about Jesus dying "instead of" us, but rather about Jesus's death and resurrection making it possible for us to pattern our own lives after him in union with his suffering and death and to participate in his resurrection. This is a participatory atonement (*kipper*) theology.

Additionally, Hebrews argues that Jesus's resurrection and ascension to the presence of God in the heavenly holy of holies are crucial to his atoning work, rather than his death on the cross. However, just as we saw how the mention of "forgiveness" is not sufficient to establish an allusion to an atoning sacrifice in Hebrews or the texts discussed in the previous chapter, the ascension is not sufficient either. That is, the fact that one of the key premises for Hebrew's atonement theology is the ascension does not mean every confession in the NT about Jesus's ascension is either inherently or likely about heavenly *kipper*.[54] That does not follow. Rather, by Hebrews' own acknowledgment, the logic runs the other way around. Hebrews develops additional meaning and relevance to the confession regarding Jesus's ascension that is new "solid food" beyond the basic elementary basic teachings of the church as repeated above (Heb 5:7—6:2). The ascension is a key "ingredient" that allows the author of Hebrews to make a coherent argument for a new theological understanding of Jesus's death built on basic early Christian confession, but this does not mean "ascension equals *kipper*."[55] Moreover, ascension at first meant kingly *enthronement* and was with reference to *David* (e.g., Acts 2:24–36), which Hebrews acknowledges is a stumbling block for then trying to think about Jesus as a *priest*, let alone a high priest who can perform *kipper* for the sanctuary (Heb 7:13–14; 8:4).

Finally, 1 John presents a truly universal atonement theology (2:2) while Hebrews presents a view of atonement that focuses on the decontamination of the heavenly sanctuary and granting believers access to the purified heavenly holy of holies, rather than a substitutionary punishment for sin. This concept of atonement is embedded within a theology of participation, with believers being seen as fellow purification offerings with Jesus as they share in his sufferings and high priesthood. In this way, the atonement theology of Hebrews is worked out through its concept of Jesus as a "forerunner" (6:19–20). What Jesus does is not "instead of" us, but rather "ahead of us." The call to follow Jesus is the call to full union and participation in the Son's indestructible life as we "bear his reproach" (13:13).

54. See footnote 41.

55. Also, the ascension itself is not the only "ingredient" or premise needed to make sense of Jesus-as-high-priest-and-agent-of-*kipper*. As we saw, another key premise is Jesus-as-non-atoning-covenant-making-sacrifice. That *change in covenant* is what grounds a *change of priesthood*, according to Hebrews (7:11–12).

7

When Jesus's Death Is Not a Sacrifice

Readers familiar with the NT probably have a list of "What about [insert NT text here]?" in response to everything discussed thus far. Although I cannot address every possible text, the following represent the "usual suspects" that people ask about whenever I have spoken or written about Jesus and sacrificial imagery. I hope this list has sufficient overlaps with yours. The main thesis for all these is the same:

> This text is not making an analogy to any Levitical sacrifice.

Since making purely negative arguments feels incomplete, I also argue positively for what I think each text is about. Yet again, it will be apparent that the theme of union with and participation in Jesus's death is emphasized, thereby further undermining notions of substitution.

1 PETER 2:24 AND THE SUFFERING SERVANT FROM ISAIAH 53

In 1 Pet 2:24 we read, "'he [Jesus] himself bore our sins in his body on the cross, so that we might die to sins and live for righteousness; 'by his wounds you have been healed.'" Peter is quoting from Isa 53:4–5 (the "Suffering Servant" passage) here.

First, before getting into the Suffering Servant song in Isa 52:13—53:12, this passage is not claiming Jesus was a sacrifice. As Shauf clarifies, "the description of what Christ did on the cross in 2:24 simply does not work as a sacrifice. Sacrificial victims did not bear sins. Sacrifices were in no sense sinful. Sins were not offered on the altar."[1] The claim here is that Jesus's crucifixion was an act of solidarity with the sins and attendant curses resting upon humanity.

Some have claimed, however, that the use of *peri hamartiōn* in 3:18 means that Jesus suffered "as a sin offering,"[2] but as Shauf demonstrates, "there is no good argument" for this interpretation.[3] "While περὶ ἁμαρτίας (singular) is the technical LXX expression for a sin offering (the *hattat*), in the plural [which is what *peri hamartiōn* is], it does not have this sense."[4]

Moreover, the context is one of imitation of Jesus's sufferings. The comment about Jesus's suffering in 3:18 is meant to ground the exhortation in 3:17. This all goes back to the framing admonition in 2:21 that relies on Jesus's death as the pattern for discipleship. The idea of "bearing our sins," as Peter goes on to make plain, means Jesus endured being treated unjustly and handled it well. He responded justly to the injustice and to the sins he suffered (2:23). Then, Peter says that Jesus deals with our inclination to sin and thus we are now able to live justly (2:24). Atonement, as we now know, is about purging holy objects in the temple, but what Peter is talking about is healing us humans of our proclivity to sin/live unjustly. Jesus enables us to live justly/righteously precisely by following his cruciform example in suffering the injustices of others (2:21–23), which means bearing their sins (2:23) and bearing their burdens (3:16–18; 4:19 compare with 2:23).

Second, the use of Isa 53 is neither evidence for "atonement" nor for "substitution." All of the NT quotations from Isa 53, except Matt 8:17 (see below), come from the LXX.[5] While in the Hebrew MT Isa 53:10 has "the one who gave his life as a redemption of debt" the LXX reads "the Lord wanted to cleanse him from the blow; if you offer sin offerings, then your souls will see eternal offspring."[6] Shauf highlights how "[u]nlike in the Hebrew . . . here [in the LXX] the servant does not suffer to redeem others;

1. Shauf, *Jesus the Sacrifice*, 172.

2. Jobes, *1 Peter*, 238; quoted in Shauf, *Jesus the Sacrifice*, 173.

3. Shauf, *Jesus the Sacrifice*, 173.

4. Shauf, *Jesus the Sacrifice*, 173; brackets mine.

5. Eberhart, "Atonement," 15. The passages that quote from Isa 53 are: Matt 8:17, Luke 22:37, John 12:38, Acts 8:32–33; Rom 10:16, Rom 15:21, 1 Pet 2:24–25; Rev 14:5. As Eberhart observes, "None of these citations depict Jesus giving his life vicariously for others" ("Atonement," 15). Matthew 8:17 is not even about Jesus's death and Paul cites Isa 53 as referring to his own apostleship (!) in Rom 15:21 and to evangelists more broadly in Rom 10:16.

6. Using Eberhart's translations in "Atonement," 15 and 16 respectively.

rather, God desires to rescue him from his suffering" and "it is the audience who is encouraged to offer a sacrifice for its own sin."[7]

Again, we might also see "the absence of evidence" in Hebrews (and 1 John) as "evidence of absence." If Isa 53 was received as such an obvious "atonement" prooftext, why didn't the two NT authors who explicitly identify Jesus with *kipper* rely on Isa 53 for their proof, especially since making this link was an obvious uphill battle (cf. Heb 7:13–14)? The answer is that Isa 53 was not read by the early Christ-followers as either about atonement or substitution.

Every direct use of Isa 53 in the NT confirms this. Matthew, for instance, quotes from Isa 53 to explain Jesus's healing and exorcism ministry (Matt 8:16–17), but he never brings it up in relation to Jesus's death! In any case, when Jesus heals or casts out a demon no one conceptualizes that event with the word "substitution." Yes, Jesus is doing something *for* someone else that they cannot do for themselves, but it is obviously not fitting to conceptualize this activity with "substitution." Surgeons do things for patients they cannot do for themselves, but no one ever says, "Thank God for my substitutionary surgeon," unless they mean that their original scheduled surgeon couldn't perform the operation for whatever reason and another surgeon had to take their place. When Jesus heals people's various ailments and demons, he is doing a surgeon-like activity *for* people, but "substitution" is an inadequate and misleading way to categorize that action.

Moreover, the reception of the Suffering Servant song in Isa 52:13—53:12, as attested in Daniel, Wisdom of Solomon, Romans, Revelation, and 1 Clement, establishes that the Servant was understood as a *paradigm for all the suffering righteous*. Isaiah 53 is read as the "script" for what it looks like for the righteous/just to live in an unjust/unrighteous world. H. L. Ginsberg argues that the book of Daniel is "the oldest interpretation of the Suffering Servant" because it repeatedly identifies the name, activity, and effects of the "Enlighteners (*maskilim*)" (Dan 11:33, 35; 12:3, 10) in Dan 11–12 with these same things from the Servant poem from Isa 52:12—53:12.[8] With respect to name, "the Servant himself is called a Maskil right at the beginning of the Servant Pericope (Isa lii 13) . . . : 'Behold my Servant *yaskil*'" since both *Maśkîlîm* and *Yaśkîl* are *hiphil* forms of the verb root *ś-k-l* relating to wisdom, insight, and understanding.[9] It is apparent that the author(s)/redactor(s) of Daniel read Isa 52:13 as something like, "Behold my Servant,

7. Shauf, *Jesus the Sacrifice*, 120.

8. I learned the following observations from Ginsberg, "The Oldest Interpretation," 400–404; here, 402.

9. Ginsberg, "The Oldest Interpretation," 403. *Maśkîlîm* is a third-person plural hiphil participle and *Yaśkîl* is a third-person singular hiphil imperfect.

the Wise One [*Yaśkîl*]" and that this figure is a typological representation of the *Maśkîlîm* ("those causing others to understand or become wise")[10] because of the tight correspondence between what happens to them and the Servant/*Yaśkîl*. Both the *Yaśkîl* and the *Maśkîlîm* "justify the many" (Isa 53:11; Dan 12:3). The *Yaśkîl* is persecuted and dies and the *Maśkîlîm* are persecuted and many die (Isa 53:8–9, 12; Dan 11:33–35). Finally, both the *Yaśkîl* and the martyred *Maśkîlîm* are resurrected ("the general sense of the difficult last 8 Hebrew words of [Isa] liii 10a"[11] and Dan 12:3). Thus, "there can be no doubt about it" that "the author of Dan xi–xii has simply identified the Servant of Isa lii 13–liii 12 with the Maskilim (Enlightened or Enlighteners) of his day, and the Many of the said passage with the Many of Dan xi 33, 34, etc."[12] This is why "the Maskilim knew that they were the Servant of the Lord of whom Isaiah . . . had spoken in Isa lii–liii, and that even if they died they would live again in order to be glorified."[13] Therefore, it is clear that the *Maśkîlîm* are patterned after the "script" for the suffering righteous in Isa 52:13—53:12.

This same idea is attested in Wis 2:12–24. Here the perspective is from the wicked who desire to persecute "the righteous person" to see if God will deliver them from torture and death (2:12–20), but then the author affirms that God will indeed resurrect the righteous (2:21–24; cf. 1–5). All this is based on an interpretation of the servant in Isa 53 as a paradigm for any righteous sufferer. Moreover, Rev 14:5 ("no lie was found in their mouth") quotes from Isa 53:9 and applies it to the saints.[14] Similarly, Paul only quotes from the Suffering Servant song to apply it to evangelists in general (Rom 10:16, quoting Isa 53:1) and to his apostleship in particular (Rom 15:21, quoting Isa 52:15).[15] All this confirms that Isa 53 was read as a paradigmatic script for what living righteously in an unrighteous world will entail (suffering, probably martyrdom, but ultimately vindication to resurrected life).

This sufficiently explains why 1 Peter quotes from Isa 53 and says this is the pattern/example to share in (2:21). Jesus *epitomizes* the Suffering Servant, but it is because he embodies the fullness of the Servant script that we are called to do likewise. While Jesus fully embodies this script, this way

10. Rillera, "A Call to Resistance," 760–61, here 761.

11. Ginsberg, "The Oldest Interpretation," 402.

12. Ginsberg, "The Oldest Interpretation," 402.

13. Ginsberg, "The Oldest Interpretation," 403.

14. Compare *en tō atomati autōn ouch heurethē pseudos* (Rev 14:5) and *oude heurethē dolos en tō stomati* (Isa 53:9 LXX). The only differences are minor: word order, the necessary singular versus the plural, substituting "lie" (*pseudos*) for "deceit" (*dolos*), and the synonyms of negation (*ouch* versus *oude*).

15. Cf. Das, "Models for Relating Sin as a Power," 57–59.

of life is not just for him, but for all the people of God. There is to be total solidarity between Jesus and his disciples. The suffering of the Servant is understood as enduring the consequences of the majority's sinfulness, which applies to both Jesus and his followers (2:21–23; 3:16–18; 4:19, compare with 2:23).

It is obvious that Peter views Jesus as the Suffering Servant *par excellence*, but what prevents me from categorizing this as a "substitution" is that he simultaneously says we are called to share in the same servant lifestyle (2:21). Substitution, by definition, *precludes any sort of participation*, as Simon Gathercole argues in *Defending Substitution*. Gathercole writes: "I am defining *substitutionary* atonement for the present purposes as Christ's death in our place, instead of us. The 'instead of us' clarifies the point that 'in our place' does not, in substitution at least, mean 'in our place *with us*.'"[16] He later employs the word "replacement," which makes clear that substitution is to be distinguished from representation even if it may be "possible that one can find an even more substitutionary sort of representation."[17] In other words, even if "some might argue that substitution is rooted in representation,"[18] I agree with Gathercole that representation and substitution are to remain logically distinct from one another in the same way rectangles and squares are. A square may be a rectangle, but not all rectangles are squares; likewise, substitution may be a type of representation, but not all types of representation are substitutionary. This precise definition of substitution is important for the purposes of the present discussion, and I will refer to it to discuss more problems with the term "substitution" for other passages.

Even though the reception history of the Suffering Servant in Second Temple Judaism does not evince either "sacrifice" or "substitution" this does not by itself rule out that 1 Peter interprets Isa 53 in a substitutionary manner (and we have already ruled out "sacrifice"). What is necessary is to see how the author makes use of that material and then decide if *substitution/replacement* best conceptualizes what that author is getting at since perhaps something like *representation* or *solidarity* better captures the author's point.

We need to appreciate how the notion of participation and solidary with Jesus as a "pattern" or "example" for Christians to conform to in 2:21 is what immediately precedes and thus informs what comes after when Peter quotes from Isa 53 in 2:24. Jesus as *the* Servant is used to say that now we have *the definitive* paradigm for the Servant rather than just the *script* in

16. Gathercole, *Defending Substitution*, 15; his emphasis.

17. Gathercole, *Defending Substitution*, 20, 20n14 respectively.

18. Gathercole, *Defending Substitution*, 111.

Isaiah for how *we* ought to likewise be servants as well. Jesus is not construed as a substitute here on Gathercole's definition, because what he is doing is not "instead of us" or "in our place" so that we are excluded from doing whatever it is Jesus did as our substitute. Rather, Jesus, and Jesus's death in particular, is held up as a model to be imitated. Whatever that is, "substitute" does not capture what 1 Peter is talking about.

First Peter says that Jesus dies as an "example (*hypogrammos*) so that you should follow his steps" (2:21; cf. 4:1). In short, Jesus's death is a participatory reality; it is something we are called to follow and share in experientially ourselves. The logic is not: Jesus died so I don't have to. It is: Jesus died (redeeming us from slavery and forming us into a kingdom of priests in 2:5, 9) so that we, together, can follow in his steps and die *with* him and *like* him; the just for the unjust (3:18) and trusting in God who judges justly (2:23; 4:19). This is what it means to "suffer . . . for being a 'Christian'" (4:15–16). It does not particularly matter *why* a Christ-follower is suffering or being persecuted; it only matters *that* they bear the injustice of the world in a *Christ-like*, and therefore, a *Servant-like*, manner.

In fact, Clement of Rome in the later first to early second century AD quotes all of Isa 53 with reference to Jesus to make this very same point (1 Clem. 16:3–16). Clement reads Isa 53 in light of Jesus, not to make some point about substitution, but to discern the following lesson: "You see, dear friends, the kind of pattern that has been given to us; for if the Lord so humbled himself, what should we do, who through him have come under the yoke of his grace?" (1 Clem. 16:17).[19] This word for "pattern" (*hypogrammos*) is the same word used in 1 Pet 2:21 to introduce the use of Isa 53 with reference to Jesus and the ethical claims that that has on Christ-followers. Like 1 Peter, Clement introduces the quote from Isa 53 with an appeal to imitate Jesus: "For Christ is with those who are humble, not with those who exalt themselves over his flock. The majestic scepter of God, our Lord Christ Jesus, did not come with the pomp of arrogance or pride (though he could have done so), but in humility, just as the Holy Spirit spoke concerning him" (1 Clem. 16:1). These bookends (16:1, 17) enveloping the quote of Isa 53 demonstrate how shallow and insufficient the word "substitution" is to convey the concept being deployed here. The notion is *solidarity* all the way down (see "through him" in v. 17). Jesus partook in the sufferings of our condition in order to heal us so that we might be able to do likewise in union with him.

19. Greek and translation from Michael W. Holmes, *The Apostolic Fathers*.

Lest I be misunderstood, I agree with Gorman that "Jesus' death as the slave/servant is both soteriologically *unique* and ethically *paradigmatic*."[20] The concluding chapter will elucidate this further, but affirming that Jesus's life and death is soteriologically unique does not require the notion of substitution. Put another way, just because something is unique does not mean it is substitutionary, especially on the definition of substitution Gathercole provides, which I am operating with due to its laudable precision. Jesus's death is unique, but "substitution" is not the word to capture that uniqueness accurately and adequately.

Jesus's death is *unique* because it creates a participatory reality. Yes, Peter says Jesus dies "the just for the unjust" (3:18), but that beneficiary "for" (*hyper*) is not as a substitutionary benefit; rather, it is a means of opening up the possibility for *shared participation in Jesus's death*. In other words, Jesus's death *generates the very condition* for the possibility of our union and participation in him. Jesus's death makes it so that we are no longer "unjust," but rather "just"/"righteous" (*dikaosynē*, 2:24). And this is how we can now follow the example of Jesus's death as we, now being made "just," can suffer or die at the hands of the "unjust" (i.e., "suffer for doing what it right" in 3:17) just like the Suffering Servant in Isaiah, the *Maśkîlîm* in Daniel, and the paradigmatic righteous one in Wisdom of Solomon.

What we nevertheless have in 1 Peter (and Rev 14:5, which quotes from the same bit of Isa 53 that Peter does) is a clear application of the theme of "bore our sins" from Isa 53 being used to support the theme of participation/union whereby *we* can now "bear" the sins of others against us in a Christ-like cruciform manner by his power and life within us (cf. Wis 2:12–24). At the end of the day, both 1 Pet 2:21–25 and Rev 14:5 apply the Suffering Servant as the pattern/example all Christians are called to imitate/follow since Jesus is the preeminent "Servant" who enacted the Servant script perfectly. This is all about solidarity and union with Jesus by sharing in his performance of the Servant script, not substitution.

MARK 10:45 AND MATTHEW 20:28

Some have proposed that the word *lytron*, which is used only in these two places in the NT (Mark 10:45 and Matt 20:28 in parallel contexts), is a clear allusion to sacrifice and therefore, atonement.[21] Neither of these is the case

20. Gorman, *Death of the Messiah*, 120; his emphasis.

21. E.g., France, *The Gospel of Mark*, 420; Lane, *The Gospel of Mark*, 383–84; Gorman, *Death of the Messiah*, 33, 117. Though note 1 Tim 2:6 (*antilytron*).

for the simple reason that the *lytron* word group is never used in a sacrificial register in the LXX.[22]

When we look at the uses of *lytron* in the LXX, it is obvious that it is usually used in financial/economic register (Lev 25 is littered with references). That is, the *lytron* is a monetary value that is "the price of liberation" as David Bently Hart translates it.[23] When that price is paid, then you get the state of *lytrōsis*, the state of "redemption"/"liberation." The verbal form of this word is *lytroō*, which means "to redeem"/"to ransom." It is no surprise that these words are commonly applied to ransoming/redeeming from slavery, either of Israel (see Exod 6:6; 15:13) or individuals (see Lev 19:20, 25:47–55). This is why "liberation" in English best captures the nuance. So then, a *lytron* is the cost/price that liberates or releases someone or something (land can be redeemed in Lev 25) from some sort of bondage or debt. Once this happens it accomplishes or brings about the state of *lytrōsis* ("redemption").

Jesus the Liberator

Now coming to Matthew and Mark, we must ask who or what are "the many" being *liberated from*? As already discussed, the Gospels frame Jesus's ministry as another exodus-like deliverance (cf. *exodos* in Luke 9:31). And, if there are any *sacrificial* aspects associated with the exodus event, it is the Passover, which is a non-atoning thanksgiving well-being offering praising God for that act of deliverance. Therefore, if these passages in Mark 10:45 and Matt 20:28 are there anticipating the sacrificialized Lord's Supper, then they still are not activating any notion of atonement. But, the use of *lytron* implies *slavery* of some kind.

Hence, a key question is to whom are "the many" enslaved? What are "the many" being delivered from? The parable of the "strong man" in Mark 3:22–30 (par. Matt 12:22–29) and Jesus's many exorcisms give the answer.[24] Jesus has come to liberate the people from Satan and his demons and all the impurities ("impure spirits") and ailments he has afflicted them with (cf. Luke 13:16). Moreover, the framing of John the Immerser's ministry with reference to Isa 40 and the Lord's Supper reveals that this liberation entails the end of the covenant curses and the establishment of the promised new

22. Cf. Hooker, *Jesus and the Servant*, 74–79.

23. Hart, *The New Testament*.

24. And, although John doesn't use the words *lytron*, *lytrōsis*, or *lytroō*, he states that Jesus's being lifted up on the cross is all about the expulsion of the devil (and thus the liberation of those under the devil's hold) in John 12:31–33 (see also 1 John 3:8).

covenant. Jesus's giving of his life functions as a *lytron* since it is construed by the Gospels by narrating Jesus's death as a proleptic embodiment of Jerusalem's approaching second exile (the destruction of the temple at the hands of the Romans just like what happened during the first exile under Babylon).[25] That is, in both Matthew and Mark, the use of *lytron* conveys an "exodus" theme and it is not a word denoting either sacrifice or atonement.

But how does Jesus's life and death as a microcosm of the coming destruction of Jerusalem function as a *lytron*? It is only able to be interpreted that way because of the resurrection. The resurrection shows that Jesus is leading the way *through* exile (the covenant curse of death) and into freedom out the other side. His resurrection proves that *his life is the liberation from death/slavery/curse*. This is liberation from the devil ("the strong man") because it is the devil who has used death to enslave Israel (and the world) in cursed and sinful societal habits and practices, depriving them of the flourishing God desires (cf. Heb 2:14–15, which summarizes this succinctly).

This Is Not a Substitution

We have established that *lytron* is not about sacrifice or atonement. So far, so good. But what about substitution? When we observe the context of Mark 10:45 (and Matt 20:28) we will see that "substitution" cannot adequately encapsulate what Jesus is saying about his death.

Jesus is doing this *for* many, but he is not doing it "*in place of*" or "*instead of*" many (despite what some English translations say). The context precludes "substitution" by definition, as defined above.

Jesus is doing something *for their benefit*, but the benefit is only activated when *they join with him in that sort of self-giving service of others.*[26] As Jesus tells James and John as well as the rest, they too will have to be baptized with the same baptism and drink from the same cup as he has (Mark 10:38–39; Matt 20:22–23). If this was "substitutionary," then this would be *only* Jesus's baptism and *only* Jesus's cup. But this is clearly not the case. The disciples must also "pick up their cross" and "follow" Jesus (Mark 8:34; Matt 10:28; Luke 9:23; 14:27). Jesus is not doing this in order that no one else has to. Rather, all disciples must follow him to where he ends up: the cross.[27]

25. This is a subtlety John maybe felt was too easily missed and so he just comes straight out and essentially says, "the destruction of Jesus's body is linked with the destruction of the temple because Jesus is the presence of God incarnate" (cf. 2:19–22 with 1:1–18).

26. Similarly, Marcus, *Mark 8–16*, 756.

27. Again, John makes more than explicit what may have gone unnoticed before (see John 12:26).

How is Jesus's death "substitutionary" in the Gospels if he says all his disciples must also pick up their own crosses and follow him to be crucified? A substitution means person A does something so person B doesn't have to. When you substitute in soy milk in your latte, you don't also mean that you want dairy sharing in the latte as well. This is why "substitute" would be appropriate here. Something is *replacing* something else. But Jesus seems to think that he is just going *ahead* of his disciples into a fate that they themselves will and must also participate in. All disciples are called to share in Jesus's baptism and cup.

This is why using "substitution" to summarize what is taking place here actually prevents us from comprehending what Jesus is teaching. To go back to the latte metaphor, if someone wanted *both* soy milk *and* dairy in their latte, no cashier would use "substitute" to convey to the barista what the customer wanted because that word would obscure and confuse what the order was. The customer does not want a substitute; they want both soy milk and dairy to have a share in the latte. Likewise, when we hear what Jesus is claiming and teaching in the Gospels, no one should use "substitute" to convey what Jesus wanted to happen.

Although there is no direct quote of Isa 53 in Mark 10:38–45, I am not doubting that Jesus read Isa 53 as the script he was called to embrace in his messianic vocation. It seems likely to me and others that this "script" informs the ethos of what Jesus is teaching here.[28] What I am doubting is that Jesus conceived of this as a solo (substitutionary) project. He plainly states this is not the case in Mark 10:38–39. Jesus did not think he was a substitute, but rather a messianic pioneer who epitomizes the righteous Servant in Isa 53 who suffers in solidarity with and because of the sins of the wicked against him and whose suffering God will use to benefit "the many." But it is nevertheless *the same script* all of Jesus's disciples are called to perform as well.

Moreover, Jesus's "life" as a "ransom" is not said in a vacuum. The saying in Mark 10:45 and Matt 20:28 comes at the end of Jesus instructing the Twelve how they are supposed to exercise their power and rule *alongside him* as the Messiah (10:35–45). As Gorman observes, "Its Christological claim is linked to a summons to discipleship."[29] Gorman further contends,

> Here [in Mark 10:38–39], we might suggest, is the ultimate origin and source of all Christian language about participation in the death of the Messiah. To pick up one's cross and follow Jesus in suffering, generosity, and love (the essence of the three

28. Marcus, *Mark 8–16*, 756–57; Gorman, *The Death of the Messiah*, 119–20.

29. Gorman, *Death of the Messiah*, 33.

> passion prediction-summonses [8:31–34; 9:31–37; 10:32–45]) is not to *imitate* as much as it is to *participate*."[30]

And, "participation in the Messiah's suffering and death has two dimensions: literal suffering and self-giving service to God and others."[31] Therefore, ironically, Jesus's pioneering "ransom" is about liberating humanity from Satan, "the strong man" (Mark 3:22–27; 8:33), so that we too can "pick up the cross" and participate in Jesus's death ourselves, rather than think Jesus's death was substitutionary, being deceived by Satan to deny the cruciform pattern of life as Peter was at first (8:33).

2 CORINTHIANS 5:21

Here we read: "For our sake he made him to be sin who knew no sin, so that in him we might become the righteousness of God."

Those who think this is about sacrifice and atonement claim that "sin" (*hamartia*) here is referring to the various "sin offerings" that have an atoning function (what I have been translating as "purgation offerings/sacrifices"). This is because the LXX uses *peri hamartias* to refer to the purgation sacrifices. But it is significant that 2 Cor 5:21 lacks the *peri*. As Shauf explains, "For Paul to have used ἁμαρτία to refer to the [purgation] offering would have required a περί or some other indication that a sacrifice was meant, and there simply is none."[32]

And, as Dominika Kurek-Chomitz argues,

> The sin-offering interpretation . . . ultimately fails to convince. The main reasons . . . [are]: the meaning of the word ἁμαρτία would need to change radically within just a few words; it is not clear what the contrast between sin offering and δικαιοσύνη θεοῦ would mean; and finally, ἁμαρτία does not mean sin offering anywhere else in the Pauline letters or the New Testament more generally.[33]

She goes on to note: "there is no explicit cultic imagery in vv. 14–21. . . . The two prevailing images for how God deals with the world affected by sin are (1) the aforementioned banking metaphor of not counting trespasses, and

30. Gorman, *Death of the Messiah*, 124; his emphasis.

31. Gorman, *Death of the Messiah*, 124.

32. Shauf, *Jesus the Sacrifice*, 171.

33. Kurek-Chomycz, "Divine Generosity," 88.

(2) reconciliation, a metaphor originating in a political, and in particular, military-diplomatic sphere."[34]

Therefore, there is insufficient exegetical warrant to support the claim that Paul is talking about sacrifice, let alone atonement here.[35]

GALATIANS 3:13

Here we read: "Christ redeemed us from the curse of the law by becoming a curse for us—for it is written, 'Cursed is everyone who hangs on a tree'—in order that in Christ Jesus the blessing of Abraham might come to the gentiles, so that we might receive the promise of the Spirit through faith."

Shauf explains, "there really is no case to be made for it [as a sacrifice]. Sacrificial victims were not cursed."[36] However, scholars such as Stephan Finlan and Shauf have suggested that Paul is evoking the scapegoat ritual on the Day of Decontamination here.[37] So not only do we seem to have Paul talking about substitution, but he may also be alluding to the Day of Decontamination. Given what we have covered so far, three observations will suffice in response.

1) The scapegoat is not about *curse* transmission. Covenant curses are not placed on the goat—the word does not appear in this ritual—but rather Israel's ritual contaminations of "iniquities and transgressions" are placed on the goat (Lev 16:21–22). The Day of Decontamination is a disinfecting ritual *for the sanctuary and its sancta* (16:33) that begins in the holy of holies, the innermost part of the sanctuary. Once the purgation blood disinfects that area, the high priest then moves to the holy place and decontaminates the curtain and the incense altar, then he proceeds to the outer altar. Once these are all purged, then he sends the "tote-goat" to the wilderness as it is ritually loaded with all the guilt, transgression, and sin contamination of the people that were just removed from each of the preceding sancta (16:21–22).

2) Daniel Streett has argued against readings like Finlan's that think this is about the Day of Decontamination or the tote-goat ritual more

34. Kurek-Chomycz, "Divine Generosity," 90.

35. *Pace* Finlan, *The Background*, 98–101 and Shauf, *Jesus the Sacrifice*, 171, who both think this may allude to the scapegoat on the Day of Atonement. However, Shauf later acknowledges the weakness of this view since "Paul could have used a verb that would have made a sacrificial sense more apparent" (*Jesus the Sacrifice*, 187n135). For another argument that 2 Cor 5:21 is neither about sacrifice in general nor atonement in particular, see McLean, "The Absence of an Atoning Sacrifice in Paul's Soteriology," 538–42. I will return to this passage in the conclusion as well.

36. Shauf, *Jesus the Sacrifice*, 172.

37. Finlan, *The Background*, 101–11; Shauf, *Jesus the Sacrifice*, 172.

specifically. This is because talk of "becoming a curse" is used several times in places like Jeremiah to simply speak about becoming an object of derision, reproach, and scorn and has nothing to do with curse transmission or anything like "sin riddance" (cf. Jer 24:9 [*katara* LXX]; 29:18 [verse not in LXX]; 42:18 [*ara* in LXX, 49:18]; 44:8, 12 [*katara* in LXX, 51:8, 12]).[38]

Before getting into how it is that Jesus has "redeemed" (*exagorazō*) those under the curse of the law (Gal 3:13), it needs to be pointed out that all Paul seems to be getting at with his use of curse language is that Jesus *shared* in the same condition plaguing those now under the curse of the law. This is the language of *solidarity*, not substitution. Like Jeremiah who talks about those experiencing the curse of the covenant as "becoming a curse," so too Paul is only saying that Jesus went so far as to become an object of reproach and scorn by being crucified in order to liberate his people. Paul is saying that Jesus underwent solidarity with the cursed plight of Israel. This is akin to the prophets like Jeremiah, Daniel, and Ezekiel being hauled off into exile, that is, experiencing the curse of the covenant along with the whole people even though they themselves were righteous. Jesus went even further than Ezekiel's sign-act of laying down to announce and identify with Israel and Judah's covenant curse (Ezek 4:4–6). Ezekiel is "place-sharing" and enacting both their curse and eventual restoration. The same logic is at work in Galatians: Jesus's crucifixion identifies with the curse of law and his resurrection announces and identifies with the promised restoration. The main point here, however, is that "become a curse" is never used to mean that curses are being drawn away from others and onto something/one else instead.

3) As it is, the tote-goat ritual is apotropaic and preemptive, as discussed in chapter 4. It is meant to "ward off" dire conditions that would threaten the community; not mitigate them once already present. This means the Day of Decontamination only has a function when there is a sanctuary to be purged to ward off the threat of divine abandonment (and it can only do this for sins that *can be* purged from the sanctuary). Once the divine presence leaves, it is too late and no amount of purgation sacrifices or tote-goating will bring it back. This is why Ezekiel only envisions a divine washing and resurrection (Ezek 36:25), not a Day of Decontamination, to end the covenant curses of exile. So whatever Paul means in Gal 3:13, it seems to have nothing to do the Day of Decontamination.

38. Streett, "Cursed by God?" McLean has likewise argued that Gal 3:13 is not about atonement or the scapegoat but rather "'Christ became a curse' is an emphatic way of saying 'Christ became the object of a curse'" ("The Absence of an Atoning Sacrifice in Paul's Soteriology," 539; cf. 538–42).

So how is Paul saying then that Jesus "redeemed" us? First, Paul says that those "of the works of the Torah are under a curse" and then quotes the covenant curse from Deut 27:26 (Gal 3:10). Then Paul says that Christ likewise came under the covenant curse from Deuteronomy by quoting from Deut 21:23 as proof that he died a paradigmatically cursed death (Gal 3:13). Thus, Paul is at pains to communicate the simple point, not that sin or curse was *transmitted* from others to Jesus at the cross, but that God's own Son *participated fully* in Israel's cursed condition his entire life. Since all those "of the works of the Torah are under a curse" (3:10) and God's Son was "born under the law" (4:4), then Paul understands all of Jesus's life from birth to death (hung upon a tree) as characterized by the curse of the law that he thinks all Israel is living under. (Paul seems to believe that Israel has remained under the curse of the law ever since Babylon—i.e., Israel was "still in exile" when Jesus was born under the law.)

The curse is not transmitted to him as sin is transmitted to a tote-goat; rather, Jesus is simply "born under the law" during a time in Israel's history where the curses promised in Deuteronomy and prophesied about in places like Jeremiah are the lived reality for all, but also that Jesus's death functions as a sort of "poster child" for Israel's condition, just as Jesus is the Suffering Servant *par excellence*. This is not about substitution, but rather seems to be better conceptualized as "(covenantal) cursed solidarity."

If it is the case that Paul is communicating Jesus's full participation in the negative conditions of Israel, then, as Hooker has asked, "[H]ow do the conclusions follow? How are the Jews set free from the curse of the law, and how does the blessing come to the Gentiles?"[39] She goes on to observe that "underlying this there is an important assumption"; namely, "the resurrection."[40] Even though the resurrection is not mentioned explicitly in 3:13, it has to be in view, even if it remains implicit (cf. 1:16; 2:20). The resurrection is the *only* way Paul's conclusions can follow. Paul says that "the blessing" (opposite of curse) comes "in Christ Jesus" (3:14) and this can only be because in Jesus's resurrection the opposite of the curse he was living under (and died under) has occurred; the curse has been overturned in his resurrection. This point about the resurrection is made explicit in Rom 4:25 where Paul says that Jesus was raised for our justification, the very concern of Gal 3:11 (cf. 2:16–17).

The fact that it is Jesus's resurrected life that breaks the curse poses significant problems for any attempts to push the tote-goat image through in Gal 3. The blessing comes not by forever banishing a once pure victim that

39. Hooker, *From Adam to Christ*, 15.

40. Hooker, *From Adam to Christ*, 15, 16 respectively.

has had a curse unloaded onto it, but rather by the one who overrules and annuls the curse by being raised up (cf. 1:15–16; 2:20) after living and dying under the curse (3:13 with 4:4). Put another way, the curse is dealt with by construing it as a judicial sentence,[41] which is an altogether different metaphorical register than sacrifice, and then reversing that judicial sentence in Jesus's resurrection life. Paul gives no hint that the curse has been carried away by permanently banishing a living creature, which would be essential if the predicate "tote-goat" is to be remotely intelligible. By living and dying under the curse of the covenant, Jesus's resurrection thus "redeems" all those living enslaved under the curse since it means that the curse does not have the final word; rather, the blessing of resurrection does.

ROMANS 8:3

Here's the passage: "For God has done what the law, weakened by the flesh, could not do: by sending his own Son in the likeness of sinful flesh, and to deal with sin [*peri hamartias*], he condemned [*katekrinen*] sin in the flesh."

First, I want to acknowledge that the concept of substitution *is* used here, but not at all in the way it has traditionally been understood by proponents of penal substitutionary atonement. *The substitution taking place is between Jesus and the law; not Jesus for other human beings.* This is therefore not about "substitution" in the way it is construed by the terms of penal substitutionary atonement. Jesus is not being substituted in the place of humans, but in the place of a particular function of the law.[42]

Second, this passage has been interpreted as Jesus being an atoning purgation offering because of Paul's use of the phrase *peri hamartias*. Again, this is how the LXX translates the *ḥaṭṭāʾt* sacrifice.[43] So, *peri hamartias* in Rom 8:3 might be an echo of atonement. But this ultimately fails to convince.

For one, throughout Rom 5–8 Paul uses *hamartia* repeatedly. Paul says throughout that "Sin" is "reigning" (5:21; 6:12), "ruling" (6:14), "enslaving" (7:14; 6:14–22), "deceiving" (7:11), and "killing" (7:11). That is, "Sin" is the personal subject of active verbs. So Paul would have to go from consistently using *hamartia* as a personified agent doing all these actions, to suddenly

41. Hence the *dikaioō* language throughout Gal 2–3.

42. The word "particular" is key here. I do not think Paul is saying that Jesus *replaces* the law. The law still has many functions, most preeminently in Romans as that of "witness" (e.g., 3:21) and the special revelation needed to know what "sin" is (3:20; 4:15; 5:13; 7:7) and what "love" is (13:8–10). It remains "holy," "righteous/just," "good" (7:12), and "spiritual" (7:14). Also, I argue for the significance of baptized Jews remaining Torah-observant in "Tertium Genus or Dyadic Unity?"

43. Shauf, *Jesus the Sacrifice*, 159–61.

using *hamartia* to mean an inanimate "purgation sacrifice." The most natural interpretation, however, is how the NRSV translates it. Paul is basically saying "and to deal with this tyrant ruler, Sin, God condemned it in the flesh, the domain where Sin rules."[44]

Another reason *peri hamartias* is unlikely to be a sacrificial reference is because when this phrase is used in Leviticus (LXX) to mean "sin/purgation sacrifice" it never is the means of "condemning" (*katakrinō*) sin as it is in Rom 8:3, but rather of "making atonement" (*exilaskomai*) (e.g., Lev 5:6; 12:8; 16:9, 15–16). Also, the *peri hamartias* is always "offered" (*prospherō*) (9:2; 12:7) or "slayed" (*sphazō*) (14:13; 16:15). And it is worth noting that in the LXX, while both atoning and non-atoning sacrifices are always said to be "offered" (*prospherō*) (9:2; 12:7) or "slayed" (*sphazō*), the verb *thyō* ("to sacrifice" [more rigidly, "to offer by burning"]) is only used for well-being sacrifices (17:5, 7; 19:5, 6; 22:29). None of these three verbs appear here. In fact, Paul never uses the verbs *exilaskomai*, *prospherō*, or *sphazō*. But, Paul demonstrates he is familiar with the nuances of sacrificial verbs because when he says "Christ our Paschal lamb was sacrificed" (1 Cor 5:7), he uses the verb *thyō* because he is referring to a non-atoning well-being sacrifice. Therefore, Shauf's comment in relation to 2 Cor 5:21 applies here to Rom 8:3 as well: "Paul could have used a verb that would have made a sacrificial sense more apparent."[45]

In any case, Paul's personification of "Sin" as an active agent in Rom 5–8 and his use of the non-sacrificial verb *katakrinō* is a strong case against any sacrificial interpretation.

So then, what *is* Paul saying here in Rom 8:3 if it is neither about human substitution nor an atoning sacrifice? Paul is first saying that God sent Jesus as a substitute for something the law aimed at doing, but ultimately could not accomplish: setting humans free from their mortal bodies of death enslaved to sin (7:14–25) so that they can put to death the deeds of the flesh (8:13). Paul says that it is *Sin* being *condemned*; not *atoned* for. In this way Paul is saying that despite what a Roman judicial crucifixion might imply, it was *Sin*, not Jesus, that was condemned as criminal. If it is *Sin* that is condemned, then it is not Jesus, not human beings, and therefore not "Jesus instead of human beings." The only thing being condemned is Sin. Therefore, not only is this not about Jesus as a sacrifice of any kind, there is

44. For a similar argument against the purgation offering interpretation that takes seriously Paul's personification of Sin, see McMurray, *Sacrifice*, 80–85.

45. Shauf, *Jesus the Sacrifice*, 187n135. Moreover, McLean notes that because "a sacrificial victim becomes neither sinful nor accursed" Jesus's identification with "sinful flesh" in Rom 8:3 precludes this verse from speaking about Jesus as a "holy sacrifice" ("The Absence of an Atoning Sacrifice in Paul's Soteriology," 538–42, here 538).

also no concept of substitution being used as if Jesus is being condemned instead of humans.

The remedy for Sin in Romans is deliverance and rescue. And this is because Paul conceptualizes Sin as a personified power and agent that deceives, enslaves, and kills and so needs to be conquered, subdued, and condemned. Sin for Paul is not conceptualized as a contamination that needs to be disinfected from holy objects through cultic atonement. Paul is using another conceptual framework than *kipper* because the verbs he uses do not match any sacrificial, let alone, atoning verbs.

ROMANS 3:25–26

Romans 3:25–26 is the ostensible "smoking gun" many point to in order to settle the case that Paul thinks of Jesus as an atoning sacrifice. This will take some time to unpack.

Some understandably think Rom 3:25 is a reference to atonement based on Paul's use of *hilastērion*. Some English translations have "atoning sacrifice" or "expiation," or "propitiation" for *hilastērion* here.[46] None of these interpretations can be substantiated by the actual use of this word in either Jewish or Greek sources, however. As Daniel Bailey notes,

> Unfortunately, past studies of ἱλαστήριον [*hilastērion*] have often allowed theological considerations to overshadow lexicography. Hence it was the *doctrine* of propitiation rather than the actual occurrences of the term ἱλαστήριον in ancient sources that dominated the English-language discussion of Romans 3:25 in the twentieth century.[47]

Paul uses *hilastērion*, rather than the word in the LXX for an atoning sacrifice, which is *hilasmos* (cf. 1 John 2:2; 4:10). Bailey makes clear through his in-depth study of *hilastērion* that "a ἱλαστήριον is always a thing—never an idea or an action or an animal."[48] Further, the problem is that "words ending in -τήριον seldom denote abstract verbal ideas, while ἱλαστήριον never does; the suffix -τήριον is very concrete."[49]

46. Douglas Moo argues God is pouring out divine wrath upon Jesus as a "wrath-averting sacrifice" (*Romans*, 236).

47. Bailey, "Jesus," 155.

48. Bailey, "Jesus," 155; for the full study see his PhD dissertation, "Mercy Seat," 31–75.

49. Bailey, "Jesus," 156.

Hilastērion as Ark of the Covenant Lid?

In the LXX *hilastērion* refers to the lid of the ark of the covenant in the holy of holies.[50] So, *hilastērion* might mean "place of decontamination" since blood is sprinkled on it on the Day of Decontamination.[51] But *hilastērion* in the LXX more regularly connotes the place of *revelation*, both in terms of divine *presence* and the place where God *speaks* (Exod 25:22; 30:6, 36; Num 7:89; Lev 16:2). It only serves as the place of *decontamination* once a year (Lev 16).

Since there are a lot of words in Rom 3:21–26 having to do with divine revelation and objects that are seen (e.g., "manifested" [*phaneroō*], "set forth" [*protithēmi*], "demonstration" [*endeixis*]), this may suggest that what Paul means by *hilastērion* in 3:25 is that *Jesus is the place of divine revelation and presence*. This would be an incarnational claim (similar to Phil 2:6–8). God becomes made manifest in Jesus and especially in Jesus's faithful obedience to the point of death (see Rom 5:6–11, 18–19; Phil 2:8).[52] In this sense,

50. Also, "cover" or "lid" is the straightforward meaning of *kappōret* (Exod 25:22; 30:6, 36). "Mercy Seat" is potentially a theologically motivated interpretive gloss that derives from the Greek root *hileōs* embedded within *hilastērion*. The connotation of "mercy" is not at all in the Hebrew root *k-p-r*. See Feldman, *The Story of Sacrifice*, 64, 188–89; Feldman, "The Idea and Study of Sacrifice in Ancient Israel," 8; Levine, *In the Presence of the Lord*, 56–57; Milgrom, *Leviticus 1–16*, 1079–84.

51. McLean, "The Absence of an Atoning Sacrifice in Paul's Soteriology," 545.

52. Although my argument here is not dependent upon the subjective genitive interpretation of *pistis* in 3:25, it would only be strengthened by such an interpretation. Here I offer an observation that to my knowledge has not been brought up in this debate. Notice that justified (*dikaiōthentes*) by faith (*ek pisteōs*) in 5:1 is paralleled with justified (*dikaiōthentes*) by Jesus's blood (*en tō haimati autou*) in v. 9. Rather than two different modes of justification, this suggests that these are interchangeable and, therefore, that the *pistis* in v. 1 and the *haima* in v. 9 refer to the same thing; namely, Jesus's death. His death is also referred to as a righteous/just act (*dikaiōma*, 5:18) as well as an act of obedience (*hypakoē*, 5:19). Paul no doubt would also think of this as an act of faith(fulness) (*pistis*, 5:1). Thus, when we find all these concepts combined in 3:24–25 (*dikaioumenoi . . . dia tēs pisteōs en tō autou haimati*), the subjective genitive coheres best. My translation of 3:24–25 would be: "they are now justified by his grace as a gift, through the redemption that is in Christ Jesus, whom God put forward [either] as 'the place of divine manifestation and revelation' [or] as 'a votive gift' [I will argue for this option below] through the faithfulness [which comes to its full expression] in his blood." In other words, Paul would be talking about Jesus's continual faithfulness even to the point of a violent death on a Roman cross similar to Phil 2:8 (cf. Rom 5:18–19) since "blood" does not necessarily mean "sacrifice" (and *hilastērion* never refers to a sacrificial *victim*, but rather to an *object*, so "blood" as "sacrifice" is all but ruled out for 3:25), but could simply refer to a violent and bloody death. On this reading, Paul would be conveying: "through Jesus's faithfulness shown in its fullest expression in his violent death upon a cross."

Jesus can be spoken of as the *hilastērion* because he is the *place* where God both *appears* and *speaks*.

But it would have been better, as G. Adolf Deissmann notes, that if "lid of the ark" was what Paul was going for, then he should have said the *cross* was the *hilastērion* and that God was made manifest *on* it in Jesus.[53] This would be keeping with the imagery in the Torah. Also, *hilastērion* is anarthrous in Rom 3:25, and that presents a significant hurdle for the lid of the ark interpretation because this is another missed opportunity where Paul could have made it more clear that he is referring to *the* specific *hilastērion* known by Greek-speaking Jews to be the object (again, not a "sacrifice") in the holy of holies just like other Greek-speaking Jews do (cf. *to hilastērion* in Heb 9:5; Philo, *Cher.* 25; *Her.* 166; *Fug.* 101; *Mos.* 2.95, 97). Granted, there are arguments that seek to overcome this difficulty, but it is not necessary for me to completely foreclose on this lid of the ark interpretation here.[54]

In any case, the Day of Decontamination would be a deficient solution to the preceding context in Romans. This is because the sins that cannot be atoned for since they contaminate the *land* (idolatry, murder, sexual immorality) are all mentioned previously in Rom 1–3 (1:23, 25, 26–27, 29; 2:22; 3:15). Therefore, it is hard to see how Paul would think cultic "atonement" could be anything like a plausible solution to these sins. Another remedy is needed. This coheres with how, just a few sentences after Rom 3:25–26, Paul places the "solution" to sins in a non-sacrificial register by quoting from LXX Ps 31:1–2 (32:1–2 MT) (Rom 4:7–8). There is no mention of sacrifices in Ps 31 (32 MT). Rather, God simply forgives those who ask (31:5–6; cf. David's confession and prayer for purification in Ps 51 that explicitly rejects offering sacrifices for this end in vv. 16–17). Paul uses this psalm as proof that God "accounts righteousness [*dikaiosynē*] apart from works" (Rom 4:6) (cf. *dikaioi* in Ps 31:11 LXX) to "the one who trusts" (*tō . . . pisteuonti*) (Rom 4:5; cf. Ps 31:10 LXX). There is no evidence in Romans (or in the rest of his letters) that Paul conceptualized sin as a contamination that needs to be disinfected from holy objects through sacrificial atonement, which is why Paul always analogizes the remedy for Sin/sins apart from *kipper*.

Nevertheless, here we can conclude that if *hilastērion* refers to the lid of the ark, then (a) it cannot mean it is an atoning sacrifice.[55] Also, (b) it likely does not even primarily mean place of *atonement* because (c) in the Torah it more regularly and explicitly means "place above which God

53. Deissmann, *Bible Studies*, 129.

54. Bailey, "Mercy Seat," 145–76. For another argument against the ark lid interpretation, see McMurray, *Sacrifice*, 61–65.

55. Bailey, "Mercy Seat," 33; Wilson, "*Hilasterion*," 6.

appears and *speaks*." This is strengthened by considering how (d) sacrificial atonement cannot be the solution to the sins Paul is concerned with in Rom 1–3 and (e) how Paul explicitly appeals to the means of forgiveness outside of the sacrificial system.

Hilastērion as a Greco-Roman Conciliatory Gift

I think Deissmann's proposal in 1901 is more promising: *hilastērion* is a votive gift.[56] The word *hilastērion* was used in the wider Greek-speaking world to name a votive gift,[57] or as McMurray calls it, a "conciliatory gift."[58] These were inanimate *objects*, such as "statues, monuments, or stelae" (cf. Josephus, *Ant.* 16.182).[59] For the purposes of this discussion I will use *gift* and *sacrifice* distinctively so that gift refers to an inanimate object and a sacrifice refers to an animal offering.[60] And, as Bailey determines, "since we do not have a single example of a ἱλαστήριον that is a sacrificial animal [in Jewish or pagan literature or inscriptions], we shall have to abandon the idea that a ἱλαστήριον is a victim."[61]

While conciliatory gifts were "brought to the deities in order to induce them to be favourable,"[62] these could also be used between two parties at enmity in order to reconcile "at the end of a conflict."[63] That is, they could be offered as a way of seeking some sort of reconciliation with another party (i.e., to pacify the other party, to turn away their enmity) by stimulating the favor of their enemy's god.

For example, Bailey points out that "the most famous ἱλαστήριον in the ancient world was the Trojan Horse," which "was called a θελκτήριον or 'charm' by Homer (*Od.* 8.509)."[64] According to Dio Chrysostom, the Trojan Horse had "*hilastērion* from the Achaeans to Athena of Ilium" inscribed

56. Deissmann, *Bible Studies*, 130–35.

57. See also LSJ, s.v. ἱλαστήριος II.2. Notably, Levitical votive offerings are never called a *hilastērion*. The LXX uses *euchē* instead (e.g., Lev 7:16) and these are animal sacrifices, not inanimate gifts/objects. Further, they are one of the three well-being offerings in Lev 7:11–18, all of which are *non-atoning* sacrifices.

58. McMurray, *Sacrifice*, 67.

59. Bailey, "Jesus," 156, cf. 157.

60. Cf. Deissmann, *Bible Studies*, 130.

61. Bailey, "Mercy Seat," 66; cf. 17, 33, 56.

62. Deissmann, *Bible Studies*, 130–31; cf. Malkin, "Votive Offerings," 1564–65.

63. McMurray, *Sacrifice*, 68.

64. Bailey, "Jesus," 156; cf. Bailey, "Mercy Seat," 46–55; McMurray, *Sacrifice*, 70.

upon it (*Troj.* 11.121).[65] And, "two later commentators on Homer also call the horse a ἱλαστήριον (anonymous scholia, ed. Dindorf [1855]; comm. by Eustathius of Thessalonica, ed. Stallbaum [1825])."[66] Virgil, writing in Latin, refers to the horse as votive gift (*votum*) as well (*Aen.* 2.15).[67] The Trojans thought the Greeks were apologizing for attacking Athena's temple and people and were beseeching her goodwill for their journey home since they decided to call off the war and make peace.

In Dio Chrysostom's (lived ca. 40–120 CE) retelling of the ancient story, "Odysseus, as a leading member of the peace embassy that the Greeks (who *lost* the war according to this version of the story) are supposed to have sent to the Trojans, is depicted as suggesting a settlement which involved the Greeks leaving behind a very large and beautiful votive offering instead of paying war reparations."[68] In *Troj.* 11.121, the peace plan was "[f]or the Greeks [to] leave a very large beautiful [votive] offering (*anathēma* [cf. 11.128]) to Athena and carve upon it this inscription: 'A *hilastērion* from the Achaeans to Athena of Ilium.'"[69] Dio aims to argue that the Trojans actually did not loose the war, but that this idea arose from a misunderstanding because the Trojans "removed a portion of the walls when the gates did not admit its [the horse's] passage" (*Troj.* 11.123) to bring it inside the city since the horse was too large to fit within the gates: "Hence the ridiculous story of the capture of the city by the horse" (11.123). The rumor spread, according to Dio, that since the "walls came down," so to speak, Troy had fallen when in fact, according to him, "The [Greek] army departed under truce in this way" (11.123).[70] In any case, Dio's use of *hilastērion* evinces how it was used to identify an object aimed at pacification and reconciliation. In fact, he says that it was given "for peace" (*hyper tēs eirēnēs*) (11.122). And, in Dio's telling, it worked! There were no hidden Greeks inside the horse. "So hostilities were brought to an end, and a truce was made between the Trojans and the Achaeans" (11.122).

Additionally, 4 Maccabees has an interesting parallel use of *hilastērion* in 4 Macc 17:22 (ca. first century CE) with Rom 3:25 with respect to the martyrdoms of Eleazar the priest, a mother, and her seven sons. Since *hilastērion* as a sacrificial victim is ruled out for the same aforementioned

65. Translation and Greek text throughout from: Dio Chrysostom, *Discourses 1–11*. I intentionally left *hilastērion* untranslated.

66. Bailey, "Jesus," 156; cf. Bailey, "Mercy Seat," 46–55.

67. Virgil, *Eclogues. Georgics. Aeneid: Books 1–6*.

68. Bailey, "Mercy Seat," 52–53.

69. My brackets and I left *hilastērion* untranslated.

70. Cf. Bailey, "Mercy Seat," 53.

reasons and because "[i]t makes no sense to speak of 'the mercy seat of their death' in 4 Maccabees,"[71] this means *hilastērion* is used "in essentially the same sense that it has in the Greek inscriptions" and it is applied to the death of the martyrs.[72] In short, 4 Macc 17:22 is an instance of a Greek-speaking Jew appropriating the Greco-Roman notion of a votive gift (*hilastērion*) to humans and this corroborates the plausibility that Paul might be doing a similar thing in Rom 3:25.

To bring further clarity as to why *hilastērion* cannot mean a sacrificial victim and why "votive gift" makes the most sense in the context of 4 Maccabees, however, it is necessary again "to distinguish between sacrifices (i.e., victims) and offerings (here inanimate things)."[73] Whereas Bailey uses *offering* to make this distinction I have been using *gift* to make this more apparent since I think *offering* is still too easily confused with (animal) *sacrifice* in English. Nevertheless, what is pertinent is "whereas one is transient [i.e., the sacrifice], the other is durable [i.e., the votive gift]."[74] As Irad Malkin summarizes, "Unlike sacrifice, where one destroys, by depositing a perceptive object [a votive gift] in a sanctuary one both loses it and makes it eternal."[75] For instance, Virgil says Aeneas, who saw into the future of Rome's destiny, saw Caesar Augustus dedicate "to Italy's gods his immortal votive gift" (*votum immortale*, *Aen.* 8.715) at his triumph after defeating Antony at the battle of Actium.[76]

The preceding co-text in 4 Macc 17 makes it clear that, as Bailey notes, "The martyrs did not make themselves to be the victims of sacrifice which are totally destroyed (or perhaps consumed) and exist no more; rather, in their death, they deposited their lives with God, losing them in this world in order to make them eternal or rather 'immortal' in the next."[77] The martyrs were "consecrated" (*hagiazō*, 4 Macc 17:19, 20) precisely because they were not perishing in their death, but rather being translated into "the blessed age" (*ho makarios aiōn*), that is currently "living" (*bioō*) and being "present" (*paristēmi*) to the divine throne (17:18: *tō theiō nyn parestēkasin thronō kai ton makarion biousin aiōna*). It is this enduring and living presence in heaven that makes the following comparison in v. 22 of their deaths to a *hilastērion* intelligible. That is, "the death of the martyrs was an *action*

71. Bailey, "Jesus," 158.

72. Bailey, "Mercy Seat," 133.

73. Bailey, "Mercy Seat," 135.

74. Bailey, "Mercy Seat," 135.

75. Malkin, "Votive Offerings," 1564.

76. Latin and translation from Virgil, *Aeneid: Books 7–12*.

77. Bailey, "Mercy Seat," 135.

similar to the *action* of presenting a votive [gift]. . . . The martyrs present their lives as one presents a votive [gift]; they are not making themselves to be like animals."[78] Thus, Bailey glosses 17:18 as conveying that the martyrs "irrevocably dedicated themselves to God in death as one dedicates a votive [gift]."[79] I would only add that this is the case specifically because we are told they were consecrated and are translated into the presence of God (17:18–20). It is the *lives* of the martyrs that are before the divine throne that allows them to function as an eternal votive gift just like earthly votive gifts are perpetually in the temples. The focus is not on their *deaths per se*, but rather, as David deSilva points out, "on the obedience and loyalty to God that leads to such a death."[80] Their deaths are the vehicle or means by which their *lives* can *now* be translated into heaven and thereby lived before the divine throne in the blessed age (7:18).

Another relevant finding comes from inscriptions found in a city in Asia Minor, Metropolis, which is between the biblical cities of Ephesus and Smyrna. Some archaeologists found pillars there in the early 1990s, which are inscribed with *Kaisaros h(e)ilastēriou* (one has a variant spelling).[81] The inscriptions mean, "the reconciling Caesar" and refer to Caesar Augustus (probably still only known by Octavian at the time these were set up ca. 31–27 BCE).[82] As Wilson comments, "[t]he use of the genitive case in Καίσαρος εἰλαστηρίου is a well-known elliptical construction in epigraphical texts wherein the genitive requires a subject, in this case ὁ βομός, 'the altar'" and thus likely means "'(Altar of) Caesar, the bringer of reconciliation.'"[83] Although the use of *hilastērion* is adjectival in relation to Caesar and does not appear to designate the pillar as itself being a *hilastērion*, the historical circumstances of these altars and the use of *hilastērion* may nevertheless be relevant for understanding the resonances Paul may be expecting his gentile Roman audience to tune into.

Briefly summarized, after Julius Caesar's death, the empire fell into a brutal civil war between Caesar's great-nephew and adopted heir, Octavian, and Mark Antony. Metropolis was loyal to Mark Antony, but Octavian ended up winning the war. Instead of punishing the cities loyal to Mark Antony, Octavian went on a grand clemency and reconciliation mission

78. Bailey, "Mercy Seat," 136; his emphasis. Also, Bailey has "offering," which I changed to "gift" for greater clarity.

79. Bailey, "Mercy Seat," 136.

80. deSilva, *4 Maccabees*, 252.

81. Wilson, "*Hilasterion*," 1, 3–4.

82. Wilson, "*Hilasterion*," 4–5.

83. Wilson, "*Hilasterion*," 5.

and initiated the Pax Romana.[84] He permitted citizens, especially those in regions once loyal to Mark Antony, to erect votive gifts that celebrated his divine virtues.[85] And these particular votive gifts were set up between 31–27 BCE as gestures of reconciliation from the citizens of Metropolis. They were set up in celebration of Octavian's clemency and to demonstrate Metropolis's allegiance to Octavian since they previously were loyal to Antony.

Although rejecting the votive-gift interpretation for Rom 3:25, Wilson argues that Paul's use of *hilastērion* in Rom 3:25 might echo Octavian's reconciliation mission of clemency, of "passing over previously committed sins" to use Paul's words, which were commemorated by these altars. But I think Deissmann and Wilson's views can be combined. Paul not only appears to be capitalizing on the votive-gift meaning of *hilastērion*, as the author of 4 Maccabees did, but he also seems to be alluding (and inverting) the scenario with Octavian with his use of *hilastērion* in Rom 3:25.

On the basis of what has been demonstrated thus far we can say this: given that Paul is writing to Roman gentiles (ex-pagans, cf. 1:5–6; 11:13, 18–24; 15:14–16) and, as noted, *hilastērion* is not the word used by the LXX for any sacrifice (let alone a Levitical votive offering) and that *hilastērion* is pervasive in texts about and inscriptions on conciliatory votive gifts, there is every reason to suspect that Paul is using *hilastērion* in Rom 3:25 in the sense of a Greco-Roman votive gift. As Deissmann observes, "it [is] quite impossible that Paul should not have known the word in this [Hellenistic] sense" and "the Christians of the capital [Rome] . . . would know what a ἱλαστήριον was in their time."[86] This would mean Paul is saying that God puts forth Jesus as a conciliatory gift *to humanity* (the opposing party at enmity with God).[87] That is, *God is the giver* (this is made clear by the syntax in Rom 3:25 because *theos* is the subject of the active verb *protithēmi*; cf. 8:32) and humanity is the recipient.

If this is a Greco-Roman conciliatory votive gift, which were meant for "advertising the donors,"[88] then it would be to show forth God's merciful good will toward ungodly humanity at enmity with him (cf. Rom 5:5–11; 4:5; 8:31–39; for the themes of "mercy" in Romans: 9:15, 18, 23; 11:30–32; 15:9). This would also cohere with the depiction in 2 Cor 5:18–20. This reconciling "conciliatory gift" is thus actually meant to turn away humanity's enmity and anger toward God so that reconciliation might take place (Rom 5:10; 2 Cor 5:18–20; cf. Col 1:21–22). The words "manifested" (*phaneroō*,

84. Wilson, "*Hilasterion*," 5.

85 Images are available in Wilson, "*Hilasterion*," 3–4.

86. Deissmann, *Bible Studies*, 132.

87. Similarly, McMurray, *Sacrifice*, 68, 70–71.

88. Malkin, "Votive Offerings," 1565; cf. Bailey, "Mercy Seat," 137–38.

Rom 3:21), "set forth" (*protithēmi*, v. 25), and "demonstration" (*endeixis*, vv. 25, 26) all fit within the context of a votive gift more broadly because the many votive gifts discovered are about celebrating a god's virtues.[89] Further, as McMurray argues, the use of *anochē* (v. 26) strengthens this case since "its primary meaning is actually that of armistice, or truce."[90] Hence, "the nub of it is that *Christ was set forth as a conciliatory gift (ἱλαστήριον) . . . in the truce of God*."[91]

Additionally, these passages all fit with the story of Octavian's reconciliation endeavors, and with his former enemies more specifically—these altars were erected to demonstrate and commemorate something about Octavian's reconciling character. It is hard to believe that this is all just a massive coincidence, that Paul's understanding of God's action toward world in Jesus Christ would cohere so precisely with Octavian's reconciliation mission and that *hilastērion(s)* (a *hapax legomenon* in Pauline letters) is a key word used in both situations. True, the altars set up to honor Octavian are not themselves *hilastēria*, but rather Octavian is described as being a merciful reconciler (*hilastērios*). For Paul, he says that Jesus himself is a *hilastērion* (Rom 3:25), the same way the martyrs in 4 Maccabees were conceptualized.

My contention, though, is that by using *hilastērion*, Paul is primarily activating the conciliatory votive-gift motif in Greco-Roman culture, which itself evokes stories of reconciliation. But unlike the martyrs in 4 Maccabees who are offering themselves as votive gifts *to God*, Paul says God put forth Jesus as a conciliatory gift *to humanity* to demonstrate God's merciful character of divine justice (*dikaiosynē*, Rom 3:25–26). Further, the word *hilastērion* itself already conveys the notion of "mercy." And, as Bailey has noted, "Philo traced the term ἱλαστήριον etymologically not to ἱλάσκεσθαι ('to propitiate *or* expiate') but to ἵλεως, 'gracious' or 'merciful'" (*Fug.* 100; *Mos.* 2.24).[92] Additionally, since incense altars had been set up to honor Octavian's merciful reconciliation (*hilastērios*), Paul's use of *hilastērion* simultaneously activates Octavian's relatively recent empire-altering campaign of mercy.[93]

89. Deissmann, *Bible Studies*, 130, 132.

90. McMurray, *Sacrifice*, 68; cf. 70.

91. McMurray, *Sacrifice*, 68; his emphasis; cf. 72 and "[t]he new peace (εἰρήνη) of 5:1 fits with truce" (76).

92. Bailey, "Jesus," 157.

93. "[I]n other eastern cities similar altars to Augustus might have been erected, possibly even in Rome. Their sole discovery in Metropolis could just be an accident of epigraphical history. Therefore, it can be hoped that additional examples of imperial inscriptions with ἱλαστήριος will be discovered in excavations at other ancient sites" (Wilson, "*Hilasterion*," 8).

Again, the words Paul uses in this context are "set forth" (*protithēmi*, v. 25), and "demonstration" (*endeixis*, vv. 25, 26). Significantly, a sacrifice is never "set forth" (*protithēmi*) in the LXX or NT.[94] Rather, as noted earlier, sacrifices are only ever "offered" (*prospherō*), "slayed" (*sphazō*), or "sacrificed" (*thyō*). On the other hand, votive gifts are said to be "set/put up" (*anatithēmi*) (e.g., Dio Chrysostom, *Troj.* 11.128; cf. 11.121), which is quite similar to *protithēmi* in Rom 3:25, which is the verb used by Gregory of Nazianzus to speak about votive gifts (*Oration 4: First Invective against Julian*, §86). Paul's verb choice of *protithēmi* means his use of *hilastērion* fits better with the Greco-Roman rather than the LXX context.

And, with Wilson, Paul's comments seem to allude to the story of Octavian's reconciliation endeavors with his former enemies for which altars such as those at Metropolis were erected all over to demonstrate and commemorate Octavian's mercy.

Therefore, since (a) *hilastērion* in Greco-Roman culture evokes gestures of reconciliation more broadly (as votive gifts) and (b) Octavian's clemency and reconciliation more specifically and (c) since the broader story Paul is telling in Romans fits precisely with these themes,[95] the simplest explanation for Paul's lone use of word here is that he is riffing on the Greco-Roman conciliatory votive gifts and not the lid on the ark of the covenant.

The story Paul is telling in Romans is that God is demonstrating his love toward his enemies in Jesus Christ and reconciling himself with them (Rom 5:5–11; cf. 2 Cor 5). God has set forth Jesus as a *hilastērion* to demonstrate his *merciful* justice toward his enemies just like, or better than, Octavian's ostensible mercy (cf. Rom 11:32; 4:5). And, just as the people of Metropolis set up the incense altars to demonstrate their allegiance to Octavian, God is demonstrating his full merciful devotion to humanity by putting forth Jesus as a *hilastērion* and nothing can separate us from that love (8:26–39). The resonance the word *hilastērion* carries for a Greek-speaking Roman audience is thus a convenient way to sum everything Paul goes on to unpack in Romans.

What Paul is claiming by saying that God put forth Jesus as a *hilastērion* is that this is proof of God's righteousness and forbearance (Rom 3:25–26). The cross is not the pre-condition for God's forgiveness.[96] Rather, it is what

94. Cf. Bailey, "Mercy Seat," 20–21, 24–26.

95. Cf. "Reconciliation in Romans is a key subtext" (Wilson, "*Hilasterion*," 6).

96. Similarly from McMurray: "Jesus was put forward as a ἱλαστήριον because God had let the preceding sins go (διὰ τὴν πάρεσιν 3:25). The sequence of events, therefore, is that God let the preceding sins go, and then put Jesus forward as a ἱλαστήριον. There is no necessary suggestion here that Jesus was the mechanism by which the sins were let go. But if God had *already* let the preceding sins go, then what did it mean to put Jesus

proves how unrelenting God's love is, even for God's enemies (5:10–11; 8:31–39). And, humanity is being saved, not from God, but from Sin and Death (e.g., 5:12–7:25; cf. 1 Cor 15:55–56). Paul thinks the cross is what God endures in Jesus as God forgives (Rom 4:7), overlooks (3:25–26), and does *not* account people's sins (4:8; cf. 2 Cor 5:18–19). The death of Jesus is what God undergoes as he loves his enemies so as to be reconciled to them (5:6–11), which requires God to enter "enemy territory" so to speak.

Paul is essentially saying:

> Look at Jesus! God is not your enemy! You are the ones at enmity with God. God is justifying you even though you are ungodly. God has put forth Jesus as a conciliatory votive gift of peace and reconciliation to demonstrate this. Be reconciled to God! God loves you! If God did not spare God's own Son, then nothing can separate you from the love of God revealed and manifested in Jesus Christ. Jesus eternally stands in the presence of God (like votive gifts stand in temples) interceding for us all.

This is a summary of the substance of what Paul is conveying in Rom 4:5; 5:5–11; 8:31–39 and 2 Cor 5:18–20 (and whoever wrote Col 1:20–22). It is clear that these concepts in these texts cohere with what *hilastērion* means in Greco-Roman culture and, therefore, it is very likely that this is why Paul uses *hilastērion* in Rom 3:25. This one word, *hilastērion*, in Greco-Roman culture carries the precise nuances that appear in Rom 4:5; 5:5–11; 8:31–39; and 2 Cor 5:18–20.

Apart from a prior external theological need to do so, it strains credulity to seek any other sense for the term. There is no reason to search for another sense when the most commonsense use of the term for Greek speakers not only poses no exegetical quandaries, but also solves the ostensible mystery for interpreter's like Moo, cited above, who think Paul wanted to say "atoning sacrifice," but used the wrong word.

Addressing an Objection to the Votive Gift Interpretation

Bailey, doubting that *hilastērion* in Rom 3:25 is a votive gift, says "no one has ever succeeded in showing how God is supposed to have presented humanity . . . with a gift that people normally presented to the gods."[97]

However, the above passages I highlighted all show exactly what Bailey says has yet to be shown; namely, that God is reversing the roles and

forward as a ἱλαστήριον?" (*Sacrifice*, 70).

97. Bailey, "Jesus," 157.

offering something to and for humanity. For instance, this is the whole point of Paul's reference to Abraham's offering of Isaac by alluding to Gen 22:12 in Rom 8:32. For Abraham, this showed his full and complete devotion to God. By reversing the roles and using this to illumine *God's* act in Jesus Christ, Paul says this shows God's full and complete devotion to humanity that nothing and no one can ever nullify for any reason (8:31–39). Moreover, it is particularly because of these types of reversals that Paul knows his gospel was considered "foolishness" (*mōria*, 1 Cor 1:18, 23) and a "cause for offence" (*skandalon*, v. 23). Deissmann articulates this point masterfully:

> God has *publicly set forth* the crucified Christ in His blood in view of the Cosmos—to the Jews a stumbling block, to the Gentiles foolishness, to Faith a ἱλαστήριον. The crucified Christ is the votive-gift of the Divine Love for the salvation of men. Elsewhere it is human hands which dedicate to the Deity a dead image of stone in order to gain His favour; here the God of grace Himself erects the consoling image,—for the skill and power of men are not sufficient. In the thought that God Himself has erected the ἱλαστήριον, lies the same wonderful μωρία of apostolic piety which has so inimitably diffused the unction of artless genius over other religious ideas of Paul.[98]

Now, some may want to claim that Paul meant both "lid on the ark" and "votive gift." Occam's razor would suggest, however, that Paul is simply capitalizing on the Greco-Roman context in his use of *hilastērion* since this is the most easily discernible context for his gentile audience in Rome. But, even if one is disinclined to accept this, the Jewish context in the LXX would allow Paul to make an incarnational claim about Jesus as the embodiment of divine revelation and God's attributes. The LXX context still does not make this about an atoning sacrifice or appeasing God's wrath.

But it is less plausible to suppose that Paul expected most of his ex-pagan audience to recognize *hilastērion* as an LXX allusion given the pervasiveness of *hilastērion* in the pagan context. Thus, the Greco-Roman context makes the most sense and accounts for all the data we find in Romans. It allows Paul to make a claim about God's devotion and goodwill toward God's enemies in order to be reconciled to them by putting forth Jesus as conciliatory votive gift, an enduring demonstration of God's merciful righteousness. In either case, though, "a ἱλαστήριον was never . . . an 'atoning sacrifice'"[99] (let alone a substitutionary sacrifice that averts God's own wrath).[100]

98. Deissmann, *Bible Studies*, 132–33; his emphasis.

99. Bailey, "Mercy Seat," 33.

100. Moo, *Romans*, 236.

As shown above with respect to Rom 8:3, the remedy for sin in Romans is deliverance and rescue. And this is because Paul conceptualizes Sin as a personified power and agent that deceives, enslaves, and kills and so needs to be conquered, subdued, and condemned. Sin for Paul is not conceptualized as a contamination that needs to be disinfected from holy objects through sacrificial atonement. As we have seen, *other* NT writers, such as the authors of 1 John and Hebrews, go this route, but there is no evidence Paul himself does. In both Rom 8:3 and 3:25 we have evidence that Paul is using another conceptual framework, especially because the verbs he uses do not match any sacrificial, let alone, atoning verbs.

CONCLUSION

As in previous chapters, the present discussions have exemplified how important comprehending sacrificial imagery is for avoiding exegetical errors when reading NT texts that talk about the meaning and purpose of Jesus's death. The prevalence of conflating any notion of the saving significance of Jesus's death with the concept of "sacrifice" and/or "atonement" makes these discussions necessary.

It is now apparent how relatively *rare* sacrificial imagery is within NT texts that address the meaning and function of Jesus's death. And many texts that modern readers often interpret to speak of sacrifice turn out, under examination, not to do so. None of the texts examined above, for instance, are making an analogy to any Levitical sacrifice.

Without belaboring these points, we can turn now to the final implications of our study.

8

Conclusion

FROM A VARIETY OF angles this study has demonstrated that while Jesus is comprehended in the NT as relating to various aspects of Israel's sacrificial and purity system, sacrifice is never about punishing the sacrificial animal with death (or suffering) in place of the offerer. We saw how Levitical sacrifice reconceptualized the necessary killing of the sacrificial animal into "not-a-killing." Neither *death* nor *suffering* nor *punishment* of the animal has any place in the sacrificial system. Therefore, all Christian theologies that attempt to derive a view of justice on the mistaken view that biblical sacrifice is about punishment or substitutionary death must be utterly rejected by any Christians seeking to anchor their views in the biblical texts themselves. There is no biblical warrant to sustain any such views. These interpretations are only possible by imposing alien frameworks and concepts onto "sacrifice" and "atonement."

Moreover, we learned how there are both atoning and non-atoning sacrifices, which are indexed by whether the offerer eats from it. If they eat from it, then it cannot be an atoning sacrifice for their sins. The primary function for the non-atoning sacrifices is to share in a holy meal in God's presence, often to give thanks for some prior act of divine deliverance. These can be individual sacrificial meals or corporate ones like Passover and covenant-making or covenant-renewal ceremonies.

Crucially, we realized that sacrificial atonement (*kipper*) is limited in what it purifies. *Kipper* is only about decontaminating the sanctuary and its attendant sancta from either ritual impurities or sin-contamination. And there is a further limitation for *kipper:* atoning sacrifices can only purge certain sins. Grave sins (idolatry, murder, and sexual immorality) contaminate the sinner as well as the land thereby exceeding the reach and capacity of atoning sacrifices. The only remedy for this moral impurity is the death of the sinner and/or exile so that the land can be cleansed.

All this makes it possible to see how Jesus is most often understood in the NT on analogy to the non-atoning well-being sacrifices: primarily the Passover and covenant-making sacrifices. This understanding is enacted in the Lord's Supper, which is a ritual sacrificialization for both.

Further, we discovered how this sacrificial understanding of Jesus's death was memorializing an act of divine deliverance since commemoration is the primary function of these non-atoning sacrifices. This divine deliverance is often framed as a moral purification on analogy to ritual purification whereby Jesus is a contagious source of holiness that purges all manner of impurities on contact. Therefore, his contact with death and subsequent resurrection encapsulates the salvation of the world, brought through the curse of death and into indestructible life.

Additionally, we saw how two NT authors (1 John and Hebrews) explicitly associate Jesus with the atoning sacrifices. Here we observed how Jesus's ascension was interpreted as indexing him as a high priest in the heavenly sanctuary. His indestructible life could therefore serve as the purgative element for decontaminating the heavenly sanctuary. But more than this, Hebrews claims that Jesus's life-blood also functions on analogy to water to purify believers. Additionally, Jesus's blood serves like the non-atoning sacrificial blood used in the consecration of priests such that believers are made co-high priests with Jesus. As well, Hebrews shows how believers are made into co-purgation sacrifices with him as they bear his reproach in cruciform suffering.

Finally, it has become clear that there are manifold problems with the notion of "substitution" applied either to Levitical sacrifice or to Jesus. Here I want to press into this by way of conclusion and delve into a few critical texts that expose how inadequate substitution is to express the meaning and significance of Jesus's death.

THE INADEQUACIES OF "SUBSTITUTION" TO CONSTRUE THE SAVING UNIQUENESS OF JESUS

I reject the concept of substitution because it obscures how Jesus's death is not only ethically paradigmatic, but also, according to the NT, *the reality* that those united with Jesus literally *participate* and *share* in experientially by the Spirit. The concept of substitution grates against the call to participate in the cross since, by definition, it conceptualizes Jesus's death as something he endured *so that others can avoid it*. Penal substitutionary atonement names the cross as what those who benefit from Jesus's death necessarily get to *escape* since it is construed as "in our place" and "instead of us." It thereby opens the door to the satanic idea that one can be a disciple of Jesus and avoid the cross (Mark 8:33). That is the exact opposite of what passages like 1 Pet 2:21–25, 3:17–18, and Mark 10:38–45 say. The consistent message throughout the entire NT is not that Jesus died *instead* of us; rather, it repeatedly indicates that Jesus dies *ahead* of us so that we can unite with him and be conformed the image of his death (Rom 6:5; Phil 3:10).

However, Jesus's death is soteriologically unique. And part of its uniqueness is because Jesus is our pioneer and forerunner, setting the pattern and paradigm for what covenant faithfulness of loving God and loving neighbor means. Jesus's death is unique, especially since it generates the singular reality that grounds Christian ethics that all can share in—or rather, will share in (Col 1:27 and 3:10–11). We are baptized with *his* same baptism of the cross, we drink from *his* same cup of the cross (cf. Mark 10:38–45). The point is union with Christ (participation and solidarity), not separation and distance (substitution).

It is solidarity and participation all the way down. Remember, all disciples are called to share in Jesus's baptism and cup (Mark 10:38–39; cf. Matt 20:22–23). Jesus was expecting co-crucifixion with his followers (e.g., Mark 8:34; 10:38–39; John 12:24–26; 13:16–17, 36; 15:18, 20; 16:1–4). And, while not happening during Jesus's actual crucifixion, this—co-crucifixion—remains the ever-present expectation and way of talking about Christian discipleship (John 21:18–22; Gal 2:20; 6:14; Rom 6:3–8; Phil 3:10–11; 2 Cor 4:10–11; Col 1:24; 2:12; 3:1, 3–4; 1 John 2:6, 3:16–18; 1 Pet 2:21). "Substitution," as defined by Gathercole in the previous chapter, logically and necessarily resists this framing of the Christian life as total union and participation in Christ, specifically and especially in Christ's death.

Jesus's taking on sinful flesh (Rom 8:3) and experiencing the curse of the covenant (Gal 3–4) is an act of solidarity and union—"cursed solidarity 'atonement'" if you like, and so long as "atonement" here means "reconciliation" rather than *kipper*. It's only a prior commitment to penal substitutionary atonement that shoehorns that concept of "substitution" into these acts of divine *solidarity*.

I have struggled to find a better analogy, but in the NT, and Paul's writings in particular, Christ is like a "cosmic voodoo doll." This is the best metaphor I can think of to convey the inextricable union of the experience of Jesus and the experience of the cosmos, especially in Paul's thinking/

writings (Rom 5:12–21;1 Cor 15:22; 2 Cor 5:14–15).[1] "Christ is all things and in all things" (Col 3:10–11) such that what happens to him happens to/is experienced by all (1 Cor 15:22; 2 Cor 5:14–15; Gal 6:14–15; Rom 5:12–21; 6:6; cf. Eph 1:10, 20–23; 2:5–6; Col 1:27; 2:9–15; 3:1–4, 11). The connection between Christ and all is inseparable. This trades in participation/solidarity logics; not substitution.

Further, in Hebrews, Jesus's suffering was not anything *beyond* the human condition under Sin and Death. It was full participation in humanity's plight. It was *for* the benefit of all, not as a "substitution," but so that by partaking of "the same [blood and flesh] . . . through death he would nullify the one who has the power of death, that is, the devil" since "he tasted death for everyone" (Heb 2:9–14, here vv. 14 and 9 respectively). Jesus's death is in full *solidarity* with humanity's death. It has saving power because of *who* it is that partook of "blood and flesh" to heal and free us. The one who partook of blood and flesh and shared in the "same" death plaguing humanity possesses "indestructible life" (7:16). Jesus has implanted this life within humanity as leaven in a lump of dough. By means of Jesus's total solidarity with humanity, his indestructible life heals and raises the whole "lump" of humanity from death (cf. Gregory of Nazianzus, Oration 30.21).

I want to emphasize that I uphold the *uniqueness* of Jesus's saving act, but I think "substitution" is a wrongheaded and misleading term to conceptualize that uniqueness. Let's use another analogy (based on a true story): If my kids are trapped to their knees in quicksand and I get in there and get muddy to rescue them, how do you conceptualize what I just did? What do you call me? I know one thing, you wouldn't call me a "substitute." Replace "quicksand" with "curse" or "Sin and Death" and me with Jesus and this is Paul's narrative of divine deliverance and the Gospels' portrayal of Jesus as the destruction of Jerusalem *in nuce*. "Substitution" does not accurately conceptualize what is happening. "Solidarity" is more on target.

Solidarity, participation, union, and co-crucifixion are by definition non-substitutionary concepts. There's a double solidarity/participation going on. Jesus first participated in the curse and death of human existence so that then we can participate *in a very real way* in his death as well as his resurrection. Again, it's solidarity all the way down.

Christians ought not insist on retaining a word like "substitution" that makes conformity to the cruciform image of Christ incoherent. If Jesus is our substitute, why do we need to take up the cross? Why do we need to

1. Though this idea is found elsewhere too (e.g., Matt 25:35–45; Acts 9:4–5; 22:7–8; 26:14–15).

have fellowship with his sufferings? Why do we need to be co-crucified with Christ?

Since we don't conceptualize many people who perform analogous acts of deliverance, rescue, or healing as "substitutes" (surgeons, quicksand rescuers, etc.), then there is no need to do that for Jesus apart from an *a priori* (and problematic) assumption about what salvation "must entail." All I know is that whatever Jesus did, the overwhelming apostolic witness is that we are called to share and participate in it. "Substitute" is a theologically impoverished way at trying to sum that up. Jesus is our deliverer and healer. He is not our substitute.

SUBSTITUTIONARY RESURRECTION?

To further expose how incoherent the notion of Jesus as substitutionary death is, it is important to see how it is the *resurrection* of Jesus that bears a lot of the soteriological significance for Paul in particular. Jesus's resurrection only makes sense as a tandem with his crucifixion. The logic Paul employs is consistently: *as* goes our relation to Jesus's death, *so* goes our relation to his resurrection (e.g., Rom 6:5; Phil 3:10–11; cf. 2 Cor 4:10; Col 2:12). If Jesus's death is substitutionary, then so is his resurrection. But if his resurrection isn't substitutionary, then neither is his death.

As demonstrated in the preceding chapters, the logic in Paul is never "Jesus died instead of us" but rather, "Jesus died ahead of us and that allows for us to share in his same death so that his life might also be made known in our bodies and to others" (cf. 2 Cor 4:7–12; 5:14–15). In this participatory logic, it would be rather jarring and incomprehensible for Paul to suddenly turn and say: "Actually, never mind the whole thing about sharing in Jesus's death; he died as your substitute."

Many insist on just this sort of understanding of Paul, however, due to a mistaken understanding of the preposition *hyper* used in a few key places (e.g., Rom 5:6–8; 1 Cor 15:3; 2 Cor 5:21).[2]

2. E.g., Gathercole, *Defending Substitution*, 71, 73–74, 79, 85–86, 103–7. Also, the fact that Paul uses the preposition *hyper* means he is unlikely to be making an allusion to any sort of sacrificial "atonement." This is because in the LXX Torah when atonement is said to be "for" someone or "for" sins the preposition consistently used is *peri* (Exod 30:15, 16; 32:30; Lev 1:4; 4:20, 26, 31, 35: 5:6, 10, 13, 16, 18, 26; 8:34; 9:7; 10:17; 12:7, 8; 14:18, 19, 20, 21, 29, 31; 14:53; 15:15, 30; 16:6, 11, 16, 17, 24, 30, 33, 34; 17:11; 19:22; 23:28; Num 5:8; 6:11; 8:12, 19, 21; 15:25, 28; 17:11–12 [16:46–47 Eng.]; 25:13; 28:22, 30; 29:5, 11; 31:50 [these are gold and jewelry that make atonement]; cf. 1 Chr 6:34; 29:24; Neh 10:34; Sir 16:7; 45:16, 23; Pss. Sol. 3:8). Therefore, there is no warrant for Gathercole's claims that "the variations in the prepositions [*hyper* and *peri*] are not particularly significant" and "[t]he prepositions are almost interchangeable"

Reassessing What "for Us" Means

Now that we can set the concept of atonement (*kipper*) aside, if *hyper* is about *substitution* when used in relation to Jesus's death, then this would also necessarily mean that Jesus's resurrection is substitutionary. By definition this would indicate no one else will ever be raised since Jesus was our substitutionary resurrection: he is resurrected so that no one else has to be. This, of course, is unthinkable!

2 Corinthians 5:15 and 21

This point can be demonstrated by attending to how Paul uses the preposition *hyper* in 2 Cor 5:15 and 21. Anyone who insists that the phrase *hyper hēmōn* ("for us") is inherently substitutionary in places like 2 Cor 5:21 needs only to read a few sentences earlier where Paul has already ruled out a substitutionary connotation of the phrase in 5:15: "And he died *hyper* all, so that those living might no longer be living for themselves, but to the one who died and was raised *hyper* them."

Grounded in his stubborn participatory logic, Paul uses *hyper* twice here to mean "for the sake of" or "for the benefit of" and it *cannot* carry substitutionary overtones.[3] Both Jesus's death and resurrection are *hyper pantōn/autōn* ("for the sake of all/them") (5:15). If there was a word to conceptualize this, it would not be "substitution" because then this would mean Jesus's resurrection is also substitutionary. The phrase "inclusive

(*Defending Substitution*, 67). The priestly authors are very precise with their verbs and prepositions, as discussed in previous chapters. This precision is attested in the NT as well since the only texts that explicitly link Jesus's death in an atoning register—1 John and Hebrews—both use *peri* (cf. 1 John 2:2; 4:10; Heb 5:3 [three times]; 10:26). The only possible places in the NT where *hyper* might be conflated with *peri* in a sacrificial context are all in Hebrews (5:1; 7:27; 10:12). However, in addition to what I argued in chapter 6 regarding 10:12 in particular, given how precise the preposition usage is in the Torah it seems most likely that *hyper* in these passages means "because of" or "by reason of" (LSJ, s.v., "ὑπέρ" 2.4) rather than being synonymous with *peri* as "for." That is, the relationship between the sacrifices and the *hyper* prepositional phrases conveys that the sacrifices are offered *because of sins*—i.e., *since* these sins contaminated the sancta, these sacrifices needed to be offered. If *peri* was used, then a different yet related aspect of the relationship between sacrifice and offerer would be highlighted; namely, that these sacrifices are offered *for* decontaminating the sin-contamination the people generated by their sins. Since the causal valence of *hyper* makes sense in all three passages, there is no need to postulate an atypical meaning of this preposition as if it were simply synonymous with *peri*.

3. If *hyper* is inherently substitutionary, then several passages that use the word become unintelligible: e.g., Acts 9:16; 15:26; 21:13; Col 1:24; Col 2:1: Mark 9:40; John 6:51; 13:37; 17:19; Heb 2:9; 6:19–20 compared with 10:19, 22.

participatory representation" might work or the word "recapitulation" that Irenaeus was so fond of (see Eph 1:10). What is clear enough, however, is both Jesus's death and resurrection benefit "all/them/us" precisely because it means that human beings not only benefit from, but also *participate in* his very death and resurrection. The benefit *is sharing in* Jesus's resurrection because we *share in* Jesus's death by our own cruciform sufferings (cf. Phil 3:10–11; Rom 6:5).

Similarly, then, when Christ was "made sin" or "became a curse" *hyper hēmōn* (2 Cor 5:21; Gal 3:13), Paul is not inserting a diametrically opposed logic—a logic of substitution—into his participatory mode of explaining the meaning of the incarnation, death, and resurrection of Jesus. Gathercole's rather astute definition of substitution rightly recognizes how incompatible each line of reasoning is. Rather, Paul is only talking about how Christ's *full participation* in the sinful and cursed conditions of humanity is a *benefit for* humanity. Similar to how both Jesus's death and resurrection are *hyper pantōn/autōn* because human beings are supposed to participate in them (2 Cor 5:15), Jesus's coming under sin and curse *hyper hēmōn* is the first logical step in Paul's thinking: human beings can participate in Christ because he *first* participated in us by coming under sin and curse as we were. And Christ did all of this for our benefit. In all cases, then, *hyper* is Paul's means of communicating both benefit for humanity *and* the solidarity and participation between both Christ and all humanity.

Therefore, when Christ was "made sin" or "became a curse" *hyper hēmōn* (2 Cor 5:21; Gal 3:13), he was not doing something substitutionary because these statements are about the whole incarnation whereby Jesus was simply entering into the same condition human beings *already were* experiencing. He is not taking upon himself something that human beings never experienced, should have experienced, but now will not have to. These statements are about Jesus fully sharing in the *already present* (albeit cursed) conditions of humanity. It was his perfect obedience (cf. Rom 5:18–19; Phil 2:8) in these conditions and resurrection from out of these conditions that allows this incarnation to be for the benefit (*hyper*) of all "in him" (2 Cor 5:21; Gal 3:13) since they are freed from sin and curse insofar as they are united *with* him in his death and resurrection. Again, if Jesus's resurrection "on our behalf" (*hyper*, 2 Cor 5:15) is not substitutionary—no one says, "Jesus's substitutionary resurrection"—then it makes no sense to think his death is substitutionary. For, if his death is substitutionary, then so is his resurrection.

Moreover, the fact that the resurrection is the basis for "dealing with sins" (cf. 1 Cor 15:3) is made clear in 1 Cor 15:17: "If Christ has not been raised . . . you are still in your sins." If it was Jesus's death alone that dealt with sins in some substitutionary way, then the consequence of Jesus not being resurrected would not be that humans are still in their sins (15:17). It would be something like: Well, your sins are dealt with (forgiven/cleansed/whatever concept you wish to place here), but we still do not know what is going to happen for sure after your body perishes (but most of us Jews believe in some sort of bodily resurrection of the dead so let us hope for that for Jesus and everyone else on judgment day; and let's just be glad we do not have to worry about being damned for our sins).

Paul is consistent with this emphasis upon Jesus's resurrection as dealing with sins in Rom 4. First, he equates justification with forgiveness in Rom 4:6–7 in his only use of *aphiēmi* ("forgiveness") in the (undisputed) Pauline letters denoting divine forgiveness of sins (and he is quoting its use in LXX Ps 31:1–2). Second, in Rom 4:25 he states that Jesus "was raised on account of our justification" immediately after saying "he was delivered over on account of our transgressions." Thus, as with 1 Cor 15:3, 17, it is the *resurrection* that effects "dealing with sins." If there is no resurrection, then, according to Paul, you are not justified/forgiven (Rom 4:6–7, 25b) and you are still in your sins (1 Cor 15:7).

Therefore, in the same way that Jesus's resurrection is "for the benefit of" (*hyper*) others and no one attempts to conceptualize it as a *substitution*, I do not think Paul is conceptualizing Jesus's death as a substitution in these passages either. The two go together hand in hand. The death and resurrection of Jesus are "for" others only to the extent that others are joined with them (e.g., 1 Cor 15:22; Rom 6:3–8).

Romans 5:6–8

This is what Gathercole does not take into consideration in his defense of substitution. He does not grasp *how* it is that Jesus's death is a benefit for others. In Gathercole's treatment of Rom 5:6–8, for example, he argues that "Paul's language about Jesus dying 'for us' echoes very closely the language used frequently in non-Christian literature to describe substitutionary or vicarious deaths."[4] That is, "the most natural link in Romans 5 is with examples of vicarious death in classical texts (broadly understood)."[5] What is most important for Gathercole is that in the classical texts "the death 'for' another is not merely a death 'for the benefit of' another—'for their sake' in a general sense. Nor is it a death *with* them. . . . These examples . . . are all about one person who stands in the place of another, and so they offer a

4. Gathercole, *Defending Substitution*, 85.

5. Gathercole, *Defending Substitution*, 90.

useful parallel to and background for Paul's substitutionary conception of Jesus's death."[6]

My concerns with Gathercole's exegesis of Rom 5:6–8 are both methodological and exegetical. I am unsure why Gathercole thinks that classical texts function as a more determinative hermeneutical context (method) than the actual co-text of Rom 5–8 (exegetical). It should go without saying that I am in favor of reading Paul in dialogue with his historical context, but I think Gathercole went about this comparative reading prematurely. That is, he went to the classical texts before considering the co-text of Rom 5–8 and this caused him to find similarity (vicariousness) where there is in fact a great difference.

Granting that Rom 5:7 indeed alludes to classical examples of vicarious deaths, after considering the co-text of Rom 5–8 we can see Paul presents Jesus's death as different in *two* ways from the classical examples whereas Gathercole only finds *one*. First, as Gathercole points out, in Rom 5:6–10 Paul shows how Jesus's death is different from the ones alluded to in 5:7 because it was for "helpless" "ungodly" "sinners" that were the "enemies" of God (as opposed to being for a "righteous" or "good person," per 5:7).[7] Second, while the reader may think immediately upon finishing 5:6–10, "I wonder if Jesus's death is substitutionary?" they will wonder no more once reading further since Paul will soon make explicit that Jesus's death is neither vicarious nor "exclusively substitutionary" as the ones alluded to in 5:7 might have been. This is because Jesus's death not only *identifies with* the current human condition of suffering in death as "the wages of sin" (6:23; cf. 5:12–21), but it also makes possible for the beneficiaries a co-death (co-crucifixion and co-burial) with Jesus (6:2–11; cf. 7:4; 8:17).

Paul's explication of Jesus's death fails to meet Gathercole's own requirements for what constitutes substitution. According to Rom 5–6, Jesus is not taking on consequences that its beneficiaries are spared. Quite the opposite. Those benefiting from Jesus's death *already were* in death and under condemnation since "death" is construed in Rom 5–6 as the current condition of humanity, already experiencing the "wages [i.e., consequences] of sin" (6:23). Moreover, humanity is enabled to *participate in* Jesus's death (6:2–11). Jesus identifies with and participates in humanity in order that humanity can identify with and participate in Jesus—if there is a word that encapsulates that concept it is not *substitution* since, as Gathercole himself is acutely aware, substitution logically rules out any notions of "with."[8]

6. Gathercole, *Defending Substitution*, 107.

7. Gathercole, *Defending Substitution*, 104–5.

8. Gathercole, *Defending Substitution*, 15, 20.

I concede that by itself Rom 5:6–8 has "room" for a substitutionary view of Jesus's death, but the passage alone by no means makes that certain. There is "room" for substitution in 5:6–8 only until we read how Paul explains the meaning of *how* Jesus's death benefits others (i.e., how it is that it is "for" [*hyper*, 5:6, 8] them). What is made clear in Rom 5–8 is that Jesus's death is a benefit to others *only to the extent that they participate in it* (e.g., 6:5)!

To be clear: it is certainly not the case that 5:6–10 articulates an explicitly substitutionary view and 5:12—6:11 articulates an explicitly representation or participatory view and readers simply have to be satisfied with the polyvalence of these juxtaposed texts. The fact of the matter is that Rom 5:6–8 by itself is ambiguous, and therefore, the reader needs to seek clarification in the surrounding co-text as to what it means for Jesus's death to be (a) "for us" (5:8) and (b) what it means for it to be *unlike* other deaths that we might be tempted to compare it with per 5:7 (where Paul is at pains to communicate that it is unprecedented).

Because Gathercole does not attend to the co-text of Rom 5–8, he seeks to relieve the ambiguity of 5:6–8 by recourse to classical texts that speak about vicarious deaths using "the same language that we find in Paul—dying 'on behalf of' (*huper*) another in the sense of 'in place of' or 'instead of.'"[9] He fails to notice, therefore, that while the classical texts indeed speak of vicarious substitutionary deaths, Paul's articulation of how Jesus's death is "on behalf of" or "for" (*hyper*) others (Rom 5:6, 8) in the co-text of Rom 5–8 rules out "substitution" as Gathercole has himself defined it. The classical texts speak about beneficiaries who do not themselves have to die (because someone died *in place of* them) while Paul speaks about beneficiaries who are themselves already suffering under death, need to be joined with Jesus's death/crucifixion in particular, and are also, then, in need of a resurrection with Jesus.

This illustrates the danger of rushing outside a given text to bring clarity to a few verses that are ambiguous on their own. What is going on in Rom 5:6 and following is Paul making clear how Jesus's death, although similar in a certain sense to classical vicarious deaths, differs from these in two important ways: (1) Jesus dies for the benefit of his *enemies* and (2) Jesus's death is only a benefit to those who are *joined* with it and *share* in it themselves. Whatever this is, it is *not a substitutionary death.*

Furthermore, substitution does not even make sense within Paul's basic narrative logic of salvation, which can be summarized thus:[10] (1)

9. Gathercole, *Defending Substitution*, 92.

10. I am distilling Rom 5:12—6:23, 8:1–25, and Phil 2:1–11 (and Col 1:15–24,

Disobedience/sin is ubiquitous in human beings because Sin's domain of lordship is mortal flesh. (2) This causes all sorts of problems for humanity and the biggest problem is that all this sin/disobedience results in death. (3) Jesus was truly human in every way, but even though he was made "in the likeness of sinful flesh" (Rom 8:3), he remained fully obedient within Sin's dominion, died, and was resurrected from the dead. (4) The resurrection means Jesus has defeated death and broken Sin's lordship over mortal flesh (cf. 6:9). (5) Therefore, if Jesus defeated the ultimate result of sin/disobedience, then he in fact defeated sin/disobedience itself. (6) Therefore, if one is united with Jesus's death (co-crucifixion), then one can walk in the newness of life—a life of obedience like his by putting to death the deeds of the flesh—and be assured of one's own co-resurrection as well. Everything Paul says on the topic of salvation either illustrates, explicates in further detail, or provides the warrants for these points.

At no point would substitution (penal or otherwise) properly conceptualize what Paul thinks is happening in Christ. If we are determined to pick a word to conceptualize Paul's thought, then Irenaeus's use of the Pauline word "recapitulation" might be it (see *anakephalaioō* in Eph 1:10). This whole thing is not "place-taking" (substitution), but rather "place-sharing" (solidarity, union, participation): Jesus, the Son of God, first shared and participated in the cursed condition of humanity albeit fully obedient (incarnation), delivered it from that condition (resurrection), and then and only then can anyone now share and participate in his divine condition (justification, sanctification, glorification) since he is the new "head" of humanity.

LAMB OF THE FREE

I wanted to expose the problems with the notion of substitution by way of conclusion because it helps bring into relief how the sacrificial interpretations of Jesus's death in the NT operate within the paradigm of participation. The well-being sacrifices activated via the Lord's Supper and the atonement and high-priestly theology in Hebrews all reinforce this basic participatory logic and exclude the concept of substitution.

Again, Jesus's death is soteriologically *unique*, but that uniqueness is not captured by the idea of substitution. Rather, Jesus is unique because he himself generates and just *is* the *condition* for humanity's participation in him and specifically in his death and resurrection.

To revisit Paul's use of the well-being sacrifices in relation to Jesus's death, no matter which way we slice it, Paul is not operating with a notion

2:9–15, 20, 3:1–11).

of substitution in either 1 Cor 5:7 or 11:25. In between these passages, Paul asks:

> The cup of blessing that we bless, is it not a sharing [*koinōnia*] in the blood of Christ? The bread that we break, is it not a sharing [*koinōnia*] in the body of Christ? Because there is one bread, we who are many are one body, for we all partake [*metechō*] of the one bread. Consider the people of Israel; are not those who eat the sacrifices partners [*koinōnia*] in the altar? (1 Cor 10:16–18)

Here we get a clear statement that Paul is working within the logic of participation. For Paul, this is all about "sharing" (*koinonia*) (1 Cor 10:16, 18, 20) and "partaking" (*metechō*) (10:17, 21) in these sacrificialized well-being offerings and thereby having fellowship with God and Jesus. And it is by *partaking* of the well-being offering that is Jesus's body that those in Christ become made participants in his broken body and shed blood and made members of the new covenant (10:16–18; 11:23–25). It is by this that we become "living sacrifices"—living well-being sacrifices—ourselves (cf. Rom 12:1). This explains why Paul calls himself a drink offering, which accompanied the well-being sacrificial feast (Phil 2:17). And he says the Philippians's gift for him can be thought of as the smoke of the well-being sacrifices that pleases God (4:18).

The well-being sacrifices are key to understanding the way Paul conceives of the relationship between Jesus and the church, which Paul calls Jesus's body (1 Cor 12:12–13, 27; Rom 12:5). The well-being sacrifices allow Paul a way to make sense of believers' very real participation and union with Jesus's death (and resurrection) because these are the only sacrifices the offerers have a share in themselves. It therefore makes perfect sense that well-being sacrifices are used to both illumine and enact the meaning of Jesus's death for a movement that saw itself as the body of the crucified Lord and called to share in his sufferings as well. If Jesus is a well-being sacrifice and we are his body and we sacrificially partake of his body and blood, then this means we become a collective "living well-being sacrifice" as a new-covenant people united to the final Passover lamb.

Similarly, as we saw in chapter 6, the sacrificial atonement theology of Hebrews is predicated on a thoroughgoing theology of participation. Jesus is a high priest according to the order of Melchizedek so that those united to him can also, as co-high priests, go beyond the veil and enter the holy of holies with him (Heb 10:19–20; 4:16; 6:19–20). Further, just as Jesus was associated with the purgation offerings on the Day of Decontamination, *so are we*, according to 13:11–13. Hebrews has a *participatory kipper* theology, not a substitutionary *kipper* theology.

The consistent testimony of the NT texts, whether sacrificial imagery is activated or not, is a theology of union and participation in and with Jesus by his Spirit. We need, therefore, to find an adequate substitute for the word "substitutionary." Using "atonement" in a broader sense than *kipper*, what the NT authors teach is a "participatory atonement" or "cursed solidarity atonement" theology.

I titled this book *Lamb of the Free* since Jesus as the non-atoning Paschal Lamb is the earliest and most common sacrificial image applied to Jesus. The Passover memorializes Israel's liberation from Egypt and now with Jesus the liberation of the cosmos from Sin and Death. But whether atoning or non-atoning, the framework within which all sacrificial interpretations of Jesus's death are comprehended is antithetical to a substitutionary one. Not only is there no such thing as substitutionary death sacrifice in the Torah, but also everything in the NT texts is aimed at grounding the exhortation for the audience to be conformed and transformed into the cruciform image of Jesus *by sharing in his death*. I also titled it *Lamb of the Free* as a play on words with the national anthem of the United States because I want to highlight how the salvation and freedom Jesus gives to the world upends the worldly notions of freedom and justice as represented in the US national anthem. Those who share in Jesus's death are "free" from the reign of Sin and Death in their mortal bodies (Rom 5–8; cf. Heb 2:14–15). They are "free" to enact a merciful justice, the very justice that was revealed in Jesus Christ (Rom 1:16–17; 3:21–26). They are "free" to enter the heavenly holy of holies as co-high priests (Heb 10:19–22), "free" to be co-purgation sacrifices with Jesus (13:10–13) and co-well-being sacrifices (cf. Rom 12:1; Phil 2:17; 4:18; 2 Cor 2:14; Eph 5:2), "free" to have fellowship in Jesus's sufferings and death so that we might share in his resurrection (Phil 3:10–11; 2 Cor 4:10–14; Rom 6:3–11), and "free" to continually offer sacrifices of thanksgiving (cf. Heb 13:15; 1 Pet 2:5).

Therefore, understanding the concepts of sacrifice and *kipper* properly is part of understanding the story of salvation the NT is telling. For instance, if we think sacrifice is all about punishment and retributive justice, then we will fundamentally misconstrue the sacrificial images applied to Jesus. This means we will misconstrue what "salvation" and "justice" mean because these terms will be informed and defined by alternative stories and frameworks. But getting the concepts and story right are crucial, not only for an individual Christian's formation, but also our collective formation as part of a common and shared tapestry faithfully witnessing to the salvation of God in Jesus Christ as his body, the church.

Understanding the NT's sacrificial imagery ought to re-frame our imaginations. For example, when we think about the story of Passover and the covenant inaugurated on Sinai, the story of the exodus, we realize that eating from the table of the Lord as the ultimate Passover lamb and mediator of the new covenant fundamentally reframes our relationship to all the nations, let alone our home nation. These are the "Egypts" from which we are being liberated, we who are being ruled over by what Paul calls the "powers"—the "pharaohs," Sin and Death—and what Peter calls "your empty way of life handed down from your ancestors" (1 Pet 1:18). Jesus is the "lamb of the free" (cf. 1:19) because he sets us free from the reign of these pharaohs and their futile disorderly forms of life, which manifest in the various idols all peoples have worshiped since the beginning; and the church has been lured into as well (wealth, security, pleasure, punishment, strength, etc.). We are being liberated to be a corporate well-being sacrifice for the life and healing of all the nations of world. We are announcing to the world the conquest of the pharaohs Sin and Death, which enslave and trap the nations in all manner of systems of oppression and domination.

So when we get the sacrificial concepts right by understanding the larger story of which they are a part, then we can find our place within that story, and as Paul says, become sharers and partakers of the body and blood of Jesus (1 Cor 10:16–17). And by so doing we become a living well-being sacrifice ourselves (Rom 12:1), narrating the death of Jesus in our bodies for the life and reconciliation of the world (2 Cor 4:10–12; 5:14–21).

Bibliography

Achtemeier, Paul J., Joel B. Green, and Marianne Meye Thompson. *Introducing the New Testament: Its Literature and Theology*. Grand Rapids: Eerdmans, 2001.

Anderson, Gary A. "Sacrifice and Sacrificial Offerings: Old Testament." In *ABD* 5:870–86.

Baden, Joel S. *The Composition of the Pentateuch: Renewing the Documentary Hypothesis*. New Haven, CT: Yale University Press, 2012.

———. "The Purpose of Purification in Leviticus 16: A Proposition Pertaining to Priestly Prepositions." *VT* 71 (2020) 19–26.

Baden, Joel S., and Candida R. Moss. "The Origin and Interpretation of *Ṣāraʿ* in Leviticus 13–14." *JBL* 130 (2011) 643–62.

Bailey, Daniel P. "Jesus as the Mercy Seat: The Semantics and Theology of Paul's Use of *Hilasterion* in Romans 3:25." PhD diss., University of Cambridge, 1999. https://doi.org/10.17863/CAM.17213.

———. "Jesus as the Mercy Seat: The Semantics and Theology of Paul's Use of *Hilasterion* in Romans 3:25." *TynBul* 51 (2000) 155–58.

Balberg, Mira. *Blood for Thought: The Reinvention of Sacrifice in Early Rabbinic Literature*. Oakland: University of California Press, 2017.

Barber, Michael P., and John A. Kincaid. "Cultic Theosis in Paul and Second Temple Judaism." *Journal for the Study of Paul and His Letters* 5 (2015) 237–56.

Bauckham, Richard. *The Theology of the Book of Revelation*. Cambridge: Cambridge University Press, 1993.

Baumgarten, Joseph M. "Messianic Forgiveness of Sin in CD 14:19 (4Q266 10 I 12–13)." In *The Provo International Conference on the Dead Sea Scrolls: Technological Innovations, New Texts, and Reformulated Issues*, edited by Donald W. Parry and Eugene Ulrich, 537–44. STDJ 30. Leiden: Brill, 1999.

Bernier, Jonathan. *Rethinking the Dates of the New Testament: The Evidence for Early Composition*. Grand Rapids: Baker Academic, 2022.

Boersma, Hans. *Violence, Hospitality, and the Cross: Reappropriating the Atonement Tradition*. Grand Rapids: Baker Academic, 2004.

Bowman, Hannah. "From Substitution to Solidarity: Towards an Abolitionist Atonement Theology." *Political Theology* 23.4 (2022) 1–19.

Brown, Raymond E. *The Epistles of John: Translated with Introduction, Notes, and Commentary*. AB. New York: Doubleday, 1982.

Buchanan, George Wesley. *To the Hebrews*. AB 36. New York: Doubleday, 1972.

Cassuto, U. *A Commentary on the Book of Exodus*. Translated by Israel Abrahams. Jerusalem: Magnes, 1967.

Cockerill, Gareth Lee. *The Epistle to the Hebrews*. NICNT. Grand Rapids: Eerdmans, 2012.

Cohen, Aryeh. "Tractate Zevahim." In *The Oxford Annotated Mishnah: A New Translation of the Mishnah with Introductions and Notes*, edited by Shaye J. D. Cohen, Robert Goldenberg, and Hayim Lapin, 3:5–61. Oxford: Oxford University Press, 2022.

Cohen, Shaye J. D. "Tractate Eduyot." In *The Oxford Annotated Mishnah: A New Translation of the Mishnah with Introductions and Notes*, edited by Shaye J. D. Cohen, Robert Goldenberg, and Hayim Lapin, 2:628–77. Oxford: Oxford University Press, 2022.

Cohen, Shaye J. D., Robert Goldenberg, and Hayim Lapin, eds. *The Oxford Annotated Mishnah: A New Translation of the Mishnah with Introductions and Notes*. 3 vols. Oxford: Oxford University Press, 2022.

Collins, John J. *What Are Biblical Values? What the Bible Says on Key Ethical Issues*. New Haven, CT: Yale University Press, 2019.

Danby, Herbert, trans. *The Mishnah: Translated from the Hebrew with Introduction and Brief Explanatory Notes*. Oxford: Oxford University Press, 1933.

Das, A. Andrew. "Models for Relating Sin as a Power to Human Activity in Romans 5:12–21." In *Sin and Its Remedy in Paul*, edited by Nijay K. Gupta and John K. Goodrich, 49–62. Eugene, OR: Cascade, 2020.

Deissmann, G. Adolf. *Bible Studies: Contributions Chiefly from Papyri and Inscriptions to the History of the Language, the Literature, and the Religion of Hellenistic Judaism and Primitive Christianity*. Edinburgh: T. & T. Clark, 1901.

deSilva, David A. *4 Maccabees: Introduction and Commentary on the Greek Text in Codex Sinaiticus*. Hermeneia. Leiden: Brill, 2006.

Dio Chrysostom. *Discourses 1–11*. Translated by J. W. Cohoon. LCL 257. Cambridge, MA: Harvard University Press, 1932.

Douglas, Mary. *Leviticus as Literature*. Oxford: Oxford University Press, 1999.

———. *Purity and Danger: An Analysis of Concepts of Pollution and Taboo*. London: Routledge, 1966.

Eberhart, Christian A. "Atonement: Amid Alexandria, Alamo, and Avatar." In *Atonement: Jewish and Christian Origins*, edited by Max Botner, Justin Harrison Duff, and Simon Dürr, 3–20. Grand Rapids: Eerdmans, 2020.

———. "Characteristics of Sacrificial Metaphors in Hebrews." In *Hebrews: Contemporary Methods—New Insights*, edited by Gabriella Gelardini, 37–64. BibInt 75. Leiden: Brill, 2005.

———. *The Sacrifice of Jesus: Understanding Atonement Biblically*. Minneapolis: Augsburg Fortress, 2011.

Feder, Yitzhaq. *Purity and Pollution in the Hebrew Bible: From Embodied Experience to Moral Metaphor*. Cambridge: Cambridge University Press, 2022.

Fee, Gordon D. *Revelation: A New Covenant Commentary*. Eugene, OR: Cascade, 2011.

Feldman, Liane M. "Sanitized Sacrifice in Aramaic Levi's Law of the Priesthood." *Journal of Ancient Judaism* 2 (2020) 343–68.

———. *The Story of Sacrifice: Ritual and Narrative in the Priestly Source*. FAT 141. Tübingen: Mohr Siebeck, 2020.

Finlan, Stephen. *The Background and Content of Paul's Cultic Atonement Metaphors*. AcBib 19. Leiden: Brill, 2004.
Fishbane, Michael. *Judaism: Revelation and Traditions*. San Francisco: HarperOne, 1987.
Fletcher, Susan, Chad A. Grotegut, and Andra H. James. "Lochia Patterns among Normal Women: A Systematic Review." *Journal of Women's Health* 21.12 (2012) 1290–94.
Fletcher-Louis, Crispin. "Ben Sira 50: The High Priest Is an Incorporative Divine Messiah and At-One-Ment Takes Place through Worship in the Microcosm." In *Atonement: Jewish and Christian Origins*, edited by Max Botner, Justin Harrison Duff, and Simon Dürr, 89–111. Grand Rapids: Eerdmans, 2020.
France, R. T. *The Gospel of Mark: A Commentary on the Greek Text*. NIGTC. Grand Rapids: Eerdmans, 2002.
Furstenberg, Yair. "Controlling Impurity: The Natures of Impurity in Second Temple Debates." *Dine Israel* 30 (2015) 163–96.
Gane, Roy E. *Cult and Character: Purification Offerings, Day of Atonement, and Theodicy*. Winona Lake, IN: Eisenbrauns, 2005.
Gathercole, Simon. *Defending Substitution: An Essay on Atonement in Paul*. Grand Rapids: Baker Academic, 2015.
Gilders, William K. *Blood Ritual in the Hebrew Bible: Meaning and Power*. Baltimore: Johns Hopkins University Press, 2004.
———. "The Day of Atonement in the Dead Sea Scrolls." In *The Day of Atonement: Its Interpretations in Early Jewish and Christian Traditions*, edited by Thomas Hieke and Tobia Nicklas, 63–73. Leiden: Brill, 2012.
Ginsberg, H. L. "The Oldest Interpretation of the Suffering Servant." *VT* 3 (1953) 400–404.
Girard, René. "Generative Scapegoating." In *Violent Origins: Walter Burkert, René Girard, and Jonathan Z. Smith on Ritual Killing and Cultural Formation*, edited by Robert G. Hamerton-Kelly, 73–105. Stanford: Stanford University Press, 1987.
———. *Violence and the Sacred*. Translated by Patrick Gregory. Baltimore: Johns Hopkins University Press, 1977.
Gorman, Michael J. *The Death of the Messiah and the Birth of the New Covenant: A (Not So) New Model of the Atonement*. Eugene, OR: Cascade, 2014.
———. *Inhabiting the Cruciform God: Kenosis, Justification, and Theosis in Paul's Narrative Soteriology*. Grand Rapids: Eerdmans, 2009.
Guggenheimer, Heinrich W. *The Jerusalem Talmud: Fourth Order: Neziqin: Tractates Ševuʿot and ʿAvodah Zarah: Edition, Translation, and Commentary*. SJ 61. Berlin: de Gruyter, 2011.
Harrington, Hannah K. *The Purity Texts*. London: T. & T. Clark, 2004.
Hart, David Bentley. *The New Testament: A Translation*. New Haven, CT: Yale University Press, 2017.
Hauerwas, Stanley. "Why 'The Way Words Run' Matters: Reflections on Becoming a 'Major Biblical Scholar.'" In *Working with Words*, 94–112. Eugene, OR: Cascade, 2011.
Hendel, Ronald S. "Sacrifice as a Cultural System: The Ritual Symbolism of Exodus 24,3–8." *BZAW* 101 (1989) 366–90.
Holmes, Michael W. *The Apostolic Fathers: Greek Texts and English Translations*. 3rd ed. Grand Rapids: Baker Academic, 2007.

Hooker, Morna D. *From Adam to Christ: Essays on Paul*. Cambridge: Cambridge University Press, 1990.

———. *Jesus and the Servant: The Influence of the Servant Concept of Deutero-Isaiah in the New Testament*. London: SPCK, 1959.

Hoskins, Paul M. "A Neglected Allusion to Leviticus 4–5 in Jesus's Words Concerning His Blood in Matthew 26:28." *BBR* 30 (2020) 231–42.

Janowitz, Naomi. "Rereading Sacrifice: The Semiosis of Blood." *Signs and Society* 3 (2015) 193–208.

Jobes, Karen H. *1 Peter*. Grand Rapids: Baker, 2005.

Johnson, Luke Timothy. *Hebrews: A Commentary*. NTL. Louisville, KY: Westminster John Knox, 2006.

Joseph, Simon J. "'In the Days of His Flesh, He Offered Up Prayers': Reimagining the Sacrifice(s) of Jesus in the Letter to the Hebrews." *JBL* 140 (2021) 207–27.

Kazen, Thomas. *Issues of Impurity in Early Judaism*. Itero 4. Stockhom: Enskilda Högskolan Stockholm, 2021.

Keener, Craig S. *The Gospel of John: A Commentary*. 2 vols. Grand Rapids: Baker Academic, 2003.

Khazardoost, Soghra, Fahimeh Ghotbizadeh, Shiva Golnavaz, and Masoumeh Shafaat. "The Relationship between Ultrasonic Findings of Postpartum Uterus after Normal Vaginal Delivery and the Duration of Lochia Discharge." *Tehran University Medical Journal* 75 (2017) 187–93.

Klawans, Jonathan. "Concepts of Purity in the Bible." In *The Jewish Study Bible*, 2nd ed., edited by Adele Berlin and Mark Zvi Brettler, 1998–2005. Oxford: Oxford University Press, 2014.

———. *Impurity and Sin in Ancient Judaism*. New York: Oxford University Press, 2000.

———. *Purity, Sacrifice, and the Temple: Symbolism and Supersessionism in the Study of Ancient Judaism*. Oxford: Oxford University Press, 2006.

Knohl, Israel. *The Sanctuary of Silence: The Priestly Torah and the Holiness School*. Minneapolis: Augsburg Fortress, 1995.

Kurek-Chomycz, Dominika. "Divine Generosity in the Midst of Conflict: Sin and Its Remedy in 2 Corinthians." In *Sin and Its Remedy in Paul*, edited by Nijay K. Gupta and John K. Goodrich, 81–98. Eugene, OR: Cascade, 2020.

Lane, William L. *The Gospel of Mark: The English Text with Introduction, Exposition, and Notes*. NICNT. Grand Rapids: Eerdmans, 1974.

———. *Hebrews 1–8*. WBC. Nashville: Nelson, 1991.

———. *Hebrews 9–13*. WBC. Waco, TX: Word, 1991.

Levenson, Jon D. *The Death and Resurrection of the Beloved Son: The Transformation of Child Sacrifice in Judaism and Christianity*. New Haven, CT: Yale University Press, 1993.

———. *Inheriting Abraham: The Legacy of the Patriarch in Judaism, Christianity, and Islam*. Princeton: Princeton University Press, 2012.

Levine, Baruch A. *In the Presence of the Lord: A Study of Cult and Some Cultic Terms in Ancient Israel*. SJLA 5. Leiden: Brill, 1974.

———. *The JPS Torah Commentary: Leviticus*. Philadelphia: Jewish Publication Society of America, 1989.

Levine, David. "Tractate Tevul Yom." In *The Oxford Annotated Mishnah: A New Translation of the Mishnah with Introductions and Notes*, edited by Shaye J.

D. Cohen, Robert Goldenberg, and Hayim Lapin, 3:219–36. Oxford: Oxford University Press, 2022.

Levinson, Bernard M. "Deuteronomy: Introduction and Annotations." In *The Jewish Study Bible*, 2nd ed., edited by Adele Berlin and Mark Zvi Brettler, 339–428. Oxford: Oxford University Press, 2014.

Malkin, Irad. "Votive Offerings." In *The Oxford Classical Dictionary*, 4th ed., edited by Simon Hornblower, Antony Spawforth, and Esther Eidinow, 1564–65. Oxford: Oxford University Press, 2012.

Marcus, Joel. *John the Baptist in History and Theology*. Studies on Personalities of the New Testament. Columbia: University of South Carolina Press, 2018.

———. *Mark 8–16*. AB. New Haven, CT: Yale University Press, 2009.

McCarthy, Dennis J. "Symbolism of Blood and Sacrifice." *JBL* 88 (1969) 166–76.

McLean, Bradley H. "The Absence of an Atoning Sacrifice in Paul's Soteriology." *NTS* 38 (1992) 531–53.

———. "The Interpretation of the Levitical Sin Offering and the Scapegoat." *SR* 20 (1991) 345–56.

McMurray, Patrick. *Sacrifice, Brotherhood, and the Body: Abraham and the Nations in Romans*. Lanham, MD: Rowman & Littlefield, 2021.

Méndez, Hugo. "Did the Johannine Community Exist?" *JSNT* 42 (2020) 350–74.

Middleton, J. Richard. *Abraham's Silence: The Binding of Isaac, the Suffering of Job, and How to Talk Back to God*. Grand Rapids: Baker Academic, 2021.

Milgrom, Jacob. "Further on the Expiatory Sacrifices." *JBL* 115 (1996) 511–14.

———. "Israel's Sanctuary: The Priestly 'Picture of Dorian Gray.'" *RB* 83 (1976) 390–99.

———. *The JPS Torah Commentary: Numbers*. Philadelphia: Jewish Publication Society of America, 1989.

———. *Leviticus: A Book of Ritual and Ethics*. CC. Minneapolis: Augsburg Fortress, 2004.

———. *Leviticus 1–16: A New Translation with Introduction and Commentary*. AB. New York: Doubleday, 1991.

———. *Leviticus 17–22: A New Translation with Introduction and Commentary*. AB. New York: Doubleday, 2000.

———. "The Modus Operandi of the *Ḥaṭṭāʾt*: A Rejoinder." *JBL* 109 (1990) 111–13.

———. "The Rationale for Biblical Impurity." *JANESCU* 22 (1993) 107–11.

———. "Sacrifices and Offerings, OT." In *IDBSup*, edited by Keith Crim, 763–71. Nashville: Abingdon, 1976.

———. "Sin-Offering or Purification-Offering." *VT* 21 (1971) 237–39.

Miller, Yonatan S. "Tractate Yoma." In *The Oxford Annotated Mishnah: A New Translation of the Mishnah with Introductions and Notes*, edited by Shaye J. D. Cohen, Robert Goldenberg, and Hayim Lapin, 1:589–627. Oxford: Oxford University Press, 2022.

Moffitt, David M. *Atonement and the Logic of Resurrection in the Epistle to the Hebrews*. NovTSup 141. Leiden: Brill, 2011.

———. "Blood, Life, and Atonement: Reassessing Hebrews' Christological Appropriation of Yom Kippur." In *The Day of Atonement: Its Interpretations in Early Jewish and Christian Traditions*, edited by Thomas Hieke and Tobias Nicklas, 211–24. Leiden: Brill, 2012.

———. "It Is Not Finished: Jesus's Perpetual Atoning Work as the Heavenly High Priest in Hebrews." In *So Great a Salvation: A Dialogue on the Atonement in Hebrews*, edited by Jon C. Laansma, George H. Guthrie, and Cynthia Long Westfall, 157–75. London: T. & T. Clark, 2019.

———. "Jesus as Interceding High Priest and Sacrifice in Hebrews: A Response to Nicholas Moore." *Journal for the Study of the New Testament* 42 (2020) 542–52.

———. "Righteous Bloodshed, Matthew's Passion Narrative, and the Temple's Destruction: Lamentations as a Matthean Intertext." *JBL* 125 (2006) 299–320.

Moo, Douglas J. *The Epistle to the Romans*. NICNT. Grand Rapids: Eerdmans, 1996.

Morales, L. Michael. *Who Shall Ascend the Mountain of the Lord? A Biblical Theology of the Book of Leviticus*. Downers Grove, IL: InterVarsity, 2015.

Moscicke, Hans M. "Jesus, Barabbas, and the Crowd as Figures in Matthew's Day of Atonement Typology (Matthew 27:15–26)." *JBL* 139 (2020) 125–53.

Oppenheimer, L. W., Elizabeth A. Sherriff, J. D. S. Goodman, Dina Shah, and Catherine E. James. "The Duration of Lochia." *British Journal of Obstetrics & Gynaecology* 93 (1986) 754–57.

Peeler, Amy L. "If Son, Then Priest: The Filial Foundation of Ordination in Hebrews and Other New Testament Texts." In *Listen, Understand, Obey: Essays on Hebrews in Honor of Gareth Lee Cockerill*, edited by Caleb T. Friedeman, 95–115. Eugene, OR: Pickwick, 2017.

Peres, Caio. "Bloodless 'Atonement': An Exegetical, Ritual, and Theological Analysis of Leviticus 5:11–13." *JHebS* 20.6 (2020) 1–36. https://doi.org/10.5508/jhs29566.

Rillera, Andrew Remington. "A Call to Resistance: The Exhortative Function of Daniel 7." *JBL* 138 (2019) 757–76.

———. "Tertium Genus or Dyadic Unity? Investigating Sociopolitical Salvation in Ephesians." *BR* 66 (2021) 31–51.

Sanders, E. P. *Jesus and Judaism*. Philadelphia: Fortress, 1985.

———. *Judaism: Practice and Belief: 63 BCE–66 CE*. London: SCM, 1992.

Sarna, Nahum M. *Exodus*. JPS Torah Commentary. Philadelphia: Jewish Publication Society of America, 1991.

Schwartz, Baruch J. "The Bearing of Sin in Priestly Literature." In *Pomegranates and Golden Bells: Studies in Biblical, Jewish, and Near Eastern Ritual, Law, and Literature in Honor of Jacob Milgrom*, edited by David P. Wright, David Noel Freedman, and Avi Hurvitz, 3–21. Winona Lake, IN: Eisenbrauns, 1995.

———. "Leviticus: Introduction and Annotations." In *The Jewish Study Bible*, 2nd ed., edited by Adele Berlin and Mark Zvi Brettler, 193–266. Oxford: Oxford University Press, 2014.

———. "The Prohibitions Concerning the 'Eating' of Blood in Leviticus 17." In *Priesthood and Cult in Ancient Israel*, edited by Gary A. Anderson and Saul M. Olyan, 34–66. JSOTSup 125. Sheffield, UK: Sheffield Academic, 1991.

Shauf, Scott. *Jesus the Sacrifice: A Historical and Theological Study*. Lanham, MD: Rowman & Littlefield, 2022.

Shively, Elizabeth E. "Purification of the Body and the Reign of God in the Gospel of Mark." *JTS* 71 (2020) 62–89.

Sklar, Jay. *Leviticus: An Introduction and Commentary*. Downers Grove, IL: InterVarsity, 2014.

Smith, Jonathan Z. "The Bare Facts of Ritual." *History of Religions* 20 (1980) 112–27.

———. "The Domestication of Sacrifice." In *Violent Origins: Walter Burkert, René Girard, and Jonathan Z. Smith on Ritual Killing and Cultural Formation*, edited by Robert G. Hamerton-Kelly, 191–205. Stanford: Stanford University Press, 1987.

———. *To Take Place: Toward Theory in Ritual.* Chicago: University of Chicago Press, 1987.

Stackhouse, John G., Jr. "Terminal Punishment." In *Four Views on Hell*, 2nd ed., edited by Preston Sprinkle, 61–81. Grand Rapids: Zondervan, 2016.

Stökl, Daniel. "Yom Kippur in the Apocalyptic *imaginaire* and the Roots of Jesus' High Priesthood: Yom Kippur in Zechariah 3, 1 Enoch 10, 11QMelkizedeq, Hebrews and the Apocalypse of Abraham 13." In *Transformations of the Inner Self in Ancient Religions*, edited by Jan Assmann and Guy G. Stroumsa, 349–66. Leiden: Brill, 1999.

Streett, Daniel R. "Cursed by God? Galatians 3:13, Social Status, and Atonement Theory in the Context of Early Jewish Readings of Deuteronomy 21:23." *Journal for the Study of Paul and His Letters* 5 (2015) 189–209.

Taylor, Joan E. *The Immerser: John the Baptist within Second Temple Judaism.* Grand Rapids: Eerdmans, 1997.

Thiessen, Matthew. *Jesus and the Forces of Death: The Gospels' Portrayal of Ritual Impurity within First-Century Judaism.* Grand Rapids: Baker Academic, 2020.

Thompson, Marianne Meye. *John: A Commentary.* NTL. Louisville, KY: Westminster John Knox, 2015.

Tigay, Jeffrey H. *Deuteronomy.* JPS Torah Commentary. Philadelphia: Jewish Publication Society of America, 1996.

———. "Exodus: Introduction and Annotations." In *The Jewish Study Bible*, 2nd ed., edited by Adele Berlin and Mark Zvi Brettler, 95–192. Oxford: Oxford University Press, 2014.

VanderKam, James C. *Jubilees: A Commentary in Two Volumes.* Hermeneia. Minneapolis: Augsburg Fortress, 2018.

Virgil. *Aeneid: Books 7–12. Appendix Vergiliana.* Translated by H. Rushton Fairclough. LCL 64. Cambridge, MA: Harvard University Press, 1918.

———. *Eclogues. Georgics. Aeneid: Books 1–6.* Translated by H. Rushton Fairclough. Revised by G. P. Goold. LCL 63. Cambridge, MA: Harvard University Press, 1916.

Visness, Cynthia M., Kathy I. Kennedy, and Rebecca Ramos. "The Duration and Character of Postpartum Bleeding among Breast-Feeding Women." *Obstetrics and Gynecology* 89 (1997) 159–63.

von Rad, Gerhard. *Genesis: A Commentary.* Rev. ed. OTL. Philadelphia: Westminster, 1972.

Williams, Logan. "Melchizedek, the Son of Man, and Eschatological Jubilee: The Sin-Forgiving Messiahs in 11QMelchizedek and Mark." *JSNT* (2023) 1–39.

———. "The Stomach Purifies All Foods: Jesus' Anatomical Argument in Mark 7.18–19." *NTS* (forthcoming).

Willi-Plein, Ina. "Some Remarks on Hebrews from the Viewpoint of Old Testament Exegesis." In *Hebrews: Contemporary Methods—New Insights*, edited by Gabriella Gelardini, 25–35. BibInt 75. Leiden: Brill, 2005.

Wilson, Mark. "*Hilasterion* and Imperial Ideology: A New Reading of Romans 3:25." *HTS Teologiese Studies/Theological Studies* 73.3 (2017) a4067. https://doi.org/10.4102/hts.v73i3.4067.

Wright, David P. "The Gesture of Hand Placement in the Hebrew Bible and in Hittite Literature." *JAOS* 106 (1986) 433–46.

Zohar, Noam. "Repentance and Purification: The Significance and Semantics of *Ḥaṭṭā ʾt* in the Pentateuch." *JBL* 107 (1988) 609–18.

Index

OLD TESTAMENT

Genesis

	13n14
1	17
1:29	17, 18
2:16	17, 18
3:18–19	17, 18
4:11	23
4:11–12	85, 132
6:14	122n92
9	124
9:3–5	22
9:3–6	17, 125n103
9:4	123n98, 229
9:4–6	119
9:5	125, 125n103
9:6	186n97, 198n128
14:18	182
22	12n14, 13n14
22:1	13n14
22:1–19	12n14
22:2	12n14
22:7	13n14
22:9–10	12n14
22:12	270
26:30	29n4
31:54	29n4
37:22	186n97

Exodus

	48, 178n77
2:6–7	146
3:45–51	48, 49
5:1–3	178n77
5:8	178n77
5:17	178n77
6:6	203n146, 250
6:6 LXX	203
6:9	59n105
6:11	59n105
6:16 Eng.	59n105
6:18 Eng.	59n105
6:19	59n105
6:22	59n105
6:26 Eng.	59n105
6:29 Eng.	59n105
7:6–10	59n105
7:15	199
7:34–36	59n105
8:8	178n77
8:25–29	178n77
10:15–16	122n92
10:24–26	178n77
11:4	146
11:5	45
12	41, 42, 42n56, 45, 46, 49, 50, 53n88, 181
12:1–23	41
12:6–11	43n63
12:8	43, 44n64
12:8–9	41, 42
12:10	43
12:11	50, 146

Exodus (*continued*)

12:12 45
12:13 45, 50, 53
12:14 44, 45, 57, 179
12:15 44n64, 46
12:19 44n64, 46
12:21 50, 53
12:22 50, 53
12:22–23 53, 63
12:23 45, 50
12:27 42
12:29 45
12:33 146
12:46 193
13:2 47, 48
13:6–7 44n64
13:11–16 47, 47n77
13:13 21, 22n47, 47, 47n77, 48, 86
13:13a 49
13:15 45, 48
15:13 250
18:15–16 48, 49
19:4–6 66n137
19:5 66, 203n146
19:5–6 66, 201, 202
19:6 66, 66n138, 70n4, 203
19:10 199, 199n132, 203n146, 232
19:14 199, 199n132, 203n146
19:14–15 232
20:22—23:19 56, 57
20:24 39, 54n90, 56, 71, 214
20:24 NRSV 31
20:25 57n99
20:26 56
21:1—22:16 56
21:14 11, 12n13, 16, 71n5, 84
21:23 125
21:29–30 113
21:30 113
21:33–36 125n102
22:1 91
22:25 169
22:28–29 47, 47n78
22:29–30 47
22:29–30 Eng. 47, 47n78
23:22 203n146
24 29n4, 35n31, 179, 179n78
24:1–11 39n48
24:3 56
24:3–4 66
24:3–8 56, 57, 66, 66n137, 175n67
24:4–8 227
24:5 29n4, 36, 39, 54, 204n146
24:5–8 146
24:6 55, 56, 57
24:7 57, 66
24:8 28, 54, 55, 57, 59, 68, 179, 186, 203n144
24:9–11 29n4
24:11 54, 204n146
25:1–7 60n113
25:8 60n111, 70, 71, 96
25:21–22 70
25:22 200n135, 260, 260n50
25–29 58
26:1–6 60n113
26:31–37 60n113
26:33 70
26:34 70
28:1—29:30 60n113
28:36–38 200n135
28:41 58n105
29 58
29:3 41
29:4 200n136
29:7 60n112
29:9 58n105, 60n113, 61n116
29:19–20 201
29:19–28 227
29:20 59
29:21 60n112, 60n113, 60n115, 200
29:22 58, 58n105

29:24–25 58n105
29:26 58, 58n105
29:28 58n105, 59, 201
29:29 58n105, 60n113, 200
29:30–36 54
29:31 54, 60
29:35 54, 58n105
29:36 51n84, 91
29:36–37 96, 97, 114
29:37 70, 70n4, 97, 168, 237, 238
29:38–46 30
29:41 31
29:42–45 31–32
29:42–46 71, 197, 214
29:43 32
30 122
30:1–27 54
30:3 146
30:6 70, 200n135, 260, 260n50
30:7–8 33n22
30:9 32n22
30:10 112
30:10 LXX 92, 221
30:12 113
30:15 122, 276n2
30:15–16 113
30:16 276n2
30:19–21 200n136
30:22 54
30:26–29 97
30:28–29 237
30:29 70, 168
30:30 60n112
30:36 70, 200n135, 260, 260n50
31:11 200n135
31:14 60n111
32 195
32:6 207n152
32:21–22 146
32:29 58n105
32:30 276n2
33:15–16 71
34 195
34:6–7 199n131
34:7 194, 195, 196, 199n131
34:8–9 196
34:9 194, 195, 196, 199n131
34:15 29n4
34:18–20 48
34:19–20 47
34:20 21, 22n47, 48, 86
34:25 43
40:10 97n27
40:14–15 60n113, 200
40:15 61n116
40:31–32 200n136
40:35 32

Leviticus

5, 9, 14, 18, 19, 24, 25, 50n81, 52, 71, 81, 85, 85n48, 121, 122n94, 126, 128, 130, 132, 135, 136, 141, 143, 149, 176, 177, 183, 184, 186, 215, 216, 226n28, 236n49
1:1–17 30
1:2–4 30n11
1:4 90, 276n2
1:5 55
1:6 30
1:9 21, 33
1:11 21, 55
1:12 42
1:13 21, 33
1:14–17 15
1–16 133
1:17 33
2 15, 37, 89n2
2:1 32n22
2:2 33
2:3 71n4
2:9 33
2:10 71n4
2:11 48n78
2:15 32n22
3 29
3:2 14, 38, 55

Leviticus (*continued*)

3:3 33
3:5 21, 33
3:8 14, 38, 55
3:9 33
3:11 33
3:13 14
3:14 33
3:16 33
4 98, 186
4 LXX 222n20
4:1—5:13 183
4:1—6:7 171
4:1–12 128, 194n121, 195
4:1–21 129
4:2 92, 95, 127, 185
4:2–35 90
4:3 29n7, 61n116
4–5 51n84
4:5 61n116
4:5–7 29n7, 94, 95, 127
4–6 138
4:6 186
4:7 21, 55, 184–85, 186
4:10 21
4:11–12 172
4:12 29, 29n7, 233, 236
4:13 29n7
4:13–21 194n121
4:16 61n116
4:16–18 29n7, 94, 95, 127
4:17 186
4:18 21, 55, 184–85, 186
4:20 111, 113, 117, 276n2
4:21 29, 29n7, 172, 233, 236
4:22 95, 117, 127, 128
4:22–26 194n121
4:25 21, 38, 55, 93, 95, 127, 184–85, 186
4:26 99n36, 100, 110, 111, 113, 117, 276n2
4:27 95, 117, 127
4:27–31 20
4:27–35 194n121
4:29 127
4:30 21, 38, 55, 93, 95, 184–85, 186
4:31 20, 111, 113, 117, 276n2
4:34 21, 38, 55, 93, 95, 127, 184–85, 186
4:35 111, 113, 117, 276n2
5:1 110, 185
5:1–5 95, 117, 130n111
5:2 185
5:2–3 74, 82, 111
5:2–4 127
5:5–13 120
5:6 99n36, 100, 110, 117, 258, 276n2
5:7–10 15
5:10 82, 99n36, 100, 110, 111, 117, 276n2
5:11 121
5:11–13 15, 21, 89, 120, 142
5:13 82, 111, 117, 276n2
5:14—6:7 Eng. 14, 90
5:14–26 90
5:14–26 MT 14
5:15 64, 91
5:15–18 127
5:16 91, 117, 276n2
5:17 110, 117
5:18 64, 91, 117, 276n2
5:21–22 91, 95
5:21–23 138n130
5:21–24 127
5:24 91
5:25 64, 91
5:26 117, 276n2
6:2–3 Eng. 91, 95
6:2–4 Eng. 138n130
6:2–5 Eng. 127
6:5 Eng. 91
6:6 Eng. 64, 91
6:7 Eng. 117

6:8 32n22
6:15 61n116
6:17 71n4
6:18–22 MT 29n7
6:19–20 116n72
6:20–21 97
6:21 157
6:22 Eng. 61n116
6:22–23 195
6:23 233, 236
6:23 MT 29n7
6:25 71n4
6:25–29 29n7
6:27–28 97, 103
6:27–28 Eng. 97, 116n72
6:28 41
6:28 Eng. 157
6:29 71n4
6:29–30 Eng. 195
6:30 29, 29n7, 127, 172
6:30 Eng. 233, 236
7:1 71n4
7:1–2 64n132
7:1–7 91
7:6 71n4
7:8 30
7:11–15 36n34
7:11–18 29, 36n34, 262n57
7:11–21 35
7:12 40
7:12–13 43
7:13 44n64
7:15 40, 43
7:16 262n57
7:16–18 39
7:18 110
7:18–20 110
7:18–21 176
7:19 80, 83n44
7:20–21 16, 37, 38, 43, 70n4, 71, 74n18, 76, 83n44, 155
7:22–27 23
7:30 33
8 58
8:6 200n136
8:10 97n27
8:12 60n112, 61n116
8:14 93
8:15 51n84, 91, 93, 96, 97, 112, 129
8:18–21 129
8:21 21
8:22 58, 58n105
8:22–23 201
8:23–24 59
8:28 201
8:29 58, 58n105
8:30 60n112, 60n113, 60n115, 61n116, 200
8:30–31 201
8:31 41
8:33 58n105
8:34 276n2
9 35n31
9:2 258
9:7 276n2
9:12–14 129
9:22–24 32
9:30 60
10:10 59, 61, 67, 69
10:17 117, 194, 195, 195n125, 276n2
10:18 29n7
10:19–20 195
11 72n14
11:24–28 73n14, 74, 140n133
11:25 199n133
11:28 199n133
11:32–33 157
11:39–40 73n14, 74, 140n133
11:40 199n133
11:44 66, 70, 70n4, 77
11:44–45 77
11:47 59, 67
12 15, 16n25, 75, 76, 105, 106, 107, 108n57
12:1 76
12:2 102, 104, 106, 106n52, 108n57
12:2–5 101

Leviticus (*continued*)
12:4 60n111, 70, 71n5, 73, 76, 101, 102n40, 104, 105, 106, 107, 108, 108n57
12:4–5 106
12:4–6 101, 102
12:5 76, 104, 106, 106n52, 108n57
12:6 90n4, 101, 104, 105
12:6–7 90
12:6–8 74, 78n32, 91
12:7 90n4, 99n36, 101, 103, 104, 105, 106, 107, 108, 108n57, 117, 258, 276n2
12:7–8 94, 110, 111
12:8 30, 82, 83, 101, 117, 258, 276n2
12:12–18 30
12:14–15 98
12:36–37 30
13:6 199n133
13–14 16n25, 51n81, 75
13:34 199n133
13:46 61n118, 65, 75, 83, 102
13:55–56 199n133
13:58 199n133
14 58, 64, 64n132, 79, 108n57, 153, 154, 163, 224
14:2 79, 81, 102, 104, 105, 153, 160n36
14:2–8 81
14:3 61n118, 62, 63n125
14:3–4 52
14:3–6 50
14:3–8 63
14:4–7 63n124, 93
14:4–8 61n118
14:5–6 148, 159
14:7–8 79, 102, 103
14:8 61n118, 75, 101, 105, 108
14:8–9 101, 102n40, 199n133
14:9 61n118, 62n118, 79, 81, 101, 102, 103, 105, 108
14:9–11 79, 101
14:10 78n32
14:10–11 81, 82n42
14:10–20 62n118
14:11 102
14:12 64
14:12–13 90
14:12–14 61, 63, 63n124, 91n8
14:13 71n4, 258
14–15 161
14:18 276n2
14:18–20 117
14:19 74, 91, 99, 99n36, 100, 104, 108, 109, 276n2
14:19–20 90, 105, 110, 111
14:19a 90
14:20 61n118, 79, 82, 83, 94, 101, 276n2
14:21 64, 276n2
14:21–22 90
14:21–23 78n32
14:22 64n131, 74, 91
14:24–25 90
14:25 61, 63, 63n124, 64, 91n8
14:28 61, 63n124, 90
14:29 276n2
14:30–31 64n131
14:31 91, 117, 276n2
14:31a 90
14:33–53 136
14:34 51, 63n125
14:41 185
14:44 51, 63n125
14:46–47 75
14:47 199n133
14:48 52
14:48–52 51, 53
14:48–53 63
14:50–52 148, 159
14:52 51n84, 91

14:53 276n2
14:54–55 51
14:54–57 63n125
15 16n25, 75, 106
15:5–8 74, 199n133
15:5–11 75
15:10–11 74, 199n133
15:11 155
15:12 157
15:13 79, 101, 102, 103, 104, 105, 148, 159, 199n133
15:13–15 106
15:14 78n32, 99n32
15:14–15 79, 82n42, 91, 99
15:15 99, 99n36, 100, 108, 109, 110, 117, 276n2
15:16 74
15–16 258
15:17 199n133
15:18 74
15:19–24 106
15:20–24 75
15:21–22 74, 199n133
15:25–30 154
15:27 75, 199n133
15:28 79, 101, 102, 103, 104, 105
15:28–30 106
15:29 78n32, 99n32
15:29–30 79, 82n42, 91, 99
15:30 99n36, 100, 108, 109, 110, 117, 276n2
15:31 71, 76, 78, 96, 99, 101, 102, 103, 109, 127, 140n133
16 9, 51n84, 127, 128, 130, 131, 134n119, 138, 171, 189, 260
16:1–28 137, 140
16:2 70, 128, 200n135, 260
16:2–28 137
16:3 93, 128, 194n121
16:5 194n121
16:5–6 93, 128
16:6 276n2
16:8 130n113
16:9 194n121, 258
16:10 130n113
16:11 93, 276n2
16:11–17 95
16:11–19 85n48
16:12–13 128, 129
16:14 129
16:14–15 128, 129, 236
16:14–19 93
16:15 93, 129, 258
16:16 78, 85, 94, 95, 96, 98, 99, 99n36, 100, 101, 103, 109, 110, 113, 127, 129, 133, 276n2
16:16–17 128
16:17 129, 276n2
16:18 93
16:18–19 128, 129
16:19 93, 96, 97, 97n27, 98, 99, 101, 103, 109, 110, 112, 113, 129, 133
16:20 78, 85
16:20–22 128, 129
16:21 14, 94, 95, 110, 127, 129, 130, 189
16:21–22 254
16:24 30n11, 90, 221n18, 276n2
16:24–25 128, 129
16:26 74n16, 116n72, 199n133
16:27 127, 172, 233, 236
16:27–28 103
16:28 74n16, 199n133
16:29 30, 137, 138n131, 215
16:29–30 140
16:29–31 140
16:29–34 128
16:30 99n36, 100, 117, 136–40, 147, 148, 215, 216, 218, 219, 276n2

Leviticus (*continued*)

16:30 LXX 215
16:31 30, 138n131
16:32 58n105, 61n116, 137
16:33 60n111, 70, 85, 115, 116, 133, 254, 276n2
16:33–34 117
16:34 94, 99n36, 100, 110, 113, 276n2
17 15, 17, 20, 21, 22, 23, 38, 72, 123, 124, 125, 125n103, 126
17:1–12 126
17:3–4 19, 23, 119, 121, 123
17:3–4 NRSV 19
17:3–5 19, 20, 26
17:3–6 23, 23n50, 38
17:3–7 123n98
17:4 19, 21, 125, 186n97
17:5 123, 258
17:5–6 19, 121
17:6 125
17:7 258
17:7–8 123
17:8 123n98, 125
17:8–9 19, 123n98
17:10–11 119, 123n98
17:10–12 123n98
17:11 16, 19, 119, 121, 122, 123, 123n98, 124, 126, 215, 229, 276n2
17:11 NRSV 119
17:11–13 125
17:12–16 22
17:13 22, 23, 23n50, 185
17:13–14 23, 25
17:13–15 121
17:13–16 124, 125
17:14 16, 19, 22, 119, 215, 229
17:15 74
17:15–16 74, 111, 140n133, 199n133
17:16 110
17–26 133, 133n118
18:6–30 84
18:20 84, 133
18:21 12
18:23–25 84, 133
18:24–29 85
18:25 84, 85, 95, 96, 110, 132, 133
18–25 166
18–26 86, 134n119, 138, 158, 171
18:27 85, 132, 133
18:27–28 84
18:28 85, 86, 95, 96, 132, 133
18:29 96
18:30 84, 133
19:2 66, 70, 70n4, 77
19:5 258
19:5–8 39, 176
19:6 258
19:8 70n4, 110
19:16 23
19:20 113, 250
19:22 276n2
19:29 84, 85, 132, 133
19:30 60n111
19:31 84, 133
20:1–3 84
20:2 85, 96
20:2–5 12
20:3 85
20:5–6 96
20:7 66, 70, 70n4, 77
20:7–8 77
20:9–18 96
20:17 110
20:19 110
20:22 85, 86, 96, 132, 133
20:25 59, 67
20:25–26 77
20:26 66, 70, 70n4, 77
21:1–4 74n16
21:1–6 16

21:6 33
21:8 33
21:10 61n116
21:10–12 16, 74n16
21:17 33
21:21–22 33
21:22 70n4, 71n4
21:23 LXX 161
22:3–7 37n39, 43, 74n16, 74n18, 76, 176
22:3–9 16
22:16 110
22:19–25 121
22:25 33
22:29 258
22:29–30 40, 43, 176
22:32 70, 70n4
23:13 31, 33
23:18 31, 33
23:28 276n2
23:32 30, 138n131
24:7 33
24:9 33, 33n22, 71n4
24:14 14
24:17–18 125
24:18 125, 126
24:21 126
25 113n62, 250
25:9 113, 191n111
25:10 LXX 163
25:36–38 169
25:47–55 250
26:14–45 131
26:31–33 174
26:31–45 96, 147
26:32–33 86
26:32–34 86, 132
26:34–35 86
26:34–43 136
26:39–41 110
26:40–43 86–87
26:40–45 87n51
26:43 86, 110
26:43–44 86, 132
26:44 86
35:31–32 113n62
35:31–33 113n62
35:33 LXX 113n62

Numbers

9, 47n77, 85, 135
1:47–54 200
1:51 56
3:3 58n105
3:12–13 47, 48n78, 49
3:13 48
3:45 47, 48n78, 49
5:2–3 61n118, 65, 71, 71n5, 73, 75, 83, 131, 151
5:3 65
5:7 91
5:7–8 90
5:8 276n2
5:11–31 71n5, 84
5:15 91
5:21–25 91
5:34 85, 132, 133
6:2–6 Eng. 91
6:9–11 91
6:9–12 64n130, 78n32, 91n8
6:11 99n36, 276n2
6:19 41
6:21 40
7:89 70, 200n135, 260
8 48n78
8:5–22 200
8:7 199
8:12 276n2
8:14–18 47, 48n78, 49
8:17 48
8:19 276n2
8:21 51n84, 91, 199, 276n2
9 42n56, 43
9:6 43n58
9:7 42
9:10 43n58
9:11 43
9:12 43, 193
9:13 43, 46
10:10 30, 43, 44, 57, 179, 180
11:1–4 195n126
11–21 195

Numbers (*continued*)
12:1 195n126
12:8 200n135
12:12 16n25, 62, 75
14 195
14:1–2 195n126
14:11–19 199n131
14:17–19 196
14:18 194, 195
14:18–19 199n131
14:19 195
15:1–13 37, 89, 180, 207
15:3 33
15:7 33
15:10 33
15:13 33
15:14 33
15:25 34n28, 276n2
15:27–29 90, 92, 95, 127
15:28 276n2
15:30–31 11, 95, 123, 164, 195, 222
16:1–3 195n126
16:41 195n126
16:46–47 Eng. 276n2
17:11–12 276n2
18:1–7 117
18:1–32 200
18:2 56
18:7 56
18:15–17 47
18:20–21 63n124
18:22 56
19 16, 16n25, 58n104, 63, 75, 78n32, 224
19:5 58n104
19:5–6 58n104
19:6 51, 51n84–52n84, 52
19:7–8 74n16, 199n133
19:9 51n84, 52n84, 58n104, 63n124, 83
19:10 199n133
19:11–19 77
19:12 51n84, 52n84, 91
19:13 16, 51n84, 52n84, 53, 58n104, 63n124, 74n18, 83, 91
19:14–15 75
19:17 51n84, 52n84, 148, 159
19:17–18 52
19:18 51, 52n84, 58n104, 63n124, 83
19:19 51n84, 52n84, 91, 199n133
19:20 16, 51n84, 52n84, 53, 74n18, 91, 110
19:20–21 58n104, 83
19:21 199n133
19:22 75
20:3 195n126
20:26 200
20:26–28 61n116
20:28 200
21:5 195n126
25:13 276n2
26:43–45 87n51
27:18 14
27:23 14
28:1–8 30
28:2 31, 33
28:6 31
28:8 31
28:13 31
28:22 31, 113, 276n2
28:24 31, 33
28:27 31
28–29 30
28:30 31, 113, 276n2
29:2 31
29:5 31, 276n2
29:6 31
29:7 30, 138n131
29:8 31
29:11 31, 276n2
29:13 31
29:36 31
31 122
31:19 51n84, 91
31:22–23 116n72

31:23 157, 159, 160n33
31:24 199n133
31:50 122, 122n92, 276n2
35:25 61n116
35:30–34 96, 123
35:31 86, 132, 191
35:31–32 113
35:31–34 121, 171
35:32–33 11
35:33 85, 86, 113, 113n62, 132, 186n97, 191, 198n128
35:33–34 84, 192
35:34 85
35:35 133

Deuteronomy

23, 133n118, 256
5:14 73n14
7:6 66, 203n146
7:8 201, 203, 203n146
12 12n14, 23
12:5 12n14
12:11 12n14
12:11–14, 17–18 20
12:14 12n14
12:15–16 23
12:15–28 76
12:16 23n48
12:21–25 23
12:23 229
12:23–25 119
12:24 23n48
12:31 12
13:5 201
13:15 203, 203n146
14 72n14
14:2 66, 203n146
15:21–23 23
15:23 23n48
16 42, 42n56
16:1–8 42
16:3 43, 146
16:4 43
16:7 41, 42
17:11 125
17:16 73n14
18:1 33
19:10 186n97, 198n128
19:13 198n128
19:21 125
21 190
21:1–9 85, 86, 132, 190
21:4 21, 22n47, 86
21:6–8 190
21:7 186n97
21:7–9 198n128
21:23 256
23:12–14 77
23:19–20 169
24:1–4 85, 132
26:18 66, 203n146
27:1–8 36
27:4–8 54, 175n67
27:7 29n4, 39
27:25 198n128
27:26 256
28:15–68 131
29:22–28 131
30:19 131
32 140
32:43 86n50, 132
32:43 LXX 140
34:9 14

Joshua

8:30–35 36, 54, 175n67

Judges

20:26 39
21:4 39

1 Samuel

49
1–2 48n78
2:12–17 41, 42
6:3–4 90
6:3–17 64
6:8 90
6:17 90
10:8 36, 39

1 Samuel (*continued*)

11:5 39
11:14–15 36
15:22–23 132, 141
19:5 198n128
25:26 198n128
25:31 186n97, 198n128
27:9 73n14

2 Samuel

3:28 198n128
4:11 198n128
6:17–18 36, 39
11–12 132
12:6 91
15:7–8 NRSV 40
24:24–25 32n18
24:25 36, 39

1 Kings

1:50–53 11, 71n5, 84
2:5 198n128
2:28–30 71n5, 84
2:28–34 12n13
2:31 186n97
2:31–32 198n128
3:15 39
6:16 70
7:50 70
8:10–11 32
8:22 57n99
8:31 57n99
8:54 57n99
8:63–64 36, 39
9:25 36, 39
18:38 32n18
19:21 41

2 Kings

3:5 94n18
5:1–14 159, 161n38
12:17 64
16:13 39
18:22–39 57n99
21:6 12
21:10–16 192
21:16 186n97, 190, 198n128
24:1–4 192
24:3–4 190
24:3–5 168
24:4 144, 186n97, 198n128

1 Chronicles

6:34 276n2
16:1–2 36
21:26 32n18, 36
22:8 186n97, 198n128
28:3 186n97, 198n128
29:24 276n2

2 Chronicles

12n14
3:1 12n14
4:10–12 239
7:1–2 32
7:7 36
15:10–15 54, 175n67
15:11–13 36
24:20–21 168
29:24 51n84, 91
29:30—30:27 68
29:30–36 175n67
29:31–35 39
29:35 36
30:1–27 175n67
30:17–20 80n37
30:22 36
30:22–27 39
31:2 36
33:16 36, 39, 54, 175n67
35:13 41
36:5d 186n97, 198n128

Nehemiah

10:34 276n2

Esther

16:5 198n128

Job

1:5 90
16:18 23n50
18:13 62
18:18–23 62
42:8 90

Psalms

132, 138
8:5–8 226
8:6–9 Eng. 226
13:3 186n97, 198n128
14:3 MT 186n97, 198n128
31 261
31:1–2 LXX 261, 279
31:5–6 261
31:10 LXX 261
31:11 LXX 261
32 132, 146
32 MT 261
32:1–2 MT 261
39 LXX 223, 224
39:7–9 LXX 223
40:6 Eng. 141
40:6–8 Eng. 132, 223
40:7 141
40:7–9 132
42:3 57n99
42:4 Eng. 40n50
42:5 40n50
43:4 57n99
50 33n22
50:5 175n67
50:5 NRSV 54
50:12–13 32
50:13–14 132
50:14–15 40
50:14b 40
50:23 40
51 96, 132, 133, 137, 138, 139, 140, 141, 146, 196
51:2 133
51:2 Eng. 133, 137, 147, 172
51:4 133, 137, 147, 172
51:7 Eng. 50, 51n84, 91, 137, 147, 172
51:9 50, 51n84, 91, 137, 147, 172
51:14 Eng. 133
51:16 133
51:16–17 261
51:16–17 Eng. 51n84, 141
51:18–19 51n84, 141
56:12–13 39, 40
69:30–31 Eng. 132, 141
69:31–32 132, 141
78:3 186n97, 198n128
78:10 198n128
78:19 186n97
79:3 MT 198n128
79:9 87
79:10 MT 186n97, 198n128
93:21 198n128
94:21 MT 198n128
95:2 40n50
100:1 40n50
103 146
103:3–4 132, 203n146
103:10–14 132, 203n146
105:38 186n97, 198n128
106:34–40 85, 86, 132
106:38 143
106:38 MT 186n97, 198n128
106:38–39 84
106:39 143n146
107 40n50
107:2–3 40n50
107:2–9 39
107:4–9 40n50
107:10–16 40n50
107:17–22 40n50
107:21–22 40
107:22 39, 40n50
107:23–32 40n50
116:17–18 40
116:18 40
129:8 LXX 203n146
130:8 203n146

Proverbs

1:11 198n128
1:16 186n97, 198n128
6:17 186n97, 198n128

Isaiah

249

1:11 132, 145
1:11–15 141, 142
1:13–15 199
1:16 147, 158, 159
1:17 142
1:18 198, 199, 199n132
1:21–23 144
1:27 203n146
4:4 147, 172
5:7–8 144
11:16 146
19:19–20 57n99
20:2–3 158n26
24:5 85, 132
24:5–6 143
26:21 23n50
27:9 146, 158n29, 172, 194, 196, 197, 204n146
27:9 LXX 196
31:5 50
32:15 218, 231n41
35:9 201
38:17 146
40 250
40:1 188
40:1–2 231n41
40:2–3 146
40:3 158
41:14 70, 201
43:1 201
43:14 70, 201
43:14–21 146, 158n27
43:18–19 146
43:25 146, 158n29, 172
44:3 217, 218, 231n41
44:22 146, 158n29, 172, 203n146
44:22–24 201
44:27 146, 158n27
47:4 203n146
48:17 70
48:20–21 146, 158n27
49:7 70
49:26 70
50:2 146, 158n27
51:10–11 146, 158n27
51:11 201
52:3 201, 203, 206
52:12 146
52:12—53:12 245
52:13 245
52:13—53:12 243, 245, 246
52:15 246
53 243, 244, 244n5, 245, 246, 247, 248, 249, 252
53:1 246
53:4–5 243
53:8–9 246
53:9 246
53:9 LXX 246n14
53:10 MT 244
53:10a 246
53:11 246
53:12 246
54:5 70
54:8 70
54:10 146, 172, 175n67, 203n146
55:7 146, 158n29, 172
55:11 3
57:19 203n146
58:3 30, 139n131
58:8 146, 158n27
59:7 186n97, 198n128
59:20 203n146
59:21 146, 172, 175n67, 204n146
61:1–2 163
61:8 141
62:12 201
63:9 201
66:3–4 145
66:3–5 141

Jeremiah

255, 256

2:7 85, 132, 143
2:13 148, 159
2:23 143

2:34 198n128
3:1–2 85, 132, 143
3:9 85, 132, 143
6:13 142, 143
6:20 132, 142, 143, 145
6:20 NRSV 141
7 166
7:6 186n97, 192, 198n128
7:9 144
7:9–10 143
7:21 36
7:21–23 132
7:22 141
7:22 NRSV 141
7:30 143n146
7:31 12
12:7 71, 143, 146, 166, 169, 174
13:1–11 158n26
14:12 141, 145
15:21 201
16:14–15 146
16:18 85, 132
17:13 147, 148, 148n150, 159, 215, 216
18:17 71, 143, 146, 166, 169, 174
18–19 158n26
18:23 170n58
19:4 198n128
19:13 143n146
22:3 144, 168, 186n97, 198n128
22:5 71, 143, 146, 166, 169, 174
22:13 144
22:17 186n97, 198n128
22:17–18 144, 168
22:18 144
23:7–8 146
23:33 71, 143, 146, 166, 169, 174
23:39 71, 143, 146, 166, 169, 174
24:9 255
26 168
26:15 168
26:15 MT 198n128
26:20–23 168
27:34 201
29:18 255
31:31–34 146, 158n29, 172, 175n67, 179, 188, 223
31:32 218
31:32–33 146
31:33–34 222
31:34 146, 197, 219, 231n41
31:34 MT 219
32:34 143n146
33:5–8 188
33:6–8 146, 158n29, 175n67
33:8 146, 147, 172, 179, 219, 223
33:8 MT 218, 219
33:15 198n128
34:13 146
34:25 172
37:26 172
38:11 201
38:34 LXX 219
40:8 219
40:8 LXX 218, 219
42:18 255
44:8 255
44:12 255
49:18 LXX 255
50:20 146, 158n29, 172
51:8 LXX 255
51:12 LXX 255

Lamentations

4:13 186n97, 198n128

Ezekiel

131, 144, 255
2:38 94n18
4:1–17 158n26
4:4–6 173, 255

Ezekiel (*continued*)
5–10 143
5:11 143n146
5–11 146
7–10 71, 166, 169, 174
7:23 143
8:17 143
9:7 11, 16
9:9 143
12:1–28 158n26
16:38 186n97, 198n128
16:59–63 146, 172, 175n67, 179, 223
18:10 186n97, 198n128
20:7 143n146
20:18 143n146
20:31 143n146
20:41–44 232
22:1–16 143n146
22:2–16 143
22:3 85, 86, 132, 186n97, 198n128
22:4 85, 86, 132, 186n97, 198n128
22:6 85, 86, 132, 186n97, 198n128
22:9 186n97, 198n128
22:12 85, 86, 132, 144, 186n97, 198n128
22:12–13 NRSV 144
22:15 147, 172
22:24–31 143
22:26 59–60, 67
22:27 186n97, 198n128
23:7 143n146
23:30 143n146
23:45 198n128
24:1–14 144, 168
24:6 144
24:7 186n97, 198n128
24:7–8 23n50
24:9 144
24:13 143n146, 147, 172
24:15–27 158n26
34:25 146, 175n67, 223
34:25–29 188
34:33 188
35:6 186n97, 198n128
36:17 147
36:17–18 85, 86, 132, 143
36:17–19 158
36:25 131, 147, 148, 159, 215, 216, 255
36:25–27 158, 172, 217, 218, 224, 227
36:25–33 231n41, 232
36:26–27 148, 159
36:29 131, 147, 158, 172, 223
36:31 232
36:33 147, 158, 172, 223
37 165, 173, 174, 205
37:1–14 227
37:1–23 224
37:5 148
37:9–10 148
37:14 148, 231n41, 232
37:23 143n146, 147, 149, 172, 223, 227, 231n41, 232
37:26 146, 175n67
37:26–28 147
37:36 223
39:24 143n146
39:29 231n41
40:39–41 21
41:22 33n23
43:20 51n84, 91
43:22 51n84, 91
43:23 51n84, 91
43:26 51n84, 91
44:16 33n23
44:23 59–60, 67
44:26–27 78n32
45:15 39
45:17 39
45:18 51n84, 91
46:20 41
46:24 41

Daniel
245, 249, 255
10:5–6 213n8

11–12 245, 246
11:33 245, 246
11:33–35 246
11:34 246
11:35 245
12:3 245, 246
12:10 245

Hosea

2:15 186n97
5:3 143n146
6:6 132, 169
6:6 NSRV 141
6:10 143n146
7:13 203
8:13 141, 145
9:4–5 141, 145
14:2–7 146, 172

Joel

2:28 Eng. 218
2:28–29 Eng. 231n41
3:1 218
3:1–2 231n41
3:19 MT 186n97, 198n128
4:19 186n97, 198n128

Amos

5:10–11 142
5:21–24 132
5:21–25 145
5:21–25 NRSV 141
5:23 142

Jonah

1:14 198n128
2:9 Eng. 40
2:9a Eng. 40n50
2:9b Eng. 40
2:10 40
2:10a 40n50
2:10b 40

Micah

144
2:1–9 144
3:10 144
3:10–11 144
3:11 144
4:10 201
6:4 203
6:6–8 132, 141, 145
7:18–19 146, 172

Nahum

3:1 144

Habakkuk

2:8–12 144

Zephaniah

1:17 186n97
3:15 146, 172

Zechariah

131
3 213n8
3:3–5 198, 199n132
3:4 LXX 199n131
9:11 179n78
9:19 73n14
10:8 201
13:1 131, 188
13:1–2 147, 172
14:8 131
14:21 41

Malachi

1:6–14 145
1:7 33n23
1:12 33n23
3:2–3 147, 159, 160n33
3:2–33 172

DEUTEROCANONICAL BOOKS

1 Maccabees

1:37 186n97, 198n128
4:53 55
4:56 54
4:59 55
7:17 186n97

1–4 Maccabees

36n34

2 Maccabees

1:8 186n97, 198n128

4 Maccabees

263, 264, 266, 267
17 264
17:18 264, 265
17:18–20 265
17:19 264
17:20 264
17:22 263, 264

Sirach

16:7 276n2
28:11 186n97, 198n128
34:22 186n97, 198n128
45:16 276n2
45:23 276n2
47:11 194, 196
50 226
50:11–13 226

Wisdom of Solomon

245, 249
2:1–5 246
2:12–20 246
2:12–24 246, 249
8:20 186n97, 198n128

PSEUDOPIGRAPHA (OLD TESTAMENT)

Jubilees

23n50, 133
1:7–25 191
1:23 191, 191n111
3:1–14 106n53
3:8 75, 106n53
3:8–14 16n25, 75
3:9–14 16n25, 76
3:10–11 106n53, 107
3:12–14 106n53
5:17–18 190, 191
6:14 221n18
7:20–39 134, 191
7:23 190, 191
7:25 190, 191
7:28–29 191
7:30–31 23n50
7:33 191
20:2–11 134, 191
21:1–25 23n50, 134, 191
21:19 191
21:19–20 191
21:20 191
23:14 191
23:14–25 134, 191
23:18 191
23:22 191
23:26–31 191
34:10–19 190, 191
36:1–17 134, 191
49:16 42n56
49:18 42n56
49:20 42n56
49:21 42n56
50:3–5 191, 191n111
50:11 221n18

Psalms of Solomon

3:8 276n2
8:20 186n97

Testament of Levi
18 169n58

Dead Sea Scrolls
169n58

1QH[a]
IX, 21–22 75

1QS
IX, 4 170n58

4Q221
IV, 4 170n58

4Q266
12–13 170n58

4Q541
9 169n58

4QMMT
80n36

11QMelch 164
II, 7–8 169n58

CD
IV, 10 170n58
XIV, 18–19 170n58
XIV, 19 170n58

ANCIENT JEWISH WRITERS

Josephus
Antiquities of the Jews
3.224 35
3.224–32 38
3.225, 228 36
3.226, 228, 231 38
3.228 36n34, 38, 56
3.230–32 36
3.231 38, 55, 123n98
3.234 48n78
3.236 39, 40
3.240 30, 139n131
3.241 130n116, 131
14.260 42n56
16.182 262
18.117 158n28

Philo
De cherubim
25 261

De fuga et inventione
100 267
101 261

De specialibus legibus
2.145–149 42n56

De vita Mosis
2.24 267
2.95 261
2.97 261

Quis rerum divinarum heres sit
166 261

RABBINIC WORKS

Babylonian Talmud

Nedarim

41a 163

Yoma

85b:7–8 133
85b:11 133
86a:1 133
86a:7–8 133

Jerusalem Talmud

Šebuʿot

1:4–5 134n119
1:6 133, 134n119
1:32c–33b 133, 134n119

Yoma

8:7 133, 148
8:44c 133
8:45b–c 133
8:45c 148

Midrash

Leviticus Rabbah

9:1, 7 41

Mishnah

64n133, 100

Berakot

8:1–2 156
54b 40n50

ʿEduyyot

2:1 80, 101
5:1 82, 101, 106, 107
5:4 80, 82, 101, 106, 107

Kelim

1:5 80, 101

Keritot

1:7 80
2:1 80, 101

Meʿilah

2:1–9 80

Miqwaʾot

1:4–8 159
1:8 148, 161

Negaʿim

3:1 154
14:3 80, 81, 101, 108n57

Niddah

1:7 106
10:7 106, 107

Parah

3:7–8 102
8:7 102
11:4–5 102

Šebuʿot

1:4 116
1:4–5 134n119
1:5 116
1:6 133n119, 134n119

Ṭebul Yom

80
2:1 101, 106
2:1–2 80, 107
4:3 101, 106

Yoma

8:9 133, 147, 159, 215

Zebaḥim

2:1 80, 101
5:1–3 185
10:5 64
10:6 64
12:1 80, 101

NEW TESTAMENT

Matthew

151, 152n4, 163n45, 173n65, 189, 192, 245, 250, 251
2:21 171
3:2–3 157, 158
3:11–12 158
3:16 161
5:21–22 168
5:23–24 169
5:27–32 168
6:12 205
6:24 168
6:33 8
8:2 152n3
8:2–4 152, 153
8:4 153, 154, 161, 169
8:16–17 245
8:17 244, 244n5
9:6 163n45
9:9–10 169
9:11 169
9:12–13 NRSV 169
9:13 132, 169
9:18–19 152
9:20–22 152, 154
9:23–26 152
10:28 251
10:38 174
11:2–6 162, 165
11:5 152n3
12:6 169, 170n58, 171n58
12:6–7 169
12:7 132
12:22–29 250
12:41–42 169
15:2 155
15:3 156
15:18–20 168
16:24 174
17:12–13 168
18:21–35 205
20:22–23 174, 251, 274
20:28 7, 203n146, 249, 250, 251, 252
23:19 168, 237, 238
23:21 168
23:25–26 156
23:27–28 151n1, 168
23:29–34 167, 186
23:30 198n128
23:30–36 190
23:30–38 168
23:30–39 168
23:35 167, 168, 186, 187, 198n128
23:35–36 190
23:37–44 166
23:38 174
25:35–45 275n21
26:6 152n3
26:17–19 171, 175
26:26–29 68
26:28 167, 171, 172, 172n62, 175, 175n67, 179, 183, 186, 190, 198n128
27:4 190, 198n128
27:6 190
27:19 190
27:24 198n128
27:24–25 189, 190
27:25 190, 198n128
27:46 174
27:50 187, 217
27:50–53 152n4, 187
28:28 171

Mark

151, 163n45, 250, 251
1:1–8 163
1:2–3 157, 158
1:4–8 163
1:7–8 158
1:9–20 163
1:10 161
1:15 205
1:21–39 163
1:24 152, 161, 162
1:40–45 152, 153, 163
1:42–44 161
1:44 154, 167, 169
1:44 NRSV 153
2:1–12 163
2:5–12 163
2:10 163, 164
3:22–27 253
3:22–30 250
5:21–24 152
5:25–34 152, 154
5:35–43 152
7 153n9
7:2 155n14
7:3 155
7:4 155n14
7:8 156
7:20–23 168
8:31–34 253
8:31–35 208
8:33 253, 274
8:34 174, 251, 274
8:34–35 7, 206
8:34–38 151, 180
9:31–37 253
9:40 277n3
10:10–12 168
10:32–45 253
10:35–45 252
10:38–39 7, 151, 174, 180, 207, 217, 239, 251, 252, 274
10:38–45 208, 252, 274
10:45 7, 113, 203n146, 249, 250, 251, 252
11:1–14 73n14
13 152, 166, 167, 173n65
14:3 152n3
14:12 171, 175
14:14 171, 175
14–15 173n65
14:16 171, 175
14:22–25 68
14:24 167, 171, 175, 175n67, 179, 186
15:34 174
15:37 187

Luke

151, 152n4, 163n45, 173n65, 204n147
1:35 152, 161
1:76–77 231n41
2:22 16n25
3:3–6 157, 158, 231n41
3:16 232
3:16–17 158
3:22 161
4:18–19 164
4:19 205
4:34 152, 161, 162
5:12–14 152, 153
5:14 153, 154, 161, 169
5:24 163n45
7:11–17 152n4
7:18–23 162, 165
7:22 152n3
7:36–50 164
7:37 164
7:39 164
7:40–50 205
7:47–50 164
7:48 164
8:41–42 152
8:43–48 152, 154
8:49–56 152
9:23 174, 251
9:31 250
11:4 205
11:38 155

11:39–40 156
11:41 168
11:44 151n1
11:49 167, 186
11:50 167, 186
11:50–51 168, 187, 198n128
11:51 167, 168, 186
13:16 250
13:31–38 169
13:34–35 166, 167, 168, 169, 186
13:35 174
14:27 174, 251
14:27–33 204n147
16:13 168
16:18 168
17:12–19 152n3, 154
17:14 154, 161, 169
18:13 210
19:41–44 166, 167
19:42 167, 168
20:35–36 75n23
21:1–38 166, 167
22:7–8 171, 175
22:11 171, 175
22:13 171, 175
22:15 171, 175
22:15–20 68
22:19 44, 179
22:20 167, 171, 175, 175n67, 179, 186, 198n128
22:37 244n5
23:46 187
24:46–47 231n41

John

152n4, 193, 196, 217
1:1–18 196, 197, 251n25
1:2 160n33
1:14 162
1:19–25 196
1:23 157, 158
1:29 193–97, 195n125
1:32 161
1:33 158
1:36 193–97
1:45–46 197
2:19–22 173n65, 251n25
4:31–34 195n125
6 193, 195n125
6:4 171n61, 193
6:47–56 193
6:48–58 208
6:51 277n3
6:51–56 171n61
6:56 193
6:69 152, 161, 162
7:38 217
7:38–39 218
7:39 217
11:1–46 152n4
12:23–26 208
12:24–26 174, 274
12:26 251n27
12:31–33 250n24
12:38 244n5
13:10 217
13:16–17 174, 274
13:36 174, 208, 274
13:37 277n3
15:3 206, 217, 218
15:18 174, 274
15:20 174, 274
16:1–4 174, 274
17:17 217
17:17–19 206
17:19 277n3
19:14 193–97
19:20 187
19:30 218
19:31 193–97
19:34 217, 218
19:36 193–97
20:21–23 206
20:22 217
21:15 195n125
21:18–19 208
21:18–22 174, 274

Acts

164, 186, 212, 213, 232

Acts (*continued*)

1:5 232
2:22–24 165
2:24 164, 165
2:24–32 180
2:24–36 242
2:27 152, 161, 165
2:31 165
2:31–32 152, 165
2:33 231n41, 232
2:33–36 232
2:38–39 231n41
2:46 167
3:1 167
3:13 231n41
3:14 152, 161
3:15 231n41
3:19 231n41
3:26 174
4:2 174
4:27 152, 161
5:28 198n128, 231n41
5:30 231n41
5:31 232
7:52 231n41
8:32–33 244n5
9:4–5 275n21
9:16 277n3
10:43–48 231n41
10:44–48 232
11:16 232
11:16–18 231n41, 232
13:23–24 231n41
13:33–39 180
13:34–39 165
13:35 161, 165
13:35–37 180
13:38 165
13:38–39 231n41, 232
13:39 180
14:15 231n41
15:8–9 231n41, 232
15:20 231n41
15:26 277n3
17:16 231n41
17:23–31 231n41
18:6 198n128
18:19 231n41
18:26 231n41
20:28 212n7
21:13 277n3
21:26 167
22:7–8 275n21
22:16 232
22:20 167, 186, 198n128
26:6–8 174
26:14–15 275n21
26:22–23 174
27:9 30, 139n131

Romans

245, 257n42, 259
1–3 261, 262
1:5–6 266
1:16–17 284
1:23 261
1:25 261
1:26–27 261
1:29 261
2:22 261
3:15 186, 198n128, 261
3:20 257n42
3:21 257n42, 267
3:21–26 260, 284
3:24–25 260n52
3:25 5, 7, 259, 260, 260n52, 261, 263, 264, 266, 267, 268, 268n96, 269, 271
3:25–26 259–62, 267, 268, 269
3:26 267, 268
4 279
4:5 261, 266, 268, 269
4:6 261
4:6–7 279
4:7 269
4:7–8 132, 261
4:8 269
4:15 257n42
4:25 256, 279
4:25b 279
5 279
5:1 260n52

5:5–11 221, 266, 268, 269
5–6 280
5:6 281
5:6–8 276, 279–82
5:6–10 280
5:6–11 260, 269
5:7 280, 281
5–8 257, 258, 280, 281
5:8 281
5–8 281, 284
5:9 260n52
5:10 4, 266
5:10–11 269
5:12—6:11 281
5:12—6:23 281n10
5:12—7:25 269
5:12–21 275, 280
5:13 257n42
5:18–19 260, 260n52, 278
5:19 260n52
5:21 257
6:2–11 280
6:3–6 206, 239
6:3–8 7, 274, 279
6:3–11 217, 284
6:5 274, 276, 278, 281
6:6 275
6:9 282
6:12 257
6:14 257
6:14–22 257
6:23 240, 280
7:4 280
7:7 257n42
7:11 257
7:12 257n42
7:14 257, 257n42
7:14–25 258
8:1–25 281n10
8:3 5, 7, 257–59, 258n45, 271, 274, 282
8:9–11 206
8:13 258
8:17 207, 280
8:26–39 268
8:31–39 266, 269, 270
8:32 266, 270
9:4 167n55
9:15 266
9:18 266
9:23 266
10:16 244n5, 246
11:13 266
11:18–24 266
11:26–27 146n148, 204n146
11:27 172n64
11:30–32 266
11:32 268
12:1 207, 208, 239, 283, 284, 285
12:5 208, 283
13:8–10 257n42
15:9 266
15:14–16 266
15:21 244n5, 246

1 Corinthians

1:18 270
1:23 270
5 176
5:6–13 176
5:7 171n61, 258, 283
5:7–8 206
6:9–10 206n151
6:11 206, 217, 232
6:20 203n146
10:7 207n152
10:16 180, 239, 283
10:16–17 180, 207, 285
10:16–18 207, 283
10:17 283
10:18 236, 239, 283
10:20 283
10:20–21 207
10:21 283
11 6, 38n40, 176
11:21–22 176
11:23–25 183n87, 283
11:23–26 68, 178n75, 206
11:24–25 44, 179, 180
11:25 171, 175, 175n67, 179, 180, 283
11:26–34 176
11:33–34 176

1 Corinthians (*continued*)

12:12–13 180, 208, 283
12:13 217
12:27 208, 283
15 187
15:1 183n84
15:3 183n84, 276, 278, 279
15:3–7 183n84
15:3–8 212
15:7 279
15:17 278, 279
15:22 275, 279
15:54 180
15:55–56 269

2 Corinthians

1:5 207
1:7 207
2:14 284
2:14–15 239
3 187
3:6 175n67
4:7–12 207, 276
4:10 276
4:10–11 180, 274
4:10–12 285
4:10–14 284
5 268
5:14–15 275, 276
5:14–21 253, 285
5:15 277, 278
5:18–19 269
5:18–20 4, 266, 269
5:21 5, 7, 253, 254n35, 258, 276, 277, 278

Galatians

255
1:15–16 257
1:16 256
2:16–17 256
2:20 7, 206, 239, 256, 257, 274
3 256
3–4 274
3:10 256
3:11 256
3:13 5, 7, 254–57, 255n38, 278
3:14 256
4:4 256, 257
6:14 7, 239, 274
6:14–15 275

Ephesians

1:7 192n113, 203n146, 204n146
1:10 275, 278, 282
1:20–23 275
1:23 208
2 192n113
2:5–6 275
2:12 203n146
2:12–13 192n113
2:17 203n146
2:18 192n113
3:12 192n113
4:12 208
5:1–2 207
5:2 204n146, 284
5:26 218n14
5:30 208

Philippians

2:1–11 281n10
2:5–8 223
2:5–11 151
2:8 260, 260n52, 278
2:17 207, 239, 283, 284
3:10 180, 207, 239, 274
3:10–11 7, 151, 274, 276, 278, 284
4:18 207, 239, 283, 284

Colossians

1:13–14 203n146
1:15–24 281n10
1:18 208
1:20 198n129
1:21–22 266

1:24 207, 208, 239, 274, 277n3
1:27 274, 275
2:1 277n3
2:9–15 275, 282n10
2:12 274, 276
2:14–15 198n129
2:19 208
2:20 282n10
3:1 274
3:1–4 275
3:1–11 282n10
3:3–4 274
3:10–11 274, 275
3:11 275
3:12 217

1 Timothy

2:6 249n21

2 Timothy

2:12 207

Titus

2:14 203n146
3:5 217, 232

Hebrews

5, 25n60, 155n13, 170n58, 177, 209, 210, 211, 213, 213n9, 214, 221–40, 225n26, 241, 242, 245, 271, 273, 275, 277n2
1:2–4 212
1:3 210, 221
2:4 277n2
2:5–10 226
2:7 227
2:9 223, 275, 277n3
2:9–10 227, 235
2:9–14 275
2:9–18 229
2:10 226, 239
2:11 226, 235
2:14 25n60, 234, 235, 239, 240, 275
2:14–15 223, 228n32, 251, 284
2:14–18 240
2:15 240
2:17 210, 221
2:17–18 235, 239
3:1 210, 212
3:11 237
3:18–19 240
4:2–3 240
4:6 240
4:11 240
4:14 212, 230
4:14–15 210
4:16 226, 226n28, 227, 229, 235, 236, 238, 283
5:1 277n2
5:2 235
5:3 277n2
5:5 210, 223–24
5:6–10 239n53
5:7 212
5:7—6:2 242
5:7–9 223, 226, 231, 240
5:8 240
5:9 211n2
5:9–10 210, 210n2, 211n2
5:10 211, 211n2, 223–24
5:10—6:2 182
5:10—6:3 210, 212
5:11 211
5:12 182, 212
6:1 182, 212
6:1 NRSV 182
6:1–2 211, 212
6:2 235
6:19–20 227, 229, 230, 233, 234, 236, 238, 240, 242, 277n3, 283
6:20 211n2
7:1–28 210n2, 211n2
7:11 225
7:11—8:2 222

Hebrews (*continued*)

7:11—10:18 211
7:11–12 222, 242n55
7:13–14 211, 232, 242, 245
7:15—8:2 226n28
7:15–16 225
7:15–28 230
7:16 152, 165, 226, 230, 233, 235, 241, 275
7:19 225
7:22 222
7:23—8:2 225
7:24—8:1 234
7:24—8:2 229
7:24–25 235
7:25 235, 236
7:26 230, 235
7:26–27 221
7:27 221n18, 233, 277n2
7:28 211n2
8:1–2 230
8:1–5 238
8:1—9:28 210n2, 211n2
8:2 229
8:4 211, 232, 242
8:5 222
8:6–7 222
8:7–8 225
8:8 175n67
9:1—10:18 221
9:2–5 238
9:5 261
9:6–7 226n27
9:7 222, 224, 226, 226n28, 227, 235
9:7–8 222
9:7–10 226
9:8 226
9–10 210, 227
9:11 229
9:11—10:22 225
9:11–12 116, 225, 230, 234, 238
9:11–20 230
9:12 224, 226, 233, 235
9:12–14 221
9:13–14 224, 225, 235n45, 238
9:13–15 224
9:14 223, 225, 227, 234, 235, 235n45
9:14–15 227
9:15 25n60, 175n67, 222, 223, 228, 228n32
9:15–20 192n113, 221, 222, 223, 224, 225, 227
9:15–22 228n32
9:16–17 25n60
9:19–20 227
9:21–22 116n72, 229
9:21–23 116n72
9:21–24 221
9:21–25 229
9:21–28 225, 226
9:22 116n72, 228n32
9:22–24 116
9:22–28 224
9:23–24 98, 222, 229, 238
9:23–25 116n72, 224
9:23–26 227, 230, 234, 235n45
9:24 229
9:25 226, 226n28, 227, 229, 235
9:25–26 229, 233
9:28 211n2, 235, 236, 236n48
10:1 222, 224, 227
10:1–2 223
10:1–4 225
10:1–15 224
10:1–18 210n2, 211n2, 224, 225
10:2 235
10:5–7 132
10:5–9 231, 233
10:5–14 226
10:6 223, 224, 228
10:7 223, 240
10:8 223, 224, 228
10:9 223, 240

10:10 223, 224, 226, 227, 229, 235, 238
10:10–11 221
10:11 221n18
10:12 223, 224, 235, 277n2
10:14 221, 223, 224, 226, 227, 229, 235, 238
10:16–17 221, 222, 223, 224
10:16–18 222, 223, 227, 228, 228n32
10:18 116n72, 222, 222n21, 223, 224, 228
10:19 221, 224, 226, 226n27, 226n28, 227, 230, 235, 236, 277n3
10:19–20 238, 283
10:19–22 222, 224, 226, 227, 229, 235, 284
10:20 226
10:22 221, 223, 225, 227, 235, 235n45, 236, 238, 277n3
10:23 212
10:26 116n72, 222, 222n21, 228, 277n2
10:26–27 228
10:27 228
10:29 192n113, 221, 223, 224, 227, 235
10:32–39 239, 240
10:33 237n52
10:34 236
10:37 236, 236n48
11:10 236
11:16 236
11:19 235
11:25 237
11:25–26 237, 239, 240
11:26 237
11:35 235
11:36–38 239, 240
12:2 240
12:2–4 239, 240
12:22 236, 236n48
12:24 192n113, 221
12:27–28 236
13:4 228
13:10 182, 236, 238, 239
13:10–11 181
13:10–13 229, 235, 238, 239, 284
13:11 182, 233, 236, 236n49, 238, 239
13:11–12 233, 234
13:11–13 207, 236, 238, 283
13:12 221, 233, 236, 237, 238
13:12–13 237, 238
13:13 236, 237, 239, 242
13:14 236
13:15 41n51, 221, 284
13:20 192n113, 221, 235
33:7 235n46
33:7–11 235n46

1 Peter

198, 201, 202, 203, 206, 247, 248, 249
1:2 203n144
1:3 198
1:3–4 204n147
1:5 202
1:13 202
1:18 202, 203, 285
1:18–19 198, 202
1:19 202, 285
2:5 202, 203, 248, 284
2:9 203, 248
2:9–10 202
2:21 7, 180, 244, 246, 247, 248, 274
2:21–22 204n147
2:21–23 244, 247
2:21–25 203, 249, 274
2:23 244, 247, 248
2:24 7, 243, 244, 247, 249
2:24–25 244n5
3:8–9 203
3:16–18 244, 247

1 Peter (*continued*)

3:17 244, 249
3:17–18 274
3:18 244, 248, 249
3:21 217
4:1 248
4:13 203
4:15–16 248
4:16 203
4:19 203, 244, 247, 248
5:9 202
12:11 202
14:3 202
14:4 202

1 John

5, 170n58, 177, 209, 210, 213–21, 213n9, 240, 242, 245, 271, 273, 277n2
1:1 218
1:7 215, 216, 217, 218, 219, 220
1:7–9 220n17
1:9 215, 218, 219, 220
1:10 218
2:1 215
2:1–2 220, 235
2:2 210, 213, 214, 215, 219, 220n17, 221, 242, 259, 277n2
2:6 7, 217, 220, 274
2:9 220
2:11 220
2:24 217
2:27–28 217
3:8 250n24
3:14–15 217, 220
3:15 220
3:16 220, 221
3:16–18 7, 215, 274
3:17 220
3:18 220
3:24 217
3:34 217
4:7 220
4:7–12 215
4:9–10 221
4:10 210, 213, 219, 220, 220n17, 221, 259, 277n2
4:11 220
4:12–13 217
4:13 217
4:15–16 217
4:20 220
4:21 220
5:5–8 217
5:5–12 217
5:6 217
5:6–8 218
5:8 217
5:11–12 217
5:16 220n17
5:16–17 220n17
7:38–39 217
14:16–17 217
16:7 217
16:13 217
19:30 217
19:34 217
20:22 217

Revelation

198, 201, 202, 203, 245
1:5 198, 202
1:6 200
1:13 213n8
3:21 203
5:6 201, 203
5:6–10 198
5:9 201
5:9–10 201
5:10 200, 203
6:9 239
7:1–8 201
7:9 198
7:14 198, 199, 199n132, 216
7:14–15 198, 201

7:15 198, 200
7:17 201
11:7–12 203
12:11 203
13:7–10 203
14:5 246, 246n14, 249
14:12–13 203
15:2 203
16:3 186
16:3–4 198n128
16:4 186
16:6 186, 198n128
20:6 200
21:2–3 201
21:22 201
22:3 201
22:4 200n135

APOCRYPHA (NEW TESTAMENT)

Epistle of Barnabas
213n8

First Epistle of Clement
245
16:1 248
16:3–16 248
16:17 248

EARLY CHRISTIAN WRITINGS

Anselm of Canterbury
Cur Deus Homo
9n1

Gregory of Nazianzus
Oration 4: First Invective against Julian
§86 268

Oration 30.21
275

Justin Martyr
213n8

GREEK AND ROMAN LITERATURE

Dio Chrysostom
Trojan Discourse
11.121 262–63, 268
11.122 263
11.123 263
11.128 263, 268

Homer
Odyssey
8.509 262

Virgil
Aeneid
2.15 263
8.715 264

www.ingramcontent.com/pod-product-compliance
Lightning Source LLC
Chambersburg PA
CBHW031433230426
43668CB00007B/511
9781666703047